P.

D1800029

The Pre-School Child

A handbook for parents from the
Open University in association with the
Pre-School Playgroups Association

Ward Lock Limited · London

Book Contents

Read On! A selection of books for parents and for children are given at the end of Chapters 1–5.

Help! Details and some organisations concerned with parents and children are given at the end of Chapters 6–7.

ISBN 0 7062 3883 4

First published in this edition 1979

Copyright © 1979 The Open University

All rights reserved. No part of this work may be reproduced in any form, by mimeograph or any other means, without permission in writing from the publisher.

Designed by the Media Development Group of the Open University

Reprinted in Great Britain by Waterlow (Dunstable) Ltd.
for Ward Lock Educational
116 Baker Street, London W1M 2BB.
A member of the Pentos Group

Introduction

The Pre-school Child is a book for parents. It grew out of a demand from parents, and people who work with parents, for a practical guide which would really help in day-to-day decision making and child care. It is the product of a joint project between the Open University and the Pre-school Playgroups Association.

So we – a course team from the Open University – set to work. We asked parents about their fears and worries, about what concerned them most. We also consulted the experts – in child development, family studies and practical work with parents and children – and drew on their knowledge and experience. For eighteen months we debated and drafted, trying to get the balance right.

This book is the result. We are grateful to our parents and consultants for their help, and to the Pre-school Playgroups Association for their involvement in the project, discussing, advising and generally making available to us their wealth of experience with parents and children in playgroups.

Parents face choices

Parents are constantly faced with choices. The kind of person a child turns out to be is influenced by the way his or her parents approach the thousands of everyday decisions taken in the years before school. In this book you will often be asked to think about a range of possibilities that lie between two extremes. In choosing which approach is right for you, you will be sharing in building relationships. Some parents seem to cope splendidly, as if by instinct. Others feel more confident with little babies – or will manage better with older children or teenagers. Many find that the years before school are particularly difficult. Their children are changing from dependent babies to the independent children they must become if they are to be happy at school. With the first child, particularly, parents have times of uncertainty. This book aims to help parents build up the skills and confidence which many learn later on.

Perhaps advice on bringing up children leaves you feeling that you could make a really good job of it if you had more money, more time, a bigger house, a garden, if you lived in the country, or the town. But whatever your situation the addition of some knowledge can help you build on the opportunities you have.

Many mothers find that when their child is over two, outside help dwindles just as they need it most. Their child begins to stay awake all day, to talk, run about, be destructive, curious. But you're not alone. Any community that has children has parents, some who will be asking the questions you are asking yourself. Talk with them.

A different kind of book

The Pre-school Child is all about the questions and problems that every parent has to cope with, but it does not attempt to lay down rules or give the right answers. It helps you work things out for yourself. No one knows better than you what your situation is, what you want to happen and what you feel most happy doing. We want you to value your own opinions, and have confidence in your own decisions.

While *The Pre-school Child* brings you up-to-date information, and lots of illustrations, these are simply a start. The real difference in this book lies in its quizzes, checklists, exercises and action plans. We hope you will try them out, because although part of parenting is learned from your own parents, you also learn from day-to-day, watching and thinking, changing the way you do things, trying out new ideas. The activities in this book should support your learning and inform your intuitions. You'll see that in some articles we refer to the baby as 'he' and in others as 'she'. What is said applies equally to both boys and girls.

How to use this book

Each chapter is written for parents with children aged between two and five and based on events in day-to-day living. We haven't split the book up into neat age-groups, or types of development. What we have tried to do is to show the varied strands of child development in different situations.

The book is designed so that you can dip into whatever interests you, or browse straight through. If you want to find out more about a particular situation, consult the Book or Chapter Contents. On the other hand, if a particular problem worries you, or a particular aspect of development interests you, consult the Review in Chapter 8 and the Indexes at the back. These show you how the articles build up different themes and relate to different questions.

You may feel that the book is too 'action packed' – open it at any page and there's a suggestion of something to do. These are simply ideas of things you could do: you may not have the time or inclination to try many of them just now. Don't feel you have to do them all – look for the things that interest you and your child. Remember too that you can learn a lot from watching other people's children who are at different stages and have different interests from your own. As your own family grows we hope you will dip back into the book throughout their pre-school years.

A word of warning: neither we, nor you, should be aiming for perfect parents with perfect children. We realise that there's no such thing. The trouble is that a tired or irritable parent with a grizzly and difficult child starts thinking that other parents cope better and that other children are easier to deal with. This is a feeling all parents have at times. Most just don't like to admit it. We hope this book will help.

Course team:

Tim Chard, Anne Clutterbuck, Sheila Dale, Corrine Dowle, Clare Falkner, Nick Farnes, Keith Harry, Carol Haslam, Barbara Keeley, Chris Maule, Roy McHugh, Wendy Moore, David Sheppard, Evelyn Spillman, Rob Waller, Roy Webberley, Jane Wolfson.

Consultants:

Christine Athey, Nick Balmforth, Peg Belson, Mike Berger, Vida Carver, Derek Cherrington, Brenda Crowe, Jen Davies, Margaret Dawson, Joyce, Donoghue, Eddie Duggan, David Evans, Tony Fairburn, Jane Farnes, Joan Fazackerley, Rhonda Flynn, Elizabeth Grantham, Elizabeth Grugeon, Dorothy Heard, Maude Henderson, Angela Hobsbaum, Roy Howarth, Morag Hunter, Gladys Johnson, Joan Jones, Pat Kidd, Barbara Lewis, Sarah Meadows, Cynthia Mitchell, Alistair Nelson, Panto Philpott, Jane Philps, Vera Roberts, Barbara Tone, Joyce Watt, Gordon Wells, David Wolfson.

External assessor:

Professor W. D. Wall (University of London).

An Open University course

This book also forms part of an 8-week home-study course for parents. Like this book, the rest of the course reflects your personal, practical concerns.

Besides this book, the course includes:

* 4 TV programmes and 4 radio programmes, transmitted on BBC 2 twice a year.

* 3 records, on language development, music-making and story telling.

* A Resource Pack of posters, leaflets, study guides and broadcast notes.

* The chance to join a local 'self-help' group to share your experiences with other parents.

* 4 optional computer marked assignments, which you can submit if you aim to gain a Letter of Course Completion.

If you wish, you can apply to the Open University to join the full course and obtain the rest of the course materials. Simply write for leaflet WL2 from: A.S.C.O. The Open University, P.O.B. 76, Milton Keynes MK7 6AN. You'll be in good company. Over twelve thousand parents so far have taken the course and many of them told us how much they enjoyed it.

Part of a series

Has your child a younger brother or sister . . . or are you pregnant again? If so, and you like this book, then you're sure to want to know about its companion volume – *The First Years of Life*. Covering the period from the start of pregnancy to your child's second birthday, it includes many practical ideas on baby care and play. But it also helps you to sort out the problems of the early years, and to decide on vital issues such as antenatal care, feeding and returning to work.

The First Years of Life is available in the Ward Lock series: just ask your bookseller for details. Again, you can sign on afterwards for the full course if you wish.

The same Open University teams will be following up *The First Years of Life* and *The Pre-school Child* with a course on 5-10 year olds in 1980, and a course on adolescence after that. For up-to-date information write for 'Parent Courses Information' to: A.S.C.O. The Open University, P.O.B. 76, Walton Hall, Milton Keynes MK7 6AN.

Acknowledgements

Grateful acknowledgement is made to the following sources for illustrations used in this book:

P. 23 to Methuen Children's Books for the second verse of A. A. Milne's 'Vespers' from *When we were young* (illustration: E. Shepard); *p. 44*, the illustrations used in the mug collage from Dean Hay, *I see a lot of Things*, Collins, 1966, Matt Liesen, *First things*, The Platt and Munk Company, New York, 1967, The Mothercare catalogue 1976, A Twining Tea Co. advertisement; *p. 78*, to RoSPA for the wall chart on safety, HS/CP8; *p. 122*, to Keystone Press Agency for the football photograph and Maidenhead Advertiser for Chess photograph; *p. 140*, page and illustration from John Burningham, *Mr Gumpy's Motor Car*, Jonathan Cape, 1973 and extract and illustration from Alice Dalgliesh, *The Little Wooden Farmer*, Hamish Hamilton, 1969; to Thurman Publishing and Roger Hargreaves for drawings of 'Mr Happy'; *p. 141*, to Jonathan Cape for David Harrison's illustration from *The Book of Giant Stories*; *p. 142* and *143* line drawings of girl and footballer from R. L. Wickstrom, *Fundamental Motor Patterns* 2nd ed. Lea and Fabiger, 1977; *p. 179*, to Franklin Watts Ltd for 'How a baby is made' and to Lyle Stuart Inc. for 'Man and Woman in bed'; *p. 186*, to Dinosaur Publications Ltd for 'Nurse'; *p. 216*, to Playleadership Greater London Council for photograph of the One O'Clock Club; *p. 219*, to BBC Publications for photograph of *Other People's Children*; *pp. 222/223*, to Amelia Fyshe for photographs in *Children with a difference*; *p. 241*, to John Rainford for photographs used in Opportunities for older children; *p. 248*, to Bernice Phillips for Diane's story; *pp. 248/249* to the Herald, Luton, for use of the crowd scene.

Chapter 1

Through the day

Routines of the day and week

Every day is a new day but some things stay the same. The routine of getting up, meals, housework, shopping, play and going to bed, give the days a familiar pattern.

The routines of the day provide a secure base for new experiences. For the young child there is always something new to be learnt about familiar activities, and there are always new activities to be tried.

Daily activities

Daily activities can be divided up into personal routines, family work, going out and play.

Many of these activities are carried out in the company of a parent, but if they both go out to work the child minder plays an important role as well. In the evenings and at weekends both parents are usually around.

Young children will not be able to do as many of these as older children. Indeed some may not be suitable for your child at all, for example, some of the 'going out' activities which are unsuitable for very young children. Children are not usually ready for a playgroup before the age of two or three, and staying away from home on their own should not be tried too early. You may think that children should not be expected to do some of the 'family work' activities.

In this book we hope that you will discover that even chores such as laying the table or washing clothes have all kinds of learning opportunities. We shall be looking at many of these possibilities; at why children find them interesting; at some of the difficulties they have; at how we help children master them and at how we can help them to learn about themselves and the world they live in.

We shall be taking a closer look at personal routines in Chapters 1 and 2, family work in Chapters 3 and 4, going out in Chapters 5-8 and play throughout the book.

Survey your child's activities

Listed below are a large number of helpful things that a young child can do. They give you some idea of the kind of life your child is leading at present – what he does all day long. If you check back later, perhaps next year, you will see how life has changed. Read through and check off which ones your child does now.

Personal routines

Wake up at the right time ☐
Wash and clean his teeth ☐
Brush his hair ☐
Take his night clothes off ☐
Choose his own clothes ☐
Get his own clothes out ☐
Dress himself ☐
Put his shoes on ☐
Undress himself ☐
Put his clothes away ☐
Go to toilet by himself ☐
Wipe his own bottom ☐
Feed himself ☐
Use a knife, fork and spoon ☐
Wipe his hands and face ☐

Family work

Help get the food out ☐
Choose his own food ☐
Lay the table ☐
Clear the table ☐
Put the rubbish in the bin ☐
Help with the washing up ☐
Help with the drying up ☐
Help put away the dishes ☐
Collect milk from the doorstep ☐
Cook his own cakes ☐
Help prepare the family's food ☐
Fetch and carry around the house ☐
Help make up the shopping list ☐
Help put the shopping away ☐
Feed the pet ☐
Clear away his toys ☐
Tidy his own play area ☐
Help clean the house ☐
Help repair the house ☐
Use household appliances ☐

Help wash the clothes ☐
Make his own bed ☐
Help make the other beds ☐
Help other children ☐
Answer the front door ☐
Answer the telephone ☐

Going out

Help with the shopping ☐
Make purchases on his own ☐
Take messages to the neighbours ☐
Go and play in other peoples' houses ☐
Go out with other families ☐
Stay with friends overnight ☐
Meet teenagers ☐
Talk to strangers ☐
Go out for walks with his parents ☐
Go to the recreation ground with his parents ☐
Go on outings ☐
Go to a playgroup ☐
Visit your place of work ☐
Travel by bus ☐
Travel by train ☐

Play

Watch the television ☐
Draw ☐
Paint ☐
Play with dolls ☐
Play with water ☐
Play with dough ☐
Look at books ☐
Sing and dance ☐
Sew ☐
Play with mud pies ☐
Play with bricks; Lego ☐
Woodworking ☐
Play with tricycle/pedal car ☐
Play with prams ☐
Share toys with other children ☐
Play mothers and fathers ☐
Play dressing up ☐
Play making dinner ☐
Going on swings ☐

Pattern of the day

To get an idea of how activities fit into a pattern of the day have a look at your child's day. For example, take yesterday. What activities did your child do and what main groups do they fall into?

● Use the chart and write in the activity your child was engaged in.

● Do this alongside the time that the activity took place.

● Don't worry about being too accurate or too detailed, the nearest $\frac{1}{4}$ hour will do, and only note down the main activity. The example gives the general idea.

● When you have written down the main activities shade in the columns to show which group the activity was in – 'personal routines', 'family work', 'going out', or 'play'. This has been done in the example.

● Some of the activities are difficult to group – mealtimes for example, may involve family work – getting out food, laying the table, as well as eating which is a personal routine. When this happens split the time half and half.

● Add up the time in each column.

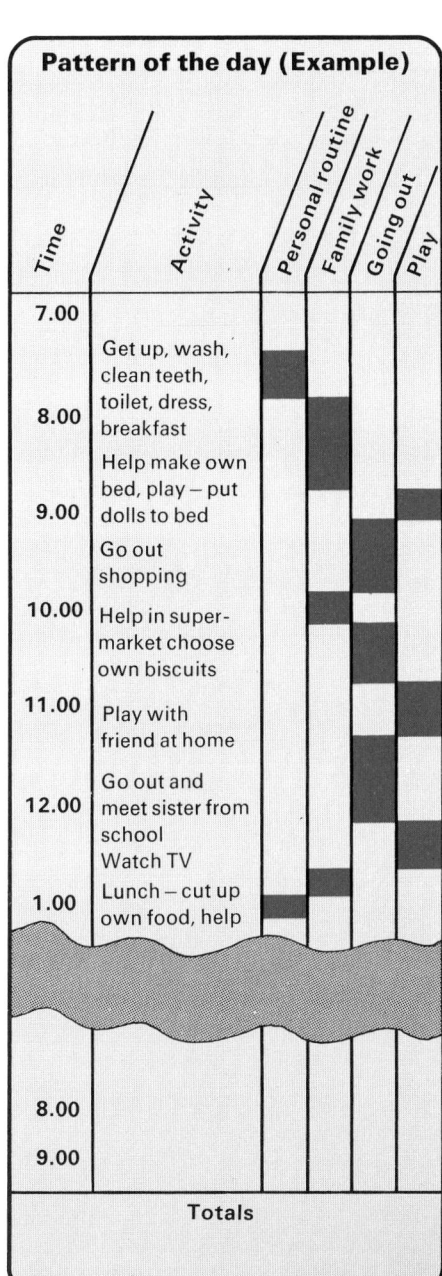

Pattern of the day (Example)

Time	Activity	Personal routine	Family work	Going out	Play
7.00					
	Get up, wash, clean teeth, toilet, dress, breakfast				
8.00					
	Help make own bed, play – put dolls to bed				
9.00	Go out shopping				
	Help in supermarket choose own biscuits				
10.00					
11.00	Play with friend at home				
	Go out and meet sister from school				
12.00	Watch TV				
1.00	Lunch – cut up own food, help				
8.00					
9.00					
Totals					

Pattern of the day

Time	Activity	Personal routine	Family work	Going out	Play
6.00					
7.00					
8.00					
9.00					
10.00					
11.00					
12.00					
1.00					
2.00					
3.00					
4.00					
5.00					
6.00					
7.00					
8.00					
9.00					
Totals:					

One of the mothers who helped us prepare this book did this exercise with her daughter Jill. Part of her chart is shown on the previous page. In Jill's day the personal routines were washing, dressing, eating and so on. Family work included laying the table, hanging up a coat and making a bed. Going out was to meet an older sister from school, on a shopping expedition, to a playgroup session. Play was watching television, dressing up, putting dolls to bed.

These groups added up to around $2\frac{3}{4}$ hours on personal routines, $1\frac{1}{2}$ hours for family work, $3\frac{1}{4}$ hours for going out and $4\frac{1}{2}$ hours play which included $1\frac{1}{4}$ hours watching television.

How did this compare with *your* child's day? It was probably different even though some parts will be the same. Getting up, eating, playing and probably going out happen in most children's days. The amount of time will vary from day to day and from family to family. Weekdays will be different from weekends and summer days different from winter days. Some families get up early, have all their meals together, have more than one pre-school child or have gran living with them and so on.

Patterns of the week

Yesterday was only one day and cannot give a picture of the pattern over a longer period. Keep a record for one week of all the main activities you do that are not on yesterday's chart. A chart like the example opposite will do, with each day divided into the groups used before.

Different activities which happened on each day are shown in the example chart; those which happen everyday, such as getting up and mealtimes, are left out.

As you read through the chapters you will have time to think about whether your child can do more for himself; think about ways that he can help with family work, how to get more out of going out, and suggestions for play; as well as looking at how you and he get on with other children. You will be able to think more about your days and weeks and whether the pattern is convenient for both of you or whether there is scope for change and more variety.

Related topics

Other topics about recording your child's routines of the day and week include:

● *Children and television* in Chapter 2.

● *All I get is questions* in Chapter 4.

● *Learning about reading* in Chapter 5.

● *Going places* in Chapter 6.

Patterns of the week

	Personal routines	Family work	Going out	Play
Monday	Hairwash	Help wash floor	Go to swings, go to playgroup	Sarah came round
Tuesday			Go to Northampton by bus	Dick and Jane came round to play
Wednesday		Help tidy under sink	Play at Sarah's house	Dresses dolls pretends to go shopping
Thursday	Sick and diarrhoea		Go to Mrs White's house	Drawing
Friday	Did not go to sleep until 9.30	Cooks own tarts	Go to library playgroup	Has fight with sister
Saturday	Gets dressed by herself	Helps paint kitchen	Goes shopping with Dad	
Sunday	Wake up early		Go to game park in Fred's car	

Children are different

Personality is not peculiar to just a few people – everyone has one. It is made up of a number of characteristics which combine to form an individual personality.

Each of the characteristics described below can be identified within a few weeks of birth. From the beginning babies seem to respond in different ways; however personality isn't fixed, it changes as a result of age and experience.

Parents have their own personalities and usually adjust to those of their children even though there are times when clashes occur. Some people are easier to live with than others. The child who is regular, adaptable, positive, approaches new experiences and reacts mildly is of the 'easy' type. Children who are 'difficult' sometimes tax even the most tolerant parents. They tend to be irregular, don't adapt, react intensely and withdraw from new experiences.

Why does my child behave like that?

This question is often asked by parents. For many people the answer given is one-sided – the parents themselves are blamed or praised. But parents are *not* all powerful. They have an important influence, but this influence is up against the personality of the child. If this is recognised and respected, clashes and unhappiness can be lessened.

Some personality characteristics

Active

The amount of *physical* activity on various tasks and in various settings

Low Activity
Play is physically calm, sits still during meals and while watching television. Bath time is quiet.

High Activity
Physically active in play, active during mealtimes, while watching television, during bathing and at bedtime.

Regular

Regularity of biological functions

Irregular
Falls asleep at different times. Difficult to know how long will stay asleep. Hungry at different times and eats varying amounts of food. 'Unpredictable'.

Regular
Goes to *sleep* within about an hour of about the same time each night. Eats about the same amount of food each day. Is hungry at about the same time each day. 'Predictable'.

Expresses Emotions

The intensity in emotional expression.

Low Intensity
When unhappy looks downcast, may whimper or whine or cry quietly. When happy smiles, chuckles or giggles. When angry looks cross or talks a bit louder than usual.

High Intensity
Cries loudly when unhappy. Roars with laughter, runs about excitedly, shouts with joy. When angry may scream shout and jump about.

Adapts

The ease or difficulty of trying to get the child to change his first reaction.

Low adaptability
Very difficult, sometimes impossible to get child to try a new food or experience first rejected.

Adaptable
First rejects new food but soon comes to accept if you try a few times. Settles in new situations after encouragement.

Mood

The balance between pleasant, joyful and friendly behaviour and unpleasant, unfriendly behaviour or crying.

Negative
Crying, fussy, angry, irritable, frowning.

Positive
Laughing, smiling, giggling, looking pleased. Generally seeming to enjoy things.

Persists

Continuing an activity despite obstacles

Low
Gives up easily if jig-saw pieces don't seem to fit. If another child takes away toy, doesn't try hard to get it back.

High
Continues to ask for ice cream even after the van has gone. Continues to ask for something even though you have said no.

Approaches or withdraws

How he reacts to a new person, situation or food when he first meets them.

Approach
Approaches or looks directly at and may immediately speak to new people. Will try new foods even though may dislike them. Enters new situations without hesitation.

Withdrawal
Will not approach and may look away from strangers. Will resist trying new foods and initially will refuse to enter new situations.

You and your child's temperament

There are examples on this page of the sorts of behaviour which are related to each characteristic. Children can be rated on each. It is not *good* or *bad* to be at either extreme or in the middle, although extremes on certain characteristics can be more difficult to live with.

Think about your child's day – yesterday.

● For each activity decide if a particular characteristic was shown.

● Then decide in general where your child fits on each characteristic.

● Circle the appropriate category in the table below.

● Do the same for yourself.

Are there ways in which you and your child differ?

Are there characteristics which you share?

If you differ how do you think it has affected your relationship?

Knowing about a child and the ways he responds gives us a basis for helping him to cope. You can try to avoid situations that cause your personalities to clash.

● An active child is likely to remain active in situations where this is not tolerated. To avoid this, for example, you would have to plan for an active child to be looked after by someone else if you were going to visit an elderly person or someone who is ill. A play-leader who is told that a child is highly active can avoid difficulty by not making the child keep still for long periods.

● The child who is withdrawn is more likely to cope if gradually exposed to new experiences. Children who tend to withdraw may have difficulty in making friends. Children who have difficulty in adapting need support and understanding in new situations. Parents and play-leaders who are aware of children's needs can adjust their level of support as a child begins to cope.

	Your child			You		
Active	low	medium	high	low	medium	high
Regular	irregular	mixed	regular	irregular	mixed	regular
Emotional expression	low	moderate	high	low	moderate	high
Adapts	low	varied	adaptable	low	varied	adaptable
Mood	negative	mixed	positive	negative	mixed	positive
Aproaches withdraws	withdraws	mixed	approach	withdraws	mixed	approach
Persists	low	varied	high	low	varied	high

WAKING

There are those mornings when children wake before their usual time. Perhaps they decide to come in bed with you. What has woken them up . . . being cold, hungry, wet, unwell, a bad dream? There is nothing they can do about these things themselves, sooner or later they must be attended to. Sometimes, as you know, a drink of warm milk or a dry nappy, clothes pulled up or reassurance will allow you both to have the extra sleep.

Jenny and her waking-up bag.

Awakenings

Remember the feeling of waking up . . .

 on holiday, or just after moving house, were you uncertain whom you would be meeting, what you would be doing, seeing, hearing, smelling, feeling . . . ? Each day is a bit like that for a child who has not had your experience of the art of living.

Sleep is a vital need, without it, life becomes distorted. Relatively trivial things like spilt milk suddenly become very important, enough to make you cry, even though you know that it is no use 'crying over it'.

Waking habits

The waking habits of children during the pre-school years change as their experience of living grows and the idea of time becomes clearer in their minds.

Alteration of clock time in autumn and spring suddenly exaggerates the change in the seasons. Babies take no notice of this at all. A pre-schooler's life is much more affected by the change to sudden dark at tea-time or the lightness of the spring evening. She begins to recognise the impact of clock time upon her life.

For the two-year-old, every day is a new day, with remembered experiences to be checked over and new things added. The five-year-old, with three years' 'worth' of memories, strengthened by listening, talking, picture books, perhaps photographs, can look to a new day with confidence and expectation. This assurance makes her quite a different person from the two-year-old. Gradually new events become part of a child's experience of life.

Think up an interesting 'waking up bag' for your child, something that she would enjoy exploring first thing the morning.

The sounds will tell you whether the bag is a success and you may have chance of extra rest. It is a good idea to change the contents from time to time, so that the child's search for a surprise is not always disappointed.

Your ideas will vary according to your resources and the age of your child. Here is a bag made up for Jenny who is two.

Perhaps you could list other things as well . . .

Given to Jenny	Use of object	What could you give your child?
Plastic cubes that screw on to a wooden stick	screw or turn	
Assorted coffee jar caps	fit	
Furry animal		
Velvet bean bag	feel – two textures	
Some raisins in an egg cup	eat	
A paperback picture book	look at	
Tinkle – a tin with a single peble or bean*	make a little noise	
Rattle – tin with a teaspoon of rice*	„	
Click – two sticks joined by a 6in. string	„	
* lids secured with Sellotape		

But what if the waking-up bag fails? Muriel remembers:

'With my first, I used to be so afraid of starting a bad habit, if James came into bed with me, I used to take him back straight away and attend to him in his own bed. Anne has a much nicer time. We have a cuddle until we agree that she would be much more comfortable in her own bed with one or another of her toys. It'll soon pass, this stage, and we might as well enjoy it!'

Muriel has her solution. But what of Suzie who plans to go to her doctor?

'I am too tired to think, even to make a shopping list! The baby wakes at 5.30am and as soon as I have finished him, three-year-old John is awake. After that, the day goes non-stop until I fall asleep in my chair after supper!'

The doctor could give her a course of tranquillising pills, which could give her a rest but would not alter the sleeping patterns of John or the baby.

Early wakers

Changing your child's rest pattern to include an afternoon period of relaxing can help – remember those antenatal classes? The same way of concentrating on relaxing one part of the body after the other will help now as it did then. Suzie has to manage on her own, she can watch for those times of the day when even John slows down a bit. What can she do to stretch out those periods of quiet contentment so that she can creep away and relax?
● switch on a television programme for him
● bring out a puzzle that he has begun to learn to do.
● bring out other quiet things to do.

Sharing children

Another solution to Suzie's problem would be to meet up with another mother, giving and taking responsibility, so that both mothers have spells with extra children and spells alone. If you have neighbours with children of compatible age, you are not likely to have big problems about this . . . but if not, where do you meet them?

In many neighbourhoods a Mother and Toddler Club will provide a neutral meeting ground for children and their mothers, where they can gradually get to know each other. In this way, the sharing of children can begin in a way that becomes a new way of life, giving mothers a change and a rest and children a wider experience of people.

Fathers are parents too!

In the way that Muriel was tough with her first child, being unaware of how quickly some stages would pass, so some husbands are reluctant to take responsibility for their children in the morning. This cuts short their night's sleep when there is a day's work ahead or worries them because they think it will mean a different pattern of relationship. A wife, unusually falling asleep in her chair, like Suzie, is a wife needing more relief than she is getting. Although she needs help it is a stage that will pass, and parents can help each other to get through it.

Children can learn!

Sometimes it is necessary to appear heartless, refusing firmly to react to blackmail. Children respond to consistency and are, however reluctantly, reassured by meeting the limits of their freedom to command other people.

What methods do you use to stall so as not to get up before . . .
● the milkman calls,
● the hands of a real clock match the hands of a toy clock that you set at getting-up time,
● you go in yourself to wake your child?
Morning sounds will vary but you can find your own time-marks and insist on them.

Late wakers

There are those mornings when, for one reason or another, you have to wake children before they have finished sleeping – perhaps you need to go out. You probably know what it feels like to be woken before you are ready to wake up – it often makes you grumpy and irritable.

When it is important for you to get an early start in the morning, because you need to catch a bus to the nursery, or to the factory crèche or the playgroup outing, it helps to speed your departure if you tell your child of your plans the night before so that she wakes in the morning ready to go.

'Don't get up until the real clock shows the same time as your clock'.

What does 'time' mean?

Have you ever thought, when on holiday or after moving house 'Only a week ago I was . . .' doing this or that. When a lot of things happen to you, you can often look back over a week and be amazed at all that has happened in that short time. It is like that for a child, every day! Have you noticed how a day with lots of excitements will tire a child too soon? Her 'inside clock' means more to her than the hours Big Ben strikes!

If you see life from your child's point of view, you can sometimes predict the times that will be tiring for her. You will come to expect that after days when two hours of clock time is like five hours of your child's inside clock, she will need a day in which her clock can have a rest, a day of leisure, thinking back over the day before, talking about it, building it into her memory.

How does your day go?

Try linking some regular landmarks of your day with the time shown by a clear clock that your child can see and read easily. This will encourage an awareness of the meaning of time.

● Talk about the nice things you are going to do during the day and bits that she will remember from another day.

● Discuss the choosing of clothes to be worn.

● Make up a story about how another little boy you knew once did something just like she is going to do.

Remember that a child's ability to look ahead is bounded by the limits of her experience, which may have unexpected gaps.

Perhaps you could:

● remark on being early or late, while looking at a clock, for example: 'It's ten o'clock and the beds aren't made yet!'

● look up times of television programmes and check by the clock so that your child can learn that you are able to read and to tell the time, so you know when something is going to happen.

● set a toy clock at the time something is going to happen, like getting up, going to bed, going out . . . then, when the clock hands say the same as the toy clock, the event can take place. Gradually, as experience of living builds up during the pre-school years, children get the idea of time outside themselves. They come to understand that if something nice is going to happen after tea, they cannot hurry it along by having tea earlier! They come to understand how the future becomes the present, that 'the day after tomorrow' is after two nights of sleeping. They learn that past events happened at different times, that last week is not the same as yesterday.

All that takes a lot of understanding; it can all happen before your child reaches the age of five.

DRESSING

Day in day out we get dressed. We don't think much about it except when a lace snaps or a zip jams. For the under-fives, getting dressed does not come easily or naturally.

Getting undressed is fun

● Most two-year-olds can take off simple garments – hats, shoes, socks, pants, vests. Most have trouble with sleeves, fastenings, and bulky garments.

● Most three-year-olds can manage all these things, and have often progressed to undoing some zips and big buttons. Familiarity with the movements make fingers quicker at doing these things.

● The four-year-old is much better and can manage most clothes.

Why? Chubby hands are slow, unco-ordinated and clumsy. They can manage pulling or dragging, the sweeping movements of undressing. These large movements are learnt before the development of the fine control needed for dressing.

Dressing requires many skills

● The co-ordination of hand and eye that will match button with button hole.

● The fine finger movements needed to push a button through its hole or pull the runner of a zip fastener, or press poppers together.

● The recognition of the difference between things that are nearly the same, for example, a right or left shoe.

● The judgement that will match a large hole to the head, smaller holes to the arms.

● The experience gained from many attempts at putting on clothes so that they come right.

All these skills are learnt slowly.

Look carefully at dressing

Think about the routine of getting dressed, the different stages of putting on clothes. Many skills are required, you can help in different ways. Can your child manage?

Look at the chart below. Put ticks in the columns to show which garments you think children aged 2, 3 and 4 can put on by themselves.

Garment	2	3	4	Your child
Bobble hat				
Pull on shoes				
Vest				
T-shirt				
Round-necked jersey				
Knickers/pants/trousers with elastic				
Buttoned jeans				
Socks				
Anorak				
V-necked jersey				
Cardigan				
Dungarees/skirt with straps				
Dress/skirt with front buttons				
Shoes with buckles				
Duffle coat				
Coat with buttons				
Lace-up shoes				
Tie				
Dress with back zip				
Dress with back bow				

The table above shows a variety of skills involved in getting dressed. Two-year-olds will have a go at putting on a bobble hat but the dress with a back zip or bow will always need adult help.

Clothes that are simple to put on will give the child the satisfaction of independence at an earlier age. They will save you time too, but the challenge of buttons and zips requires a child to develop further skills. Small buttons are more difficult to manage than large ones. To catch the runner on a zip and pull it so that it doesn't catch needs considerable judgement.

To tie a bow on lace-up shoes takes a great deal of practice. It helps if you and your child sit at a table with a shoe in front of you. Many children are able to tie bows before the age of five if they have had this kind of encouragement. This is the sort of preparation for school that makes a real difference to a child.

Mastery of physical skills gives him independence that leaves his mind free and ready to learn. This mastery, gained by repeated practising with different kinds of clothes, different shapes and fastenings will give your child freedom to enjoy trying on and wearing a greater variety of clothes than if you had been content to offer him only the simplest ones.

Look back after six months at the skills that your child had then, and see what he has learnt.

Learning dressing skills

Your child's ability to perform dressing tasks will depend on his own special rate of growth. Some children find certain things easier to do than others. They show considerable differences in their hand-eye co-ordination and finger control. The process of dressing is largely centred around the gaining of certain skills and if, as parents, you know what these are, you can provide opportunities for children to practise them in ways that are enjoyed.

● *Dolls and teddies*

Most children have an assortment of dolls, and you can provide an interesting pile of clothes. Which clothes fit the dolls? Expert judgement develops through enjoyable games.

Boys enjoy dressing and playing with 'people toys', in the same way that girls do. Putting on the jackets and trousers, doing up the buttons of dolls and teddy bears gives them a chance to learn the skills that will help them to dress themselves.

'Action man' type dolls are rather fiddley for under fives, and are better kept for older children.

● *Make a 'fastening doll'*

Dolls clothes can include a wide range of fastenings such as velcro, zips, big buttons, hooks and eyes, press studs, toggles, big laces.

● *Dressing up*

A 'dressing up box' will help your child develop skills – but to him, that box is a 'magic carpet'. Acquiring dressing skills is a by-product: what he enjoys is the pretending play that turns him into a different, exciting person when he dresses up.

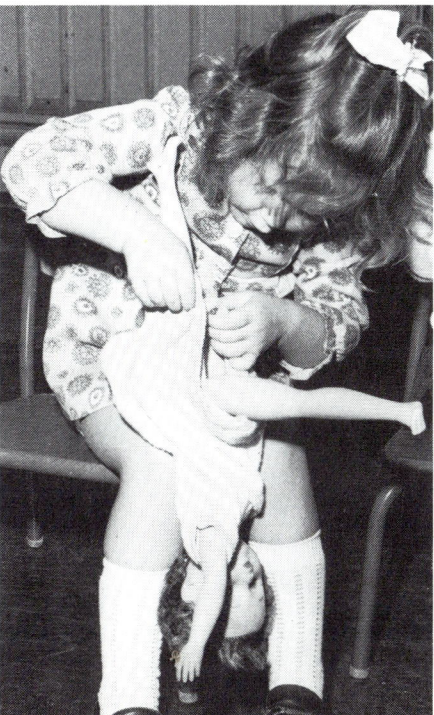

How about a box which might contain hats, grown-ups' shoes, bags, jewellery, costumes, old spectacles etc? A variety of fastenings on the garments and a long mirror will add interest and challenge. The mirror helps the young child develop awareness of his size and shape, and what other people see when they look at him. Children need to know what they look like! That growing awareness of self in which self-confidence is rooted is to be found here.

Repetition reinforces learning

Whether adults or children are learning, repetition helps in the acquiring of skills. Your child needs to practise undressing and dressing many times. Can you spare the time to allow him to proceed at his own pace? If we do everything for him without trying to start him off towards self-help, we get through the business of dressing and undressing more quickly. But if we don't make time to help, we miss a chance to help him achieve an early independence, and we lose lots of fun and chances of talking on the way. If we, as parents, take a little longer over all these efforts at the beginning, and show patience in helping and encouraging the child to do things for himself, in the end we will save many hours of needless waiting on him – as well as bad temper!

 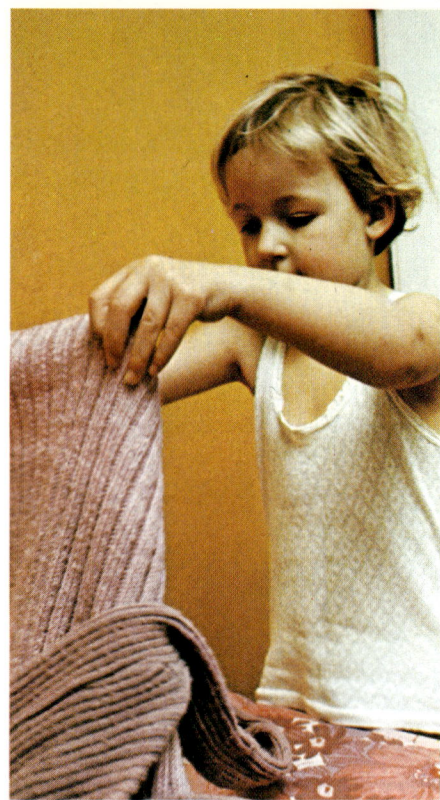 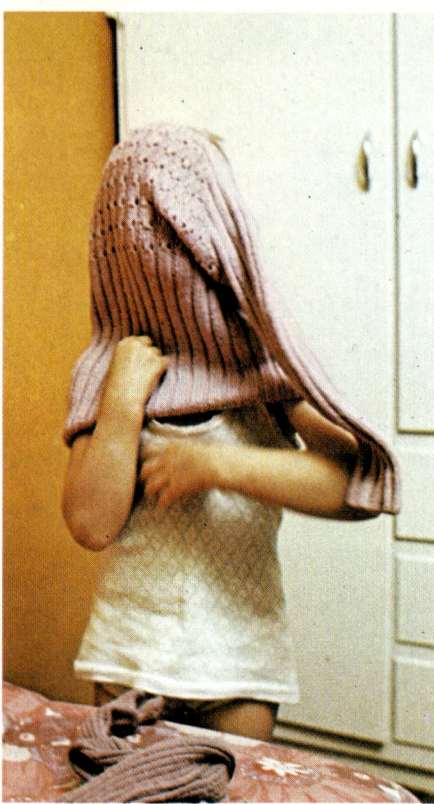

Helping him learn to choose

Should your pre-school child choose what he wants to wear?

Most two- and three-year-olds don't care what they wear – they want to get on and play.

It is unwise to create confusion in the young child by expecting him to make choices before he is ready. With a *four-year-old* you may like to try to present a limited choice of appropriate clothes, to see if he wants to choose. But often choice is governed by whether the ironing has been done!

By all means encourage a child to express his likes and dislikes but if you're still waiting at coffee time for him to choose between two sweaters, don't be surprised, deciding can be difficult.

They often dislike a garment because of its texture and tight fit – for example polo necks are not always popular with young children, nor are scratchy jerseys.

Helping him to help himself

You've overslept and are in a rush to get out to playgroup. Your three-year-old screams when you try to dress him in a hurry. He's frustrated because he wants to do it himself. But you know he's not yet capable of doing the whole job and will take all day without help. What do you do?

(a) Insist, making him more angry.

(b) Let him fumble, getting frustrated.

The result of (a) will leave you starting the day with feelings of exasperation and guilt; (b) will delay you and you will still feel guilty. No happy way out! How could you prevent a repeat of this confrontation? How can you help him to help you? Try laying out his clothes the night before – so that he can start off properly. One morning he will triumphantly appear in your bedroom already dressed – you've made it!

You know from having completed the chart on page 12, where the difficulties lie in dressing. So you could choose the clothes and lay them out bearing this in mind, for example the sweater front downwards with the welt towards the child, then it's ready to slip over the head. Usually clothes are laid out starting from the skin upwards or working in a left to right direction. You'll know what's right for your family. In houses with cold bedrooms, children often get dressed and undressed downstairs. A pile of clothes arranged in the right order can be carried to a warm place.

Saving him frustration

Let him do what he can; and be patient about helping him to do what is difficult at present. Children are quick to sense your irritation. They become more clumsy and awkward as they anxiously try to please – and may fail. Avoiding confrontation is an art, especially where young children are concerned. You will learn it through your success and failures.

Do clothes matter?

You might think that there are more important areas in a young child's life than his clothes – especially today when most are simple and practical. But we mustn't underestimate the fact that mothers are often very anxious that their child presents a good appearance to the outside world. The way the child is dressed is seen by some people to be an indicator of the care shown by parents. This sometimes causes parents to be over-anxious about their child's dress as they don't want to lose status in front of other mothers.

Mothers often lack confidence in their mothering skills, especially with the first child. Joining a Mother and Toddler Club can re-assure mothers that their child is neither as bad nor as good as they imagined. Providing tough gear so a child can relax while he 'works' and not worry about what mum is going to say will perhaps help mother and child to enjoy early childhood.

We have to resign ourselves to accept the difficulties of the whole business of dressing – the constant hunting for the lost shoe; the toddler who undresses whilst your back is turned seeing to the baby; getting wise to the fact that if you dress junior too soon if you're going somewhere special, he'll need to be re-dressed by the time you've got yourself ready! You always need resignation and acceptance of the fact that the more you try to hurry them, the slower they become.

But don't worry! This stage will pass and, thanks to being left to struggle, with only occasional help, the skills will be learnt, and independence gained.

Avoiding confrontations

There are other times at which your reaction can make all the difference between something going smoothly or becoming a fight.
For more about this see
● *Clean and dry* } in this Chapter
● *Mealtimes*
● *Wills of their own* in Chapter 2
● *Talking about sex* in Chapter 6

MEALTIMES

The most important thing about mealtimes is that your child should come happily when you call out 'dinner time'. Battles over food can't always be avoided. But start on the positive side and look at some of the natural learning that can take place at mealtimes.

Getting to grips

In *Dressing* we looked at the difference between large movements and fine control of the hands and fingers. Most of the skills used at the table are fine control skills. Your child has to learn to make very 'neat' use of his hands and fingers.

Remember your baby's first attempts to feed herself – fingers into everything, food everywhere, followed by a battle over the spoon? By two she's probably managing a spoon quite well. But the fingers have a long way to go, from those early attempts, through the spoon stage, to getting a grown-up grasp on things.

Compare the way you and your child pick up and use the following objects.

Tick 'fist' if you use the whole hand, and 'finger' if you grip the object between your fingers and thumb in some way.

Fist grip on a spoon

Object	Your child		You	
	Fist	Finger	Fist	Finger
Spoon				
Fork				
Knife				
Cup				
Beaker				
Jug				

You'll probably find that your child makes greater use of his whole hand for holding these objects, while you tend to grip more with your fingers. To find out what this difference means, try holding a spoon in a fist grip and eating from it. You'll notice that you need to make much larger movements with your arm this way, it's less easy to control the spoon and harder to eat properly.

Helping messy eaters

We need to accept that small children are likely for a time to be messy eaters. Natural 'maturing' of the body will do most of the work for us. Finer movements will follow from the large arm movements and the fist grip as the child's body becomes more physically able. It's the same as learning to walk – you can encourage a child when the time is right, but you can't make her walk before she's ready.

This doesn't mean you shouldn't give your child a knife and fork. Many children make rapid strides in self-feeding when given a set of their own cutlery. In addition you may be able to help by:

● providing a special small child-sized set of cutlery. You can buy spoons and forks with specially shaped handles – hold one to see the advantage for a fist-gripper.

● providing a dish with straight sides to push food against to get it on the spoon or fork more easily.

● providing toys such as simple jig-saws or shape-fitting boards which will give your child practice at grasping and handling small objects precisely.

● not worrying! Anxiety and constant comment on your part won't help. A very rough guide of what to expect at what age is given below – but as with all physical development children vary enormously.

At 2 years . . .
Uses a spoon well. May manage a fork. Can lift and put down a cup with two hands. May go back to fingers occasionally.

At 3 years . . .
Uses fork and spoon quite tidily. Can hold a cup with one hand.

At 4 years . . .
Uses knife, fork and spoon, though may need help with difficult cutting. Can serve himself from jugs and dishes.

Table-laying maths

Listen to a three-year-old chanting numbers: 'one, two, three, six, seven', unaware of the gaps. She knows *number names* but she doesn't really know what numbers are.

There's no such thing as a 'five' – it's an idea, a symbol that can stand for things. A child needs to handle five things, many times over before she gets the *idea* of 'five' or any other number. She needs to learn that five things, whatever they look like, are five.

Grouping and matching

Everyday a young child puts things into groups or 'sets', or sees things grouped by adults, according to something they have in common. It may be shape (the *large* plates) or colour (the *blue* mugs), or where they're kept (the things in my handbag), or because they're alike (my *favourite* toys) – and so on.

Sets of things like this can be made up of any number of objects. To grasp the idea of 'five', or any other number, it helps if a child can *match* sets of the same number of things together. (This is sometimes called 'one-to-one correspondence'.)

Eventually at school your child will be dealing simply with sets of numbers – equal sets of tens which make up sets of 100, for example. In the pre-school and early school years though, it's the practical handling of objects that counts. Table-laying in particular gives lots of opportunities for matching and counting equal sets.

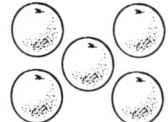

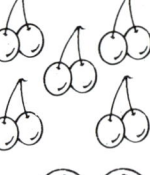

Three different sets of five

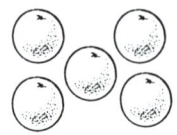

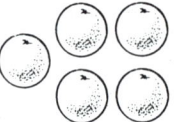

The same set of five oranges arranged three different ways

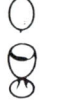

Five eggs for five egg cups

The 'fiveness' of five

See if you can find out how much your child really understands numbers with this activity.

The child needs to learn that five things, however they're arranged, are still five:

1 Put out 5 cups like this

Can your child tell you how many there are?

2 Now rearrange them like this

Does she know how many there are now?

A child also needs experience in matching equal sets of objects:

3 Put out 5 saucers with the 5 cups.

Ask her to give each cup a saucer. Can she match them like this?

4 Cups and saucers go 'naturally' in pairs. Try something less closely related – put out five knives and five plates and ask if she can put a knife by each plate.

matched together make

5 Put out two rows of spoons like this

Ask your child if there's the same number of spoons in each row.

6 Now rearrange the first row like this

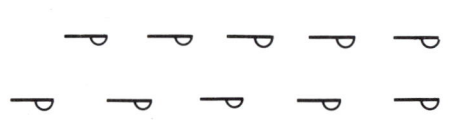

Ask her again if there's the same number of spoons in each row.

This exercise is for you to find out what your child understands about numbers. Most of it will be beyond the grasp of two-year-olds, and many children won't get all the items right until around the age of seven. So don't make your child feel bad about wrong answers – and stop if she loses interest or gets at all upset. Only use the suggestions (right) for help with numbers if your child is interested – forcing numbers on her will more likely put her off.

If your child is not sure that there are 5 cups in items 1 and 2, she needs more experience in making up and handling groups of objects, counting as she goes.

Items 3 and 4 are fairly straightforward – a child doesn't even need to know there are 'five' things in order to match them one-to-one with her hands. Item 5 requires the child to match in her head, by looking and comparing the two rows.

Item 6 is harder because the first row now occupies less space, even though it still has the same number of spoons. If your child now says there's more in the second row, or less in the first row, she's still being 'tricked' by the look of the arrangement. It takes the child several years to trust her ideas more than her eyes. You can help her by counting the spoons in each row, and by showing how to match the two rows as in item 5.

Table talk

Talking at table may seem a luxury you can do without, particularly if you and your child are going through a battle-field stage where he either won't eat what you've prepared, or makes a constant mess. But table talk still takes place – although mostly in the form of you telling the child to shut up/eat up/ use his spoon/not to drop any on the floor/stay at the table and so on. Sounds familiar?

Such 'controlling-eating' talk from you gives the child little chance to do anything except to eat – or fight you over eating. It certainly doesn't encourage either you or him to see meal-times as an opportunity to relax and chat. But table talk together could be one way of getting through mealtimes without too much fuss, simply because it takes attention off the actual eating.

Read through this conversation recorded at lunchtime by the mother of a two-year-old. In the box alongside, mark with a C those statements by the mother which are to do with 'controlling' the child's eating. Mark with a G those which are simply general remarks (for example, about the food being eaten).

☐ M. Here's Jane's dinner, and here's my dinner.

J. Dinner. (Comes to table and points at carrots)

☐ M. Yes, carrots, you like carrots, don't you?

J. Yes. (Begins to eat. Dog can be heard barking)

J. Pip, Pip

☐ M. Yes, that's Pip barking. I expect he's just going for his walk.

J. Walkie. (Finishes carrots and holds out plate)

J. More now.

☐ M. You can have some more, but you must eat your meat and potato as well.

J. 'tato.

☐ M. Yes, potato. Where's your potato?

J. Dere (pointing at it)

☐ M. Well eat it up now.

J. All gone, all gone.

☐ M. There's a good girl, you've finished it all.

☐ M. Now, do you want some cream on your peaches?

J. Keem, keem.

☐ M. Use your spoon then. (Sound of aeroplane flying over the house)

J. Sky, sky (points out of window)

☐ M. That's an aeroplane in the sky, coming into the airport near where Aunty Nan lives.

☐ M. No more? All right. Wait until I get the flannel to wipe your face. (Wipes J's face and gives her the flannel).

☐ M. Wipe your hands before you get down.

J. Keem, keem (pointing to mouth)

☐ M. Yes, there was cream around your mouth, but I wiped it all off.

☐ M. You can get down now

J. Down, down . . . .

A place to talk

Finding the balance in table talk isn't always easy, particularly with more than one child to feed. You might like to try recording a table conversation in your own family (by tape, or making notes) to hear what's actually happening. If all your talk is 'control talk' – can you cut it down, or make five minutes for a cuddle and chat afterwards? In the early years you can do much to help or hinder your child's language development. Finding suitable times and places for unharrassed talk is the first essential – table or sofa will do. Or talk while you work – see Chapter 3.

Food, glorious food?

Mealtimes chat may sometimes take your child's attention away from food he doesn't like very much. But what do you do when he's really being difficult or faddy about his food? Does it really matter what he eats? See *Food, glorious food* in this chapter.

Answers

The mother's talk falls into this pattern: G, G, G, C, G, C, G, C, C, G, C, C, G, C – equally balanced between 'controlling' talk and more general chat. It's worth noticing, too, the different ways she answers little Jane's gestures and short statements. Sometimes she expands and checks what Jane had in mind ('tato' 'Yes, potatoes. Where's your potato?') and sometimes, as with the aeroplane she adds more information and explanation. And in 'controlling' she offers limited choices 'do you want cream on your peaches?', 'more carrots if you eat your meat and potato'.

Table-laying exercises

Here are some ideas for discovering numbers through laying the table. Laying the table can give your child helpful experience in matching equal sets, and sorting out and counting equal sets of objects. As she gets more confident you can make it harder.

● *Matching one-to-one* You lay the table in place settings, except for, say, the spoons. Give her the right number of spoons, and tell her to 'give each mat (or place) a spoon'. Gradually you can do less, until eventually you can give her the sets of objects, and ask her to lay places for whoever is going to be at the meal – one of each thing for me, for you, for Fred, and so on. Now the child is matching the objects to 'people I know are here for tea.'

● *Sorting out the equal sets of objects* Once she's handled the things in these 'matching' exercises, your child should quite soon be able to get out the right number of things for herself, before laying the table. She can check if she's right when she actually comes to lay the table in place settings. 'One for you, one for me,' and so on, may help again.

● *Other matchings* Matching is useful at many other times too – for example matching mugs to hooks, or taking the right number of biscuits from the tin to give one each to her friends. Matching the right button to the right hole, the right top to the right jar, or the right lid to the right pan all require a child to match one-to-one things that 'go together'.

● *Natural numbers* As we've seen, it's the practical numbers that count. But 'counting' nursery rhymes are fun, and you can begin to help your child recognise number symbols, reading left to right: the 61 bus, your house number, numbers on birthday cards and so on. Numbers which stand for years of age don't always mean much to a young child who's not sure when 'next week' is, let alone 'next year' but see how these four-year-olds have translated age into things they can understand:

Adult: 'How old are you, Jane?'

Jane: (holding out her fingers) 'I'm all these but not my thumb.'

Tim: (playing in the sand) 'I've made a birthday cake. I put some candles on it – one, two, three, four, five. So it's not for me. I'm not as big as that yet!'

More on maths

● handling numbers in *Launder and learn* in Chapter 3.

● ideas about length in *Woodwork* in Chapter 4.

● weights and quantities in *Cooking* in Chapter 4.

● sorting things into groups in *Tidying up* in Chapter 4.

● making collections of objects in *Sorting things out* in Chapter 5.

Food, glorious food

Food is often the cause of argument, anger and frustration for both parents and young children. Considering the child's point of view can be revealing and may help avoid food-time conflicts.

The case of the giant potato

When you next have a meal, note the height of your child's head above the table. When you have a moment to yourself, kneel down at the table so that your eyes are on the same level as his. Close your eyes, and imagine a dinner plate of sausage, peas and roast potatoes. You are three years old and two feet six inches high.

The plate is nearly two feet across, the sausages nine inches long with a tough, leathery skin. The potatoes are as big as tennis balls, and the peas like green marbles. Worst of all, the knife and fork are nearly fifteen inches long and heavy in your hands. Your shoulders are only just above table level, so when you try to cut the sausage, you push forwards rather than downwards, and the thing skids off the plate.

From the moment they leave a high chair, children are faced with mealtime equipment made for people two or three times their size. They may look cute at the table, but have you taken their size into account? Mealtimes needn't be a battle-field. Tantrums may be more to do with posture than peevishness!

Ask yourself:

● Are your child's shoulders more than 6 inches above the table?

● Can he reach right across his plate from his chair?

● Can he cut up his food?

● Can he use adult-sized cutlery?

● Would smaller cutlery help?

A fork's okay for sausages but not such a good idea for baked beans so – would he find it easier to use a spoon for some, if not all, foods?

Mealtimes

There are three ts at mealtimes: taste, texture, temperature. Food looks the same to all of us – but our nose and our taste buds do not stay the same as we grow up.

Let's start with TASTE, and do a little chemistry.

Take an eggcup of water, and add the smallest possible pinch of salt – two or three grains if you can. Stir till the salt dissolves, then taste it. If the amount is really small, it probably won't taste salty. Keep on adding tiny pinches until you can just detect the salt. Make a note of how many pinches you used.

Now take a fresh eggcup and the same amount of water, but add only half the amount of salt you needed to taste it. Stir till dissolved. Try this out on a child who does not know what's in the eggcup. If he can't taste the salt, keep adding tiny amounts until he can. Unless your child has a cold, he will probably detect the salt before you did.

The older we are, the more likely it is that we've lost some of our sensitivity to tastes of various kinds. This helps to explain why children and adults do not always agree about what tastes good. Babies will instinctively reject sour or bitter-tasting foods because instinct warns them that these could be dangerous to their digestion. But you have probably noticed that some men like their bitter! Adults stay most sensitive of all to bitter or acid tastes. Pre-school children gradually grow out of their sour or bitter flavours; their dislike of them may have more than a trace of instinct about it.

TEXTURE seems just as important as taste. At the back of the throat is a spot which will cause vomiting if tickled or irritated. Dry, crumbly food or greasy substances can stick to the palate and make a child feel ill, and try to get rid of what's causing the trouble. Children are more sensitive in this way, just as they are over the sense of taste. A beaker of water is an excellent companion for foods such as meat, biscuits or apple crumble.

If you cut up your child's food, try a piece for TEMPERATURE. Is it as hot as your own? If so, try again in a few minutes. Because it was cut up, it has probably cooled more quickly. A change of temperature may change both the taste and the smell of food. Does it still taste as good now that it has cooled? If your child eats too quickly, is it because his food cools too quickly? You might like to try this checklist:

	liked by you	liked by child
Taste Sweet Sour Bitter Salty Savoury		
Texture Creamy Crunchy Crumbly Rubbery Greasy Dry Moist		
Temperature Very hot Hot Warm Tepid Cool Cold Icy Frozen		

Why do we eat?

Can you remember a time in the last week or month when you felt hungry? How did you feel?

- stomach pains
- felt cold
- had a headache
- bad tempered
- other (explain)

Did you show signs of impatience for your meal?

A hungry child is not a sociable child. A child's body burns up energy more quickly, cools down sooner, than an adult's. His feeling of hunger may not always fit in with your planned mealtimes and hunger can be worrying and uncomfortable. Note when your child first complains of feeling hungry, and watch his reactions at the same time for the next few days. If he seems to feel hungry at the same time each day, perhaps you should think whether mealtime needs changing.

Only puppy fat?

Babies develop a layer of fat to keep them warm, but there is a danger that the body will get used to storing fat.

Cells for storing fat in the body develop mostly in the first year of life. What's more important, fat storage cells never go away once you've got them. A fat baby becomes an adult with a large number of fat storage cells, who puts on weight easily. He also finds it more difficult to slim than the adult who, as a baby, developed few fat storage cells.

Take a look at the tables below. In the first the adult overeats so his cells get larger. In the second the baby actually develops more cells.

Food for comfort

Think of a hungry baby, kicking, yelling, totally helpless. Once given the breast or bottle, he is at peace. To him, food is the most important thing in the world; comfort and food are, as often as not, the same thing. But babies are not the only ones to find comfort in food. For some children and even some adults, food continues to be the way to peace of mind and they may become seriously overweight. Most children, may comfort-eat to some extent. The child returning from playgroup may not only be hungry, but unsure of himself. A meal is a sign he is back at home with mum.

ADULTS AND CHILDREN

Fat storage cells before	Over feeding	Fat storage cells after
	Too much sugar, cereal, biscuits, cakes, bread, potatoes, rice	Fat cells much larger

BABY (UNDER 1)

Fat storage cells before	Over feeding	Fat storage cells after
	Too much sugar, cereal, biscuits, cakes, bread, potatoes, rice	Fat cells much larger and more fat cells

Puppy fat doesn't always disappear. A chubby child can grow into a self-conscious overweight teenager . . . a common problem nowadays.

Eating out

Eating out can be a muddle of offers, refusals, slaps and tantrums. Each time you swear never to take them out to a meal again. What *are* the problems of eating out with children?

To begin with, eating out is an excellent way of showing children that other folk, besides their parents, observe rules at table. The 'dos and don'ts' of table manners appear not only as demonstrations of mum's and dad's bad temper, but as something everyone does. If it is chosen carefully, food at a cafe, or restaurant can be more exciting.

Unfortunately, restaurants and cafes are even more purpose-built for an

adult world than the average home. Go back to the questions at the beginning and apply them to a cafe. If things are not satisfactory, do not hesitate to ask the waiter for help. Most restaurants will serve children's portions when asked, whether they are on the menu or not. Children in a restaurant are often self-conscious. They are in a strange place, with unfamiliar tables, cutlery and food. If you can turn their tension to curiosity, and point out items of interest, such as the waiters, the glimpses of the kitchen, their self-consciousness may disappear and your outing be an enjoyable experience.

Have you said to your child . . .

'Eat your greens or you'll get no pudding'?

If he doesn't like greens he's not likely to suffer from not eating them. There's plenty of goodness in other foods and there's no evidence to suggest that any one particular item of food is essential.

You're punishing him before rewarding him and making life difficult for yourself. He's sure to learn that he can use food to test you out whenever he feels like it. If you don't want to throw away good food, it's best not to give him what he doesn't like.

We all make demands

Throughout each day there are many occasions when parents and children make demands on one another. These demands include very simple requests for help and requests to stop doing something. Who makes the most demands and are these demands mainly positive or negative? What are the responses to these demands? Does a child always do what is asked of him and does a parent always do what a child wants – almost certainly 'no'. This topic takes a closer look at these questions and invites you to think about what happens between you and your child.

The demands made by parents and children on one another can be either positive – 'Do this' – or negative – 'Stop doing that'. Parents try to control their children's behaviour, stopping them doing some things and encouraging them to do others. Similarly children control the behaviour of their parents, by asking them to do things and attempting to prevent them from doing other things. Parents and children act to keep each other's behaviour within limits by objecting to behaviour that goes above the limit and encouraging behaviour which is acceptable.

Some people think that children should be unquestioningly obedient. But it's worth considering whether we should 'do unto others as we would be done by'. How can we expect children to have standards of behaviour towards us that we don't in turn show towards them? How can we expect respect for our demands if we don't have respect for our childrens demands? 'Well' we say 'children don't have the responsibilities of adults – running a house, etc'. Complete equality is impossible but it may be possible to have more than at present. Equality doesn't mean

being totally child centred – it is to recognise that we cannot expect our children to meet more of our demands than we are prepared to meet of theirs. In other words if we meet only some of their demands it is unreasonable to expect them to meet all of ours.

There is a nice illustration of this from a mother quoted in *Four Years Old in an Urban Community*:
'. . . she said 'I can't, Mummy, I'm busy' – so I said 'Well, all right then' and left it at that, because it wasn't very important at the time; and then it happened again, and I thought, well I'm not going to let her just get away with it, like, so I said 'Now you must do what Mummy tells you *straight away*'. And she said 'Well, when you're busy you always *tell* me when you're busy!' – and she'd just got me over-bowled, and I didn't know what to do; but by that time it was too late to enforce the law . . .'

The following exercise will help you to look at what happens during you and your child's day, to see what demands are made and whether these are positive or negative and how they are responded to.

The demands of the day

● If you have noted down your child's activities for a day very recently, go back to your notes. Otherwise note down your child's activities yesterday or if you prefer, make notes during the day.

● Ignore occasions when you are both doing something together and concentrate on when you were doing one thing and your child another.

● Note down, in a chart like the one on the right, when and how one of you made a demand on the other. For example, you were washing up, he was playing, and you asked him to take the milk bottles out, or when you were ironing and he asked you to wind up a clockwork car, or when you asked him to stop jumping on the furniture.

● Note down the responses either you or he made to the demand.

● Either while you are making the note or later check off who made the demand and whether it was positive or negative. (See example opposite.)

● If you wish to, give it a break for an hour or so and then record another $\frac{1}{2}$ hour say – but try to record when you are busy because your responses will be different from when you have plenty of time.

● After you have got quite a few demands noted down add up the ticks in each column.

● Then add how many positive and negative demands to give you the total demands you and your child made.

Time	Demand	Response	Parent Posi-tive	Parent Nega-tive	Your child Posi-tive	Your child Nega-tive
7.30	He says 'Stop cleaning your teeth, I want to clean mine'.	'Wait until I have finished, then you can'.				✓
7.35	He says 'Find my blue trousers'.	I go and get trousers out of drawer.			✓	
7.45	I say 'Your breakfast is ready'.	Comes and sits down after 5 minutes.	✓			
7.50	I say 'Stop banging your knife on the table'.	Stops		✓		
8.30	'I want a drink'.	I give him some juice.			✓	
8.45	He screams to get attention.	I pick him up and comfort him.			✓	
9.00	'Stop playing and put your coat on.'	I have to drag him away.			✓	
	NUMBER OF TICKS		1	2	3	1
	OVERALL TOTALS		3		4	

How does the pattern shape up. First, what about the totals:

● Who makes the most demands, you or your child?

● Who makes the most positive and the most negative demands?

The totals give you a clue but you may feel they do not give an accurate picture. Do certain times of the day alter the pattern? When your child is carrying out personal routines does this give rise to a different pattern of demands to when he is playing on his own? Are mealtimes occasions when everyone makes more demands on each other?

It is not possible to say what are the right or wrong answers to these questions, different families will have different patterns. But in considering them you may gain insights as to what is going on in your relationship with your child and you might wish to alter the demands you make to see whether this alters your child's demands. Carrying out the exercise later may help you see how things are changing over time. Over a longer time the demands a 3-year-old makes are certain to be different from those of a 4-year-old. Younger children are much more demanding, they are less able to do things for themselves and therefore have to make more demands on others.

Time	Demand	Response	You Posi-tive	You Nega-tive	Your child Posi-tive	Your child Nega-tive
	Number of ticks					
	Overall totals					

Responding to his demands

So far we have been looking at who makes demands but an equally important question is – how are these demands responded to? Look at your notes and at your responses first. For each of his demands what did you do? Did you:

(a) meet his demand immediately?

(b) meet his demand after a delay?

(c) distract his attention away from what he wanted?

(d) offer a deal such as 'If I do this for you, you will do that for me'?

(e) not meet his demand and explain why?

(f) say 'No'?

(g) ignore his demand?

(h) respond in some other way?

You probably did all these, but some of them more often than others. Perhaps (a) and (b) are the most usual responses. With a younger child (c) often works well but an older child is more likely to be prepared to do a deal (d).

The next step is a crucial one – he has made a demand – you have responded (not necessarily doing what he wants) – what happens now? Often this is the end of the matter and you both carry on with what you are doing. But sometimes this is only the first skirmish in what becomes an all-out battle.

Responding to your demands

Sort out his responses. For each of your demands what did he do? Did he:

(a) meet your demand immediately?

(b) meet your demand after a delay?

(c) distract your attention?

(d) say – 'Wait a minute' – or something similar and not meet your demand?

(e) not meet your demand and explain why?

(f) say 'No'?

(g) ignore your demand?

(h) respond in some other way?

These are a similar set of possibilities – although (d) has been changed because pre-schoolers are unlikely to offer deals. You may feel that it would be very cheeky if your child said 'wait a minute' or 'I can't because I am dressing my doll' – when you have told him his dinner is ready but remember the earlier example.

As in the previous section the next step is crucial here. You have made a demand – he has responded – what do you do now? If he has done what he was asked OK, if not there may be a good reason why. If you don't think he has a good reason for not doing it, or that he just has to come with you to the bus now – you may be in trouble.

Demands on each other

We have looked at the demands children and parents make on one another and then at how these demands are met. The question is, do parents meet their children's demands and do children meet their parents' demands? Some parents may be very demanding and have children who do not do what is required of them, or maybe it is round the other way. Other parents may make few demands but expect these to be obeyed, and so on.

Bathtime is much more than an occasion to remove the day's dirt. It can be a relaxing, or private quiet time, or it can be playtime. Think of the bathtimes you have known, from your very earliest childhood. You can probably remember what the baths were like, and picture the bathroom in your mind. Hopefully, you can remember too, the way bath time was not just a cleanser of dirt, but of the day's frustrations too.

When it's been one of those days when everything has gone wrong, a peaceful bathtime and tucking up in bed can express without words 'We haven't liked each other much today, but we know we really love each other – so let's forget today and look forward to tomorrow.'

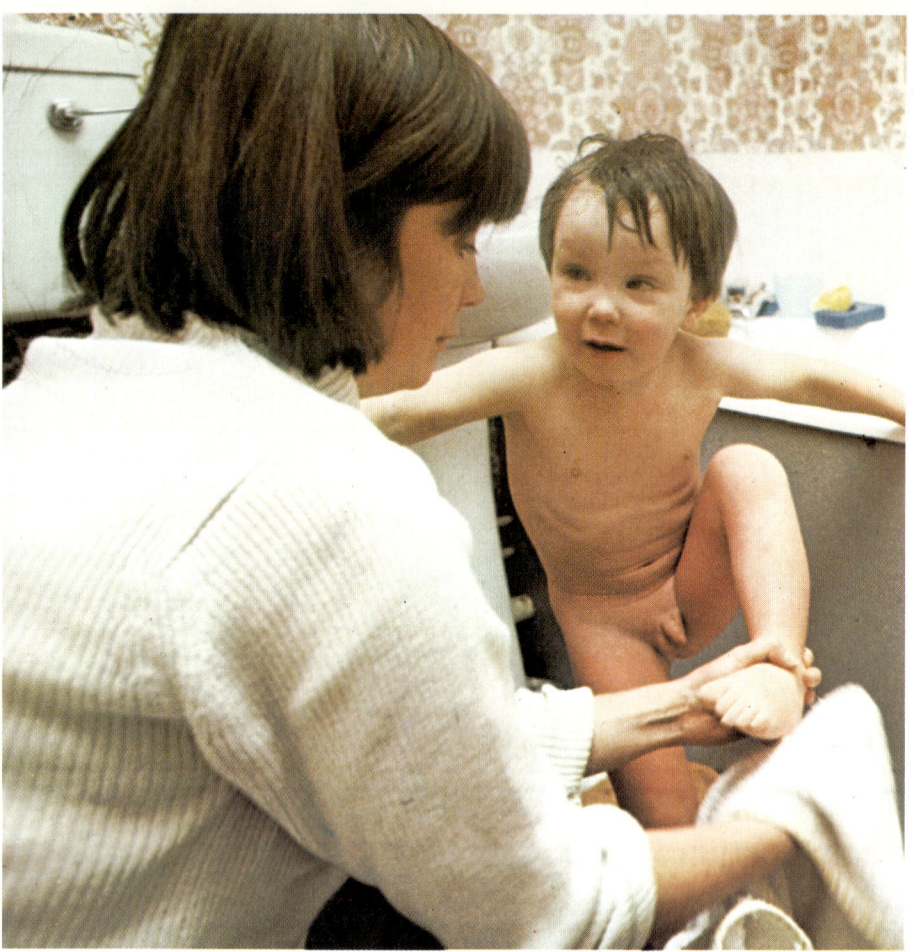

Bathtime

You may find bathtimes are an important and precious part of your childhood memories. Or your childhood memories may be painful. Your own children offer you the chance to outgrow the bitterness of your own childhood and start afresh, or to recreate your own childhood happiness. Bathtime can offer so many simple pleasures.

Nothing to play with?

Bathtime toys and games aren't always needed. Children can be given so many distractions that they miss out on the exploring and discovery that comes to those who seemingly have 'nothing to play with'.

Young children need practical experience as a foundation on which to build their ideas. Height, volume, temperature and so on are all ideas we use when handling the physical world. As a child, for example, did you ever:
● *put the soap rack across the bath and try to swim under it without touching it?* If you did, you began to find out in a practical way about height, depth, width and length.

● *discover that you could reduce the discomfort of a bath growing cold by lying submerged in the water?* (or even finding you could float as a distraction

from the cold!) Probably you discovered that more hot water would temporarily get rid of the cold – until the hot ran out, or the bath got too full. Whatever you did, basically, the longer the bath, the colder it (and you) became.

Only when children 'know' these things with inner certainty is the foundation well and truly laid for later learning. Repeated experiences are necessary if the child is to move from the accidental discovery – 'Look what's happened!' – to the certainty that – 'If I do this, that will happen.' Take soggy soap. As a child, did you ever:

● *lose the soap only to dredge it up later all soft and pale and soggy on the outside?* And then proceed to remove all the soggy part until it was hard again? You needed to rediscover this many times before you were sure in your own mind that 'Everytime I lose the soap in the bath it becomes all soft, pale and soggy.' And you needed many more discoveries before you could extend the 'soggy soap' rule to apply to anyone leaving soap in baths, bowls or buckets of water, or sponge bags with wet flannels.

The 'Why does it happen?' stage comes some time after the first acci-

dental discovery. Meanwhile, you may be concerned by waste or mess. Sometimes you have to draw the line – but you can use a mess to give your child more positive discoveries. You can save the soggy bits of soap to wash stockings, and see how it hardens in the airing cupboard. You can point out that this is why you have a soap rack or tray. And you can demonstrate the danger of making the bath slippery with soap.

You don't always have to scold 'Look what you've done – all this work/cost for me'. You can instead explain why you don't like something – and get your child to help you clear up. For example, as a child, did you ever:

● *use the sloping end of the bath as a water chute?* True, it can't be encouraged because of the splashing, but as you mop up you can explain that the *idea* was clever, but not very practical.

● *draw with your finger in the steam on the walls or tiles – and find the marks were still there next morning?* Now if you want to remove your children's marks, let them help. They'll probably treat cleaning up as another sort of play. After all, play's an attitude of mind to work, for adults as well as children.

God bless Mummy. I know that's right.
Wasn't it fun in the bath to-night?
The cold's so cold, and the hot's so hot.
Oh! *God bless Daddy*—I quite forgot.

Bathtime games

A bath on its own can be fun. But sometimes its nice to have someone, or something, to play with as well.

Wash yourself games Make these up to help your child learn the names of different parts of the body, and to wash himself thoroughly. You may have washed him in a certain order, but make a game by varying it. 'Can you wash your tummy? Now your eyebrows . . . now your toes . . . now your elbows . . . now your eyelids?'

This is an easy way in which to introduce the word 'penis' as early as you introduce the words 'elbow' or 'armpits': but if you can't then use whatever word you have decided upon – but don't avoid this part of his anatomy or show any emotion if he gives his penis the same detailed care that he has given to his thumbs.

Later on, you can make it more difficult 'Can you wash your biggest toes . . . and your little fingers?' Your child has to recognize the words and link them with the right part of his body. When he can do this confidently, change the game around. Get *him* to tell you in advance which part he's going to wash next. This gives him an opportunity to use words to plan what he's going to do next. At first he may find this more difficult than following your instructions He has to think which part he's going to wash, remember its name and say it – all before he does anything.

Tip-and-pour games A plastic duck is a plastic duck. It floats and that's about it. Tippers and pourers – plastic mugs and jugs and so on – can be used in many more ways than the traditional duck. Try for example:

● yoghurt pots, or plastic beakers, for filling and pouring over knees, hands, arms, tummies, and even down backs

● a small carton and a larger one, so that the contents of one can be tipped several times into the other

● plastic jugs, metal teapots and small watering cans, all of which pour in different ways

● funnels and tubes for bubble blowing – and many other things

Water play in the bath reduces the chances of spills and wet clothing. But waterplay – and water 'work' – in a bowl is enjoyable too, and need not be too messy. (See *Water in the sink* – Chapter 3). And in the summer, a bowl of water, and a hose outdoors will provide endless delight.

What time's bathtime?

Sometimes your child won't want to end an enjoyable bathtime when you do. He defies you to get him out. If bathtime really has to end, or he's going through a phase of 'testing' you out to see where you'll draw the line, you could try the following tactics. None of them involves you in winning or losing battles of will, and all are less harsh than a slap, or a scold:

● *Explanation:* 'I wish we could both stay here, but Daddy will be in in a minute, tired and hungry, and I must cook our supper now.'

● *Compromise:* 'All right, just a few minutes more while I wash my stockings/comb my hair.'

● *Calculated action:* 'All right, I'll pull the plug out and you can stay there until the water has all gone.'

● *Direct action:* If all the above have failed, lift him out firmly, but without fuss. A large towel wrapped firmly round an angry squirming child is restraining in a comforting way, and a calm voice talking about tomorrow's doings, will often bridge the gap between the real disappointment of having to leave the water and the pleasure of the good-night kiss.

If the battle is frequent despite these tactics, ask yourself why. It could be your child really feels deprived of this kind of play he so enjoys. Ask yourself: could bathtime be made longer after all? So often parents tie themselves up with rules they have made – like bathtime 6–6.15 – so that they can't see how easy it could be to change or break this sort of rule. Perhaps you could start bathtime earlier, and do some of your own jobs in the bathroom – mending, or letter writing, or feeding the baby. Or you could shift bathtime to a less rushed part of the day – like the mother who puts her son in a bath on a plastic sheet by the living room fire while she and her husband read the papers on Sunday afternoon. Other waterplay during the day, in the kitchen or the garden, may also help relieve bathtime pressures.

Bathtime fears

Occasionally, for no apparent reason, the bathroom can turn into a battlefield. Hairwashing, bathing and going to the toilet are common examples of everyday events that can get associated with feelings of anxiety or distaste in young children.

Children's fears are very real. You won't make them go away by ignoring them. You need a plan of action. The first step is to recognize and accept your child's feelings. Face, body movements and tone of voice will tell you a lot, even if he can't put the reason for his fears into words.

The second step is to identify the cause of the fear. Children vary in how they respond to new places, people and things, or changes in routines. Some adapt very quickly, for others an initial 'nasty' feeling caused by the experience may turn into long-lasting fear. Your child may not be able to put his fear into words – but you may find out through listening to a 'play version' of the feared event. ('Let's wash dolly's hair' – for example.)

Some fears arise from a lack of understanding – in which case your child is unlikely to understand, or believe your reasoned explanation. (For many young children, explanations that 'you're far too big to go down the plughole' don't help because their fear is not so much of the hole, as of the feeling of being sucked down or drawn along by the water.) The fear may be to do with feeling physically insecure – perched on a high toilet seat, for example. Or it may be to do with their lack of control over what's happening to them. Get someone else to blow your nose for you. It's not very nice, is it? On the other hand if you like the way your hairdresser washes your hair, you're happy to put yourself in her hands.

So – Step 3 is to change the nature of the feared event to make it more pleasurable or at least neutral. And – if necessary – Step 4 is to re-introduce your child to the experience gradually, giving him control where possible, and allowing him to set the pace.

Other fears

If necessary, you can apply the plan of action to other fears too. Once you've recognised the fear, and done your best to work out the likely cause– whether it's the sound of the Hoover, or a fear of large dogs or motor bikes –

then you've got to work out what you're going to do. In every case, in Steps 3 and 4 you're trying to help the child stop associating fear with the object or event concerned. You can sometimes do this by changing the feared event to provide extra distractions which catch his attention and help him forget the fear. But you may also need to re-introduce him to the feared thing gradually. The child needs to feel relaxed and in control – so that when he says, or shows by his face or body 'that's enough for today' he knows it will stop. He needs you to help him not to be afraid.

In the case of Hoover noise, it may be enough simply to let him help you control the machine and find out that he – and you – can always stop the noise with a push of a button. Dogs – or noisy motorbikes – in the neighbourhood aren't so easy to control. They may need a longer programme – perhaps watching them from afar, going a bit closer each time but leaving when he wants. Then finding a friendly dog or motorbike owner who is patient enough to spend time helping you build up your child's courage to get closer and finally touch the feared object. It does take time – but your acceptance of your child's fears, and sensitive help to overcome them is usually all that's needed.

The table summarizes the four steps in the plan of action, and gives two examples of what some parents did about their children's fears of the plughole, and of hairwashing. Only you know your child and his fears – so the next time you have a bathroom fear to deal with think through Steps 1-4 along these lines. But for practice you might like to fill in Steps 3 and 4 for what you'd do with John (a small 2½ year old) who dislikes the big bath.

Steps	Plughole	Hairwashing	Big bath
1 *Recognize feelings* – (from face, body, voice)	Cries and wriggles when plug pulled out	Waves arms and says soap 'hurts'	Huddles up miserably, can't wait for it to be over
2 *Identify cause* – (try to think about it from child's point of view, particularly if you've made changes recently. Playing it out may help too.)	Seems to get frightened when the water starts to gurgle and swirl around at the end	Could be doesn't feel safe standing on a chair at the sink. Perhaps shampoo really stings his eyes	Only just started the big bath. Used to love his small baby bath. Perhaps it's the amount of water and size of bath
3 *Make feared event more enjoyable* (what 'extras' could you add?)	Something to play with as the water goes down might take his mind off it	A shampoo and Daddy doing it helps – he's better with him. A towel 'turban' at the end is a treat – but he still doesn't like it	
4 *Gradually re-introduce the child to the whole experience*	Something to play with didn't work. So, in slow stages: At first lift him out before pulling the plug, let him pull the plug from outside, so he feels he can control the water. Now we let him stay while we or he pulls the plug, but lift him out at the first sign of stress	These seem to help: 1 back-washed his hair in in the bath instead 2 didn't use soap for two weeks, and washed it less often 3 gave him a flannel for his eyes 4 ask whether we'd done all over his head 5 let him do the final rinse	

With John, some suggestions are: Step 3 – foam or toys might distract him while he gets used to it. Step 4 – start by standing him in an empty bath while he's washed from a bowl. Next time, stand him in a very little warm water while he's washed from the bowl. Encourage him to bend down and splash. When he's ready to sit, gradually put in a little more water. Let him turn the taps, or at least tell you when he's got enough water for the day.

clean and dry

The washing of the last nappy, somewhere between the ages of two and five is a great occasion. It passes almost unnoticed because you have become so used to washing nappies that you cannot believe it will be the last! Whether it happens sooner or later depends mostly on your child, and each child is different. But, as in everything your feelings and attitudes affect this development. The big difference between learning toilet control and most other skills is that there can be a certain amount of conflict between you and your child over the very personal question of the emptying of bowels and bladders.

Learning control

From the age of two to three, a child is exploring the power to be independent. She discovers that control of her bodily functions stirs up feelings in herself and in you. If you exaggerate the expression of your feelings, she learns that these processes are of great importance to you, and learning to control them gives her power not only over herself but over you. She can assert herself and draw attention to herself if she feels ignored. Moderate your responses to success and failure . . . not too much joy or crying of shame. This will allow development to take place naturally.

Thinking yourself into your child's mind is, perhaps, the greatest skill you need as a parent. A sense of comfort and relief will best reflect her feelings when she shows you her potty. 'I bet you are more comfy now' will be most in tune with what she is feeling. Your approval matters, but she relieves herself for her own benefit, not yours!

The way you feel about body products is shown by the fact that there is no one word that everyone uses for the body's waste. 'Shit' used to be the universal word but when that was driven underground, a lot of words took its place. To help your child, you need to give a matter-of-fact explanation that your family words are not those used by everyone. Poo, big, poops, motions, number two are all different names for faeces. There is the same variety for urine. Loo is beginning to replace toilet, WC, bog, and that is a help for the child when he goes to different houses and public places.

Here are some of the feelings that are involved at one time or another. How many of them have you experienced yourself, either with your own or your child's emptyings. Put ticks if you have met them:

Good feelings

	You	Your child
Comfort	☐	☐
Satisfaction	☐	☐
Glee	☐	☐
Pleasure	☐	☐
Interest	☐	☐
Pride	☐	☐
Relief	☐	☐
Hilarity	☐	☐

Bad feelings

	You	Your child
Discomfort	☐	☐
Anger	☐	☐
Guilt	☐	☐
Fear	☐	☐
Irritation	☐	☐
Disappointment	☐	☐
Anxiety	☐	☐
Pain	☐	☐
Disgust	☐	☐
Embarrassment	☐	☐
Resentment	☐	☐
Shame	☐	☐

There are probably more 'good feelings' ticks in your child's column than in yours. The workings of the body are a source of great interest, curiosity and enjoyment to children. Most of their 'bad' feelings are stirred up by adult reactions.

The ways of the large bowel

Right through the day and night, our digestive system is quietly working independently, thank goodness, without our having to think about it. From the mouth . . .

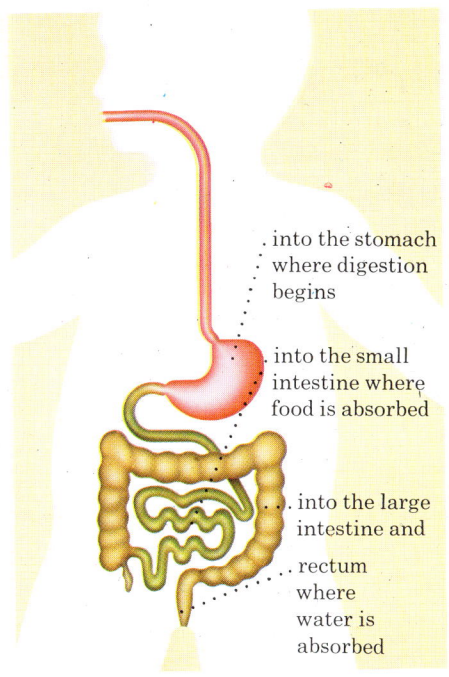

. into the stomach where digestion begins

. into the small intestine where food is absorbed

. into the large intestine and

. rectum where water is absorbed

The waste material in the baggy, expandable rectum is neither poisonous nor harmful while it is in the body. The longer it is in the rectum, the harder it becomes as water is drawn from it.

Regularity is a convenience and, as such, could be encouraged. Some small children quickly become creatures of habit, perhaps with a morning motion following breakfast. It is easy to catch the moment and slip them on to a comfortable and solid, not wobbly potty and, bingo, with a few quiet straining noises, all is well! Being sensuous creatures they show how satisfying that feels.

One convenience of regularity is that it makes life easier if you are going out. Little children often do not like strange loos and will sometimes suffer agonies of discomfort rather than visit an unfamiliar lavatory. For this reason it is a good idea to pack some medicinal paraffin if you are going on holiday with a child. Certainly before going to playgroup and school it is an advantage and a convenience. But you cannot compel a child by making a big issue out of failure to 'do a big job' every morning ● ● ●

Control – call it 'training' if you like – is learned in an atmosphere that is usually one of acceptance, love and understanding. Apart from the bother of nappy washing for the parents, there is no real reason why control should not be delayed into the fourth year. All that is needed is patient, tactful help from parents, who avoid making control an issue with a very small child. When she becomes worried and made uncomfortable by being soiled she will want to learn how to control her motions herself.

Occasionally, a child may utterly refuse to sit on a pot or toilet. This will date back to that peak of experimenting in independence that happens at about the age of two. Sometimes there will be a triggering incident like falling off a wobbly potty or having to use a loo that is dark and full of clanks and gurgles. Or it may be due to jealousy of a baby or some other stress. A child may not get over this easily even with the help of toys and endless stories. It may need professional help, especially if the child hangs on to a motion for too long and has to strain anxiously to pass some hard rocks! Treating with medical paraffin is a beginning but the real cause may need further enquiry.

Widdling at will

Our kidneys make urine to keep the balance of salts and water in our bodies right and to take away some waste materials. The bladder that stores urine is made of special stretchy material which gives way until it is half full without our knowing it.

At about three quarters full, the feeling of discomfort begins, increasing as the bladder stretches to full capacity. Up to this last urgent stage, a muscle ring around the exit tube, the urethra, automatically holds the water. In a baby, emptying happens automatically because the nervous system that controls it has not developed. When development of this nervous equipment is complete, conscious control of this muscle is learnt – first in the daytime and then at night. The key to learning this is the avoidance of alarm and fear. Encouragement can be given by help with difficult clothes when the need to go to the loo is shown.

Night-time waterworks control

A sleeping baby collects and lets go at least one bladder full in ten hours. The useful development of waking up when the bladder is full happens at different times in different children. Most children learn it around the age of three and four, but occasional bed wetting is common enough in older children. If the skill is not learnt at the usual time, for whatever reason, it seems harder for the child to learn it later.

Wetting at night is a continuation of, or return to the baby's automatic emptying cycle. Since it happens when the child is deeply asleep, there is absolutely no chance to exercise control by will power. Some bed wetters are extremely deep sleepers, others are extremely sensitive, easily upset by worries or changes.

Very little is known about how to establish night-time water holding. One approach, however, is to think about how the child might be made apprehensive and tense about its bladder performance. This can happen if the adult focuses too much attention on water holding, praising it over much when it is dry, making a great fuss when it is wet. Another anxiety is made if the parents and child feel that other children don't have this problem. Some do, of course!

The giving of comfort and relief can be the only 'right' response – but parents are only human and most parents of older bed wetters will admit to lapses into impatience and exasperation. GPs will give advice on your problem, perhaps recommending for older children the use of an alarm device that rings a bell when the first trickle of urine leaks out. But up to five, and even beyond, it is the basic comforting and encouraging that is needed to console children who have every reason for wanting to be dry at night.

Stresses may cause regression

Feelings caused by stresses of one sort or another may cause some children to slip back in the progress towards toilet independence. A worry about one parent or another . . . or both, the birth of a new baby, half-understood knowledge about all sorts of things can create fears that cause a set back in development. Comfort, acceptance, understanding, reassurance are the only things that really help . . . which does not mean to say that the occasional lapse will do untold harm!

Privacy

Clinging, insecure two-year-olds follow their mothers to the loo, three-year-olds will often enjoy the company of playmates, but gradually a desire for privacy grows naturally. There is no need for you to feel that there is anything deliberately rude or unhealthy in the way children are interested in lavatory happenings. They have a lot to work out about the strong feelings that they experience and meet in connection with emptyings of bladders and bowels – help them to learn!

STORIES

From the beginning we all want to know who we are; how we fit into the world. The most important story for all of us is the story of our life. As children we need to hear about ourselves and as adults we need to talk about ourselves

The story of my life

Every family has its own history and life-story. Children develop their sense of time, and who they are, by listening to stories which can be told time and time again. They need to hear stories about themselves, about you and their grandparents. You will soon discover what their favourites are – 'Tell me about when you and Dad got married' – or – 'Tell me about when I fell off the wall' – or – 'What happened when I went to Gran's?'. Out of the web of stories about past events children build a picture of themselves in the present.

The story about 'when I was a baby' may be one of the most important stories they hear because it tells them about a time in their own lives which they cannot remember. They usually love to hear about:
● how they were born, especially about how everyone else thought about their birth,
● the small events of their baby years like outings, holidays, birthdays,
● their first achievements like walking or riding a trike.
They want to hear these stories and to tell them themselves time and again. Photographs can be a very useful focus for the telling of these stories.

A book about me

Stories you tell 'about me' can become some of your child's first books. Choose an event in your child's life which you know he enjoys talking about and make a small book about it.

Fold a large piece of paper like a concertina and put a picture and some story on each page. Keep the book short. Use photographs or pictures from magazines and your own drawings – matchstick men will do, you don't have to be an artist, it's the story that matters!

Alternatively you could start with a photograph of a pregnant mum, or proud parents with a very new baby and write a story about his birth. 'Once upon a time, Mr and Mrs Smith came home to 6, Park Drive with their new baby . . .' put in the details your child wants to know, such as how much he weighed, the colour of his eyes, whether he had any hair and how much he cried!

If your child likes his book—make others about different events in his life. You're helping him 'find' himself in this sort of book—and showing him how books generally can hold interest for him.

Stories and imagination

Telling stories about real events is important. It helps your child to understand what has already happened in his life and how he will relate to different people and places in future. But telling imaginary stories is equally important.

From a very early age children need to be aware of things which are not part of their everyday experience. Have you noticed how often a child has an imaginary friend or invents a favourite toy with all sorts of human and super-human attributes? Their stories and conversations about these imaginary characters tell you a lot, about your child. Take James, with his 'Humphrey', a furry seal:

'Humphrey doesn't want to go to the party. He doesn't like children.

My Humphrey saw a tiger coming and he didn't run away. Do you know what he did? He ate it all up!

Humphrey took Christopher's gun away and he shot everyone in the whole wide world – except you Mummy.'

Telling stories to themselves

Almost as soon as they can talk children start telling stories to themselves about what they know, what they don't know, the frightening things in their lives and what they would like to happen. You can sometimes eavesdrop on this storytelling when they are playing on their own, in the bath, or in bed, just before they go to sleep. It can be a guide to things that are worrying them or things that particularly interest them. In their games, cars crash, people get lost, go to the swings, have endless lollies and ice-cream, wolves come out of forests, and Dad drives trains, tractors, submarines and helicopters.

As children get older their stories become more complicated but still deal with experiences which are important to them. The books you read to them and the stories you tell them add to their own stories and help them make sense of the world. Young children don't always distinguish between the real and the imaginary in the way adults do. Stories extend the enjoyment of imagining things and show them ways in which their imaginary and real worlds can safely overlap.

Me on holiday by the sea
Here I am having an ice cream / What a mess!
I had a paddle / It was wet and cold
A wave hit dad / He got wet
Mum lay in the sun She got very pink
We all went home / I slept in my carry-cot all the way

A lot of the stories you read and tell your children are about the familiar world of small children and their families. But stories *can* be about almost anything. Simple stories about little children or animals who are helped out of difficult situations help children to recognise and interpret their real life experiences.

Stories which begin – 'Once upon a time' – and end – '. . . and they all lived happily ever after' – allow them to think about things which could be frightening, safe in the knowledge that everything will be alright in the end.

As long as children understand and sympathise with the characters in the stories they hear, it doesn't matter whether they are folk tales, religious stories or imaginary adventures. When the hero comes home safe and sound, or the problem is solved by a big hug, then stories can be about things which are familiar, fantastic or even a bit frightening.

The familiar

Stories about familiar events are important because everyone needs to know that they are like everybody else. Small children identify with the children or the animals in the story who simply wake up, go through a routine day and end it by falling asleep again.

There are the stories about high spots, or moments of drama within the familiar routine – like – 'when we had a puncture' – or – 'the day we went to the seaside'. Books about other children who play at dressing up, have parties, go to the dentist or go on holiday, are important because they confirm and extend familiar experiences.

The frightening

Some parents wonder whether folk tales and fairy stories are too frightening. But witches, wolves, giants and trolls seem to have a particular fascination. Children do need to explore the darker aspect of life, just as much as they need to be reassured by stories about their everyday world.

Sitting safely on your knee, your child can listen to stories about people who are cruel, ugly, greedy and who often come to a bad end – and realise that life is not always comfortable and good.

The fantastic

The nice thing about fantasy for the two- to five-year-old is that anything is possible. They accept stories about the impossible adventures of rabbits and tigers, dinosaurs and dolls houses in much the same way as they accept our tendency to spring new, and sometimes quite odd things to do upon them. That is – they accept both when they take place within a secure and familiar framework. Improbable and often hilarious stories take place in the recognisable settings of homes, streets, shops and gardens. Such stories feed a child's imagination and are entered into their own world, where the boundaries between what is real and what is not are still being established.

Enjoying books

Enjoyment of books is not something that happens all by itself. You wouldn't put the ingredients for making a cake in front of a child and expect him to know instinctively what he should do with them. Children have to be helped to discover what different books have to offer and learn how to cope with them – and there are as many ways of doing this as there are ways of baking a cake. One thing seems certain – the stories read and the books you look at together, provide the foundation for an interest in learning to read and a real enjoyment of books.

Reading and telling stories

But you don't always have to read. If you're happy about doing it, a story made up and told by you will often fulfil what your child needs when he says – 'Tell me a story'. Stories about familiar events are probably the easiest for you to do – you can remember what happened. 'Props' can help too – like photographs or a box of objects around which you can tell the story. Sometimes you and your child can make the story up together – take turns to say what happened next, or lay out picture cards and weave a story around them.

Perhaps the most important thing your child needs from you is your time and attention. You don't have to be a 'professional' story reader – your child wants a story not a star performance. A story shared is double the fun – but if *Cinderella*, told for the twentieth time, is getting you down – try a different story this bedtime.

day's end

We all need sleep to refresh both body and mind. But how much and when varies . . . as with adults, so with children.

Sleeping pattern

As parents, we usually have clear ideas about how much sleep our children need – or how much we want them to need! Already you will have found changes in your child's sleep patterns: ticking this chart will help you to remember the changes since your first night as a parent. Never mind if you can't remember every period exactly, you are sure to remember enough to remind you of the changes.

Sleeping pattern	Age up to		
	6 mths	1 yr	2yrs
Two daytime sleeps			
One daytime sleep			
No daytime sleep			
Broken nights: many – big tick some – small tick			
Awake before 7			
Unbroken nights			
Going to bed readily . . .			
reluctantly			

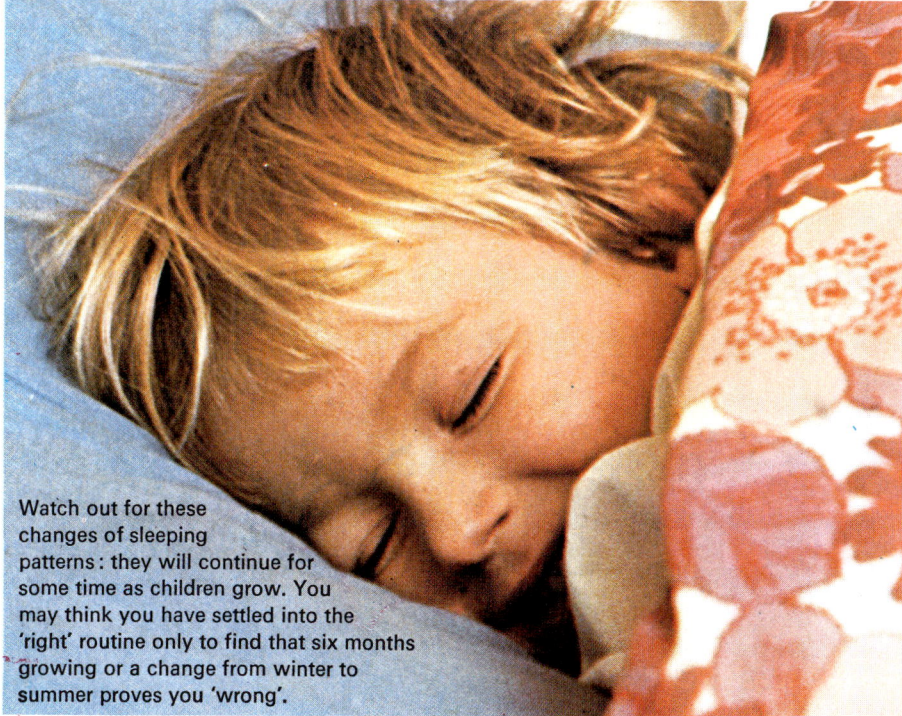

Watch out for these changes of sleeping patterns: they will continue for some time as children grow. You may think you have settled into the 'right' routine only to find that six months growing or a change from winter to summer proves you 'wrong'.

Children will sleep when they are tired and are content to let their bodies relax. Think a bit about your own approach to sleep. In the two tables below, tick the boxes to show how you and your child feel as you get to the end of your days.

How do you recognise tiredness?

	You	Your child
Tired body, ready to be still	☐	☐
Slow clumsy movements	☐	☐
Yawning	☐	☐
Tired eyes needing rubbing	☐	☐
Getting irritable	☐	☐
Losing interest	☐	☐
Nodding off	☐	☐
What else?	☐	☐

What keeps you awake?

	You	Your child
TV or other sound	☐	☐
Feeling too hot or too cold	☐	☐
Being hungry or thirsty	☐	☐
Vigorous movements	☐	☐
Interesting doing, thinking or talking	☐	☐
Being afraid	☐	☐
anxious	☐	☐
worried	☐	☐
unhappy	☐	☐

Children are very similar to adults in these respects. It is a mistake to assume that being tired and going to sleep are different for you and for your child. The art of getting a child to bed happily rests upon that understanding. A tired, happy, contented child ready for bed at a time that is convenient for you is evidence that you are really understanding your child.

Not tired at bedtime?

The fact that a neighbour's child or an older brother needed the sleep does not mean that your child does. Which solution worked for you . . . or could you try?

● Tiring your child out in the afternoon. Any healthy adult can outwalk a child. If you can't walk far, try taking another child. Two children will use up more energy than one on his own.

● Keeping your child up later, with something quiet to do.

Early bedtimes for children are not the custom in every country – but be prepared for baby-sitter problems if you follow this one!

● Give him something to play with in bed

● Staying with him. Are you prepared to create a pattern that depends on you?

● Something else.

● Have you built up a pattern or routine about going to bed so that he knows that one stage is going to follow another?

Learning a pattern

Often in this book you will find that learning depends upon recognizing a pattern, getting to know it with such certainty that your child can tell you what is coming next. After the gaining of this mastery, security and understanding comes a stage of confidence that gives freedom to vary and experiment, knowing that any time, he can go back to the familiar pattern.

What marks the pattern of your child's going to bed?

Is there anything particularly nice about going to bed that will be better than any rival attraction?

Television and company need some beating. What has a bedroom, lonely or shared, that can rival it? What is your solution to this one?

special relaxing playing kept for bedtime ☐

a routine that has specially valued things like a bath, a read, a cuddle and talk ☐

a tired child ready for sleep, left with door open, low light on . . . ☐

a firm instruction to go to bed and stay there ☐

bath time ☐

reading a book ☐

quiet talking that settles the day's problems, picks out nice things from today and tomorrow . . . ☐

telling a story ☐

turning off the television ☐

And so to bed . . .

but that may not be the end of the day!

Interruption of parents' lives and sleep by the wakefulness of children is one of the most common problems of young families. The simple solutions are the caring ones that you will be familiar with – sleep will not come if a child is hot or cold or hungry, thirsty, or wet. But a child not settling to sleep may be

● afraid of the dark

Who is not? Fear is our natural reaction to danger; it is the protection that causes us to draw back to safety. To a child, with little experience of living, there are many things to be afraid of. Alone in the dark, even in a familiar room, with people in the house, he can frighten himself by what he thinks or imagines. From the information he has, he can work out logical arguments that may seem silly or mad to an adult who has more knowledge. A child is often sorting out the differences between the real world and one that he makes from his imagination. Alone, in the dark he can become confused and believe that what he has imagined is real and is going to happen. A child frightened like this needs an accepting, calm, sympathetic and confident person who will listen and then explain the fear away, who will move the talk on to another subject when the child is ready to listen to something else.

Confidence is infectious, your sympathetic help will help him to build up the confidence that will let him grow up to handle his own fears.

The compromise of a dim light puts many of these fears to rest, but make sure, especially in a strange place, that you talk with your child about the caves of darkness or unexplained shadows.

Familiar things may make strange shadows

● wanting attention or company

'Mummy, can I have a drink of water?'

You know he can't be thirsty, and you spent plenty of time putting him to bed in the usual way. So you go to him once, and draw the line firmly. But this may be like treating the symptom instead of finding out the underlying disease. Asking for a drink of water may be a convenient way of getting your attention. If you simply say, 'He can't be thirsty', you may be ignoring an important problem. The call for attention at night may really be due to a need for more variety of things to do in the daytime, new places to go to, more people to meet . . . or for more of your time.

Your children grow and change so quickly that with every change of season, you need to think again about the new person you are living with. If children are satisfied with the variety of living and go to bed tired, content and secure, with plenty to think about, they are more likely to be able to rely upon themselves until they fall asleep.

If this is your problem, can you . . .

Find a new outing ☐

Look for a new playground ☐

Walk further than you have walked with your child before . . . whatever the weather! ☐

Play a new game with him ☐

Let him do some cooking ☐

Making changes

Sooner or later you are going to want or need to change the pattern of going to bed. A tiny baby can be taken about and fall to sleep anywhere. By the age of one, surroundings matter more than people and he will go off better in a familiar bed with a known baby-sitter than with parents in strange surroundings. So, unless the family's life is to be ruled by the child's needs entirely, occasional variation of the routine will be needed and can do no harm.

Light summer evenings will keep children awake, so will older children's playing and other people's television. Being over-tired or the beginning of an illness will make them drowsy earlier. Your child's own internal clock is more important to him than your idea of time. Sometimes he will want or need

to break the regularity, sometimes you will.

Many variations can be managed if some trace of that familiar pattern is kept, perhaps the talking or the singing, whatever is most important . . . and possible! A lullaby that brings back memories of many happy settlings, with full tummy and fresh clothes, will bring contentment to a child in the strangeness of a hospital bed or a different house.

Flexibility at night requires the freedom to be flexible in the morning. If going to work demands a regular waking time, is it fair to allow the start of the night to be irregular?

Children need to wake up at their own time in the morning and if there is a fixed time for getting up it is important that they should have been able to

get all the sleep they need. Occasionally cutting it short can do no harm; there are children who need less sleep than others anyway. But for many children repeated late nights coupled with fixed early rising can be harmful to their health.

It is worth thinking out various answers to this problem, looking at them again as the seasons change and children get older. If children want to stay up, look at the section on the previous page and see whether some change in the pattern of what you do will help them get sufficient sleep. Sleep can't be forced, but children can be persuaded to relax ready for sleep. That gradual unwinding will help to prepare for the next day.

See also *Babysitters* in Chapter 2.

And so to sleep . . .

but that might not be the end of the day!

Sometimes children wake at night in fear and, if this wakening becomes a habit, it is a great trouble to the parents. There are two kinds of 'bad dream', *nightmares*, which are vivid, frightening dreams that wake the child up and can often be remembered; and *night terrors* which happen about an hour after going to sleep and happen during sleep. The child may start up and, for anything up to twenty minutes can show real terror, crying out even though he may seem to be asleep . . .

He may call out for someone he knows. Sometimes he clings in terror, sometimes struggles as if to fight off people who want to help. He looks frightened. If his eyes are open, he seems to look right through you. All this is more frightening for the adult than for the child who, after one of these attacks will go back to sleep and remember nothing in the morning. About three per cent of all normal children have night terrors at one time or another, sometimes accompanied by sleep-walking and sleep-talking. Usually they go as suddenly and inexplicably as they come.

Nightmares and night terrors happen during different kinds of sleeping. Through the night, periods of light, dreaming sleep alternate with times of deep sleep. In dreaming sleep, the eyes move under closed eyelids as if looking round. People woken up from

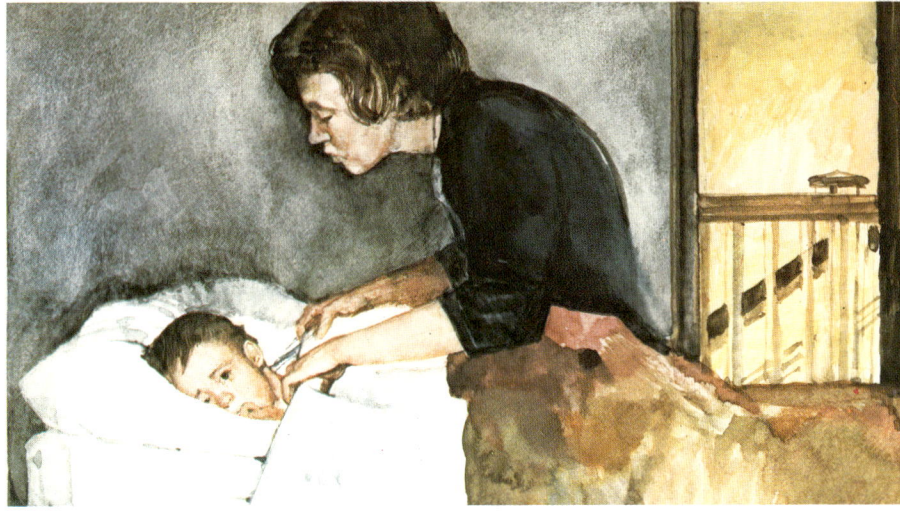

this kind of sleep can always describe a dream even if it fades away quickly. We need our dreams: if people are woken often from this kind of sleep, they become very upset even though they have had plenty of deep sleep. In young babies about half of the sleeping time is spent in dreaming sleep. By the end of the first year, the proportion drops to about a quarter of the whole and stays so afterwards. Nightmares happen during times of dreaming sleep.

Night terrors happen during periods of deep, non-dreaming sleep. It is not known why some children have them, any more than why some children wet their beds at night. Anxiety and stress seem to make terrors worse, or the child may be anxious about something

that is happening which his parents may not even know about.

If your child suffers night terrors repeatedly, you will find understanding help from your GP. You will probably be encouraged to think over:

● your approach to your child's bedtime – is it calm reassuring, quiet. Does it give plenty of time for talking?

● any worries that your child may have, uncertainties, anxieties or fears. You must look at life from his point of view when thinking about this possibility.

Most children come through spells of night terrors quite unaided, perhaps learning through their own experience that a fear was ungrounded. Others are helped by support and care from their parents.

Room for another one?

Simple nightmares or the stranger night terrors may draw your child to the comfort and security of your bed. What then? Do you . . .

take the child straight back ☐

let him join you for as long as he likes ☐

let him stay awhile and then take him back to his own bed ☐

To take a child straight back to the bed in which he has just had a terrifying dream can do no good. But, if he finds that a bad dream is an excuse to leave a lonely bed for the comfort of company, a habit can begin that can interfere in the relationship between father and mother. Being aware of both pitfalls, you can decide which will be the best middle course.

You can help your child by helping him to learn, at his own pace, to handle his fears, building up the confidence that will help him to enjoy his own bed and independence. If you take him back gently and firmly, once he is comforted, and then survive one night of resisting further calls, the chances are that you will have established the next step towards your child's maturity.

Some books to borrow or buy for your child

Here is a list of some of the books your children might enjoy. Use it as, and when, you will. Don't worry if most of the books you and your child like best are not mentioned – your own preferences are more important than any list. The books are listed under the following headings: *Stories* in Chapter 1, pages 27 and 28; *Looking at books* in Chapter 2, pages 44 and 45; and *Your child's own books* in Chapter 5, pages 139–41.

Baby's First Book
Margaret Borrett
Ladybird Books, 1973
This has straightforward, clear pictures of familiar and very ordinary things, with attention to detail.

In the Busy Town
Ali Mitgutsch
Collins, 1972 (HB)
This is a big picture book with no text. The double-page illustrations are detailed and fun.

Meg and Mog
Helen Nicholl and Jan Pienkowski
Picture Puffins, 1975
There are lots of Meg and Mog books. They are all zany stories with the same brilliant colours, simple lines and games with the text. Meg is an incompetent witch, Mog her long-suffering cat.

The Best Word Book Ever
Richard Scarry
Hamlyn, 1964 (HB)
Like all books by Richard Scarry, this is for looking at and enjoying again and again. The pages are crammed with little animals – driving cars, buses, lorries and aeroplanes, shopping and cooking, going to the beach, staying indoors.

Busy Wheels
Peter Lippman
Picture Lions, 1973
Cars, and things that go 'brrm' and 'beep-beep', are some of the things to excite very small children. Here there are pages of vehicles in action, dustcarts, ambulances, fire-engines, racing cars, bulldozers – lots to look at and talk about.

Where's My Baby?
H. A. Rey
Chatto, 1976 (HB)
A book for reading with Mum. The picture facing the text shows the mother animal; lift the flap to make the page bigger, and there are all her babies.

Circus
Dick Bruna
Methuen Children's Books, 1965 (HB)
This is one of a series of small, sturdy books. Dick Bruna's drawings, one on each page, are simple and brightly coloured. These are ideal for one- to three-year-olds who are just discovering these things and have the added pleasure of seeming to be able to read them on their own.

My Teddy
Jill Murphy
Blackies Chunky Books, 1973
A first real story book; easy to follow, with simple illustrations.
Companion books by various authors are *My Hamster*, *My Puppy* and *My Kitten*.

Facts and information

When your child wants books with more than simple pictures of single objects, then look out for the Ladybird *talkabout* books. The illustrations in these books have been planned to help increase a child's vocabulary and understanding through conversation – and there are useful suggestions to help you to make the most of them. Highly recommended in this series are:
talkabout baby
talkabout shopping
talkabout clothes.
When your child starts getting interested in specific things – making things, growing things, and so on, then the Macdonalds Starters are useful. The science series is particularly helpful for non-scientific families – try *Wheels* or *Floating Things*. The information is simple and precise, the illustrations extremely lively and colourful.

ABC
John Burningham
Jonathan Cape, 1974 (HB)
Each page is filled with one large object or lots of the same objects – P has twenty pigs, big, little, fat, thin and all different colours. H has rows of houses. It's a super book for prolonged browsing at home or in a playgroup.

Numbers of Things
Helen Oxenbury
Heinemann, 1976 (HB)
This book counts its way from 'one lion' to 10 animals, 20 balloons, 30 penguins, 40 fish, 50 ladybirds and ends with the splendid question 'How many stars?' This is one of Helen Oxenbury's best books, and is worth looking out for.

Find your A.B.C.
Richard Scarry
Picture Lions, 1976
The familiar little animals do alphabetical things at home and indoors.

The Ladybird abc
G. W. Robinson
Ladybird Books, 1962

Numbers
M. E. Gagg
Ladybird, 1959

Nursery rhymes, folk and fairy tales

The Mother Goose Treasury
Raymond Briggs
Puffin, 1976
This is a big, boisterously illustrated collection of all the nursery rhymes you ever knew – and lots more. It is for reading and re-reading, and for looking at the funny details in the pictures. It is a twin paperback pack with *The Fairy Tale Treasury* – and it's a best buy.

The Fairy Tale Treasury
V. Haviland and R. Briggs
Puffin, 1976
Virginia Haviland has selected traditional fairy and folk tales from all over the world. These are illustrated with humour and energy – and this matches the tone of the stories well.

Folk Tales for Reading and Telling
Leila Berg
Piccolo, 1976
A selection of short stories which no family should be without. These tales are re-written for you to tell.
As well as collections of fairy stories, you may want books of individual stories. Old favourites like 'The Three Bears' and 'Red Riding Hood' can be found anywhere, but are not always well told and are often very crudely illustrated. Versions published as picture paperbacks can be good.

The Story of the Three Little Pigs
William Stobbs
Picture Puffin, 1976
This familiar story is dramatically illustrated.

Chapter 2
Feeling their way

Chapter 2

Feeling their way

1

2

3

4

5

6

Your child is ready to draw the moment he can hold on to a chubby wax crayon. He will soon begin to bang it on paper and will be surprised and pleased to see the marks that are left behind.

Drawing

Drawing and painting start the first time a child spills his food on the tray of his high chair. He will put his fingers in it and begin to re-arrange the shape on the tray. He may also take one finger and trace a path through a blob of food. Later on, if he is given magic markers, chubby wax crayons, chalk or paint and a brush, he will gradually and naturally take himself through the 'scribble-line-drawing' sequence until he is producing the 'big head' figures we all know.

Stages of drawing

There are many clear stages in children's drawings. Your child may go through all of them. He will certainly go through most of them, but – DO NOT RUSH HIM – let him discover them for himself.

A child between twelve or eighteen months – will probably produce scribble like one of the first three stages of children's scribble. It can take many months for a child to move from Stage 1 to Stage 3.

Stage 1

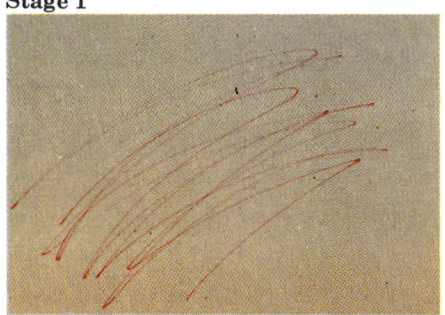

Here the child is able to hold the marker and move it backwards and forwards easily.

Stage 2

Now he can lift it from the paper and move it in different directions

Stage 3

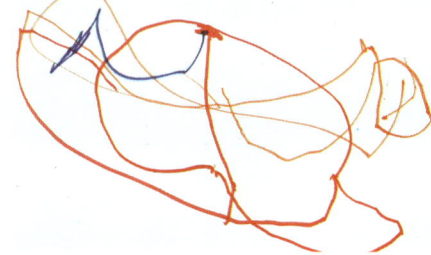

Further progress is shown as he begins to scribble circles.

The next stages will look something like this:

Stage 4

Stage 5

Stage 6

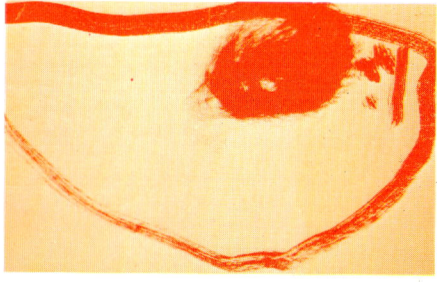

As the child progresses through these stages he is showing a greater ability to control the marker, developing a greater link between hand and eye and showing more and more observation of the world around him. After Stage 5 the child is well on his way to 'drawing'.

Stage 7

Gradually, there comes a single roughly circular shape. This is a great moment because the child has now discovered the first 'symbol' for the human form which he can reproduce at will. Given the opportunity he will proudly produce circle after circle (with varying numbers of dots inside which 'do' for eyes, nose and mouth) and tell any adult willing to listen, 'that's my mum' or '– my dad' or '– the postman' or even '– my dog'.

Stage 8

Here the circle has a large number of lines added which are placed all round and anywhere.

Stage 9

By now the lines are arranged in bunches to represent legs or perhaps hair.

On page 35 there are six examples of children's drawings.

See if you can judge which stage of drawing they represent. What clues do you use when making your decision? Fill in the table with your answers. Number the top two pictures 1 and 2, the next pair 3 and 4 and the bottom pair 5 and 6.

It isn't always easy to tell one stage from another as there can often be overlaps. Practice helps.

If you have kept your own child's drawings see if you can spot which stage they represent, and how they develop.

If you have the chance to visit a local playgroup or Mother and Toddler Club, look at the children's drawings. You will probably find they represent different stages, as each child develops at his own pace.

Picture	Stage	Clues used
1		
2		
3		
4		
5		
6		

To create and destroy

Sometimes you will see a child paint or draw a picture and then scribble or paint over it so that nothing of the original can be seen. This sometimes upsets the adult, but don't worry. If a child builds a sandcastle he will very likely jump on it to knock it down the next minute. If he builds a tower of bricks – listen to the squeals of delight as he knocks it down. What seems to us to be destructive may be something entirely different for the child. If he paints out his picture it's probably because there's little else left to do with it.

Stage 10

Notice the smaller number of lines placed below the circle (legs) and straight out at the sides (arms). There are other extras such as hair and fingers. This stage lasts for quite some time.

Stage 11

Stage 12

Stage 13

Once Stage 11 is reached, Stage 12 and 13 follow quite quickly. The body is formed at Stage 12. Then at Stage 13 clothes are added. Sometimes children get particularly interested in one part of the body or in an article of clothing and include it in every drawing they produce for a while – like Robert who gave everyone knobbly knees for many months and Linda who became very interested in Wellington boots.

Drawing is important

● Drawing helps a child to express his feelings and record his experiences, when it may be too difficult for him to put them into words. So drawings give clues as to what is important or interesting to the child at any one time.

Mary's favourite uncle took her out to a fair, so she drew this picture. In spite of being thrilled that uncle took her out, the person who is most important in her eyes gets most space.

Elaine's mother had a new baby. Who is to say if Elaine is lovingly protecting her new baby or about to trample on it! It is a mistake to 'interpret' children's paintings too precisely or read too much into them – but it was probably very important to Elaine to have this way of recording the fact that someone had come to share her mother with her.

The picture below was painted on Lindy's return to playgroup after she had been away with severe ear-ache. Her drawings never showed ears before or after that date.

● Drawing helps a child to express his fears and his fantasies. Children can't always tell the difference between what's real and what isn't.

The drawing used to illustrate Stage 5 was declared to be 'Milna Dumpy' by three year old Melissa who drew it. 'Milna Dumpy' had to have a place laid at table and was Melissa's constant companion for many months. By drawing it she was able to talk about it to her playgroup leader.

Fantasy in drawing is not only expressed through fantasy companions though. Gavin drew suns and snakes and crocodiles all in one picture and told many adventures about them.

Sometimes drawing is used just to make the world as the child wants

it to be. Jane wanted plaits but her mother kept her hair very short so Jane drew a picture and proudly declared 'me and my pigtails'. She was not telling lies – just feeling herself in complete control in a way she could never do in the 'real world'.

Helping your child along

You can help your child's drawing along by:

1 providing a variety of drawing materials

2 providing experiences

3 talking about his work and showing interest.

1 Exploring before drawing

Try giving your child different materials on different days, for example wax crayons, coloured pencils, chalk, an old lipstick, a piece of charcoal. Make sure they are all non-poisonous. Then put them all out one day and without making it too obvious see if you can observe:

Which one your child chooses first?

Which one he uses the longest?

If there are any he doesn't use at all?

If he has an obvious preference?

If he uses each material for a different purpose?

Watch also to see what he does with these materials besides drawing with them. Does he:

● smell them?

● put them in his mouth?

● rub them in his hands?

● draw on the kitchen wall?

You perhaps found that your child was more interested in the different properties of the crayons, etc., which you provided than in producing a picture. This is why the paper may be left blank while everything else around gets covered in chalk marks. Your child is experimenting with various textures, surfaces and learning about the physical world. This is okay for him but not so good for you if you've got to do the cleaning up afterwards – and wallpaper isn't easy to clean. You will have to set 'limits' for him to observe.

For a child it's the 'doing' that counts – not the finished article. When your child tells you a story about a drawing or a painting, try putting it out of sight for a few weeks and then bring it out again. The chances are he will have forgotten what it was all about.

2 Meeting the world

Usually a child starts by drawing people then gradually he begins to add other shapes which he will tell you are houses, trees, cars, animals or anything he sees in the world about him. His drawings may not develop in this way if he doesn't have experiences which will excite him enough to be worth reproducing. These don't have to be vastly exciting by adult standards but can be very simple events.

Going on a bus ride or train journey, watching workmen in the street, walking on a windy day, visiting a zoo – all these provide rich material for a child's imagination especially if you share these experiences and talk about them with him.

Take notice of the things your child chooses to draw. He may be remembering things that happened some time ago or thinking about something soon to happen – a birthday, a visit – events that interest him or which he feels are important.

3 Tell me about it . . .

Give your child plenty of opportunity to talk about his drawings but beware of guessing what they represent. Children can be upset if you guess wrongly – like Robert who spent a long time lovingly drawing the family dog only to have a well meaning but thoughtless adult say 'What a lovely baa-lamb'. Although when a similar thing happened to Stephen *he* said 'Gran – 'course it's not an elephant – it's an 'orse'.

If the child's earliest scribbles are received with appreciation by the adults around him, he will get used to the idea that drawing activities are something pleasurable and will naturally want to talk about his pictures when he is able to. Many children will tell a long tale about an apparently meaningless scribble.

Next time your child does a drawing at home or brings one home from playgroup, look for the opportunity to say – 'Tell me about it'. He may not want to talk about it at that moment, so don't push. But if he does begin to tell his story, show interest and help develop his thinking by making the right sort of comments.

Which of the conversations do you think is more helpful to John, and why?

Mr Grumpy with toothache

The sun shining and the rain raining on the pussy

Mum: Who's that?

John: The milkman.

Mum: The milkman doesn't look like that, does he?

John nods.

Mum: Where's his van?

John: He leave it at home.

Mum: He'll get tired carrying all the milk!

Mum: Tell me about your picture.

John: The milkman.

Mum: What's he doing?

John: Bringing milk for us.

Mum: What else does he bring?

John: Cream and eggs for supper.

Mum: Yes, he's a useful person to know!

Although these are very short examples the main difference lies in the reaction of 'Mum' to her child's drawing. In the first example 'Mum' is suggesting that the drawing is not quite right so her child might get the message that he's no good at drawing. In the second example 'Mum' is asking simple questions and is involved with her child and his drawing.

Don'ts

Don't . . . insist that your child talks about his drawing.

He may get cross and make up something just to please you – something which probably bears no relation to what he has just put down on paper. He may then begin to draw to please the adult, rather than as a spontaneous expression of his own thoughts.

Don't . . . read too much meaning into your child's drawing.

Treat them at their face value and let your child speak for himself on their importance.

Don't . . . ever try to change a child's drawing to make it 'better' or more accurate.

What this usually means is 'to make it more acceptable to me' and this can upset a young child's confidence. It will only make him feel that the drawing is not his or that he can't draw.

What is help and what is interference with a child's natural development? This needs much careful thought. Your child will always need encouragement and frequently need extra stimulation – but you must be careful not to swamp him with your ideas and so take over his play to the extent that he has no need for original thought and indeed, eventually becomes incapable of it.

Useful hints

The easiest place for a child to draw at home is on the floor. Keep a sheet of plastic to protect the floor.

In good weather drawing can be done outdoors – in the garden or yard.

It shouldn't be necessary to buy paper. Save odd ends of wallpaper. See if there's a firm with a computer near where you live – they will have a lot of old computer paper.

Keep your child's drawing materials in a place where he can easily get them for himself and put them away when he (or you) have had enough.

> ## Painting
>
> Much of what is said about drawing can also be said about *painting*.
>
> Read the topic on painting in Chapter 3 for more ideas about how to find out what interests your child and how to help develop these interests.

Children and television

Many children of school age spend more time watching television than they do in class. How much time does your child spend watching, what programmes does he watch and what effect do these programmes have on him?

The facts

Although we don't know how many hours' television pre-school children watch each week, we do know:

1 Some children between 5 and 15 years spend as long as $3\frac{1}{2}$ hours every day watching television, which adds up to $24\frac{1}{2}$ hours per week.

2 When 16-year-olds leave school many will have spent more time watching television than doing any other single activity, including being in the classroom.

3 On average adults watch $2\frac{3}{4}$ hours of television every day – or $19\frac{1}{4}$ hours each week.

your child watch?

Before you go on think about last week – about how many hours do you think your child spent watching television over the whole week? You probably found making this estimate quite difficult. In order to get a more accurate idea keep a record over the next week. Use the TV chart alongside. Start on any day of the week:

● Write down the titles of the programmes your child watched, alongside the box with the day of the week in it.

● Place a tick against the programmes you (or another adult) watched with your child.

● Write down the length of the programme (check with *Radio Times* and *TV Times* or the newspaper).

● Next estimate how long your child spent watching the programme. If he watched all of it then the two times will be the same, if he went out to play after ten minutes but came back for the final five minutes, write down the watching time.

● For each day add up the time your child spent watching.

● At the end of seven days, add up all the times to get the total watching time for the whole week.

What did you find out?

First compare the total time with the time you estimated. You will probably find that your estimate was on the low side – it's surprising how the time adds up!

Does your child watch the programmes all the way through or does he watch part of some and all of others? He may (like us) watch only the first part to see if he likes it – or he may watch on and off all through the programme.

What kinds of programmes?

Children's programmes are usually shown before 5.45pm each weekday; family programmes run from 5.45pm to 9.00pm and from then on the programmes tend to be for 'adults only'.

Look at your TV chart and decide how many programmes your child saw which were designed for:
● under 5s
● school-age children
● family viewing
● adults only

Pre-school children will probably watch quite a lot of programmes before 5.45. During the day there are a number of programmes designed specially for young children. There may be school broadcasts that interest your child and occasionally a family programme may be watched before bed. It is unlikely that many pre-schoolers will watch programmes after 9.00 pm (except perhaps at weekends or on holidays), unless they wake up or are ill – beware of letting this become a habit!

Day	Programmes watched by children	Tick if watched with adult	Length of programme	Time spent watching	Total
Example:	Play School Blue Peter Softly, Softly	✓ ✓	25 mins 25 mins 50 mins	10 mins 15 mins 45 mins	1hr 10 mins
Monday					
Tuesday					
Wednesday					
Thursday					
Friday					
Saturday					
Sunday					
				Total	

Children and television

The attractions of television

What is the great attraction of television? Tick those that you think are most important.

- ● TV is enjoyable, interesting and stimulating. ☐

- ● TV is able to teach a great deal. ☐

- ● TV watching with mum or dad provides something to talk about. ☐

- ● TV is passive – you don't have to use much energy watching. ☐

- ● TV is great company if there is no one for a child to play with. ☐

- ● TV is helpful for a tired mum when she can have a little peace while her child watches the television. ☐

- ● TV watching can be a bribe for bedtime. ☐

- ● Mum and dad watch and children like to join in watching. ☐

- ● TV watching is great when there are other children there too. ☐

- ● There is nothing better to do than watch TV. ☐

- ● Children need to watch TV because their friends do. ☐

Television can widen children's experience and give them a window on the world. Through this window they can see people, animals, places and events which children without television could never see. This can stimulate them to ask questions and follow trains of thought. Viewing with a parent or with both parents can involve comments on what is happening and on the programme generally.

Children can be helped to discriminate between programmes. Ask your child at the end of a programme what he thought of it – Did he like it?; What did he like about it?; Was it better than yesterday's programme? and so on. Also encourage your child to choose which programme he wants to watch out of a variety of programmes.

Television can be useful to keep children occupied. When a group of children watch they may well pass comments on what is happening. Television can lead to activities, for example, children will imitate television characters and copy their actions and their conversation.

Violence on television

A lot has been written about television violence because there is a lot of violence on television – for example, a 15 minute cartoon has about 7 violent incidents usually with people laughing on the soundtrack. Detective programmes have at least one murder or beating-up in each episode. Westerns and spy stories may have gunfights, house-burnings, beatings – even rapes – at a rate rarely less than six an hour.

Children see many of these (though television programmers try to keep too much violence off the screens during the day and in the early evening).

- ● However, no-one yet has shown convincingly that violence on television really does make people more violent. Equally, no-one has shown that it doesn't.

- ● In some experiments, a group who have seen a violent film will be violent if put into a similar situation, while a group which hasn't seen the film doesn't act so violently. In other experiments, there's hardly any difference in how people react after seeing violent films. By watching how your child reacts you can gauge whether or not to let him watch.

- ● Some children may want to copy the violent people on television: but some recent research suggests that viewers are sympathetic to the victims. It may be that seeing a lot of violence may make some children more frightened of violence, instead of making them violent.

- ● Ask yourself whether your child would be frightened if you threatened him with the police – or do you have other 'bogey-men'?

Do children believe television?

Very young children – often up to five-years-old, or even older, quite simply believe that everything they see on television is real. A magician weaves real magic, a cartoon character is as alive as a newsreader, an advertiser says brand X is the best soap powder and space travel through the galaxies is not only possible, but it actually happens. When an actor is shot in a cowboy film and the tomato juice runs, children believe the cowboy is dead. Even adults believe enough to send telegrams and letters when a character dies or gets married in long-running serials.

Children also become attached to the presenter of a programme: for this reason many of the more recent programmes for under-fives have a variety of presenters so that the information in the programme becomes more important than the person who's presenting it, therefore *Jackanory* has a new story teller each week.

It seems also that young children find the story in a programme hard to follow, and they remember especially well the parts with the brightest lights, sharpest detail, catchiest tunes, and memorable catch-phrases. This is especially true of television advertisements.

- ● Choose your child's favourite television programme. A couple of days after it has last been shown, ask him or her to tell you everything remembered from it.

- ● Talk to your child about the events he sees on television. Ask him if he really thinks people behave in that way and whether he thinks they should or should not.

Watch with mother

Look back at your TV chart. How many of the programmes did you or another adult watch with your child?

Some programmes for the under-fives expect a grown-up to watch with the children. *You and Me* has regular pauses for grown-ups to help children with answers. *Playschool* suggests activities for children to do with adults. And *Watch with Mother* assumes that they will be viewing together and help both of you to enjoy learning together.

All these programmes are designed to teach things. How many of the programmes your child watched were mainly designed to teach and how many were designed mainly for enjoyment, for example – cartoons?

The more you can watch with your child the more you can talk about what's in the programme and the more you can do the activities suggested in them. This will help your child to get a better grasp of what he is watching.

Do you censor your child's viewing?

The quiz below is to start you thinking; you may find that none of the choices fit what you have done recently – or that you want to change one slightly.

1 When there's a programme on that you don't think your child should watch do you:

    a switch off the TV

    b send the child out of the room

    c let him watch

2 If you think your child has watched enough TV for the day do you:

    a switch off the TV

    b find another activity for your child

    c let him watch

3 If it is bedtime and your child wants to watch TV do you:

    a switch off the TV and send him to bed

    b keep watching but send him to bed

    c let him watch

4 If you want to watch one programme and your child wants to watch another do you:

    a switch off the TV

    b switch over to your programme

    c switch over to your child's programme

Obviously if all your answers have been 'c's then you do not censor your child's viewing at all. If you have answered all 'a's you are an extreme censor and would rather censor yourself than let the child watch when you would prefer he didn't.

I expect your answers are more random, although you might not like the idea of censoring viewing, you draw the line on occasions such as bedtime or a particularly unsuitable programme.

In another test with a large number of parents, over half the parents did in fact censor their children's viewing. This was because they thought too much television was being watched rather than the programmes were unsuitable. One in five of the parents did not make any effort to limit their children's viewing at all.

Children will watch a lot of television. Rather than you deciding how much and what kind, you should whenever possible encourage your child to decide for himself. If children have a range of activities and a number of friends they will not want to spend all their time watching television. When they do watch they should make an active choice as to which programme it will be and should be encouraged to talk about and comment on the programme.

'Square eyes'?

Looking at books

As soon as you can balance a baby on your lap with one hand and hold a book with the other, you can look at the pictures together. Make reading and telling stories a habit. Have books of all kinds in your home and let your child learn how to handle and enjoy books with you.

What is a book . . .? A child's eye-view

When a child is first big enough to sit on someone's knee and watch as the pages of a book are turned for her, all she notices are colours, patterns and the pages rustling. Soon, the patterns become things she knows, with sounds she recognises – 'ball', 'cup', 'meow'. She learns to turn the pages herself and points to objects, trying out their names – 'house', 'car', 'man'. Later the pictures begin to tell a story – 'Who's that?' 'That's the milkman bringing your milk.' Soon she will tell the story herself – 'There's a mummy going to the shops with her baby. He wants a lolly'. Books become part of a world of stories for your child; stories people tell her, stories she tells them and stories that books tell, in words and pictures, in many different and exciting ways.

First books

By the time they are two, most children enjoy naming familiar objects. Looking at anything which has pictures, whether in books, magazines or catalogues, can be an absorbing activity.

The first 'book' your child appreciates may be a catalogue full of objects that she recognises before she knows their names. Children want to go on looking at pictures – 'That's *my* jumper', then 'That's like Robert's jumper' and later 'We've got a bottle thing like that' – so don't throw away old catalogues and magazines. But what else should you have? From the start have some proper books; Ladybird first books, board books with shiny pages, good colours and clear objects, books that are good to look at and firm for a child to hold.

Have some home-made books too. Making your own story book involves a lot of talking, as you select and organise pictures together, choose things to stick, cut and colour and decide what to write.

Making a picture book

In the same way as you made your *Book about Me* (see *Stories* in Chapter 1), make a book about something which interests your child. Using catalogues, magazines and materials you have in your home, make a small book with your child. If she can, let her cut out or stick in the pictures.

Choose everyday objects and events – 'going shopping', 'our clothes' or 'my toys' – and write a short caption under each picture using your child's own words. This sort of book isn't meant to last forever – just for as long as your child's interest lasts.

A mug is a mug . . . there's variety even in pictures of familiar objects

Nursery rhymes and fairy tales

Listening to stories is a way we all come to learn about ourselves. Once, story-telling was the only means of passing on the history, values and beliefs of a society from one generation to the next. Nowadays when a mother bounces her baby on her knee and sings 'Ride a Cock Horse to Banbury Cross', or lulls her child to sleep with 'Bye Baby-bunting' she is drawing on a spoken and sung tradition *her* mother passed on to her.

Most of us have no idea about the origins of nursery rhymes or singing games. Thinking about them makes them seem pretty nonsensical. But most of us know some rhymes. They are often a baby's first contact with the sort of words that convey feeling and emotion rather than direct meaning. The three-year-old sings 'with silver bells and cockle shells and pretty maids all in a row' for the sheer pleasure of the sound and rhythm of the words. She chants, 'I'll huff and I'll puff and I'll blow your house down' and enjoys the repetition and rhythm of 'run, run, as fast as you can, you can't catch me, I'm the gingerbread man'.

Unfortunately most mothers can't miraculously dredge up nursery rhymes and folk tales from a pool of childhood memories when their first child arrives. Most need reminding. Starting the story of Hansel and Gretel and suddenly realising that you don't know how it ends can put you off telling other stories you thought you knew. How many parents know *all* the verses of Jack and Jill?

So what every parent and child needs is a small reference library, a selection of nursery rhymes, fairy stories and folk tales. A good collection will have a large number and variety of rhymes or tales with illustrations which have plenty of detail. Children need pictures to pore over when they look at these books on their own. Books like this are a good present for new babies, for they will provide enjoyment for many years.

Pictures help children to understand stories in books and stories about themselves.

Pictures and stories

You can compare different ways of story-telling in order to see which your child enjoys the most.

Here are three possible variations:

1 Listen to a story with your child on the radio programme *Listen with Mother.* (Many young children find it hard to concentrate.)

2 If you have a record player and a children's story record, try to match listening with looking at some pictures in the story book. (Pictures are nearly always a helpful 'prop' in story-telling.)

3 Tell the story yourself from the book using the pictures. Encourage your child to help you tell it. Unlike a record, your voice is familiar and if your child joins in you will respond to what she says.

Try to leave a day or so between each story-telling session. Each time, note down afterwards what your child's reactions were, by ticking the appropriate boxes in the next column.

	Radio	Record + book	You + book
1 Fidgets	☐	☐	☐
2 Does not seem to listen	☐	☐	☐
3 Talks to you about something else	☐	☐	☐
4 Walks away	☐	☐	☐
5 Listens with interest to part of the story	☐	☐	☐
6 Listens with interest to the whole story	☐	☐	☐
7 Joins in the telling of the story	☐	☐	☐
8 Talks about the pictures	☐	☐	☐

Many children will find stories read by a strange voice difficult to follow. You will probably notice an improvement when you match listening with looking at pictures. Does your child attend and seem to understand the story better?

The third time should be most successful. The pictures now guide and support shared story-telling. The combination of pictures, story and parent should be the best experience for you and your child.

Reading to your child

Armed with your fairy tales and nursery rhymes, there are still a lot of questions left.

● How often should I read to my child?

● How do I choose the right story at the right time?

● Is telling better than reading?

● How do I know whether they are enjoying the stories I read?

Some or all of these questions will probably occur to you and there are no hard and fast rules. Most important of all is to follow your child's lead – listen to what she says and what she wants and some of these questions will be answered. *When* you read to your child depends on her asking for a story and you finding time to sit down to read or tell it. Sometimes you will be very busy. Stopping to read a story would be impossible!

Yet repeatedly turning down a child's request for something will lead to the child losing interest. You need to consider just how busy you really are, and whether ten minutes or even half an hour reading a story might not do you both good. If your child comes in asking for a drink you would probably give her one. So perhaps you have to consider whether a child's inner, imaginative life needs as much nourishment as her physical one.

You will know when your child has enjoyed a story when she asks for it again – and again! Favourite stories – read or told – are the ones children get to know well, picking up the rhythms and words, filling in gaps, correcting you if you make mistakes, joining in, laughing and taking parts. There will be some stories you and your child know so well that you can share in the telling of them. Then you know you have chosen the right story.

Skills and ideas grow out of children's experiences of play and of everyday living. Children can learn at any time – but certain times and experiences are more likely than others to encourage learning. Children are different too. So how can you recognise a learning moment for your child? And what should you do about it?

Learning moments

Detecting the right conditions
Think about the following questions:

Q1 Are you really sitting comfortably . . . ?	Yes/No
Q2 Do you feel hungry?	Yes/No
Q3 Is this the time of day when you feel you learn best?	Yes/No
Q4 Does background noise disturb you?	Yes/No
Q5 Do you like having other people around?	Yes/No
Q6 Does the idea of learning anything at all make you feel tense?	Yes/No

Adults vary in the ways they prefer to learn things. The right conditions are those you feel happy in. Children vary too – so let's look at these questions with your child in mind.

Q1 and 2   A child's idea of comfort may not be yours. If your child really seems happiest lying face down on the floor, then that is up to him. What matters is that he is comfortable enough to be able to concentrate on learning. It seems such an obvious point – but can you remember trying to learn sitting on a hard chair in a stuffy classroom? A hungry child is also likely to be an inattentive one.

Q3   Some people are definitely more alert at night than in the morning, for example. More important, your child's 'best time' may not be the same as yours.

Q4   Too much noise can be distracting, but otherwise familiar surroundings and noise provide a comfortable background to learning through play.

Q5   More difficult play, or more complicated problems *may* mean that your child needs more contact with you. Ask yourself: 'If he does this, how much will he want me around?'

Q6   Anxiety can be passed on. If you tend to feel tense about learning, you may pass this on to your child. Stand back occasionally and let the child learn by himself. Only you can judge whether this may be happening. In other words, there's not much point worrying about learning moments if the setting for learning is not right.

Attention

Adrian is five and Jonathan is three. Adrian is cross because Jonathan couldn't stick to the rules; Jonathan didn't know there were any rules, to him Adrian seems bossy. The two, in fact, are at different stages of attention development. Adrian has reached a point where he is able (and prefers) to focus on one topic for a fairly long time; Jonathan begins with, say, cars on a race track, but his attention soon shifts sideways to another possibility, and may shift again several times. He might begin a drawing of a tree, and end by calling it a man or an aeroplane.

Thinking about learning moments – what does this incident suggest about the ways Adrian and Jonathan learn? Try answering the following questions:

1   If both boys are playing for half an hour at activities which are suited to them, whose shoulder should you look over most often?

2   Who is likely to use the most play material?

3   Who should you spend longest with at any one time?

4   If you are on the look-out for learning opportunities, how would the difference in the amount of attention shown by the children affect your comments on what they are doing?

5   Should they show each other what they are doing? Should you encourage this?

Comments

1 Probably Jonathan's, as he'll change his activities more often. Each change may supply a different learning opportunity – how to hold a pencil, how to fold paper, possibly finger-paint. If both are to remain occupied by the same activity, it must provide enough variety for Jonathan and enough interest for Adrian. Play involving drawing, clay, building blocks or water should enable each child to play at his own pace and in his own way. Avoid co-operative or competitive games; these are likely to include rules – and trouble.

2 Very likely Jonathan will use the most material. It's not a bad idea to prepare a 'tool-box' with crayons, paints, scissors (and an apron cut from a plastic tablecloth) and let him help himself.

3 Probably with Adrian. If he is concentrating on one drawing for example, he may have more to tell you about it – and you may have more suggestions to make.

4 In Jonathan's case, you may have to start afresh each time you come back to him; it would be a mistake to say 'But I thought you said it was a tree' when he's just told you the object is an aeroplane. On the other hand, Adrian may be old enough to enjoy being reminded.

5 This is a difficult one, as it could lead to conflict or misunderstanding – with the younger child likely to be the worse off. **Needs treating with caution.**

'That's all very well, but my kid doesn't light up to show me when he's learning. How do I know a learning moment when I see one?'

Children start off as babies with two important tendencies: to be sociable and to learn. Every experience – seen or heard or felt – sets up an idea in the baby's mind, and these ideas grow together as experience builds up. The child acquires a set of ideas gained from his experience which makes up a model in his mind of what his world is like and what he can do with it. All his success and failure is related back to this model, altering it accordingly. The child tries out his new ideas on the world, and the world or child is changed as a result of the experience. Take these two examples.

Example 1: *Mike* is two. He has a plastic board into which he can fit circles, triangles and squares. He is given a board which also contains ovals, five-sided shapes and oblongs. He spends some time trying to fit this new bit of the world to his present stock of experience, and confuses ovals with circles, triangles with five-sided figures, squares with oblongs. But soon he sees the difference.

Tim is also two. He has not played with the simpler puzzle before being given the more complicated one. He takes much longer to learn the differences and makes many more mistakes.

Example 2: *Susan* is just four. She has been using a knife and fork for some time, but has trouble spearing meat with her fork, because she holds it with the points curving upwards. One day she tries turning it over . . . Later she discovers that a knife can be used as a stop as well as for cutting.

Mike and Susan have one important advantage over Tim: *the new item learned is built on something they already know*. Mike would not have discovered how to distinguish between circles and ovals so rapidly if he had not known about circles first. Susan already knew two ways of handling a knife and fork.

Learning moments

'So now I know a learning moment when I see one. But what do you want me to do – make up a list of things for him to learn – or what?'

Don't think you need to go around with a plan for your child's learning. It's much more a question of looking over your child's shoulder at what he's doing. Pre-school children are not ready for formal teaching. As adults, we are far more effective if we can spot the right moments in a child's play, to get a helpful idea in edgeways, and then leave it up to him.

When the next play-session occurs, try asking yourself the following questions:

● What is he *trying* to do? (Not 'What is he doing' – or you may see nothing!)

● Is it a fairly limited activity, or are there lots of possibilities? (Time spent playing is a reasonable guide.)

● Does he seem aware of all the possibilities?

● Is he having any problems with the activity?

● Should I help him solve the problem, or let him work it out for himself?

● Is there anything I can point out, or comment on, that would add to his general knowledge and interest? (But don't give a lecture.)

Macaroni necklaces

Presented with macaroni, string, cochineal and ink, some six-year-olds with lots of play experience could say: 'I will make a necklace with pink, blue and white beads'. They have learnt all the skills they require to do this.

Few two-year-olds will continue long enough to complete a necklace at one go. From that stage of learning and skill to the spontaneous idea of the six-year-old, experiences have to go through many stages.

The chart gives an indication of the age at which your child might be able to do each stage on his own, with encouragement, or with your physical help. Use the symbols to fill in the line for your own child.

1 Divide the macaroni into three cups. Dilute both cochineal and ink in the proportion of about one teaspoon to half a cup of water.	2 Just cover the macaroni in one cup with cochineal, and in another with ink.	3 After a few minutes, strain off the dye solutions and spread the macaroni on kitchen paper to dry.	4 Make a stop at one end of the string by knotting in a section of macaroni. Make firm point at the other end by rolling the string in half an inch of sellotape.	5 Start threading. No need to suggest any colour sequence, but you might be interested to point out any patterns that emerge.	6 When the necklace is long enough, knot up and wear!	
						age 2
						3
						4
						your child

child probably needs your physical help with these stages – his ideas and skills on their own aren't enough

child is beginning to manage these stages himself, but your encouragement helps him persevere if he's having trouble

child can cope with these stages himself

Wills of their own

In the first 18 months of your child's life you will have learnt a lot about adapting to life with a baby. But now you both begin to learn that she has a will of her own. She finds that she has ways of controlling her behaviour and the workings of her body that give her control over you.

By now your child has very definite ideas on what she will or won't do. This 'negative' stage can discourage some mothers, making them feel quite hurt. But it is part of growing up – it is a child's way of testing the reactions of adults. Have you noticed how often your child can sense just when you are about to expect something of her? If she does not want to go along with you, she learns that, by word or action – or both – she can say no. It happens to everyone!

Trying you out

Many mothers meet trials of strength over daily events like, for example:

● *eating* A healthy child doesn't suffer from stop-start eating, but if you have prepared the food that you think she needs, *you* may get upset. Sensing your anxiety, your child finds she has discovered that by refusing food she can distress you. If you are not upset by her refusal to eat, she does not get this feeling of power.

● *dressing* If you are in a rush to get ready to go out somewhere, your child may find that by dawdling over choosing or finding clothes, she can irritate you.

● *bathing* Sometimes there is a great fuss to avoid getting into the bath, followed by an even greater protest when it is time to get out. Hair brushing or washing can become another battleground.

● *sitting on a potty* can evidently please mother, so by refusing to do so she can displease her, even at the price of her own discomfort.

● *going to bed* or getting into bed with you in the middle of the night, are other ways in which a child can cause worry or concern.

Action and reactions

Just as you are affecting the way your child behaves, so she is having an influence on you. It is important to recognise what reactions your child's challenges awaken in you. Parents may find that they feel bewildered, threatened, roused to equal anger . . . like these:

'Sometimes I feel I'm dealing with a wise little adult.'
'Sometimes I feel I'm being pushed back by a giant force.'
'Unless checked now, he may become a tearaway, a delinquent. I do hope these aren't the first signs.'
'I couldn't tell this time whether it was just a bit of ordinary, mild bloodymindedness, or some *really* strong opposition to me.'
'Damn, she's won again! This *must not* happen!'

Recognition of your own feelings will sometimes help you to understand what your child feels. Perhaps just talking about your differences will help.

This can be a very discouraging, tiring stage. No one likes having to say 'No' all the time. But look, and you will see from your child's refusals and challenge signs that she is growing up, that she is beginning to understand that she is an individual, a separate person. This kind of behaviour tells you that she is

● beginning to practise her powers of choice,

● showing signs of confidence and security by choosing someone fairly loving and close to practise refusals on!

● exploring the weird ways of adults.

Your child is testing the limits of permitted behaviour and your authority, in the way that a blindfolded person finds the limits of a room by blundering about. If her challenges are *always* met by instant restraint, she begins to feel that exploring is a bad thing to do, her initiative may dwindle. Sometimes, like you, she needs to 'win', but by providing consistent limits you can reassure her by showing that you care, and that you can protect her from more freedom than she can cope with at this time in her life.

This stage passes!

The development of this negative stage reaches a peak at about the age of two. It then usually tails off to very little by two and a half to three . . . but you can make it last one or two years longer! Inviting head-on collisions, threatening and confusing a child will prolong the stage. Offering acceptable alternatives or luring her to enjoy the course you want her to take, will help it pass.

What would you do . . . ?

Here are some situations that are met by parents of children who are passing through this negative stage. Some responses to these situations are suggested. As you read through mark item as follows:

X = will increase child's resistance
XX = will make matters even worse
√ = the best way out in your view

Your knowledge of the way your child thinks will help you to judge which course will provoke the greatest fight or confusion and which will end in agreement

Situation		You say	
Choosing clothes		1 This is the shirt for you today. 2 Do you want to wear this red, stripy shirt or the blue one? 3 Why do you make me so angry? You knew we were going out today so why did you put on your dirty shirt?	
Sharing toys with a visitor		4 If you don't let Mike play with your bricks you must go up to your room. 5 I will count up to five and then you must let Tim have a go on your bicycle. 6 Let Sharon play with your gun and then we can all go down to the swings. 7 All right, don't share your Lego. But you will find that Peter won't want to come and play with you on another day when you want him to.	
Time for bed		8 If you don't come up this minute I'll call a policeman. 9 If we go now there will be plenty of time for you to play in the bath while I sew these buttons on. 10 Come to bed now or else you won't see any television tomorrow.	

Some possible consequences?

Here are examples of the kind of thinking that might result from reactions to these situations. Of course they are not the only reactions possible, but are just suggestions as to what might happen.

Choosing clothes

Answers: 1X; 2√; 3XX.
1 gives a child something to disagree with right away while 2 leaves the burden of decision with her . . . you have set the limits, but within them there is some freedom of choice. The suggestion in 3 that the choice of the dirty shirt has been made purposely to anger can only confuse a child – there is too much for her to cope with here.

Sharing toys

Answers: 4XX; 5XX; 6√; 7XX.
4 and 5 invite head-on collisions. No reasonably attractive alternative is offered, there is no freedom of choice. 7 shows just

the kind of sulkiness you don't like your child to show! However 6 offers enough of a compromise to avoid fights!

Time for bed

Answers: 8XX; 9√; 10X.
Threats like 8 are a bluff that your child will see through eventually, though not before unnecessary fear may well have been created. 10 might work but it would be a reluctant child that came to bed, and not one ready to enjoy the shared experience promised in 9.

All these reactions are ways in which parents can exaggerate the importance of trivial incidents, 'making mountains out of mole-hills'. The effect of these reactions is to reinforce resistance and prolong the 'no' stage, to the satisfaction of no-one.

But just as mishandling can prolong this stage, understanding reactions can help children to grow through it without too much distress. Here are some ideas to try when you meet a challenge.

● wrap the disagreement up in a joke;

● make a distraction 'Just *look* out of the window!';

● fix something curious that will provoke her interest in what you want to do, like a surprise in the bath or something nice hidden in the bed;

● arrange a treat, something like a story and a cuddle when the job is done, reminding her of it before a little disagreement becomes a big fight;

● try to remain kindly but casual, appearing quite neutral, uninterested and unimpressed by the first signs of refusal.

Have you already tried any of these? Challenges are most difficult to meet when you are feeling low, so it is worth thinking out which ideas work best for you so that your mind is prepared before you meet your test. For instance, if you want to get out in the fresh air, decide to offer her a walk in the playground or to the shops, and not a choice between going out and staying in.

New characteristics

You may meet the beginnings of two different character traits at this early stage. They may be inconvenient now, but quench them and you undermine characteristics that can go with success in later life or career. Meet:

● James (age 3) who came rushing, furious, towards his mother with the two halves of a biscuit. 'Mend it, mend it!' he screams in fury.

● Daniel (age 2) who is just plain stubborn, rather like his dad – and grandpa too! He is a real chip off the old block.

We need people to care, like James, when whole things are broken. There will always be some people, like Daniel, more stubborn than others. At about the age of two, your child's character is beginning to emerge, whether you like it or not, and how you respond to the challenges of the two-year-old will affect your child's growing ideas about herself and the world she lives in.

Security

A child achieves independence from feelings of security. That security, a comfortable sense of well-being, begins in the early attachments of baby days. A baby can spot something changing in his field of vision very quickly. The moving patterns of your face are registered and remembered. Other senses are also registering:

● within a week or so a baby can tell his mother's breast scent from that of another woman,

● the sound of voices become associated with familiar faces,

● the way a child is held by familiar people is registered so that at six to eight months a child will look quite dismayed if handed over to a stranger. Back in the security of familiar arms, she scrutinises the unfamiliar adult.

At the age of two a toddler given the chance rarely strays far from familiar company. Some stay very close, even to the extent of insisting on coming with you to the bathroom. Others are quite happy if they can pick up other signals that you are near. Perhaps they will pop in to show you a toy, unconsciously checking that you're still there.

If your child is going through an uneasy stage, how can you make your signals stronger? Would it help if you sung or hummed, or turned the radio off so that she could hear YOU! Or if she has something of yours, perhaps a scarf that she can feel and stroke and smell.

Small children usually make attachments easily but it is the selective attachment to special people that matters. Too many different people confuse a young child and make the building of that inner security, which is the basis of independence, very difficult.

Regression

All too easily it is possible to revert back to earlier stages of growing up that had been left behind long ago. Adults often do it when ill or under stress. Quarrelling husbands and wives act like ten-year-olds without realising it. And if one adult behaves childishly, another can be provoked to anger.

But regression can be delightful. It can give comfort and joy in lovers' talk and sex play.

Sometimes the babyish behaviour of a three- or four-year-old is a cry for the remembered comforts of being a baby. Think of Debbie's situation:

She was nearly four when her baby brother was passed round among visiting relatives. She suddenly went all helpless and sat on the floor. Should her Mum react to this demanding babyish behaviour:

● sharply telling her not to be a baby, she was a big girl now;

● or giving her an extra cuddle and snuggle?

A cuddle and the acceptance of babyish behaviour helped Debbie to grow up again. It satisfied her need and helped her worry to go away as quickly as it had come.

Regression may happen in other ways, reverting to bed-wetting, remembering food fads, a returned reluctance to be alone, thumb-sucking . . . different kinds of behaviour all saying 'Let me act like a baby for a bit, I need to!' Remember this: the same kind of behaviour will come again in adolescence. The same acceptance will be just as important then as it is now.

Babysitters

A reliable babysitter who gets on well with young children is a boon to any family. Parents will feel happy to leave their child in such capable hands and confident that if anything unexpected should happen their babysitter will be able to cope. You can help each babysitting occasion go smoothly by preparing everybody concerned.

What should you tell your babysitter?

To look after your children well while you are away, your babysitter must have certain information. Keeping a babysitter's notebook reminds you what to say even if you chat about it beforehand. It's also a reminder for the babysitter, should anything arise in your absence.

Doctor's name is Dr. Pagett telephone number is......

The emergency number is......

Make sure that David's door is always slightly open and the hall light left on.

There's ready made squash and Ribena on the fridge if he wakes and asks for a drink.

Coffee/tea/biscuits are on the shelf over the sink.

First aid etc. is in the hall room cup

Going to friends for the evening. Their name is...... and telephone number is......

Back about 11.30pm.

David knows where we're going and the people we're visiting and that you'll be here 'till we get back.

He's been waking up occasionally late evening and may want you to stay with him for a while, or take him to the toilet.

He's been looking at books

Preparing your child

Depending on the age and understanding of your child, you should tell him you are going out for the evening and who is coming to look after him. If he wakes up and you haven't told him, he may feel frightened and deserted. He may worry that you might go out again without telling him and feel insecure.

Some children get upset if they don't know the babysitter very well, others are able to take this in their stride. Some children are happier with people who don't fuss over them, whereas others need plenty of cuddles and attention. You know your child, and the kind of person he'd respond to best.

Tell the babysitter what you usually do if your child wakes up, so that she can do the same. Your child expects that kind of treatment, and will feel happier with the familiar.

If your child experiences short separations from you without any problems he'll learn that you always come back. Perhaps going to play with a friend for the afternoon, or staying with grandparents or a neighbour for an hour or two will allow him to get used to the idea of occasionally being looked after by people other than his parents.

Babysitting circles

You only need about five members to make such a circle work, although the more people that are involved the better. Usually each member is given tokens to pay for a number of hours of babysitting, perhaps ten hours' worth. To keep a stock of tokens each member has to do some babysitting, so the circle is of mutual benefit to all. Husbands are invited to join too.

Every member should have a list of all the people in the circle.

Who makes a good babysitter?

Grandparents who live near make good babysitters but can be taken for granted. Because they are well known to the child and usually very popular with him, you are unlikely to have worries about leaving him with them. Occasionally their ideas may clash with yours and problems can arise.

Neighbours and friends can make good babysitters because again they probably know your child quite well. But if they don't have young children and you can't return the favour you may feel reluctant to ask.

Teenage girls often advertise locally for babysitting, usually to earn a little pocket money. Their ability to look after young children varies considerably. Many have a genuine interest in children and hope to work with children eventually.

You and your child should get to know your babysitter first. This applies to any babysitter. Invite them round during the day so that your child gets used to them and the babysitter used to your child. Let her handle the child and possibly do something for him, take him to the toilet, play and talk to him.

You will be able to decide if this person is suitable to look after your child when you go out.

If you are lucky enough to belong to a *babysitting circle* or *bank*, all the sitters will have children of their own. You know what the quality of babysitting is like because you babysit for each other and therefore have similar expectations. For this reason parents may well feel happier leaving their children with someone from the circle. If you prefer it, you would also be able to choose someone who has children about the same age as yours.

Breathing space

However much we enjoy our family life, most of us, at some time or other, like the feeling of having the house to ourselves for a few hours. No-one else to worry about or see to – a time to unwind and take stock. Most children also have this need to 'get away from it all'.

To each his own

You've probably found, if you have more than one child, that children differ in their need and reaction to quiet and space. Like Sheila (aged four and the younger of two children), who creeps away to her bedroom when too many visitors appear on the scene. Although Tom, the same age and one of five children, is so used to a noisy house that he doesn't like being alone when it's quiet.

Moods vary too. Have you noticed how sometimes you just want to get away from it all and be on your own? On other days, you're dying for someone to talk to. It's the same with children. Some days they'll hang around you wanting to be cuddled and hugged, on other days when you try to make a fuss of them they push you away and don't want to know.

Many children feel the need at some time or other to be quiet on their own – somewhere away from the demanding adult world, where they can enjoy privacy and 'do their own thing'. It's easy to understand this need but not so easy to provide for it. In many homes where two or more children share a bedroom, where kitchen and living room are all in one, where rooms are small and crowded with furniture, space is a luxury and it's not always possible for a child to find a space of his own.

It doesn't take too much effort, though, to organise some small corner for private play. Children soon learn to set it up for themselves and if it's really to be 'their corner' they should be responsible for keeping it clean and tidy. The one rule should be no interference from you provided they keep their side of the bargain to clear away when they've finished.

You can always find some small corner for children to play in

A time and place for everything

Most of this book is concerned with the day-to-day *active* involvement of parents with their children. It's important to remember, however, that there's a time and place for everything. You shouldn't feel it necessary to constantly 'develop' your child's interests.

Remember the times your child goes on and on asking questions. You answer patiently for as long as you can and then reach the point where you want it to stop but it doesn't. He has yet to learn your need for quiet. At least you are able to recognise when he needs time to himself, and, hopefully, you will be able to use this time as a breathing space for yourself as well.

A child has to learn to live in the world as it is. This learning is greatly helped by dolls or teddies that become 'person-toys'. With these toys a child can act out lots of things that happen to her during the day.

So often in a child's life someone is in control of her, telling her what to do and what not to do. Sometimes a child finds this very difficult to cope with. Why does the world treat her like this?

Equally, the way people behave towards each other is sometimes difficult for a child to understand. Why does Mummy keep talking to her friend and not take any notice of me? Why does Daddy get cross with Mummy? All this going on around her can be better coped with if she is able to play out similar situations with her teddies and dolls.

When she plays with such toys, she is in control and they can be made to take on any role she wishes. Perhaps a baby to mother, a naughty little boy to scold, a family to feed. The child can act out any emotion – she can love, hate, be cross, be tender to her dolls and they will accept it. Such toys make perfect companions, satisfied with the inferior role, ready for anything – but never demanding it.

What does your child do with her person-toys?

Below is a list of activities children do while playing with dolls and teddies. Watch your child, see what she does and tick where appropriate. Does she:

1 talk to it? ☐
2 cuddle it? ☐
3 feed it? ☐
4 take it for a walk? ☐
5 dress/undress it? ☐
6 wash it? ☐
7 put it to bed? ☐
8 scold it? ☐
9 smack it? ☐

What emotions does she show towards her toys?

1 love ☐
2 tenderness ☐
3 protection ☐
4 anger ☐
5 hate ☐
6 jealousy ☐
7 sympathy ☐

Dolls and teddies

A lot of a child's play involves copying how you and others behave towards her. She does this so that she can put herself in the position of others and find out what it's like to behave and feel as they do. To watch your child play is often quite an eye opener into the way you behave.

If your child shouts at and smacks her doll, look at your own behaviour towards her, from her point of view. You may well see yourself in a different light. Is your child sometimes gentle and loving towards her doll? This may well be a reflection of how you behave towards her. Listen to her language, does she talk down to her doll, punctuate her sentences with 'Darling', 'Sweetie', 'Angel', etc? If so, do you do this?

The beginnings of person-toy play

How does this begin? And at what age? A mother, when encouraging her toddler to eat, may hold the spoon to Teddy's mouth; later, the child feeds Teddy, putting himself in Mother's place, and Teddy in his place. Again, a mother, comforting her little daughter after a fall, passes her a doll – 'There, you love dolly better – she was hurt too.' From these simple beginnings grows the complex role-play of the older pre-school child. Sex differences develop fairly early, but are more usually due to the expectations of parents regarding their young son's and daughter's play, rather than something inborn in the child.

Boys and girls person-toys

Parents usually decide for their sons and daughters what toys they think they should play with. Here are a list of toys you might buy for your child. There are two columns alongside, one for boys, and one for girls. Tick the toys you would buy and for whom. If you haven't got a son and daughter pretend you have so that you can do this activity.

Toy	Girl	Boy
Doll	☐	☐
Teddy	☐	☐
Action man	☐	☐
Pram	☐	☐
Cot	☐	☐
Pushchair	☐	☐
Doll's clothes	☐	☐
Doll's bath	☐	☐
Action man kit	☐	☐
Doll's tea set	☐	☐

No doubt the girls will have more ticks. But boys need to understand what's going on around them just as much as girls. So they too need just as much play with person-toys. It's a pity that boy's dolls have to be 'fighters' to make them acceptable. Don't discourage your son from playing with dolls and prams. It's a stage he needs to go through. Usually little boys see more of their mothers than their fathers. So much of their person-toy play will be modelled on the sorts of things mothers do.

The best kind of person-toy

What is it that makes a child like one person-toy and not another? Find one of your child's favourite person-toys and use the table below to try and find out what attractive qualities it has.

Qualities

What is it?...............................

What size is it?.........................

What is it made of?.....................

Does it have clothes?...................

Are the clothes removable?.............

Is it washable?.........................

What is its face like?..................

Is it an elaborate toy – for
example, does it talk?.................

How does it feel?.......................

Which of these characteristics do you think are important to your child? If you do the same exercise with another, unpopular toy, you may find that it lacks some of these qualities.

Do the requirements of what makes a good person-toy change with the age of a child?

As children get older they are able, for example, to dress dolls more easily and their interest may move to more elaborate toys.

Developing person-toy play

As person-toy play is so important in helping the pre-school child to adjust to the realities of life, it is worth considering ways in which this play can be widened and deepened without imposing them on your child. At first the play is purely imitation, but later imagination comes in. The play, though still based on the child's everyday life, becomes an outlet for her impressions and emotions.

Here are some suggestions:

1 Provide some more clothes for the toy, for example bibs, nappies, etc.

2 Make a wardrobe from an old grocery box.

3 Suggest things your child can make for the toy, for example a necklace from cut-up straws, a headdress from feathers.

4 What about a birthday party with other children and their dolls?

5 Make a cot from an old shoe box.

6 Make a high chair from cardboard boxes.

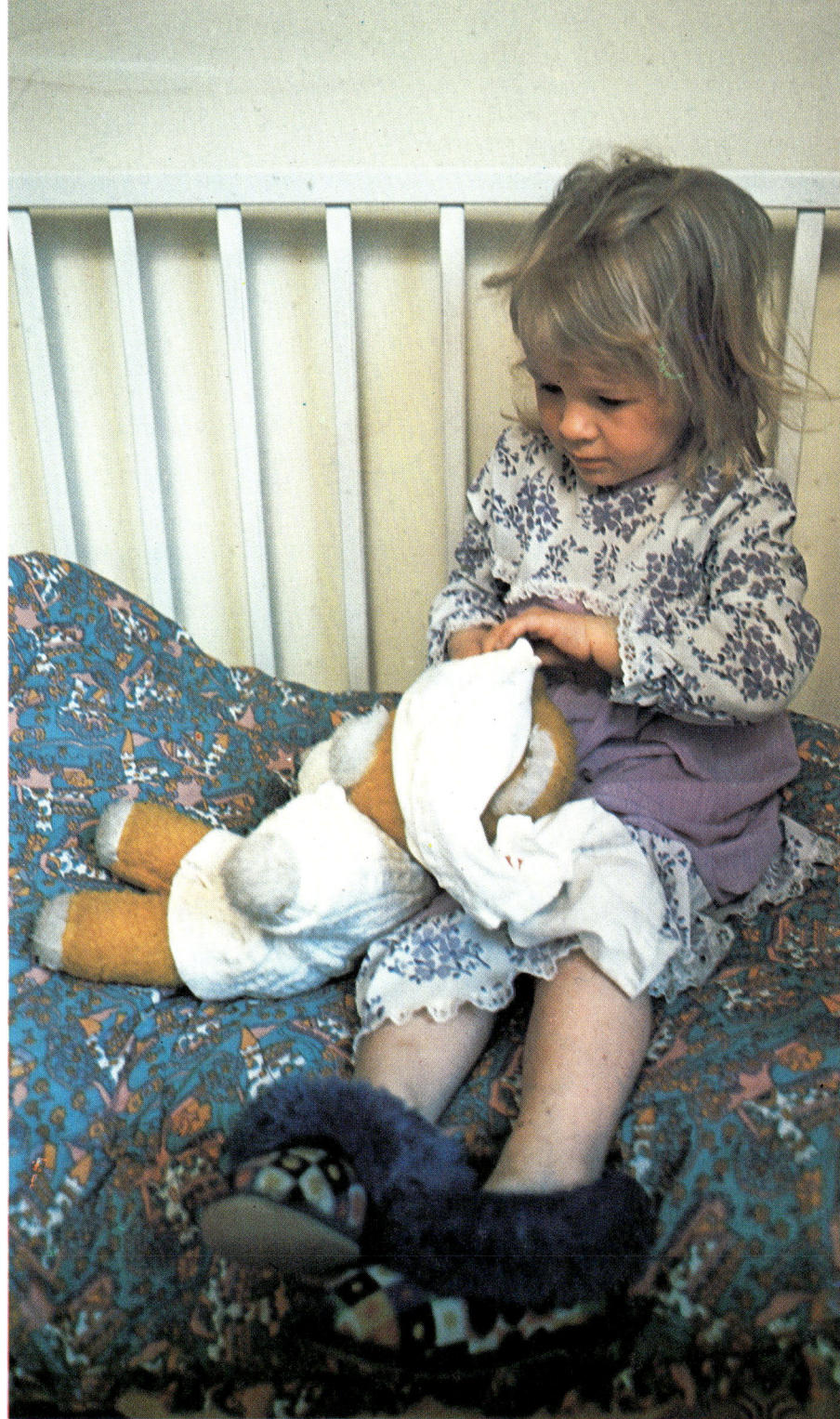

Comfort objects

If you have been able to observe several children, perhaps in a pre-school group, you will probably have noticed that one or two have a comfort object rather than a favourite person-toy. This object may be a piece of rag, a tattered baby blanket, a piece of fur, a nappy, even mother's once-best cardigan.

The object, however shabby it may appear, has become of great importance to the child and may, indeed be vital to her emotional security; although she may forget it for many days together, at times of stress she needs the reassurance of its feel and look and, sometimes, even smell! Some children are remarkably efficient at ensuring that their comfort object is always within reach however. It may be un-obtrusively moved around so that it is always to hand, with the result that it is seldom needed just because it is always there.

What starts as rather an endearing habit quickly becomes well established and many parents may find it rather a nuisance. The cuddly has to be found before going out and taken everywhere, it gets dirty and falls to pieces, and it looks pretty awful.

Don't blame it all on the child. There are times when parents positively encourage their child to have a comforter. Perhaps a child is being trouble-some about going to sleep and one night she quickly drops off cuddling an old shawl. The parents will give it to her the next night in the hopes that she will go to sleep again without any trouble – cuddling the shawl. But they may be setting up difficulties for them-selves without realising it. At the time it seems the easiest thing to do but in the long run can be far more tiresome.

Rather than encourage your child to have one cuddly, encourage her to have a range of them, then any one of them will be acceptable. By doing this you do not run into the kinds of problems described above.

In time the intensity of feeling for toy comforters can be expected to fade and these objects to be outgrown, though this is likely to be a gradual process.

Mum and Dad are often the two main characters in children's play. This sort of play is important now and for the future. Things like washing up, making dinner, and getting the shopping are essential parts of home life.

Take time off to listen . . .

Try to find time to watch your child play but be careful not to disturb him. It helps to appear involved in something else – like writing or knitting or watching the television, while you watch and listen to his play.

Some things to notice

● What sparks off play – an accident, a conversation, new dressing-up clothes, etc.?

● Where is this play carried out – sitting room, hall, back garden, bedroom, etc.?

● What are they pretending to do – cooking, feeding and changing their babies, mending a car, etc.?

● What props are being used – chairs, beds, boxes, yoghurt pots, dolls, clothes, etc.?

● What role does each child play – mummy, daddy, little girl, little boy, baby, etc.?

● What tasks does each child carry out – washing-up, laying the table, pushing a pram, giving instructions, going on errands, etc.?

We're making dinner

Lucy (four) and Sophie (three) are sisters. They have started a game because of a suggestion from Dad. They are playing in a bedroom but pretending to be in a kitchen/diner. They are 'making dinner' and using two dolls, a large teddy bear, a table, chairs, boxes, plastic plates and yoghurt pots. Lucy is mummy and Sophie is a big girl. Lucy is organizing things, laying the table, serving the food and feeding the dolls. Sophie eats her dinner and feeds the dolls.

As you listen to children role-playing, you will notice that they spend time in setting up the game, and during the game they occasionally revert back to their normal roles to deal with a problem. Once the game has been set up and the roles decided, most of the time will be spent 'in role'.

In the example below most of the extracts are mainly about role setting. The first extract is from the beginning of the game, the second after the arrival of other children which required changes in role.

Extract 1:

Sophie: We're making dinner.

Lucy: I'm Mummy. I'll have to go and get baby now. They're sitting up aren't they?

Sophie: I'm a big girl.

Lucy: This is Tessa (a doll) there, and that's Helen (a doll) . . . and this is Ben (a large bear). John (not present) is Daddy at work.

Sophie: Who am I?

Lucy: Sophie – or do you want to be a different name?

Lucy: Come on everybody – have dinner.

Extract 2:

(Later they are joined by two older friends, Suzy (six) and John (six).

Lucy: Hello! That's soup and that's soup.

Suzy: What is this? (Points to box on chairs).

Lucy: High chair.

Suzy: Can I use the high chair for my baby?

John: What's that, is it a draining board?

Lucy: That's . . . you have to pretend washing-up – wash, wash – like that.

Suzy: What's that?

Lucy: The oven.

Suzy: Can I be Mummy?

Lucy: I'll be a big girl.

Sophie: I'll be a little girl.

Lucy: John can be Daddy. Daddy go and work . . . I think the car's just broken down– I think you'd better go and mend it, all right?

Lucy: My doll's cot can be the car – Yes?

Suzy: No, the car's in the car park.

Lucy: I'll get the car (the pedal car.)

Suzy: We are not allowed to take it inside the house.

John: Where's the washing-up basin? (He finds one and 'washes up'.)

Playing mothers and fathers

To compare these two games, fill in who (including the dolls, etc.) plays the roles in each game.

Role	Extract 1	Extract 2
Mummy		
Daddy		
Big girl		
Little girl		
Little boy		
Baby		

You could compare the games you listen to at home in a similar way and complete the next table. First list the tasks and then write in who carries out each one in each game – like this:

Task	Game 1	2	3	etc.
Setting up the game				
Handling the baby				
Serving food				
Washing up, etc.				

● How well do the children adapt to different roles?

● Do the most important roles always go to the older children?

● Do boys always play male roles and girls female roles?

● Do girls and boys do the same tasks?

Words of warning

You may recognise yourself in your child's play as a much stricter parent, but you must resist the temptation to say – 'But darling, I *never* speak like that.' Remember – you must only watch and not interfere.

Sometimes boys will want to be mummy and girls to be daddy, boys may want to be nurses and girls firemen or soldiers. There is no reason why you should worry about this, it is all part of growing up.

But why do they do it?

Young children come to understand a situation and come to terms with it through play. Adults can usually accept the tensions of everyday living as a normal part of family life but young children, even from the happiest homes, need to work through situations of stress for themselves.
● Why is Mummy suddenly cross?
● Why must I be specially good for some visitors?
● What do Mummy and Daddy do when I'm in bed?

A child may ask such questions and receive answers that do not help him understand because, although words give the facts, they do not explain the feelings which colour the facts. A child who can go off to play 'mothers and fathers' with other young children can, by bringing stressful situations into his play, learn how it feels to be a hurried daddy, a cross mummy, and, more important, learn that a hurried daddy, a cross mummy, are still the same loving parents underneath. Of course, this is not done consciously: a child unconsciously role-plays 'cross mummy or daddy' and this has the effect of helping his emotional growth and so lays a foundation for mature relationships in later life.

How can I encourage play?

You have listened to children playing, and thought about what lies behind it. You know how important it is and you want to do something to encourage this play. Here are some suggestions:

● Look critically at your child's play space. Has he somewhere to call his own? Has he room to have a friend or friends to play in? Try to plan where he can have a 'home area':
   in a corner of the living room
   in the hall or a bedroom
   even under a table!
Can you define this area for him? Throw a sheet over a clothes-horse, hang a curtain on a string, arrange a wall of chairs.

● Take your child to a jumble sale – after the first rush is over – let him choose dressing-up clothes, an old saucepan, some odd cups and saucers.

● Make things with your child that will add to his home play. Thread necklaces, make cushions, a door knocker, collect packets for the 'larder', make toy money.

● Look out for picture-stories about mummies and daddies. Make picture scrap books about home and families.

● Sort out your own priorities:
   tidy homes versus untidy play
   peace and quiet versus visiting playmates
   watching TV versus reading a story
Remember that children have rights, but so do parents!

Something to make: a doll's house

The doll's house need not be too elaborate. Inhabitants can be made very easily from pipe cleaners or cotton reels, with a bead stuck on for a head and two holes drilled through the cylinder to take pipe cleaner arms and legs. Furniture is easy to improvise – match-boxes, conkers, pill-boxes, tiny cartons, all can be converted. Rooms can be arranged in a series of boxes, papered with the child's drawings or with left-over scraps of wallpaper. Consider the play value rather than the fun you will have making it!

A miniature home

Playing with a doll's house is 'mothers and fathers' on a small scale. It is different from 'home area' play, less active and does not involve the child in the same way. On the other hand, because everything is on a small scale, a child feels able to handle the situation. He can move furniture, and the people around the house, sometimes dropping them casually on the floor as he loses interest, sometimes shutting the baby in the wardrobe, throwing the mummy on the bed, and even forgetting the child who has fallen head first down the toilet!

Don't try to read too much into this play. Doll's house play simply brings relief from tension, as well as bringing emotional satisfaction.

Is it worth it?

You might like to jot down some interesting aspects of your child's home play – the things he says, the events he plays out, the incidents he invents, the use he makes of the equipment you provide.

Rival or friend?
Plaything or playmate?
Your child's feeling about other members of
the family will depend a lot on the way
in which he learns about what is
going to happen within that family.

New baby in the family

Spacing pregnancies

Whether children who are already established members of a family will welcome or resent the arrival of a new baby often depends on clever spacing.

The Victorians may have produced a baby each year under the pressure of their dreadfully high infant loss rate. Since then, British generations have tended somehow towards a 2½-year interval, averaged out. This gap allows the first-born to learn to walk and talk and to pass through the very active exploring, independent stage before having to learn about accepting another child in the family.

There are various pressures affecting this most private and personal decision. Among them there's something to be said for arranging to be through the toddler stages before having another baby (and possible competitor) to add to your family group.

Avoiding transmitting worry

By the sixth week of pregnancy you can be fairly sure that a new baby has been started and mixed feelings often dominate. It's worth remembering that children are like little radar sets and will pick up snippets of talk through a kitchen door ajar or from overhearing their parents talking in bed. They may well sense from neighbours' and relatives' carefully camouflaged comments that something puzzling and new is in the air.

You may have fleeting fears and imaginings about the baby growing inside you, but it is important that you avoid passing on indigestible worries to an older child who may seem unusually understanding and attentive.

Avoid giving your child second hand feelings of discomfort or morning sickness! Be aware of the need to prevent him overhearing the conversation of a friend who delights in recalling the pangs of labour or who treats pregnancy as an illness.

This can be tricky if it's someone like a grandparent. Feel your way through these difficulties, bearing in mind the ideal of giving your child the impression that the inconveniences of pregnancy matter less than the pleasure of having another child.

Conflict at home

● Do you usually get on well with Gran?
● Do you sometimes have rows at home?
Quarrelling parents are a worry to children at any time, but especially when a big change is in the air.

Some conflict is normal in the 'organised' chaos of most homes, but it is an important part of family democracy to respect a child's special need for happiness, contentment and well-being at this time.

Talking about the baby

'The baby growing in Mummy's tummy' is a classical start. By three months, the womb can just be felt, about grapefruit size, behind the pubic bone. Young children have in the past been confused by being told that 'You were once a little piece of jelly' or 'At one stage it had a tail like a tadpole or a fish'. They need to visualise something rather more human, and of course so do grown-ups. In fact by three months, although the baby is so small it could lie in the palm of your hand, it is really a perfect tiny human being.

Look around for children's picture books that show how babies develop in the womb. These sorts of pictures can be valuable conversation starters.

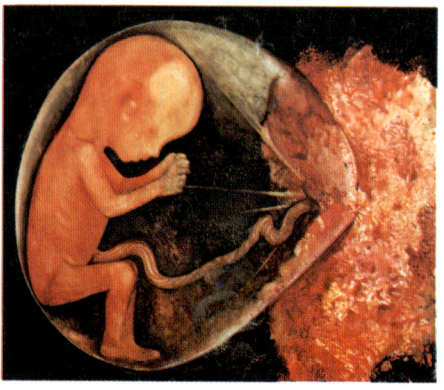

How do I tell him?

Below is a list of ways of telling your child about the new baby. Think about each one and tick those you think you might say.

1 Father Christmas is going to bring you a present soon.

2 We are going to save up our pennies so that we can go and buy a new baby.

3 Mummy's going to go to hospital to choose a new baby.

4 We are going to have a new baby for you to play with.

5 You're such a nice little boy that we thought we'd have another one.

6 There's a baby growing inside Mummy's tummy.

7 Would you like a new baby?

8 Have you noticed Mummy's tummy getting bigger? Why do you think that is?

9 You know your friend Martin had a new baby sister, well, we're going to have a new baby too.

10 Do you remember when Karen had a big tummy there was a baby inside? Well Mummy's going to have a baby too.

If you tell him something that's not true, like 1, 2 or 3, it may be difficult to keep the story going. He's bound to find out sooner or later that you've been spinning him a yarn and then how will he feel? If you use 4, 5 or 7, you'll have problems if he answers no! It may be easier to talk about things he knows already so that through 6, 8, 9 and 10 you both move towards talking about reality.

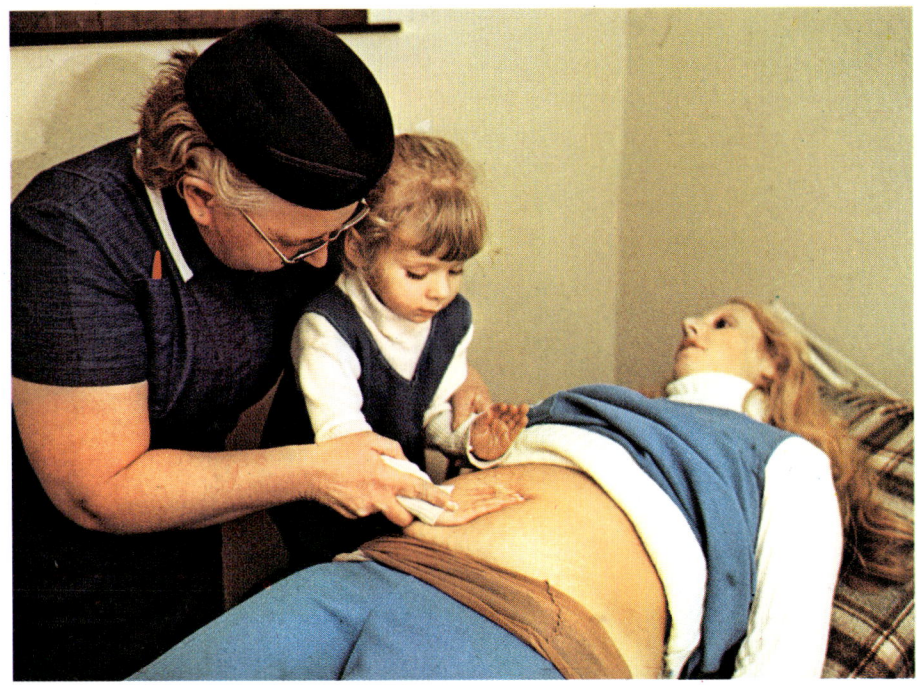

By five and six months they love to know that 'the heart is beating now' and that 'soon it'll be kicking about to try out it's arms and legs'. As soon as a kindly midwife lets you listen to the baby's heartbeat, don't forget to give the little one alongside a go at the stethoscope – it could almost be a message from outer space.

Once bumps and kicks can be felt through the tummy wall, you can imitate the baby's elbow-shoving and leg kicking and make it into a funny experience. Try putting a cup of tea onto your pregnant tummy and letting the children watch what happens? Morning tea-parties made by kind husbands are very helpful at this time; they can make your child feel loved.

The way it gets out

At this stage, children are bound to ask how the baby will come out, so you will have to give a sex education lesson. The idea that the vagina is constructed of special stretchy material that becomes even more specially elastic as the time of birth approaches, is quite acceptable to children, who can't imagine really just how big the baby's head will be.

They may well ask 'Will it hurt' – meaning also of course 'Did *I* hurt you when I came out? – and they appreciate an honest 'Yes, it *did* hurt, but I was actually so pleased to see you I forgot about the hurting'.

It is a constant experience that, when you are telling children of all ages about a baby growing inside the womb, they are thinking of themselves. 'Was I *this* big?' 'Did I kick like that?' 'Has it got fingers and toes yet?' This question also says 'Has it got a penis yet, and so would you have known I was a boy or girl by then?' Above all,

they love to hear how you were thinking and feeling about them while they were growing inside the womb and it's quite likely that what you say they'll remember for a long time.

This fundamental curiosity about conception and birth is altogether natural and is an important part of childhood. Answered questions allow a child to go on and think about something else.

If you watched youngsters seeing how a calf is born, either as it flops down in a boneless heap on the floor or in a television wildlife programme, you'll be reassured by their interest in all the details. How the animal licks her child, perhaps eats her placenta, nuzzles the baby and learns its smell and cry, all this intrigues them greatly. They'll appreciate its grip on life and its fight for survival, with great sympathy and understanding.

We were all babies

This isn't a bad time to pull out those early family photographs of them as infants and to fill in with plenty of anecdotes. Stories like: how they yelled at the wrong moment or did outrageous things, mildly shocking the grown-ups. It emphasises to them how *they* mattered, and what a grip on life they also had.

Don't forget 'parents-when-we-were-babies' pictures are good for a laugh and another mood-setting warm-hearted thing to do.

They may like you to recap on how it all worked out when they were born, what time of the day it was, even whether it was snowing at the time and even what you'd have named them if they'd been the other sex (but of course how glad you were that it was in fact a little . . . .).

The approaching delivery

As the baby grows to full size, toddlers and older children might like to lay hands on it, feeling it inside mother's tummy. Your midwife will tell you how the baby is lying, left-about or right-about or whether it is in a head-down position. Children are always intrigued by this.

At about 36 weeks, with 4 weeks to go, you can feel the solid round head low down, with the curve of the back above it. On the opposite side those interesting knobs and lumps appear from time to time where it thrusts and kicks its limbs forwards. After about 36 weeks you can't demonstrate the head so easily because about then it tends to descend a few inches to lie within the pelvic brim.

To get an idea of the size of the baby it helps to show them the tiny clothes you are getting ready, particularly little socks.

Now is the time to offer an older child the chance to help choose names. One way of bringing them in, and a good exercise in 'family democracy', might be to give them the power of veto, a guarantee that a name to which they react badly will not be chosen – 'At least we've *all* decided it won't be Montmerency or Ermintrude'.

Ladybird Books have produced an excellent, illustrated, simple little book for the younger child expecting a baby brother or sister, called *Talk-about Baby*. It's talking points include preparing baby equipment together, visiting hospital, the baby's arrival home and a number of incidents including jokes, each making a good point.

Besides such aids, it's not a bad idea to try to get acquainted with a neighbour's or friend's new baby, preferably when it is being handled and perhaps not only looking alert and smiling, like the Ladybird examples, but also yelling a bit!

Separation from mother needs careful planning, whether in infancy or as a toddler. With any luck you'll have chosen a relative or friend whom the child knows and perhaps has visited and been left with, so that he feels at home. If father is able to take time off work to do this caring, a build up of extra play and talk with dad before the birth, with his seeing to all baths, and tuckings-up in bed, will help.

The thing to remember is that the very young child of 1½, 2 or 3 can make a quick and strong relationship with a stand-in parent figure. This means that the earlier 'bridging' exercise, the getting-to-know-beforehand, may well need to be put into reverse rather gently.

A sudden jump back to mother and home after sleeping in another person's home and living intimately with them, may after only a week be surprisingly disconcerting for the child. The odd visit back (both ways) in the first few days, may be welcomed.

Home again

Keeping the playgroup attendance going, visits to the usual shops, friends and pets, give continuity. Youngsters nowadays visit their mothers in a maternity ward as a matter of routine and like to see them knitting, making tea, doing familiar things in familiar clothes.

They expect quite normal mothering for themselves and not necessarily a baby-adoration session. It can be quite difficult after the hectic success of childbirth, when you are involved in intensive 'bonding' experiences yourself with the new baby, to think into the mind of the small toddler wanting to talk about everyday things and be admired and cared for as usual.

Getting to know him

Breast or bottle feeding they'll enjoy and if the former you may have been able to show them some of the extra-rich milk which can be pressed out of the nipple in the days before the birth – explaining that although it becomes bluish and watery looking in the next few days, it is a very special mix.

Let them explore the baby's body:

● feel the soft fontanelle of the mid upper skull-bones,

● test the grasp reflex and pulling,

● stroke its cheek, see it following the end of a finger hoping for a nipple.

All this will satisfy their curiosity for facts. It gives a more interesting image than a swaddled baby would, when it is obscured almost to the nose.

They'll need to know that the baby can watch them and hear them, even though it will not react with smiles until about six weeks. They may have no wish to kiss the new baby and would

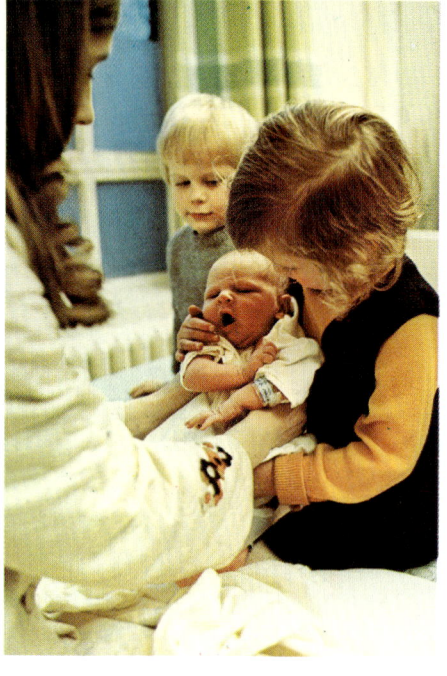

much rather observe and be told '*You* used to do this, just the same way and we loved watching you'.

Back home, when you may be incredibly busy, their need for regressive (baby-like) play and physical handling may crop up at any moment. While the new baby is being fed and loved they may need their own special time alone with each parent. At this time, their own space for toys and possessions may be specially important, with their personal treats and birthdays mapped out in advance.

Some like helping with the bath, a little girl will want to have a good look at her brother's tiny penis. Most like to play, but others don't. Tactful checking may be needed at this stage if the older child makes the baby shriek with laughter repeatedly. The baby will not be able to keep up as he is not so strong.

Baby becomes child

You can expect very reasonable feelings of jealousy and resentment to appear or grow once the baby begins to crawl and pulls down toys. You will find yourself refereeing little conflicts, trying not to blame but rather put their natural hostility into words for your older child . . . 'Oh dear, you must have felt cross when the baby pulled your train over . . . '

If you sense your older child's emerging resentment, why not take time to give him your full attention when the baby is sleeping. Leave the housework, that can wait . . . your child matters. There are plenty of ideas in this course that will allow you to introduce something new – dough and water, buttons and paint will give you plenty of chance to play together.

It is important that there are regular reminders that even though there is a baby, your older child is still loved.
'You're my oldest daughter now . . . '
'You helped to choose his name, didn't you . . . '
'He can do that, but *you* can do . . . . '
'He'll be glad to have you to play with when he's older.'

In any situation that crops up, try to avoid negative thinking. 'I'll put a stop to that idea, I'm too busy right now . . . ' Instead be encouraging, 'Oh yes, come over here and tell me about it while I do this.'

With the passing of time, the baby becomes more of a playmate. The smile of recognition is a sign that playing peep-bo can start. Show your child how she can cause a smile, then a laugh of relief, by re-appearing from behind a head scarf held up to hide her face. Later games are:
● hunt the teddy – or some other large toy – with a crawling child,
● hide and seek with a toddler.

Sharing your baby

A final thought. Might you be prepared to share your baby with other small children? Do you know the schoolteachers locally? Would they invite you in, perhaps starting with the pregnancy, to see how a baby is handled, measured and fed, particularly if you can breast-feed comfortably with others watching?

Many schools nowadays welcome such a project and older secondary school boys and girls gain much more from baby-observing if they've been prepared as part of the expanding child-care courses for the mid-teens.

You may find that your nearest playgroup or nursery class would welcome a visit from you and your baby. Not all little children have babies at home, very few would have both boy and girl. Watching the bathing of a baby can be the highlight of a playgroup morning, as you can see!

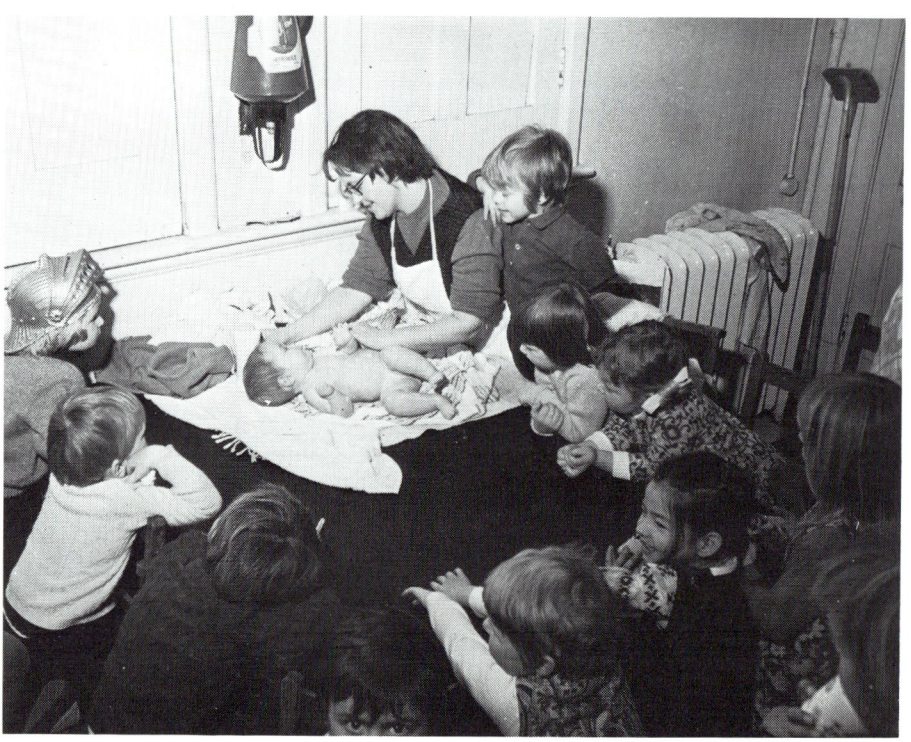

Family relationships

What do parents think children should do – or be? Do mothers and fathers agree about what they expect of their children and about what they expect of each other? What happens if they have different expectations? This topic and the next give you an opportunity to explore these questions.

Mrs B
'I don't seem to be very successful. Other people's children seem to be more polite and less cheeky – it sometimes makes you wonder what they do that I don't do. I've often felt like crying, you know – say I've smacked them a bit harder than usual; it's very upsetting because I love kids . . .'

Parents' views about children

All families have different views about what children should do and what they should be like. This is reasonable as no one can say what all children should be like, as all children are different. The views parents have about children will not only affect their relationship with their child but will affect their relationship with each other.

In this topic you can look at your own and your partner's views about your child. To help you do this there is a simple check-list which, of course, does not have any right or wrong answers. It merely provides a way of opening up discussion about different views. You will want to go into more detail and to qualify many of the items in the checklist – but use it as a starting point. For example, the first item – 'children should be obedient' – you may agree in general and so may your partner but the circumstances in which you expect your child to be obedient may differ.

You may feel obedience is particularly important when you are visiting other people – or when your mother-in-law is staying with you. Your partner may agree about visiting friends but not agree that obedience is important when 'in-laws' are staying, and so on.

What do you expect of your child?

Work through the checklist quickly on your own, then cover up your answers and hand it over to your partner to fill in.

√ = Yes
X = No

● Please add any items that you think are important. Some of those noted may seem unimportant so just note down, in the space provided, the things that you think are important and see whether you both agree.

● When you have both filled it in have a look at each item. If you both agree you may still want to qualify your agreement and check that you are really agreeing about the same things. It is best to do this by discussing things your child has actually done and see whether you both agree about them.

Should children:	Wife thinks	Husband thinks
be obedient?	☐	☐
be polite?	☐	☐
be quiet at home?	☐	☐
say 'Please' and 'Thank you'?	☐	☐
ask their parents to wait?	☐	☐
answer back?	☐	☐
be cheeky?	☐	☐
eat all their food?	☐	☐
interrupt adults?	☐	☐
speak until they are spoken to at mealtimes?	☐	☐
swear – mildly, for example say 'Damn'?	☐	☐
tell lies?	☐	☐
get into their parents' bed?	☐	☐
run around naked?	☐	☐
touch their sexual parts?	☐	☐
stand on their own feet with other children?	☐	☐
hit other children?	☐	☐
share their toys with other children?	☐	☐
play with guns?	☐	☐
be physically active?	☐	☐
be thoughtful?	☐	☐
be outgoing towards other children?	☐	☐
do housework?	☐	☐
look smart?	☐	☐
hang up their clothes?	☐	☐
keep their bedrooms tidy?	☐	☐
make a mess?	☐	☐
wash hands after going to the toilet	☐	☐
clean their teeth?	☐	☐
....	☐	☐
....	☐	☐
....	☐	☐

Mrs J
'I said "Go and hit him back, then – go and fight your own battles". Because I mean they've got to learn to stand on their own feet – its no good really molly-coddling them is it?'

Mrs M
'I think he would quite willingly let me take him to the toilet, look after him and clean his teeth and wash him, you know. He would quite willingly let me but I think he should start.'

Do you agree?

It will be very surprising if you both agree about everything. The purpose of the activity is not to stir up disagreement but to bring into the open things you may have been disagreeing about for a long time but have never quite put your finger on. If you know what you disagree about then you can do one of two things – either discuss the question and end up agreeing, or agree to disagree. If you agree to disagree you will have to try to ensure that your child is not confused by your conflicting views. If he understands that one of you disapproves of certain behaviour while the other does not, he can learn to avoid the behaviour when both parents are around and to only do it if the approving parent is around.

For example:

Mr and Mrs Brown

Mr Brown doesn't mind his child interrupting him, asking him to wait, playing with guns and looking untidy. While Mrs Brown does object to being interrupted, being asked to wait, playing with guns and expects her child to look smart when they go out. Here the child can learn one way of behaviour towards his father and another towards his mother. He also has to learn not to play with guns while his mother is around and to put up with looking smart when she takes him out.

Children are quite capable of learning to relate differently to different people and this is of course, an important part of social learning. If they related to both parents in exactly the same way this would not give them much practice in learning to relate to the other different people they are going to come across. There can be problems when the views of parents are incompatible and the child has no way of pleasing them both.

Mr and Mrs Weston

As an example Mrs Weston doesn't mind her child climbing into her bed during the night for a short while. Mr Weston objects strongly. One night the child has a nightmare wakes up and knowing the conflicting views of his parents is made doubly anxious about seeking comfort from his parents. This difference of views is also likely to lead to tension between Mr and Mrs Weston.

When they discuss it Mr Weston explains that he thinks that it is bad for the child to intrude into parents' privacy in bed. Mrs Weston suspects that he may be a little jealous of her affection towards her son especially when it is expressed in their bed. They agree to disagree on this one and Mrs Weston decides to comfort her son in his own bed when this is necessary.

What does the husband expect to do as a father and what does the wife expect to do as a mother? What does a wife expect her husband to do as a father? What does a husband expect his wife to do as a mother?

Parents' views about each other

These questions are important ones. At the moment there is considerable change in our assumptions about what mothers and fathers do. The distinctions of the past are being questioned and people are asking whether fathers should necessarily be fatherly and mothers motherly. Why shouldn't fathers be motherly if they want to be? With working parents and single-parent families the money earning father and the housewife mother are not as common as they used to be. Some families have even swapped roles, the woman going out to work and the man staying at home doing the housework and looking after the children. There is no reason why this should not work as well as the more traditional way.

With things in a state of flux it is quite likely that young parents are not too sure what the roles of mother and father mean anymore. With change there is likely to be disagreement between parents as to what they expect each other to do as mother and father to their child.

A checklist has been devised to help you and your partner look first, at what you expect of yourself, and second, at what you expect of each other. This is only to provide a starting point for discussion. The questions you are asked in the checklist do not have a right or wrong answer and you may find it difficult to give a straight 'yes' or 'no' response.

The second item for example asks the father (1) whether he thinks he should 'be strict', (2) whether he thinks his wife should 'be strict'. It asks the mother (3) whether she thinks she should be strict and (4) whether she thinks her husband should be. Obviously these questions hinge on what's meant by 'be strict' and you may wish to think of it as 'be stricter than you are now' or 'be strict under certain circumstances' and then go on to think about under what circumstances you think you should 'be strict'

What do you expect of each other?

Work down the checklist quickly on your own filling in either the first two or the last two columns.

● Then cover up your answers and hand it to your partner to fill in.

● Add any items you think are important and have been left off.

● When you have both filled in all the columns have a look at them together.

● Take each item in turn, even if you agree, and check that you are agreeing about the same thing. If you disagree you will need to discuss this. Do this with reference to examples of what you both do or would like each other to do.

The patterns of disagreement are quite complicated and are discussed in more detail below. First, fill in the checklist before you start thinking about sorting out what the various patterns mean.

Should mothers/fathers:

	Father thinks:		Mother thinks:	
	he should	his wife should	she should	husband should
be loving towards their child?	☐	☐	√ = Yes	☐	☐
be strict?	☐	☐	X = No	☐	☐
be kind?	☐	☐	☐	☐
be soft?	☐	☐	☐	☐
kiss and cuddle their child?	☐	☐	☐	☐
discipline their child?	☐	☐	☐	☐
smack their child if necessary?	☐	☐	☐	☐
dress their child?	☐	☐	☐	☐
bath their child?	☐	☐	☐	☐
help their child with his toilet?	☐	☐	☐	☐
take their child out?	☐	☐	☐	☐
entertain their child?	☐	☐	☐	☐
read stories to their child?	☐	☐	☐	☐
help their child to dress dolls?	☐	☐	☐	☐
help their child to play with cars?	☐	☐	☐	☐
help their child with woodwork?	☐	☐	☐	☐
know what to do?	☐	☐	☐	☐
be interested in what their child does?	☐	☐	☐	☐
give time to their child?	☐	☐	☐	☐
do the things their child asks?	☐	☐	☐	☐
teach their child new things?	☐	☐	☐	☐
answer their child's questions about sex?	☐	☐	☐	☐
tell the truth to their child?	☐	☐	☐	☐
get up for their child in the night?	☐	☐	☐	☐
not be seen naked by their child?	☐	☐	☐	☐

(Others, fill in here)

.... ☐ ☐ ☐ ☐

.... ☐ ☐ ☐ ☐

.... ☐ ☐ ☐ ☐

.... ☐ ☐ ☐ ☐

Comments from Mrs Barnes

'My husband and I were quite surprised at how much we disagreed about what we expect from our children. We talked about this and thought it might be something to do with what our own parents expected of us when we were kids. We were a bit worried that our children might be confused because their Dad expects one thing and their Mum expects something else.

We then did the checklist about what we think each other should do. We agreed over most things, then we thought it might come out different if we ticked the things we actually *do* rather than what we think we *should* do. It came out completely different. My husband thinks he should do lots of things for the children, but in fact he doesn't. We tried to work out why.

Our idea of a model mum and dad was the same, but in real life it worked out differently. My husband says it's because he has to go to work and isn't around as much as I am, so he doesn't get to do much for the children. When he is around they tend to come to me because they are used to me doing things for them and I just get on with it and he tends to keep out of it.

Then we remembered about our disagreements over the first list. It suddenly occurred to us that if my husband doesn't have the same expectations of our children as I do then he isn't going to be very keen on helping me carry out what I think is right, and the children are more likely to behave as I want them to because I am with them more. We find we agreed on most things when we were answering what we *should* do. We then completed the answers for what we *actually* do. There was much more disagreement.'

What does it mean?

Let's take as an example the item 'be soft'.

Look at the ways the question could be answered.

Should mothers/fathers be soft?

Father thinks:		Mother thinks:	
he should	his wife should	she should	husband should
☑	☑	☑	☒

Here the father, Mr Green thinks he should 'be soft' he also thinks his wife should be. His wife, Mrs Green, thinks she should be soft but – she thinks her husband should not be soft. Let's imagine the kinds of disagreements they could have.

To make it more realistic let's say Mrs Green also expects her husband to be strict and to discipline their child. Mr Green does not want this role – in addition to thinking of himself as soft, he does not consider he should be strict or should discipline their child. This is bound to lead to tensions between them and it may confuse their child. Suppose Mrs Green threatens the child that 'he will be for it when his father gets home' – she does this because she is in fact soft, not strict and cannot discipline the child herself. Mr Green, on arriving home, refuses to live up to his wife's expectations and dole out punishment – instead he wants to 'be soft' with the child. The child would see his mother's authority undermined even further by this. She would feel that not only has she shown that she cannot cope with punishing the child but her husband had let her down in front of the child.

The conclusion isn't that all fathers should be strict, it means that parents should be in reasonable agreement about what role each of them will play towards their child. If the husband wants to be soft and his wife knows and accepts this then this is okay. And if she and her husband agree whether she should be soft or not then the child will know where he is. This state of affairs could be shown like this:

Should mothers/fathers be soft?

Father thinks:		Mother thinks:	
he should	his wife should	she should	husband should
·☑	☒	☒	☑

However, it would mean that Mrs Green would have to be less soft in order to keep her child within certain limits of behaviour.

The problem above would not arise from the pattern below, where another set of parents both agree the father should not be soft.

Should mothers/fathers be soft?

Father thinks:		Mother thinks:	
he should	his wife should	she should	husband should
☒	☑	☑	☒

63

Books about everyday life

Lucy and Tom's Day
Shirley Hughes
Picture Puffin, 1973
The leisurely day which is pictured here might seem rather old-fashioned, but children love the domestic details.

Lucy and Tom at the Seaside
Gollancz, 1977
The beach is crowded and wind-swept, the picnic plagued by wasps. Most families have had outings like this and the excitement and detail of the drawings will bring back all the memories.

Emma has the measles
Gunilla Wolde
Brockhampton, 1974 (HB)
Little brother is poorly, Mum is worried, Dad takes his temperature and gets the doctor. Emma feels left out . . . This short family drama of anxiety, naughtiness and frayed tempers is very popular.

Thomas Goes Out – and in his hurry gets all his clothes into a marvellous muddle.

Thomas Goes to the Doctor – he enjoys having his throat and ear examined, loves the stethoscope and cries a lot when he has an injection. But he likes the plaster and gives teddy an injection and a plaster, once he is safely back home.

Thomas Bakes a Cake – with very little help from Dad. His recipe is there for everyone to try.

Emma's First Day at Nursery School
Hodder, 1976

Topsy and Tim go on Holiday
Jean and Gareth Adamson
Blackie, 1965
Judging by the number of titles in this series, the twins are very popular. They give a very comfortable and reassuring view of childhood.

The Blanket
'When I go to bed I always take my blanket. One night I could not find my blanket . . .'
The story is about the search for the blanket. Any parents whose child chews a ragged piece of cloth or takes a tatty teddy everywhere will recognise the drama.

The Baby – this deals very perceptively with the mixed feelings of an older brother when a new baby arrives.

Kate's Bouncy Ball
Inger and Lasse Samberg
A. and C. Black, 1976 (HB)
This little book is very good value in hard cover. It is about Kate who discovers a big, round, squashy ball that bounces. Look out for others in this series.

Kate and Sam Go Out
Kate and Sam's Tea
Michael and Joanne Cole
Methuen, 1975
Kate and Sam are great at imagining all sorts of things which are going to happen – and which then do happen. Short, simple and satisfying.

Just Awful
Whitney A. Marshak
Collins Picture Lions, 1976
James cuts his finger in the playground and feels just awful; but when he goes to the nurse for treatment, it's not as awful as he'd feared.
The illustration by Lillian Hoban show the little boy's fear with a comical understanding of the way small children feel.

Goggles
Ezra Jack Keats
Picture Puffin, 1975
Peter and Archie find a pair of goggles on the rubbish dump. A gang of boys try to take them away. Willie the little dog helps out and they manage to outwit the gang. The illustrations are interesting; look out for picture books by Ezra Jack Keats – he makes exciting use of lines, shades and textures to create collage pictures of city life, like *The Snowy Day*, Picture Puffin, 1975, and *Peter's Chair* (HB).

Going to the doctor – and all that

Stories about these worrying events are often more effective than attempts to explain, in a rather general way, what they are like. Topsy and Tim or Thomas cover these topics. Otherwise the Dinosaur series are as good as anything.

Going to the Doctor
Althea
Dinosaur Publications, 1973
This is a very straightforward account of seeing the doctor at home, or in his surgery. It explains and illustrates black bags, stethoscopes, torches for looking down throats and ears, prescriptions and medicine. It goes to the hospital for an X-ray and to the clinic for the dreaded *injection*. The child, in the rather clumsy, diagrammatic drawing, looks resigned; he is not yelling blue murder! There's the same sort of approach in Althea's *Visiting the Dentist* – though it is a helpfully calming description of what really happens. 'He uses some silver stuff which squeaks when he pats it down.' More of the same helpful details are in *Going into Hospital*. A five-year-old who was waiting to have his tonsils out found this a book to hang on to. In much the same way, *Starting School* is a sensible and reassuring book to buy for any four-year-old.

Sex

At pre-school stage, parents are the best source of information on this subject. Books with two dimensional illustrations which are rather funny or indistinct are confusing. If you have one small girl or boy, then *Thomas is Different* is a good little explanatory book.

Thomas is Different
Gunilla Wolde
Hodder and Stoughton, 1975 (HB)
Thomas and Sarah *look* identical. It's hot, so they take off their shirts; they are still the same – two nipples and a tummy button! It gets hotter; they take off their shorts. 'But look, they do not look so much alike now. Where Thomas has a penis Sarah has a little slit' – and there is a delightful picture of them both peeing on the grass.
If you are going to have another baby and feel you need a helpful book then turn to Dinosaurs again.

A Baby in the Family
Althea
Dinosaur Publications, 1975
This is a serious, straightforward account, very simply illustrated. It explains making love, conception and birth. It's a book you need to read with a small child, as some of the pictures are difficult to understand.

The fantastic and the familiar

Fantasy and reality mix freely in books for the very young. In the list are a number of books where fantastic events are firmly anchored in familiar settings.

Bread and Jam for Frances
Russell Hoban
Picture Puffin, 1977

Bedtime for Frances (Faber 1969) – is an understanding story dealing with children's resistance to going to bed.

A Baby Sister for Frances (Faber 1969) – is exceptionally sensitive about the problems of jealousy. The illustrations by Lillian Hoban are a delight.

Chapter 3
Work and Play

Chapter 3

Work and play

Family work is essential to support the life of a family. Food has to be bought, meals have to be prepared, clothes have to be washed. Children learn that certain jobs are vital and when they are allowed to help they feel they are a valued member of the family.

Family work

Work and play

You may feel that for pre-school children there's not much difference between work and play and that, as long as a child is enjoying himself, it's all play. But is this the case? Are there differences between what a child learns when 'playing' and what he learns when 'working'?

Let's look at some activities and see whether it's possible to classify them into work and play. Listed below are a number of activities. Tick the 'play' column if you think the activity is mainly concerned with play or tick the 'work' column if you think it is mainly concerned with work.

	Play	Work
building with toy bricks	☐	☐
making a sandwich	☐	☐
laying the table	☐	☐
dressing dolls	☐	☐
shaping dough	☐	☐
playing mothers and fathers	☐	☐
taking messages	☐	☐
making cakes	☐	☐
writing greetings cards	☐	☐
drawing	☐	☐
hammering nails into wood	☐	☐
tidying the bedroom	☐	☐
arranging animals in a toy farm	☐	☐
pretending to make dinner	☐	☐
pouring water down a tube	☐	☐
dressing up	☐	☐
putting the shopping away	☐	☐
sorting clothes for washing	☐	☐
cleaning teeth	☐	☐
vacuum cleaning	☐	☐
making a plastic animal	☐	☐
washing up	☐	☐
washing the car	☐	☐

● In general, what is it about the activities you called 'play' that makes them different from those you called 'work'?

● What is it about the ones you called 'work' that makes them different from 'play'?

● Do these differences mean that your child is learning something different with play activities and work activities?

The following questions help sort out these differences in important ways.

● Take three of the activities you have called play and three you have called work.

● Write them in the table.

● Put a √ for yes and a X for no.

● Add up the number of ticks for each activity.

	Play			Work		
1 Does the activity lead to something that is useful to other people?	☐	☐	☐	☐	☐	☐
2 Does the activity involve real household materials or equipment?	☐	☐	☐	☐	☐	☐
3 Does it matter if the child does something wrong in carrying out the the activity?	☐	☐	☐	☐	☐	☐
4 Does the quality of the end product of the activity matter?	☐	☐	☐	☐	☐	☐
5 Is it an activity that adults do?	☐	☐	☐	☐	☐	☐
6 Is the activity supervised by an adult?	☐	☐	☐	☐	☐	☐
Total ticks						

When this exercise was carried out it was found that all those activities called 'play' had three or less ticks while all the 'work' activities had four or more ticks.

For example, building with toy bricks got no ticks and six crosses. Even though this activity is useful in other ways, it is not useful to other people – except that it keeps a child busy and allows Mum to get on with something else. Also it does not involve real household materials, it doesn't matter if a child does something wrong, or how good the play is; and it doesn't require supervision. It is not an activity adults do – except when they are playing with a child.

Putting shopping away, on the other hand gets six ticks because it is useful to other people – it is one less job for Mum to do; it involves real household materials; if the child does something wrong or does the job badly it may make it difficult for people to find food, and it is a job adults do.

Hammering nails into wood is borderline because hammering is an important work-activity but it is not being used in this example to make something useful.

Work

Work activities often lead to something useful and, because they are activities adults do, a child can learn about adult work and the business of living. He can learn to handle real equipment safely and will be able to see the results of what he does. He will gradually learn that the care he takes affects the quality of the end product. Work usually involves adult supervision because of the danger from equipment like sharp knives, or because the tasks are difficult enough for mistakes to spoil them, like putting the wrong ingredients in a cake. This supervision means that an adult and a child will work together, helping the child to feel he is a member of a team sharing an important job.

Shared or solo work

Some parents feel that a pre-schooler's life should consist entirely of play and that it is unreasonable, or that it takes too much time, to involve them in family work. Others find that their children want to be involved and that it is easier to give them tasks to do than to tell them to go away and play.

As we have seen, there are important reasons why children should be involved in family work. But there are tasks, where it is sensible to encourage them to play by themselves while you get on with your work.

Listed opposite are some tasks.

● Which ones could your child be involved in and which ones are best carried out by you alone with him playing on his own?

● For the shared tasks note down what your child could be doing to help.

You may find that there are ways to involve your child that you hadn't thought of. But your child might not be able to share some of them because he hasn't learnt enough to be helpful. Putting shopping away, for example, will only be helpful if he knows where at least some of the items go. Some tasks are too dangerous for your child to share, for example window cleaning.

Play

Play provides *different* opportunities, often important ones. Play is open-ended and directed by the child. Play materials can be interesting in themselves and provide props for a child's imagination. Because they are safe children can usually play on their own without constant supervision. It doesn't matter if they make a mistake. The fact that adults don't play may be an advantage – children need some things that belong to their own world, a world where they have control over what they do. Play provides opportunities for learning and practising skills rather than simply applying them. Furthermore it usually involves activities that are artistic, imaginative and exploratory.

Work and play everyday

There seem to be real differences between work and play. Both provide important opportunities for acquiring and applying skills. In the topics in Chapters 3 and 4 you will have a chance to look at some play and family work activities more closely.

In *Routines of the day and week* in Chapter 1 you looked at your child's activities. Go back to this and look at your results. How do the family work and play activities work out when you ask the six questions on page 67?

When you reach the end of Chapter 4 you might carry out another survey. Concentrate on family work and play. See if the ideas you get from Chapters 3 and 4 change the pattern of your child's day.

Task	Shared	Solo	Child-sized task
Making cakes			Mix ingredients, put cake mix into baking tray.
Using the sewing machine			
Tidying the bedroom			
Sorting clothes for washing			
Cleaning the cooker			
Making jam			
Cleaning windows			
Washing up			
Laying the table			
Painting the house			
Putting the shopping away			
Making a sandwich			
Wall-papering			
Repairing the TV			
Writing greetings cards			
Ironing			
Servicing the car			
Vacuum cleaning			

Shared work

1 Linda is glad to get home. The shopping bag is heavy and Ken is tired. They all need their tea. The baby is asleep in the pram. With Ken's help Linda can get the clothes in and the shopping put away before the baby wakes up. Then they can all relax together for a little time after tea.

2 For two years Ken has been learning what goes in the low cupboards and he sets about his work confidently. He is just finishing as his mother comes in with the clothes basket. 'Great! Now, can you lay the table while I heat the beans and make the toast?'

3 By suggesting another child-sized job for Ken as he was finishing the first, Linda had been able to hold his interest in working with her. He knows how to lay the table, unwrap the swiss roll, and put it on a plate, pour a bottle of milk into a jug, and collect the tea things and put them out.

What makes a good child-sized job?

● It must be something you really want doing – if you pretend, your child will find out eventually.

● He must be able to see how his task fits into the job you are doing.

● He must know enough and be skilled enough to carry out parts of the job on his own – if necessary with help from you occasionally.

● It must be accepted with thanks immediately he has finished.

● Even if the quality of his work is less than you would expect yourself, you must accept whatever he has been able to manage gracefully. If it is essential to put finishing touches to it, wait until he has gone before you improve on what he has done.

● It must not require too much strength or persistence.

● It must not be too dangerous – you will not be able to remove all the danger as real tasks often involve some risk. However, you should be sure that you can prevent serious accidents.

Solo work

1 Cleaning windows is a job Linda prefers to do alone. Hearing that Ken is busy with his cars, she collects a model village and a bag of farm animals. With these, she might be able to keep him playing on his own until she has finished the windows.

2 Linda had just finished the first window when Ken comes to look for something different to do. He could make a world for his cars to drive round with the model and as Linda works she can talk to him. Ken arranges the houses in a street and a square but after a while begins to lose interest.

3 By leaving the animals nearby, but hidden in their bag, Linda is able to suggest a way to extend the interest of this game. She has to do more talking now, asking questions, making suggestions to hold his interest until she has finished. She puts away her tools and then helps Ken to clear up his toys.

Playing while you work

What helps to make playing-while-you-work a success?

● Planning play activities before you start work.

● Encouraging play that your child has enjoyed on his own before.

● Showing an interest in the play. Watch and listen and make occasional comments.

● Leading his play on to different stages by introducing new ideas. Often the chaos-making-stage comes when his interest wanes. If you can tell when this is approaching, a suitable suggestion may direct him on to something else that is interesting.

● Older children usually play for longer on their own. You cannot expect a two-year-old to keep busy for long just playing on his own.

● When his interest wanes deal with it as quickly as possible so that you will have more time to finish what you are doing.

Home making

There is no need to involve your child in all family work because some of it will be unsuitable.

Your child will appreciate being involved in the more essential jobs and in those essential tasks that are central to family life. He will be valued for his contribution and value himself as well. He will learn that housework is not a chore but the essence of home making.

All in a day's work

How can parents help their children carry out household tasks and learn from them? What about possible dangers? This topic introduces these questions.

Making cakes

A first step to helping children help you is to break the job down into small, 'child-sized' parts. Making chocolate fairy cakes involves the following steps:

- Get out the ingredients and utensils
- Open cake mix
- Tip mix into bowl
- Add 5 tablespoonfuls of sugar
- Mix
- Add 3 tablespoonfuls of milk
- Break egg into cup
- Add drop of milk to egg
- Pour into mix
- Put mix into paper cartons
- Put tray into oven

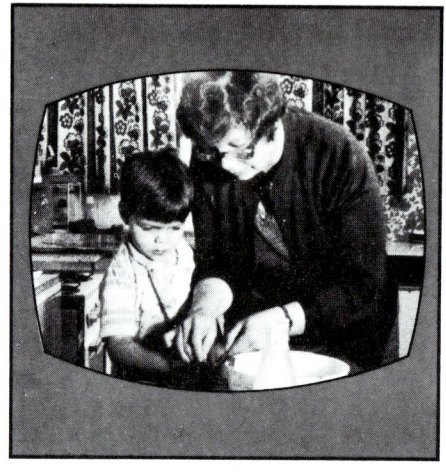

Robert makes fairy cakes, while Tracey tackles a sandwich

In this chapter and the next we look at washing, sewing, cooking, woodwork and tidying up in some detail. These are all jobs children can do and enjoy doing them with you. They learn about grouping and sorting, about weight and length and order, about how a series of small sizes builds up into a task well done.

On the opposite page we look at the two main ways in which you can help – with words and with actions. It's important to be sure a child understands the instructions. And it's important to remember that small children aren't very skilled with their hands. But they do learn with practice.

All work and no play would make Jack a dull boy indeed. So in this chapter and the next there are also play ideas for when you want to get on on your own. Or you can take time off together – see below.

Dismantle a mincer... and put it together again!

EXPLORING ANI

Ordinary kitchen objects can be objects of delight. Take time off from the chores to explore them with your child.

How to help

There are two main ways you can help:

1 Verbally
● by asking questions, *for example, what do we do next, how many?*
● by giving instructions, *for example, mix it up, prise it apart with your thumb*
● by giving encouragement, *for example, that's it, good boy!*

2 Physically
● by doing it for him, *for example, get out utensils and ingredients*
● by guiding his hands, *for example, helping him stir the mix, lift the baking tray*
● by helping him do it himself, *for example, pouring the milk into the spoon while he holds the spoon.*

Parents do many things to help, sometimes they give verbal help, sometimes physical help and sometimes both together. But there are occasions when one kind is more appropriate than the other. For example, it may be necessary to physically prevent a child from hurting himself, while on another occasion the child may be quite capable of doing the right thing if you tell him what it is. Younger children whose ability to understand instructions and whose physical skills are not so well developed will require more physical help than older children who can be helped verbally. (See *Instructions and explanations* in Chapter 4.)

The nature of the task

The nature of the task affects the kind of help required. Obviously more difficult tasks require more help. Tasks involving physical skill will require more physical help than tasks requiring conceptual skills such as sorting or matching, which require more verbal help. For example, there are a lot of physical actions involved in making cakes or a cheese-and-tomato sandwich. There are therefore, more likely to be times when physical help is offered. Whereas sorting out clothes before or after washing (see *Launder and learn* in this chapter) does not require very complicated physical actions, merely picking out and putting clothes in different places. It does require ideas of matching, like sizes and like colours together; and sorting 'whites' from 'non-whites' and each person's clothes in a separate pile. Verbal help such as 'Find me another red sock like this one', 'Whose vest is this?' breaks down the task into child-sized jobs and helps children apply the 'relevant' concepts.

Risk of danger

The difficulty arises when it is a task that has a risk of danger, for example using a sharp knife. In order to become skilled in using a knife children must have opportunities to learn. This must be done under adult supervision. So, with a three-year-old, a knife and something to cut, what do you do? Children of this age have had some practice and have seen people using knives and they usually have an idea of what to do. In the section above various kinds of help were suggested. Let's start with an instruction – 'Cut up the cheese'. Other instructions or questions may be necessary – 'Hold the handle of the knife', 'Which way up is the sharp side?' If the cheese moves you can give physical help and hold the cheese. You may need to give verbal warnings 'Mind your fingers', or physically intervene to move the child's fingers out of the way. You could help the child more directly by holding the hand that holds the knife and guiding him. As a last resort you could do the task for him.

When to give help

The difficulty for parents is knowing when to give help. One question is – do you tell a child what to do before he starts or after he has started and seems to be in difficulty? The answer to this depends on the points made above about the child's skill and knowledge, the nature of the task – whether physical or conceptual – and the risk of danger. It also depends on what kind of help we are talking about – physical or verbal.

Obviously if the child has the skill and knowledge to carry out a task on his own the question doesn't arise. If the child is physically capable but simply needs verbal help you can either give an overview at the beginning of the whole task or step-by-step help as difficulties arise – perhaps in the form of a question such as 'What do you do next?' In this way parents avoid telling the child what to do when he already knows. Children are usually very sensible in knowing what their limits are and will ask if they want help.

'When to help' is of course a matter of judgement. On the one hand you do not want to impose help on a child that does not need it, and on the other you do not want *not* to give help when a child needs this – especially if there is a real danger. You can do everything to keep the danger to a minimum and when you are present a serious accident is extremely unlikely. Even if the child is likely to cut himself, this will not be serious as you will be able to physically intervene in time. Therefore you will be using your judgement and detecting the appropriate moments to give verbal or physical help – if you are in doubt whether this is needed you can ask the child. If the child seems to be getting into difficulties you will offer verbal help and have physical help at the ready. By warning a child of danger you can teach him to anticipate what might happen so that he can take the right action himself.

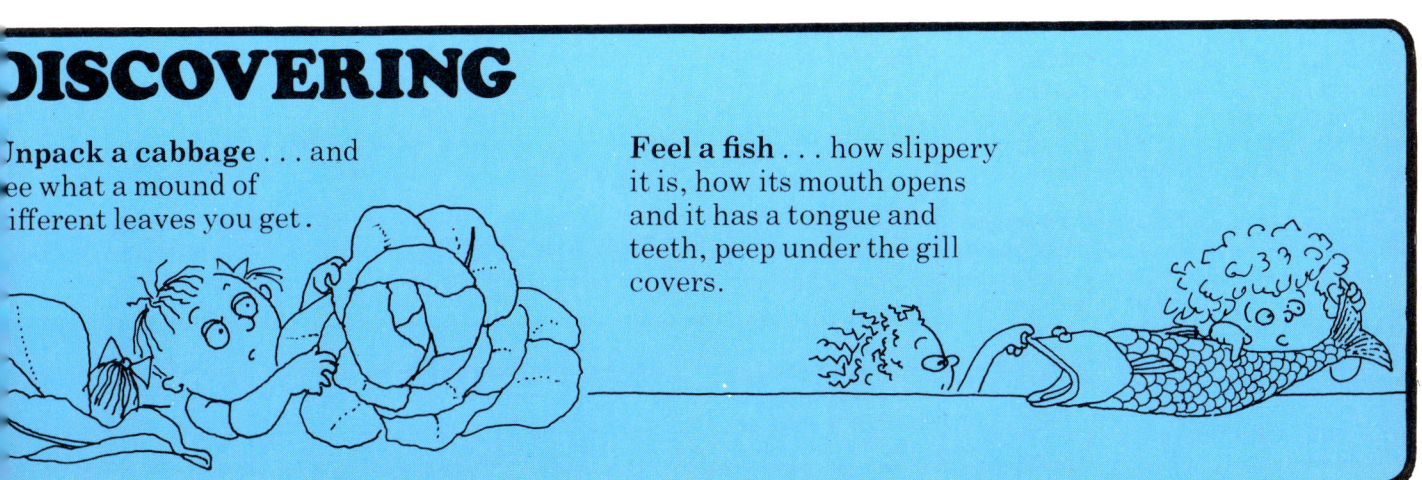

DISCOVERING

Unpack a cabbage . . . and see what a mound of different leaves you get.

Feel a fish . . . how slippery it is, how its mouth opens and it has a tongue and teeth, peep under the gill covers.

Launder and learn

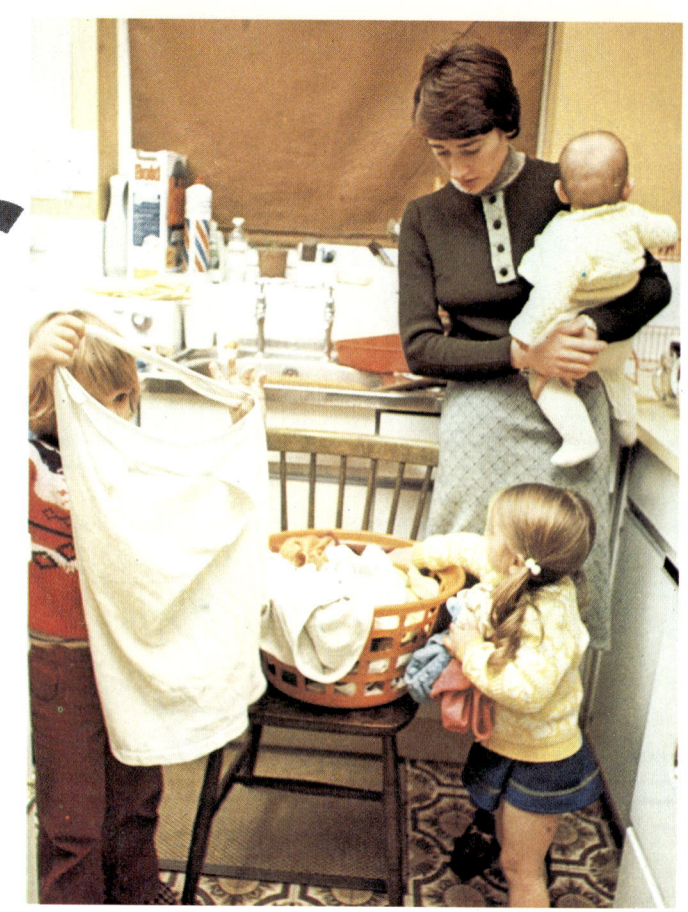

Remember sitting at a desk in your primary school 'doing' sums and tables? In the pre-school years particularly, it's lots of practical 'doing' that counts – making, moving and handling things. Forget sums and take a look at washday instead.

What's this, Mummy?

Your three-year-old may be driving you up the wall with this cry. Sometimes it's just to get your attention. More often it's because he really wants to know, or check he's got it right. As well as learning the names of things, your child is trying to work out what things 'go together'.

Every day we group people and things into many sorts of 'sets' according to what they have in common, or what makes them different. Nice/nasty; mine/yours; big/small; red/blue and so on. ('Big-and-red' is hard for young children because *two* similarities are involved.)

Sorting is a part of life, and it begins early on. The baby sorts out mum from strangers and the toddler will sort out 'toys-I-want-to-play-with'. But to begin with children are very self-centred, so you may find your make-up or your spanners get classed as a set of toys!

Sorting and grouping into sets is an essential part of the maths your child will do at school. The idea of numbers grows out of many practical experi-ences of seeing, handling and playing with sets of the same number of objects (see *Mealtimes* in Chapter 1). Similarly, the ways children will eventually 'handle' numbers – adding, taking away, multiplying and dividing – grow out of practical experiences of putting together and splitting up sets of objects. The mathematical names and signs (add; +, etc.) mean nothing to the very young child and shouldn't be pushed on him. But what you do with your washload *will* make sense. See the examples in the chart.

Learning in the kitchen

- *Mealtimes* in Chapter 1
- *Talking while you work* } in this
- *Family work* } chapter
- *All I get is questions* }
- *Cooking* } in Chapter 4
- *Tidying up* }

Add – putting two separate sets together	T shirts and towels together make	One washload (T shirts and towels)
Take away – what's left is the important thing	8 sheets take away 2 sheets for another load to leave	One maximum washload (6 sheets)
Multiply – really just repeated adding	1 wash load and 1 wash load and 1 wash load together make up (or × 3)	Total of 3 washloads for the day
Divide – splitting one set into groups each with an equal number of things	14 socks sort into pairs to make	7 pairs

Sorting into sets

As the chart opposite shows, washday involves putting sets together, and breaking them up. Your child can help with these operations – and you can help by simply talking through with him what you're doing, why, and maybe counting as you go.

● *Dirty clothes* are sorted into sets by colour, and the type of wash they need. To make sets you need to know in what important way things are alike and how they differ. You can help your child to recognise washing sets by getting him to hand you all the whites, or all the shirts, or whatever. With practice he may even be able to make the separate sets (piles) of clothes himself.

● *Washed clothes* are sorted into sets for ironing or just drying and then sorted again according to who they belong to, or where you keep them. Again your child can help to make the piles. Socks go in sets of two – can he make them into pairs? (Sometimes there'll be the odd sock left over.)

Ordering

The order of washday goes something like this. Five things need to be done, in their right order – can you find something for your child to do at each stage? Can he tell what's got to happen next?

1 *Find the clothes* – can he find the things you ask for?

2 *Sort them for washing* – can he help, or do it?

3 *Wash them* – can he help fill the measuring cup with powder, put it in the machine (or the sink) and – if you want him to learn – push the buttons or turn the dials?

4 *Sort for drying and ironing* – can he help? Can he iron tea-towels standing safely on a chair? (Practise with a cold or low iron first.)

5 *Put away the clean clothes* – can he sort out all his own clothes, or what goes in the airing cupboard? Can he help fold easy things like underwear and towels, and put away things that go on low shelves?

Talking

You don't need to give a Grand-National-type running commentary – children learn best by *doing*, not listening. Use words to interest and help your child in the 'doing'. Younger children enjoy learning to put names to things and actions, and being able to carry out simple instructions. Try to explain simply *why* you're doing things – why so much soap, why you don't mix some sets, such as jerseys and sheets. There'll always be questions! Older children will like some puzzle questions – 'What would happen if we forgot the soap?', 'What shall we do if it rains?' – that makes them work out what needs to be done, when and why.

Washday blues

Very few children are totally colour-blind. But you may begin to wonder when your child holds out a yellow building block and proudly says 'red'!

The trouble with colours is that often they're not really necessary. Take the difference between a black-and-white and a colour television. Colour may look nicer, but we don't need it to know what we're looking at on the screen. We identify things mainly by their shape and size, by their particular features and what they are used for. Another problem with colours is that they shade into each other, and there's no real reason for the names we give them. It's just tradition that we call red red, and at a certain point stop calling it red and start saying it's orange, or purple.

Colours can be quite a puzzle for young children. They can see colour differences, and quickly learn to rattle off colour names, but getting the two together takes time. It's a bit like numbers. You cannot touch or hold a 'five' or a 'red' – the idea of 'five' or 'red' has to grow out of practical experience.

Next washday, take a few minutes off to find out what stage your child has reached with colours:

1 Choose some items in your wash pile that you are sure your child can name, like panties. Now write down in the table examples of these items in several plain colours.

2 Ask your child to pick them out in turn – 'Please find me a red sock', 'Can you pass me the white jersey' – and so on. (Make sure there's more than one jersey or whatever, otherwise he doesn't have to make a colour choice.)

3 Put a tick or cross by each article in the 'Picking out' column of the table, according to whether your child chooses right or wrong on the first attempt – don't give hints! If he gets some wrong, he may be guessing, so try this simpler task:

4 Hold out an article of which there's another in the pile (underwear or linen are most likely) and ask your child to – 'Find me one that's the same colour, like this.' You're making it easier by giving him a colour to match. Put a tick or cross in the 'Matching' column.

Article and colour	Picking out	Matching
1		
2		
3		
4		
5		
6		

The tables of two neighbours who did the activity together looked like this. You can see how Sarah (nearly 4) has a firmer grasp of colours than John (just 2). John's still having problems even with matching colours.

You can give your child practical help in recognising and naming colours whether for clothes or for building bricks: 'A brown one like this . . . No, that's a yellow one . . . *Brown* like this one . . . That's right, well done'.

Sarah

Article and colour	Picking out	Matching
1 Brown sock	✗	✓
2 Grey sock	✓	✓
3 White panties	✓	✓
4 Red panties	✓	✓
5 Yellow jersey	✓	✓
6 Pale blue jersey	✗	✓

John

Article and colour	Picking out	Matching
1 Brown sock	✗	✓
2 Grey sock	✗	✗
3 White panties	✗	✓
4 Red panties	✗	✓
5 Yellow jersey	✗	✓
6 Pale blue jersey	✗	✗

Water in the sink

Water fascinates young children. Because it can be so messy, it's wise to plan ahead so that your children can enjoy playing with water at home without you always saying – 'No'.

What is water?

Adults take water for granted. But children think water is marvellous – it is something that delights and surprises them. Water is so varied in what it looks like and feels like and in what it can do.

The wetness of water: wet sleeves, or socks or pants can chafe and be uncomfortable – but a wet swimsuit in the sea has no feel of wetness at all.

The temperature of water: a warm bath is lovely – but if it's too hot or too cold the sensation on the skin changes completely. When the air is cold the water feels hotter than it does on a warm day.

The colour of water: we call the sea blue, but it can look green or grey; and a bucketful poured out has no colour at all. Puddles can be clear, or brown, or blue from the sky, or rainbow-like from oil.

The shape of water: water has no shape – but it takes the shape of what contains it, or what it runs out of. Compare water poured from a jug with water draining through a colander. The same amount also *looks* different, depending on the shape of the container it's in.

Magic water

It's only through experience that children learn about the many ways other things affect what water is. Water loses some of its early 'magic' as children come to understand, for example, that it is a drop in temperature which causes puddles to freeze. But even adults remember some of that early magic, for example, when

a sudden snowfall brings a smile of wonder and pleasure, even though it may also mean the buses will be late.

What water does

Water can affect the way other things (and people!) behave. For example:

Water gets absorbed by some things, and changes their nature – a wet jumper becomes heavy, wet fur loses its fluffiness, wet window leathers feel slimy. Water absorbed by flour makes something new – dough – that can't be turned back into water and flour.

Water marks and cleanses Water splashed on wallpaper makes dark marks. Yet water on dirty hands lightens most dirt marks or removes them altogether. Water on a painting makes the colours run and change, but they never disappear.

Water can make adults cross Everybody is inconsistent in their attitudes sometimes, but from a child's point of view it can be bewildering. We buy gumboots and then say – 'Come out of that puddle!' We're pleased with ourselves when we wash the floors, but if *he* spills water we rush to mop it up in the same way – only he's naughty.

Finding out about water

You can help your child find out about water in two ways. You can give her opportunities simply to explore the nature of water or you can let your child help with jobs around the house

which use water. She won't think one is play and the other is work, even if you do! The basic rules are the same for both:

1 *Set your child up so that you won't be forever having to nag about mess – and be clear in your own mind where you'll draw the line over spilt water.*

● Explain what you're doing, and let her help:
'If there's water in the sink *then* you may get wet, *so* let's roll your sleeves up, and you must have an apron on.'

She'll sense that you're very happy for her to play with water *as long as* the floor and her clothes stay dry. You're implying 'be careful' without nagging.

● Be prepared for accidental spills – but don't invite trouble by giving large saucepans that are too heavy to control when filled, or fill the bowl too full.

2 *As far as possible let your child get on with the task in hand by herself.*

● If you think she's not doing a good enough job rinsing plates, you must decide whether you can tactfully point out the bits she's missing, or whether to do it again later. Nagging from you is unlikely to encourage her to continue being happy to wash up.

● If she's absorbed in water play on her own don't break in on her concentration. She will tell you by 'bored' signs, or asking you questions when she wants you to share the experience with her.

Watching water play

You need:

- A bowl or sink about half full of water.
- *At first:* just one or two objects – say a yoghurt pot and a plastic cup
- *Later:* other things from around the house which differ in the way they pour, or float and sink, or absorb water. Add these slowly – too many things at once and your child won't know where to start.

1 **Watch** as she plays – out of the corner of your eye if you can – for:

- the expression on your child's face which indicates what she's feeling
- which actions your child repeats many times.
- Signs of boredom when she turns away and loses that 'concentrating' look or when her hands stop being purposeful and make random movements.

2 **Fill in** the chart to keep a record of what you've provided and your child's reactions. Try each of the four groups of objects on a different day (Spaces are left for you to add your own ideas, for example, another variation is to change the water itself – make it soapy for bubble play with pipes sometimes). By the side of each object you provide, enter how long your child spent playing with it. Length of time is a measure of interest – you may find a 'league table' of favourite objects.

Make notes on what she does, for example fills and empties, or pours from one container to another. Face and questions indicate interest too – make notes on these as well.

Watching quietly, you will notice clues as to when it's time to produce something new, to talk – or to simply call it a day. As your child repeats something many times, she becomes ready to put her discovery into words:

3 **Talk** There are different groups of questions that can help your child think things out for herself.
'Could you . . . ?' questions – for example, . . . fill the mug with a teaspoon.
'What would happen if . . . ?' questions – for example, . . . you put the cork in the cup before you filled it up with water from the teapot. (If this sort of question leads to new discoveries, fade into the background again.)
'I wonder why . . . ?' questions – for example, . . . the cork floats. (If you get an answer "Cos it's brown" – try suggesting she finds out whether other brown things float too. Some will, some won't, which may lead her to look for another reason.)
Quantity questions – for example, how many jugs of water does it take to fill your teapot? (Even if the answer is 'Two!', don't assume your child automatically knows the reverse – that the pot will pour two mugs of tea.)
'Is it the same as you had before?' – does your child know that the water she's pouring back and forth between different shaped containers is the same, even though it looks different.

Water work

1 **First plan your child-sized jobs**
Tick the following objects as appropriate:

Which of these would you let your child wash up?

plastic plates	☐
china plates	☐
glasses	☐
spoons	☐
knives	☐
saucepans	☐

Which of these could your child get clean enough for your standards?

socks	☐
panties	☐
jerseys	☐
face-flannels	☐
floors	☐
table-tops	☐

If you haven't ticked anything at all – look again. A lot does depend on the age of your child and her skill with her hands. But some things are safer and easier to clean than others, and some can have another wash soon if they're not perfectly clean.

Objects	Time spent	Notes
1 Pourers Beaker Jug Funnel or tube		
2 Tricklers Tea-strainer Squeezy bottle with holes in the side		
3 Floaters and sinkers Cork Pingpong ball Nailbrush		
4 Absorbers Felt Plastic Cotton		

Your child needs to start somewhere. It means nothing to warn a child – 'Be careful, that will stain' – if she's never tried to remove a biro stain. She needs to try, and fail, to understand what 'stain' means. On the other hand, 'dirty' is less threatening if she knows 'dirt' comes off most things – especially herself – quite easily.

2 **Choose your time** The next time the cry comes – 'Let me do it, let me help' – is the best time to choose. You'll be prepared with positive ideas about what you're happy for your child to do. If you're in a rush, it may be better to suggest another day, explaining why – and meaning it – rather than hurry your child through.

3 **Keep a check** Note what jobs your child enjoys playing with, whether it's washing up, washing the car – and let her do them again. With praise her confidence will grow and as her skills increase so will her standards of cleanliness. She's learning that water jobs have to be done – but that they can be pleasurable too.

Sewing

Knowing about fabrics, how to cut them out and stitch them, are the skills involved in sewing. Even dressmakers have 'disasters' – the frayed seam, the two right sleeves, the drooping hemline.

Understanding the nature of the materials we use is important. Thin, thick, soft, hard, stretchy – your child needs to experience the feel of things. At first he'll need help, with cutting and stitching. He needs plenty of time, too, to find out what he can do with fabrics and the sewing kit before you advance to practical projects like making trousers for teddy.

Fabric games

Give a child a rag bag and what does he do with it? He will triumphantly pull out bits of material that are soft, rough, smooth, stiff, brightly coloured, patterned or plain. He feels, looks at, smells and pulls the material and rubs it against his skin.

Just feeling and looking at fabrics is the first step. When your child wants something more, try these fabric games. They'll help him use his hands and eyes to tell the difference between materials, and put like ones together. While you're playing, *talk* about the different feels and colours, to help him keep the experience in his mind.

Dominos – take six different remnants and cut them into squares to make a set of dominos. (Stick them on card for a longer life.) Instead of matching dots, you take turns to match the fabrics by colour and texture. You don't have to play to win or lose – instead see how long you can make the line between you.

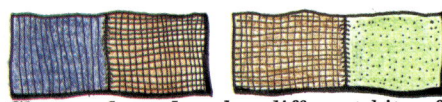

Chequerboard – glue different bits of fabric onto small squares of card. Make a large square of card with fabric squares glued on to match the individual squares. Let your child match the pairs. (This can be played blindfold for extra fun.)

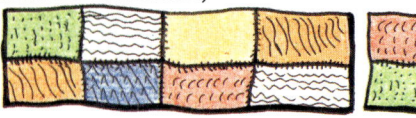

Snap – when you're both bored with dominos or chequerboard, cut them up into individual squares to make cards for fabric snap. Turn up cards in turn, and when there's a matching pair, the first person to call snap collects all the cards on the table.

Feely games

Don't get stuck on fabric. Other things have feels, too!

A feely box

Cut hand-sized holes in the side of an old card-board box. Put a selection of toys and everyday objects inside and close the lid. (Or use a draw-string bag.) Can your child tell what's in there just by putting his hands in and touching?

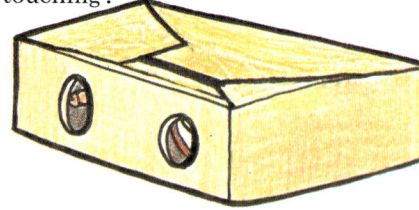

Wax rubbings

Cover anything that has a partly-raised surface, such as wood-chip wallpaper, (or even the manhole-cover on the pavement outside) with thin kitchen paper, and rub with the side of a wax crayon. Watch your child's face as the pattern come through.

Collage

Provide a large sheet of card, glue, and a boxful of bits and pieces (for example, eggshell, rubber, wire, straw, tea-leaves, as well as fabric) for your child to stick on as he likes.

A fur hunt

Talk is important in finding out about materials. If your child asks 'Is this fur?', and you just say 'Yes', what has he gained? Not much. But if you say – 'Yes, it's white nylon fur. Can you think of any other fur in the house?' – then you're off on a fur hunt.

As you find the cat's fur, Gran's fur coat, the rabbit fur lining of his gloves, you're enlarging his knowledge of fur. Talking about fur helps your child to think about fur, to remember other

Discovery time

Just watching is a good way of finding out what your child can do. Simply give him some scraps of cloth, a large bluntish needle and stiffish thread, and sit back to see. (Don't stare! Watch out of the corner of your eye as you read, or sew.)

● How does he handle the cloth?

● Which material does he choose?

● What does he do with the needle?

● Does he attempt to thread it?

● How many stitches can he make, how well?

● How long did he play for?

If your child can't cope with the needle, go back to simpler threading and fabric games. If he's just about stitching, let him experiment further first with one bit of cloth, then two to join together. Sewing on buttons can be fun too.

You might like to compare 'free' sewing with sewing cards which you can make or buy. Jot down how your child handles them:

● Can he follow the outline?

● Does he (or do you) feel he should follow it?

● How long did he do it for?

● Did he give up before completing the picture?

Sewing cards offer less scope for imagination than 'free' sewing. But the 'doing' can give great pleasure, particularly if the card can be finished before the child gets bored or frustrated by the quite high level of skill it requires.

furs, and make the link between animals and the fur we use. When he comes to read about fur, he will link it with these early experiences.

Developing skill

To sew, the fingers make small, controlled movements and work closely with the eyes. As we saw with eating and dressing, young children need time to get this control. Don't expect too much too soon of your child.

By the age of two your child should be able to use his fingers to *pick up* small objects such as a needle and thread. But he'll need more practice at *handling* small objects – doing up buttons, threading beads, putting pegs in holes – before he can thread a needle or control scissors. At $3\frac{1}{2}$, if he's interested, he can probably make a successful attempt at cutting.

Cutting and threading

Success is the key to further effort. Make cutting and threading practice fun – but as he plays, watch out for your child's difficulties. Help if you can, and try something simpler if he gets frustrated.

Scissor practice Use small, round-ended scissors that cut well, not blunt or plastic scissors. Thin card is easier to cut than paper or fabric, so start by chopping this up. You can help by sitting in front of the child and holding the card or fabric tight across the cutting edge of the scissors.

Threading Practice at threading helps your child when he comes to the more difficult task of actually using a needle. Try:

● threading big beads on to shoe-laces (or string, with the end stiffened with Sellotape),

● threading laces through collander holes, or small pieces of pegboard,

● making a mobile for a baby with milk bottle tops threaded on to string – it makes a lovely noise in a breeze and the tops catch the sunlight,

● feeding the birds with peanuts in shells, squares of toast and bacon-rind strung on to nylon thread,

● making necklaces or bracelets from pieces of coloured plastic straws threaded on to wool.

Needles

At first your child will simply be interested in getting the thread through the hole. Start him off with a large, fairly blunt needle (like a bodkin), and thick thread. Sewing will be easier if you double the thread and show him how to knot the ends together. This will avoid the frustration of the needle coming unthreaded in the middle of sewing.

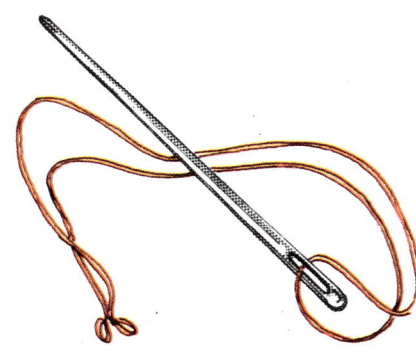

Trousers for Teddy

Is this scene familiar to you? Mum is trying to sew. Mark, aged four, wants to sew too. His Mum suggests he makes trousers for Teddy. She tells him:
'First sew these two edges together'. Mark finds that the material slips and slides, the stitches wander and the cotton tangles.
'You've sewn it all together', says Mum. 'How will Teddy fit in there?'
'Come on, let me do it.'

Young children need time to get to grips with the skills involved in sewing before they're able, or want, to make something useful. It's the same as with drawing, or playing with bricks or sand. As a general rule, the first interest is in the 'doing'. Making things, particularly lasting, useful things, comes after the child's had time to explore the materials in the world around him, and to practise his skills in handling them.

Read more about it

In Chapter 4 we'll be looking in some detail at how your child becomes more skilled with his hands, and how his ideas develop from looking and touching things, and talking about them. Look out for:

● getting the feel of things in *A dollop of dough*

● using his hands – and his head in *Cooking* and *Woodwork*

● the talking that goes on in *All I get is questions* and *Instructions and explanations*

● how to use those bits and pieces in *Making things*

● your expectations and his abilities in *I can do it* and *Styles of learning*.

Safety in the home

Safety in the home is guaranteed to bore most of us who expect to be told a string of rules that we ought to follow, but know we won't. These rules, though based on sensible ideas, often don't work in preventing accidents because people haven't thought about the ideas behind them. Rules don't work for children if they do not understand them.

Safety checklist

The questionnaire below is about safety in your home. The questions are based on safety rules. Rules only take us so far; however, they should help you identify some areas where further consideration might be required. (Indicate these by ticking the box in the ? column.)

The questions concern you, your child and other children. This is because you will probably have other children in your home to play. But remember there may be other areas in your home that are not covered by the questions so make a note of any that occur to you.

                                    YES NO ?

1 Do you keep poisons, cleaning fluids, disinfectants in a place where children cannot get at them?

2 Do you keep all medicines and pills in a secure place where children cannot get at them?

3 Are razor blades kept in your house in a place where children cannot get at them?

4 Do you allow children round the cooker when you are cooking?

5 Do you keep pots and pan handles from sticking out?

6 Do you allow toys in the kitchen?

7 Could children find matches around your home?

8 Are all your open fires (coal, gas and electric) guarded?

9 Are your child's nightclothes flame resistant?

10 Do you leave your child in the room you are ironing in when you go to answer the door bell?

11 If you have a car does your child wear a seat belt?

12 Do you allow your child to use a sharp knife?

13 Do you allow your child to use real tools such as a hammer, a saw or a screwdriver?

14 Does your home have safety electrical sockets which make it impossible to put hairclips etc. in the holes?

15 Do you use multi-way adaptors so you can plug in more than one appliance to a power point?

Go back over the questions and think through what lies behind the rules they are based on.

For example, question 10 is based on the rule:

Don't leave the ironing

Ironing is *dangerous:*

● It's easy to fall over the wire

● a toddler can pull the iron down on top of him. But what happens when the door bell rings or the baby cries? You can't put the iron away because it's hot, besides you will return in a minute or two to carry on ironing. Removing your toddler is an easy precaution.

Question 12 is based on:

Don't let the children play with knives

Everyone agrees that knives are dangerous and that children should not play with them. But this does not mean that they should not touch a knife at all. If it did, how would children ever learn how to handle a knife?

Question 15 is based on:

Don't use multi-way adapters

There are good reasons why you shouldn't use adaptors:

● there is the increased risk that the power point will be overloaded and may overheat

● there will be wires going in all directions and someone may trip over them.

But there are also good reasons for using adaptors:

● modern hi-fi equipment, for example, usually requires a number of separately powered units

● the cost of having extra power points put in is very high.

If you make sure you do not overload the power-point (this is very unlikely with hi-fi equipment) and that you tuck the wires away, then there is very little danger.

Recognising danger signs

It's all very well having rules and understanding them but if you don't recognise danger signs you cannot apply your understanding. Equally, understanding something makes it possible to recognise danger and to take steps to avoid an accident. As a simple exercise to see whether you are sensitive to danger signs look at the poster on the left produced by RoSPA. It applies to the kitchen, and concerns two children. Note down the danger signs that you can see in the picture.

The danger signs are reprinted below. You probably found many of them and perhaps you found some that are not given. But you may have overlooked a few.

1 Boy standing on biscuit tin on top of stool.

2 Broken milk bottle lying on the floor.

3 Milk bottle standing on edge of surface.

4 Opened tin on working surface.

5 Squeezy mop propped up against stool.

6 Bleach opened and standing on sink.

7 Iron left on the ironing table instead of heat resistant stand.

8 Iron flex left to trail across floor.

9 Pills on top of washing machine.

10 Pan handle protruding from the cooker.

11 Spilled liquid on floor.

12 Contents of pan spilling onto cooker.

13 Knife carelessly lying on edge of table.

14 Towel on cooker and overhanging the hotplate.

Now go into your kitchen and carry out the same exercise only this time for real. Note down the danger signs you can see.

You might not find as many danger signs as there were in the poster but it would be surprising if you did not find any, especially when a young child is around.

Children's understanding of rules

Children do not find it easy to stick to rules for keeping away from danger. Their curiosity can easily over-ride a half-remembered instruction 'not to touch'. This is why we must remove as many dangers as possible when there is a young child about. As children's curiosity grows so their understanding of danger must grow too.

The poster produced by RoSPA can serve two purposes: first it serves to make *us* aware of danger signs that could lead to accidents; second it can be used to provide talking points with children. By talking to your child it is possible to find out what he understands about safety in the home.

Talking to your child about safety

Before you talk to your child, read through the types of questions and answers below.

● Questions that direct the child's attention:
'What is this boy doing?'
'What's this over here?'

● Questions that require the child to predict or explain:
'What might happen here?'
'If he stands close to the cooker what might happen?'
'Is it a good idea to do this?'

● Questions that apply to his own life:
'Are you allowed to stand on chairs?'
'Do you go near Mummy's cooker?'
'Have you ever been burnt?'

The types of answers you are likely to hear are:
● Descriptive answers:
'He's standing on the chair.'

● Predictions and explanations:
'He will get burnt.'
'. . . because he is not allowed to . . .'
Notice that sometimes children explain why they should not do things by referring to the dangers. On other occasions they know they are not allowed to do things but they do not appear to know *why* they are not allowed to. They do know that if they do them Mummy will get cross.

● Applications:
'You don't let me go near the cooker!'

Now talk to your child about the poster

Use the types of questions above and look out for the types of answers.

How did your discussion compare with the extract below?

Here we have Sharon (S) aged 3½ and her Mother (M) talking about the poster. The questions and answers illustrate the types described above.

M Here's a nice picture of two children in their kitchen – can you see their Mummy?

S Where's the Mummy?

M Perhaps she's upstairs – what's this child doing?

S Making the cooking.

M Do you think that's a good idea?

S Yes!

M Do you? What might happen?

S He might burn himself?

M Are you allowed to use our cooker?

S No, only when you let me put my cakes in.

M What else is happening?

S One of the children is standing on the chair.

M What could happen?

S It might break.

M Then what would happen?

S You would be cross.

M Why isn't he allowed to stand on the chair?

S 'Cos, he's just not allowed to.

M I see . . . why isn't he allowed to go near the cooker?

S 'Cos he'll get burned.

A poster like this can provide an opportunity to see how much your child understands dangers but it only has a limited value in helping children to be safety conscious. Real situations are where the lessons have to be learnt – hopefully without there being an accident. You can explain to your child about why he should not do certain things. Your child will come to understand that there are real dangers and it is not just one of those rules, like saying 'thank you'.

What's naughty and why?

The things that children do, which are often disapproved of by adults, cannot always be called 'naughty' because such behaviour is often quite normal for the child's age. It may be a remnant of babyish ways which he has not yet given up or controlled, or it may be part of striving towards greater independence. What makes children behave in a certain way and why do we sometimes disapprove?

What's naughty?

The word 'naughty' isn't very useful except as a vague description of something that you disapprove of. It does not say much about the behaviour; but, worse, it suggests that all behaviour labelled 'naughty' is bad, and should be punished or scolded in some way. What lies behind a 'naughty' act is not 'badness'.

The first step in discovering what is meant by 'naughty' is to look at what motivates your child – the reasons why he behaves as he does and your reasons for disapproving of his behaviour. Your response should help him learn, encourage him to develop ways of behaving appropriate to his age and acceptable to you and others.

Reasons and examples

A number of reasons why you might stop or discourage your child's behaviour are listed. A second list contains examples of behaviour, grouped by what motivates the child. As you read each example decide whether you would try to discourage it – and if so, for which reasons.

Compare your reasons with other people's ideas if you can – your husband or wife, friends, play leader or nursery school teacher. What do they disapprove of and why?

Reasons why you may stop or discourage behaviour

You think it:

A   is dangerous

B   is unhygienic

C   causes distress, a nuisance or inconvenience

D   causes damage, expense or extra work

E   is against rules or conventions

F   is babyish

G   makes him 'too big for his boots'

H   is bad manners or impolite

I   is disobedient

J   prevents people from getting on with what they are doing

K   prevents you giving attention to others

L   is irritating or embarrassing

M   is bad tempered or emotional

N   is a lie or dishonest.

Examples of behaviour

Curiosity/imitation

1   Your child pokes a pencil in an electric socket. *A*

2   Your child washes a dolly's hair in the toilet. *B*

3   He cuts his coat with scissors after watching you dressmaking. *D*

4   He draws on the sitting room wall with a felt tip pen. *D*

5   He smacks his younger sister when she does something he was scolded for. *C*

6   He digs up a patch of ground where he 'helped' you sow some seeds. *D*

Self-centred/possessiveness

7   Your child pushes over his baby sister when he sees her sucking one of his toys. *C*

8   He will not let a friend have a turn on his tricycle. *H*

9   He eats a cake that was meant for tea. *D*

10   He will not give one of his sweets to a friend. *H*

Body functions

11   He wets the bed after being dry for six months. *F*

12   He wets himself at a pantomime. *PL*

13   He has a bowel accident just as he gets home after a day out. *L*

14   He plays with his penis.

Control over others

15   He will not hold your hand in a busy street. *A*

16   He says 'Wait a minute' when you ask him to come and eat. *IC*

17   He insists that you stop dressmaking and play with him. *J*

18   He will not help put his toys away. *ID*

19   He smacks you because you didn't get him a drink immediately. *G*

20   He smacks his sister because she won't give him a toy. *C*

Attention seeking

21   He keeps asking you to do little things while you are talking to a visitor. *K*

22   While he's playing he keeps calling 'Mummy, Mummy' even though you keep going over to him. *J*

23   He keeps on making 'rude' noises with his mouth. *HL*

24   He says 'Silly old bugger' in front of visitors. *HL*

Anger/frustration

25   He throws a toy car across the room because he can't open its boot. *AM*

26   He stamps and screams because he can't button his doll's clothes. *M*

27   He smacks his baby sister after you have scolded him. *C*

28   When you insist a visiting child has a turn on his tricycle he has a tantrum. *M H*

Anxiety/fear

29   He insists on holding your hand at the children's zoo even though it is unnecessary and inconvenient. *F*

30   He says he did not eat the cake even though he did. *N*

31   He says go away to a visiting aunt who wants to kiss him. *HL*

32   He wakes you up by screaming in the night. *C*

I throwed it away 'cos you only wanted three

Disapproval

Often we disapprove because of the effect it will have on

● *himself* – for example, hurting himself

● *you* – for example, prevent you from attending to others, or getting on with your work

● *other adults* – for example, rudeness, impoliteness

● *other children* – for example, hurting other children, smacking, being selfish.

As far as the child is concerned his immediate interests and motivations dominate and he can't see beyond them.

Let's go over some of the examples and possible reasons for disapproval.

Once or twice is OK

Many of these examples are okay at first but if they are repeated or continued they can invoke parental disapproval and annoyance. Drawing on the sitting room wall once is understandable even though you may be dismayed at the thought of repapering. But drawing on the wall twice in a week would be a bit much. Banging a spoon on a tin lid is the beginnings of music but after ten minutes (especially if you want to talk to a visitor) it can invite a sharp 'Stop that for goodness sake!' Even asking questions, which is an important way for children to learn about the world, becomes very annoying if it continues – especially as many of the questions are impossible to answer.

Children asking for something to be done when you are busy is likely to be annoying if they insist on help immediately. They often persist in doing things even when they are asked nicely to stop, and refuse to carry out reasonable and simple actions, or worse still seem not to hear any requests at all. All these undermine parents' intentions to remain calm and pleasant and their resolutions not to get angry.

Most parents reactions to behaviour, like that in the examples, is required by an immediate situation. But the kind of reaction is usually based on ideas about the future and what they hope their child will become. They take action now in order to enforce limits which will affect what sort of person their child becomes.

For comparison with your own views, here are some suggested reasons why you *might* discourage the types of behaviour listed opposite. The numbers refer to the example of behaviour, the letters to the reasons why you might want to discourage it. You will probably disagree with some of the reasons and think that there is no reason to disapprove of behaviour in some of the examples.

1 A; 2 B; 3 D; 4 D; 5 C; 6 D; 7 C,M; 8 H; 9 D; 10 H; 11 D; 12 D,L; 13 D; 14 L; 15 A,I; 16 G; 17 J; 18 D,I; 19 G; 20 C; 21 K,G; 22 J,C; 23 H,L; 24 H,L; 25 A,M; 26 M; 27 C; 28 H,M; 29 F; 30 N; 31 H,L; 32 C.

Curiosity/imitation

A child's curiosity and learning by imitation are vital but can lead to danger to himself, breakages, a mess and extra work for you. We have to compromise between the different needs of children to learn by 'doing' and our need to keep them safe and our homes in a reasonable condition. When your child cuts up his coat after watching you dress-making, he is imitating you and expressing his curiosity. Using scissors may be dangerous and cutting up his coat will involve extra work or expense for you.

Self-centred/possessiveness

Self-centred actions are often disapproved of by parents who value ideas of sharing. Rules or conventions about being unselfish and having a concern for others, are important in governing behaviour towards other people. If this is not done it is considered bad manners or impolite. Even so, a child finds it difficult to be unemotional if someone else takes his prized possession.

Body functions

Accidents with body functions are babyish but understandable at this age, none the less they involve extra work and may be embarrassing to parents. Playing with sexual parts is something that parents worry about even though it is only part of growing up.

Control over others

Control over other people is a way of getting things done if, like all young children, your child is not yet very good at doing things himself. Also not doing what he is asked to do is a way of showing that he has a mind of his own. Both are part of becoming independent and standing on his own feet. Even though most parents recognise that children do need to assert their independence, they often feel in certain circumstances their child is getting 'too big for his boots' for example, if he resorts to smacking *them* or if he refuses point blank to do what he is told. When he tries to exert control over other children you may intervene to prevent fights.

Attention seeking

Attention seeking is quite reasonable except when you are busy or giving your attention to someone else. Even though he might be feeling left out, your child's constant interruptions are bad manners and embarrassing. You can try to prevent this by making sure he has something else to do and that you spare him a minute every now and again.

Anger/frustration

Parents often feel that uncontrolled emotional outbursts are bad in that they are what babies do and not what grown ups are supposed to do. Tantrums are particularly trying for parents and they will often let things go rather than risk a confrontation that could lead to an all out tantrum. Uncontrolled aggression against other people is also disapproved of by most parents especially when there is danger to younger children.

Anxiety/fear

Anxiety and fear normally result in a return to more babyish behaviour – wanting to hold hands, hanging around mother and so on. Occasionally lying may be for fear of telling the truth. Parents are usually very disturbed when they find their child has lied and it is worth looking for the reasons before taking any action. Fear of strangers is quite natural but may be embarrassing to parents if their child expresses this to relations.

What does a young child understand about what's naughty; how does he learn this; what does he think of rules and does he consider the reactions of others in what he does?

One way to find out what children think about being naughty is to ask them. Find a quiet moment and then ask your child the following questions, using them as a starting point; but don't hesitate to ask others that occur to you.

Questions	Comments
1 What do you do that's naughty?	1 You may get a list of answers to this question, for example, 'Not eat your dinner', 'Scribble in Daddy's book', etc.
2 Why is it naughty? (Repeat this question after the others if your child says something is naughty.)	2 Young children often say that an action is naughty because scolding or punishment results or is threatened.
3 Is it naughty to hurt people?	3 The answer to this question will depend on whether your child has much close contact with other children. If he has a brother or sister you may have had to stop many fights and may have scolded them for hurting one another. On the other hand you may feel that children have to learn to look after themselves and accept their fighting, even though you still comfort the loser.
4 Is it naughty to run across the road?	4 Your child may explain that this is naughty because 'You will get knocked over by a car' – rather than because 'You will get smacked'.
5 Is it naughty if you make a mess?	5 Making a mess is usually regarded as being naughty even if you allow your child to make messes on occasions.
6 Is it naughty to break something?	6 The same applies for this as for making a mess.
7 A little girl was helping her mother to wash up and she accidentally broke three plates – is this naughty?	7 Children usually say this is naughty.
8 Another little girl threw a plate on the floor and broke it because she was cross – is that naughty?	8 Children usually say this is naughty – or very naughty.
9 Which little girl was naughtier – the one who broke three plates when she was washing up or the one who broke one when she was cross?	9 This is a difficult question for pre-schoolers. When they understand it they almost always say that the girl who broke three plates is naughtier.
10 Are Mummy and Daddy ever naughty?	10 Children sometimes say that adults are never naughty. Perhaps parents should help children to see that they also do things they shouldn't do. Other children say adults are naughty when they do something the child doesn't like – or has been told off for doing himself – such as 'shouting'.

WHAT'S CI

CHILDREN'S IDEAS

Young children know something is naughty through the reactions of parents or other authority figures. If punishment follows they call the behaviour naughty.

They regard acts that have the greatest consequences to be the naughtiest – without taking into account the intention behind it. So in Question 9 the child who broke most plates is seen as naughtier even though she was helping her mother and it was an accident.

Also young children do not judge an act in terms of what it would be like if it was done to them. They are unable to take the view of another child or adult and see how their behaviour would affect others.

Children say that the more severe the punishment the less likely a child is to be 'naughty' again. It is not until they are teenagers that they say explanations and discussions will help to stop someone doing something naughty again. The reasons behind naughty behaviour is then seen as important and the effects of the behaviour on others is recognised.

Now find out what your child thinks about rules.

NAUGHTY-CHILDREN'S VIEWS

Keeping to the rules

If your child has learned to play a simple game with only a few simple rules – such as snakes and ladders, ludo or snap, ask him to show you how to play the game and tell you what the rules are . . .

● Does he put the rules into words as well as demonstrate them?

● Does he make up new rules for the game?

● Does he think a new rule (suggested either by him or by you) would make the game 'fair' for someone playing with him?

● Ask him what happens if you don't obey a rule.

Next, play the game with him and look at the way he responds to the rules in practice.

● Does he always take turns?

● Does he interfere with the dice or the cards?

● Does he obey the penalties – such as always going down a snake?

● Does he play the game properly or does he convert it into a game of his own?

● Does he ignore rules when it suits him?

● Does he expect you to stick to the rules?

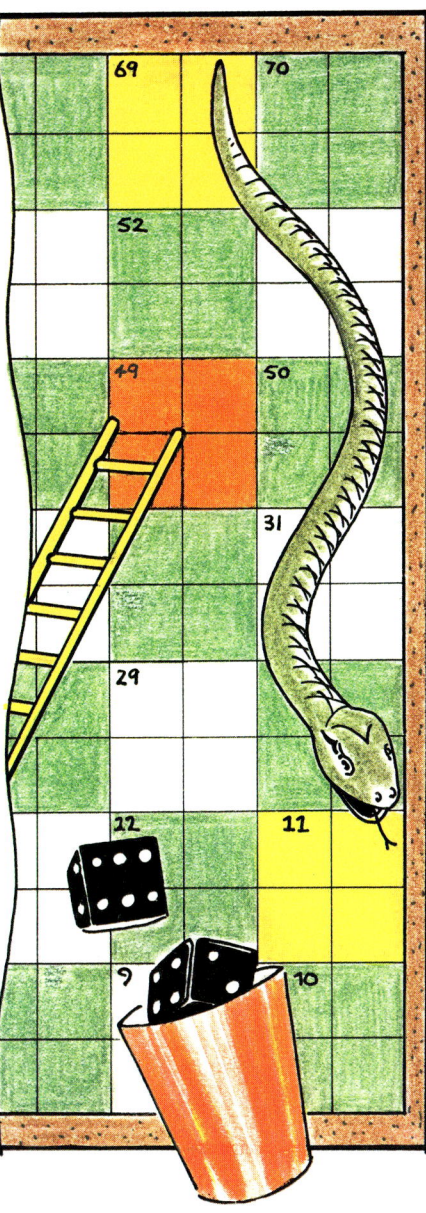

Young children only begin to use rules between the ages of 3 and 5 years. Before that they use the materials of the game to play with in their own way, for example pretending the counters are people, or the board is a house, or just stacking them up or making a pattern.

Even when pre-schoolers do begin to play games by their rules, they usually impose their own personal view on the game and ignore the rules if they don't suit them. It is only when children are in their school years that they learn to play games amongst themselves using the rules.

Sometime after the age of 3, children begin to show some knowledge of rules and regulations. The way they talk about rules is very different from the way rules are actually treated. They see rules as important because they are laid down by trusted and powerful adults but they do not act as though the rule came from inside. Limits have to be set on children's behaviour from outside. In other words, children can understand rules so it's worth telling them, but they cannot always keep to the rules because there are powerful selfish forces pulling against them.

Consistency

One of the pieces of advice most often given about young children is the need for parents to be consistent in what they call 'naughty'. It isn't so much which particular behaviour you disapprove of as long as you are consistent.

Obviously you should not insist on one thing one minute and then encourage it the next. This is not as unusual as it sounds. You might think of examples that actually occur from time to time with your own child when you make it confusing for him –

'Why don't you help me mix this cake?' and later –

'Stop mixing up your food.'

'Don't be naughty, you must not touch this note paper, it's mine and not to be touched by anyone.'
and later –

'Don't be naughty, you must let Sandra share your paper so that she can draw a picture as well.'

Being able to notice from parents the clues as to what is and what is not allowed in different situations, requires a lot of learning and skill. This is very much a feature of a child's social learning at this particular stage of life. He has to learn, for example:

● when it's all right to be dependent and when it's not;

● what he can and cannot touch;

● when it's good to be independent and when he's 'getting too big for his boots'.

This learning is not entirely one way. Parents also have to learn to accept their child's definition of the situation. When a child is frightened and acts dependently, parents should be prepared to take this into account. It is often a question of balance – on the one hand children have to learn when certain behaviour is acceptable but on the other parents have to learn to take into account a child's needs as far as they can in the circumstances.

Children frequently get it wrong by parents' standards, and sometimes parents are not as helpful as they could be in making the differences between situations clearer and explaining these to the child. The fact that behaviour is approved of in some situations and not in others makes life more complicated than if there was 'always right' and 'always wrong' behaviour. But if children grew up in a family where there was complete consistency they would become mechanical and inflexible and unable to respond appropriately to different social situations. This may well involve responding in one way on one occasion but not responding in this way on another. Different rules do operate at different times. A child must learn to consider things like changed circumstances, the moods of others, and adapt accordingly.

THAT GIVES ME 25 MINS. TO MAKE THE BED, HANG OUT THE WASHING, HOOVER THE CARPET, PHONE THE PLUMBER, PUT ON THE DINNER.....

Talking while you work

Sometimes the chores just have to be done, and fast – and television or toys are a blessing if they'll keep the kids quiet. But talking is a very 'educational' activity for your child, and it needs little more than being in the same room together. So whenever there's time, don't whistle while you work – talk and listen!

Finding out what your child knows...

When your child first begins to speak it is fun to keep a list of the words he uses (until you can't keep up with him). 'More' and a lot of words for food and drink will probably take up much of the list. Nevertheless as you write down each new word it is worth remembering that *for each word your child can say, there are many more that he understands.* You can discover some of the words he does know and some that he doesn't by playing the simple game in the next column. Don't do it for too long or he'll get bored.

Learning new words

Finding out what your child does and does not know is not an end in itself. It's a useful first step when you are helping him to learn new words. The best situation for any sort of learning is when the child has a reason for learning. Helping with household tasks can be a good opportunity for using words to stand for objects and to describe the order of events.

Words for all occasions

Some of the most useful words are not tied to any particular object or action, but occur in almost every kind of situation. Children usually understand *position* words like 'in', 'on', 'under', by the time they are three-years-old. *Time* words like 'before' and 'after' are not usually understood until a year or two later. *Quantity* words like 'some', 'all', 'more', or *size* words like 'big', 'long', 'thin', are used in many different situations.

1 Choose a place where you both spend a lot of time together – like the kitchen – and make a list of words which you might use in giving simple instructions. You can use this list and add to it, or make one up to suit your own home.

2 Now give simple instructions which use these words. For example :
  Wash the spoon.
  Show me the *kettle*.
  Find me the *brush*.
  Close the *cupboard*.

3 Tick the words your child knows on your list. (Make sure he is not guessing by asking him to select one item from a group of different objects – don't ask for the kettle if only the kettle is on view).

4 If he finds this easy, go on to give him more complicated instructions using words from more of the columns in the table. For example :
  Put the bowl on the table.

And then make it more complicated :
Put the little yellow bowl by the jug on the table.
Open the cupboard under the sink.
Bring me the towel from the drawer.
Put the dirty spoon into the sink.
Push the stool under the table.

Objects	✓	Actions	✓	Qualities	✓	Quantities	✓	Position	✓
bowl		sweep		dirty		some		in	
table		wash		blue		more		on	
brush		push		big		all		under	
kettle		put		heavy		one		behind	
cupboard		close		new		both		inside	
....		....		....		....		....	
....		....		....		....		....	
....		....		....		....		....	

It goes on top

Listen to this mother helping her child to learn the meaning of the word *top* – both as an object – the top that goes onto the basket – and as a position – *on* top. Notice how patiently she keeps on until he seems to have understood what she means.

Stephen (aged 2 years 4 months) is waiting for his mother to finish the washing up and play with him.

Stephen: Play, Mummy? Finished washing up?

Mother: Just let me dry my hands.

Stephen: All right. Here you are. (Hands a towel to his mother.)

Mother: Just a minute . . . will you put the top back on the washing basket please?

Stephen: On there? (Points to the laundry basket.)

Mother: No, not the towel in there! (Stephen wants to put the towel in the basket.) The top of the basket, on it!

Stephen: All right on there? (Puts the lid on something else.)

Mother: Put the *lid* . . . on top of the *basket*. (Stresses the words and simultaneously indicates the objects.)

Stephen: Oh, on there?

Mother: Yes please.

Stephen: Mummy, play! Play, Mummy!

Mother: I will play if you put the top on the basket.

Stephen: All right. (He finally puts the top on the basket.)

84

Object lessons

Knowing what an object is called is important, but equally important is knowing how it works and what it is used for. So when your child asks what something *is* or comments on something he can see, you can tell him what it is *for* as well.

'What's that?'
'A brush, to sweep dirt up – like this.'

This gives him the name, and shows him how the word is used in a sentence, and relates language to the situation it describes. Whenever it is possible try to extend his interest with a related piece of information.

'What's a saucepan?'
'We're going to use it to cook the potatoes for your dinner.'

I spy what things are for

'I spy, with my little eye something we go to sleep in.'

Choose objects whose names are familiar to your child and you will give him the satisfying experience of success. Encourage him to listen carefully to your descriptions of the objects. After a few turns, he will probably want to try making up clues himself. Extend the game to other types of clue, such as shape, ownership, position, and so on – 'I spy with my little eye something in front of the big saucepan,' 'I spy something brown and woolly that belongs to Paul.'

Traditional 'I-Spy something beginning with . . . ' is hard for young children because they are only just beginning to understand the relationship between letters and the words they speak.

Sorting and grouping

But what makes a chair a piece of furniture? Why is a giraffe not a horse?

Children need help in sorting out these confusions. Cut pictures from magazines and catalogues and let them group them in any way they want – you will be surprised at the number of different groups they will make. Talking to you about what they are doing, grouping things, according to colour, shape, uses, or even private stories they make up, will introduce them to new words and help them to use them confidently. Sorting and grouping comes into family work (see *Launder and learn*, this chapter and *Tidying up*, Chapter 4).

House game

The house game is something to do when you are *not* working – but it should give you some ideas for talking when you are working! Using the house game can help you to find out which words your child knows, and which he doesn't, so you can think of ways to help him learn 'top' or 'more', for example. It gives your child a chance to make sure of the words he knows and helps with sorting and grouping. It also gives him the pleasure of successfully naming objects, saying what they are for and where they belong.

The 'house' in the picture was the work of a mother with scissors and her $2\frac{1}{2}$ and almost 4-year-olds. The children selected items from catalogues and pasted them in the appropriate rooms. The game involved a great deal of talk about what things go where and in which rooms. It gave the mother an opportunity to discover what kinds of things they could recognise and how far their language could cope with grouping and relating objects. She also 'eavesdropped' when talk turned into a family game about the people who lived in the house.

To make your house game more permanent, you could draw out simple rooms on a large piece of card. The objects could be made more lasting too.
It is easy to make household playing cards by cutting out pictures in magazines and sticking them on old cereal packets for a longer life.

You can use the cards and house for a number of different games, as long or as short as you and your child wish.
For example you could:
● name objects on the card;
● put objects or room cards where they belong;
● talk about what the objects are used for;
● sort and group the objects in various ways (by room, or by ownership – mine, Mummy's – for example);
● play a card game where one of you turns up a room card or an object card at a time, and the other has to put it where it should go in the house.

Getting away from here-and-now

A very young child can't bring you his coat if he can't see it in a familiar place. When he is older he will remember that he left it upstairs on his bed and go to fetch it. When this happens the word *coat* has become a bridge between an object which isn't there and the appearance of that object.

Now you can say – 'Shall we go to the swings?' – and he knows what you mean. *He* can say – 'Want a sweetie?' – when there isn't one in sight. He can understand and use words to conjure up in his mind things and events that aren't present in the here-and-now of what he can see.

You help to develop his use of words as substitutes for objects when you ask him to find things which you need – 'Can you go downstairs and bring my duster from the hall?'

Time and the order of events

'Is it Christmas?'

Not yet.

When?

Soon.

When is soon?

Next week.

Is it after this day?'

Even when they are three, thinking beyond 'this day' is difficult. Today, yesterday and tomorrow are a puzzle.

'Am I going to playgroup, today?' asks James who is nearly four.
'No, you go tomorrow.'
'Well it *is* tomorrow, today,' he says trying to make sense of it all.

Sorting out the order in which he has done things seems to be causing trouble too. Showing someone three paintings he has brought home from playgroup he says – 'I did that one first and I did that one after and I did that sooner.'

Gradually the span of time over which a child can link speech in the present with events in the past and future begins to extend. He begins to be able to talk about activities that happened earlier in the day or yesterday, or that can be expected to happen in the not too distant future.

How you help

1 First ask questions which call upon the child's memory of a recent particular event. For example – 'Where did we leave the dustpan just now? Could you go and get it?'

2 Later you can ask questions about what objects will be needed for a job that still has to be done – 'What will we need to polish the floor?' This question calls for a more generalised memory of past events.

3 More difficult questions still are the ones that ask for the correctly ordered sequences of events – 'What will we have to do to make a cup of tea?'

Thinking and talking about the future

Mother: Would you like to go into town this afternoon?

Paul: Yes.

Mother: And buy your new shoes?

Paul: Yes. Can we go on the bus?

Mother: Perhaps Aunty Jane might take us in her car.

Paul: I don't want Aunty Jane to take us, then we can go on the bus.

You can probably remember having had conversations like this. They happen frequently and may seem unimportant, but they provide a child with an opportunity to use language to think about possibilities and alternative courses of action. These can be considered and their consequences *imagined*.

'*Or I could plant them tomorrow*.' Simon (aged 4 years 9 months) has just eaten an apple. He is explaining to his mother what he might do with the pips. Notice how he is thinking through a course of action and considering alternatives:

'A pip is a seed.

So he can grow . . .

And we *might be able* to grow some now.

Got some apple seeds – apple pip seeds.

And *if I put* even more . . .

Daddy and me *might go out* one day which isn't a rainy day –

And we *might be able* to plant the seeds.

Or I could plant them tomorrow.'

Words like *might, could, perhaps, if,* are words used during thinking about what might or might not happen; words used to think things out for ourselves. They are very important.

You can encourage this kind of thinking when you are doing things together. Let your child 'try it out in words' so that he can check what he expects against what actually happens.

Will it float? . . . What colours do you need to mix together to get green? . . . What do you think will happen if you put the ice in the water jug? . . . and so on.

Talk, talk, talk

You don't *teach* children to talk . . . they learn. The world they live in is a talking world and learning to talk is the biggest act of independence a child ever makes. As he learns to talk he learns to think, to organise and understand the world. It is a two-way process happening all the time he is awake, from the moment you say – 'Breakfast time, let's get that nappy off' to 'Night night, see you in the morning' – he is listening, absorbing, practising, trying out and inventing. All the people in his life, parents, other children, people he knows and lots he's never seen before contribute to this learning process. It never stops. Right through the day, you will see it happening if you look out for it. Learning to talk is involved in every activity in every topic – in the kind of questions your child asks, in the new words and ideas your child may learn, in the conversations that go on all the time. Listen to what other children say and notice the ways their parents answer them.

Rhymes, songs and finger plays

What do children enjoy about songs and rhymes? Paul's mother is rocking him and singing. What do you think Paul is finding so enjoyable about this experience?

Like most mothers, Paul's mum isn't a trained musician. So what is it that he finds so enjoyable?

It's secure and comfortable. A child never forgets being held close to his mother, feeling her warmth and smelling her familiar smell, hearing her heartbeat and the sound of her voice. Every time you sing with your child you draw upon the power of this early experience, even when the child is too old or too big to sit on your lap. Adults still feel its strength as they sing together in football crowds or campfire groups.

Paul and his mum are sharing the song, and each other. At this moment nothing else in the world is important.

What use are action songs?

Young children learn much from action songs and rhymes. When you both play a game like 'Wee Wiggie' your child sees your hands moving; he feels their touch on his toes; he senses your other muscles moving against his body; he hears the words (and also feels the vibration of the sound and the warmth of your breath against his cheek). All these sensations are felt together, so the pattern of the rhyme is experienced simultaneously through several senses. This makes its impact much more powerful.

Joining in

Actions are also the easiest way for a young child to join in with a song or rhyme. With a baby you have to do the actions for him, wiggling his toes or clapping his hands, but by the time a child is three (if not before) he'll be able to say the rhyme and do the actions for himself.

However, this is much harder for him. He has to:
- remember the pattern of the rhyme,
- pick up the speed at which it is being spoken,
- control and match his own movements and speaking,
- make them fit in with yours.

Is singing meaningful?

Learning from songs and rhymes depends on the songs being about something within the child's experience. Without such meaning either he will switch off or he'll change the song to something he knows about, and so not learn what you expect. Think of children's versions of hymns and prayers that have no meaning for them. Have you heard about the village whose local bobby was called Arthur Heffer? The children in the village school always prayed 'Our Father, with Arthur Heffer' . . . a very meaningful prayer to them!

How can you make songs and rhymes meaningful? . . .
- by doing them *yourself* and not relying on records or on other people,
- by giving your child opportunities to join in in his own way, especially with actions,
- by making songs fit his experience, to the extent of changing the words, if necessary.

Rhymes, songs and finger plays

Learning from songs

As a parent you've probably found:

● your child doesn't have the same attitude to performance as an adult. He likes to 'do' the rhyme, but he may do it in his own special way;

● he isn't bothered (or indeed may not notice or know) when he does something 'incorrectly'. At this age a child can't check his performance mentally — he has to sing the song in order to see how it comes out;

● he has a strong drive to master something new, provided that he feels secure and confident. But he can't master everything at once. So he picks out one or two things he feels he can do and tries those. Success leads him to try other parts, and he gradually masters the whole.

Don't misinterpret this drive to master new material. It doesn't mean that he is ready or willing to be 'taught' new rhymes or songs however sensitively you do it. Indeed, that may well destroy the confidence and enjoyment which he has built up by sharing your pleasure in the songs and rhymes you have already done together.

When you 'share' a song with him...

● you take pleasure in his company and in his enjoyment,

● you let him choose his own ways of coping with difficulties and his own level of participation,

● you value his contribution, however limited,

● you encourage him.

When you 'teach' him a song...

● you demand that he demonstrates his ability and skill,

● you confront him with his difficulties and dictate his level of participation,

● you judge his contribution by your own standards,

● you threaten him.

MAKING SOUNDS

WHEN GIVE A CHILD HAS PICKED HIM A CHANCE TO E

Clappers – flat pieces of wood with cotton reels glued and nailed to make handles,
halves of coconutshells with a hole in each that takes a string that gives handles and keeps the halves together,
two pieces of broom handle to click together.

Shakers made from detergent bottles or tins with beans or rice or pebbles inside. Let your child help you make them.

Jinglers made with bells. Stitch them on to wristbands of folded ribbons gathered by elastic, with more ribbons that fly. Knot them onto a string and tie into a groove notched near the end of a dowelling wand, then decorate with a flourish of flying ribbons.

A drum f plastic lic and fit a Make hol skewer an them to se spoon mal

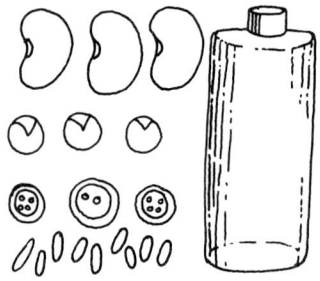
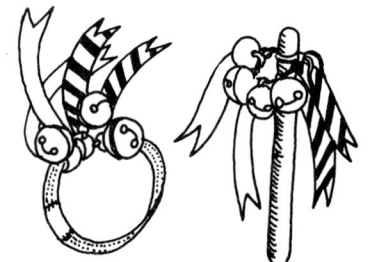
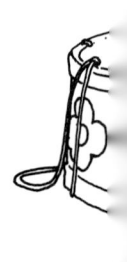

Are songs and rhymes 'just good fun'?

Children enjoy songs and rhymes very much, we know, but they also learn from them the fundamentals of thinking. Human beings love noticing and making patterns from the complexity of the world around them. Art, language, logic, mathematics, sports and games all depend upon this ability to see pattern, so anything that makes a child more sensitive to pattern and more confident about making his own patterns will increase his ability to learn.

Many kinds of human pattern-making are too complicated or too sophisticated for young children to appreciate. Songs and rhymes, though, have a pattern that they can take in. So when you sing a simple song with your child you're giving him one of his best opportunities to appreciate human pattern-making and you're helping him to feel that he can do it too. Such understanding and confidence carries over into other things.

A simple action song helps you see something of this. Sing one you know until you're sure your child can follow it. Then alter it:

● leave out some verses;

● change the order of the verses;

● combine two or three actions in one verse;

● make up some new verses (just think of simple actions that your child can do and sing out the instructions!).

Observe his reactions to the changes – he may well:

● want the new verse repeated immediately,

● laugh with pleasure at a new verse (or be angry!),

● tell you that you've left something out,

● suggest a new verse or action himself.

Any of these reactions tell you that he has understood some important things. Hearing the song the first few times has made him familiar with the pattern. He begins to learn that from knowing a pattern he can make something new.

We've been talking about a simple action song, but you can see that the pattern of thinking is a basic one and one which is seen in many other areas of young children's exploration and learning:

Repetition gives understanding of a pattern. It leads to:

Mastery – confidence and control of the pattern. This gives:

Freedom – to invent, create, change, adapt the basic pattern.

RHYTHM SE IT.... WITH HIS HANDS OR FEET, WITH SOUNDS FROM OTHER THINGS...

coffee tin with a out the bottom lid to each end. e lids with a hot d string through e lids. A wooden umstick.

Scrapers with notches sawn in bamboo or broom handle, scraped with a teaspoon or stick.

Danglers – different objects dangling from a coat hanger that can be tapped very gently with various different 'hammers' to make different sounds.

89

Paint

Painting can be a messy business and requires preparation so if you are short of space and time you might not want your child to paint at home. But children really enjoy painting so it could be a pity not to provide your child with the chance of doing so.

Very young children are not trying to paint pictures. They are more interested in experimenting with the paint, almost in the same way as they would play with a stick and a muddy puddle. Only much later on does paint become a 'tool' with which a child can describe his world.

Pictures 1 and 2 show the child's most usual first experiments with paint. Don't worry if your child seems to stick at this stage. Give him time to enjoy seeing the colour appear on the paper and let him enjoy just playing.

Many children will then quite deliberately make more 'formal' patterns as in pictures 3 and 4. The child

1

Getting down to painting

Drawing is mainly concerned with lines and painting with patches. Just as there is a sequence in the development of drawing which you can easily recognise, (see Chapter 2) so there is in painting.

Try and find two or three children of different ages, for example 2 years, 3½ years, and 4½ years and compare their ways of painting. Perhaps you have a neighbour or friend with an older child. If so compare notes. It would be easier to observe each child one at a time rather than in a group.

Give each child a large piece of paper, a brush and two pots of well mixed paint of different colours – see *Mixing it up*. Sit where you won't be too obviously intruding on the child's play and see what is happening. Tick which statement applies to which child.

What he does . . .

	Child 1 Age:	Child 2 Age:	Child 3 Age:
He puts the paint on the paper at once	☐	☐	☐
He listens to the noise of the brush as it plops about in the paint	☐	☐	☐
He stirs the paint	☐	☐	☐
He looks at the colour on the brush before putting it on the paper	☐	☐	☐
He puts his finger in the paint pot	☐	☐	☐
He keeps the brush on the paper while he's painting	☐	☐	☐
He uses both colours	☐	☐	☐
He keeps the two colours separate on the paper	☐	☐	☐
He paints one colour on top of the other	☐	☐	☐
He makes blobs	☐	☐	☐
He paints lines	☐	☐	☐
He paints patches	☐	☐	☐
He covers the whole paper	☐	☐	☐
He paints a recognisable picture	☐	☐	☐

You probably noticed that the younger child was playing with the paint rather than painting a picture but the older child took more interest in actually painting.

It seems that paint has a fascination all of its own and young children tend to spend more time exploring the materials in painting than in drawing.

5

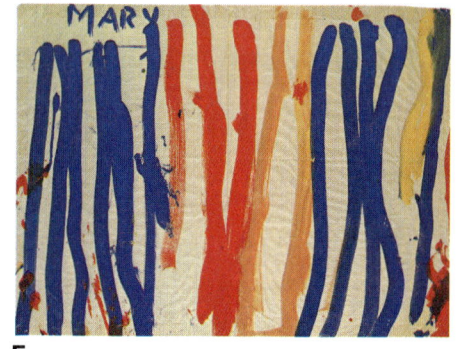

looks as though he is mastering the paint and brush not simply splashing about but making the colour work for him and go where he wants it to.

The next discovery is that paint will go on top of paint and his paintings may become 'decorated'. Pictures 5 and 6 show this pattern emerging. Soon he will also begin painting people, houses and things he sees around him, as in pictures 7 and 8.

Can you tell roughly which stage each of the children you observed has reached?

Going back

As a child goes through the various stages in drawing and painting he will often get to one stage and then go back to an earlier stage. This is nothing to worry about – he may be finding the new stage a bit difficult and so seeks reassurance in what he already knows. If he seems to stick at his earlier stage without going forward again try to help him along by using some of the ideas in 'When does he need a change?', on page 93.

Suggestion
Read the topic on *Drawing* (Chapter 2) together with this topic. Drawing and painting have much in common, especially in the ways you can help.

What is it?

The objects a child paints may not always be recognisable to us but we must treat them with respect. While the child is painting them they are important to him and we must listen while he tells us about them. If he says this blue splodge is the cat who visits from next-door, then that is what it is!

3

4

2

6

7

8

Painting at home

You can protect your floor with a plastic sheet and protect your child's clothing by making an apron out of an old plastic mac or an old shirt of dad's turned back to front with the sleeves cut short.

What you need...

An easel

A child can paint with the paper on the floor or on a table – but it is best if an easel can be provided. On a table, particularly if it is too high, the child has difficulty in reaching the far edge of his painting and cannot see what is happening very easily.

An easel is relatively easy for a handy person to make. It shouldn't be too high and ideally there should be a tray for paints at the bottom. If this is not possible a plastic milk bottle carrier for four pints will do but it should be placed near the easel. Another idea is to have a board – half blackboard and half soft board to take drawing pins – hung in your child's bedroom or elsewhere. He can then scribble or hang paintings as he wishes.

Paper

The rougher the paper the better. It is best to have large pieces of paper – about 55 cms x 40 cms. Use old wallpaper, sugar paper or computer paper or old newspaper – the kind with more print than photos. Attach the paper to the easel using clothes pegs or drawing pins.

Brushes

A paint brush will do, or an old decorating brush providing its not too large and will fit into the paint pot. If you want to buy brushes then size 10 or 12 round ferrule hog-hair brushes are best. They may seem expensive but they last a long time and make the paint flow in a very satisfying way.

Paint pots

Make your own from old washing-up liquid containers. To do this cut off the neck and cut the remaining bottle into three pieces as shown in the diagram. Discard the middle piece. Turn the 'dome' piece upside down and place in the bottom piece. If the pot is upset there is less spilling, so less mess to clear up.

Paint

Powder paint is best. You can buy it in art shops and the larger the tin you buy the cheaper it works out. Get together with other parents to buy in bulk and share the cost. Try to provide at least three colours with a separate brush for each.

cut off

finished pot with brush in

Mixing it up

Before giving paint to your child try some yourself – put some powder in a container and add water – experiment with it very thin, very thick and just right. Which do you find most satisfying? Chances are your child will agree with you.

A good test for the right consistency for a child is to try a blob on paper on an easel. It should flow easily from the brush – but not run down the paper.

You can thicken the paint by adding cold water paste (be sure it's free from added fungicide) or a good quality washing up liquid or some household flour. Practice will tell you how much to use.

Wot, no brushes?

People painted long before brushes were invented. So why not give your child the chance to explore other ways of painting.

Using fingers

Children like the feel and the freedom of using their fingers to paint. Ideally you need a hard, washable board for this but strong paper secured to a hard flat surface will do. The paper must be secure so it doesn't move about. Your child will also be less likely to put his fingers through it. Have a sponge and clean water handy for mopping up and cover the floor and your child.

Mix some paint with paste, making it fairly thick and put about two table-spoonfuls on to the board or paper. Watch what your child does with this. Does he:

● touch the paint with one finger or more?

● put his whole hand in the paint?

● use both hands?

● touch it gently or charge in?

Let your child mix his own paint by giving him some ready mixed water paste and a small amount of different coloured powders in a half-dozen-size egg box with a lolly stick for mixing. Does he:

● mix all the colours together?

● seem to prefer one colour?

● talk to himself or to you while he's doing it?

● spend more time mixing than painting?

Using straws

The paint will need to be runny for this. Give the child a straw and show him how he can make patterns with the paint by blowing it in different directions. Colours can be put on top of each other and blown through each other to produce rainbow effects.

Printing

You will need a small piece of foam cut up to fit into a lid – for example from a coffee jar – to make a paint pad. Find also bits and pieces suitable for printing – a cork, a cotton reel, a wooden brick, a small piece of real sponge. Soak the plastic foam in well mixed paint and put it beside some clean sheets of paper. Do *not* show your child what to do but watch what happens. Does he:

● put his finger on the paint pad?

● explore the objects before choosing one for printing?

● use all the objects?

● pull and push the object back and forth across the paper and prefer to finger paint?

If he does prefer finger painting don't stop him. It probably means he is not yet ready for printing. Put it away and try again much later.

Printing should remain an activity in which the child explores the materials and discovers for himself what they will do. It is only too easy for an adult to turn this into a demonstration which takes all the initiative away from the child. He will probably not be ready for these discoveries until he is about four – but once he is used to the idea of transferring shapes to paper he can be encouraged to make his own collection of things to print with.

Special events

At Christmas time or birthdays your child's drawings and paintings can be important.

When paintings are still wet sprinkle some glitter on them. When they are dry they will make gay wall decorations for parties.

Children can make birthday and Christmas cards in the same way if provided with small pieces of folded card. As soon as they are able, they can write their own messages in them too!

When does he need a change?

From watching your child painting you will have learnt what his interests are and which aspects he finds most pleasing – particular colours, shapes, printing objects, textures.

You have noticed perhaps that some days he will spend an endless amount of time on the same activity, for example painting trees, and on other days he will soon become bored and be in need of new ideas. If your child seems to get bored quickly this does not mean he can't concentrate. Concentration doesn't only mean how long he stays with one activity, but also how deeply he is involved with the activity.

Can you tell when your child is getting bored? Does he begin to look around him, paint over what seemed to be finished or stop looking at what he is doing?

You can help to extend your child's interest by keeping back some different materials and ideas to be introduced when the signs of boredom appear.

Don't put out all the materials at once. Just give two colours, and only a few sheets of paper. Then later on you can introduce a new colour, a different size brush, a sheet of coloured paper or embossed paper for a patterned effect. When printing is introduced put away the brushes; see if you can find different surfaces for printing on such as old scraps of material, cardboard, eggboxes.

Talk with your child about things he has recently experienced or enjoyed as this will give him ideas for stories to paint.

Pictures on show

Find a suitable place to put up your child's paintings and drawings – perhaps in his bedroom if there's room. There need only be space for two recent or favourite pictures and these can be changed as new ones are made. Let your child decide which ones should be on display and let him pin them up by standing on a chair or table with you nearby to see he's safe.

All sorts of music

All children are born with an interest in sounds. Whether this develops into an interest in music depends partly upon the child but mostly on the opportunities and encouragement that you give her. You're not musical? All the more reason to think how you can begin to open this world to your child. There's plenty you can do.

Listen to silence

Start by listening to the sounds of silence. Do this anywhere – at home when there is no radio, record or television and outside, as far from any traffic as possible.

'Let's listen,' you say and then concentrate for as long as your child's interest lasts, whispering the name of each sound you hear. It's a good game and will usually end in an outburst of laughing or shouting or wildness . . . a relief from the concentration of listening.

When you have finished write down the names of the sounds you have heard.

Inside	Outside
tap dripping	
footsteps outside	
passing car	
bird singing	
clock ticking	

This may seem a far cry from music, but unless you can listen carefully, you can't make or enjoy music. You hear a lot of sounds all day long, and get accustomed to hearing without listening. There is music in shops, sometimes the television or radio is on all the time. Continual sound *prevents* your child from learning to listen. Try this observation on your wife, husband or another adult:

Watch them one day when you have background music on. Do they change what they are doing when the music changes, or show that they notice it in any way? Try turning it off and ask what sort of music it was, what the song was about or anything else that would tell you how much they were aware of the music itself.

You do not notice very much when you are just hearing music, *listening* is the key to learning.

Then listen to rhythms

After listening to silence, try listening to rhythms and share with your child the playing of her first instrument . . . her own body.

The rhythm can come from anywhere – radio, record, nursery rhyme.

If your child is cradled in your arms, pat her bottom or thigh, and rock her. If she is on her feet, let her hold your fingers and move your arms to and fro, up and down, moving in time with the music or rhyme. Help her to feel the rhythm.

Always carry on just as long as the child's interest lasts so that you build up memories of shared pleasure that were about listening, making rhythms and repeating them, then, much later, making music.

Catch a rhythm

After listening come the skills of recognising, learning and repeating . . . then of remembering! Here is something you can do using various parts of the body to keep the rhythm. How many different kinds of body rhythm can you think of?

Clapping   – palms together.

Tapping   – two fingers on the palm of the other hand; feet on the ground while you are sitting; hands on your thighs; fingers on your blown-up cheeks.

Tongue clicking – mouth open or closed.

Finger noises   – snapping, drumming on a table.

These are just a beginning . . . you could probably add to the list.

Begin by using one of these ways of making a rhythm. Choose a time when your child is content to be quiet with you . . . and play a rhyme in taps. You can use a code for short (●) and long (■) taps. Humpty Dumpty would go like this:

Humpty Dumpty sat on a wall
■ ■ ● ■ ● ■ ● ●

Humpty Dumpty had a great fall
■ ■ ● ■ ● ● ● ■

A rhythm game

Start with a simple rhythm, asking your child to play the rhythm back to you. Repeat the same pattern a few times and then change it for another. Play the rhythms slowly so that your child can catch the details of the pattern. Here are a series of patterns that become longer and more difficult. How far down the list can your child go? Put ticks by the rhythms she catches to-day. Try doing this sort of thing now, and then after a week try the series again and see whether you get any further.

Can your child get the rhythm

	now	after a week
1 ▬▬ ▬ ▬▬	☐	☐
2 ▬ ●▬●	☐	☐
3 ▬ ● ●▬ ●● ● ●●	☐	☐
4 ●●▬▬▬●● ▬ ▬●	☐	☐
5 ▬ ●▬ ● ● ▬ ▬ ▬	☐	☐
6 ●●▬ ▬● ▬ ● ● ▬	☐	☐
7 ▬ ▬ ● ● ▬ ▬ ● ●	☐	☐
8 ● ● ▬ ●●▬ ● ▬● ▬	☐	☐

If your child can do all these, invent some more, picking out the rhythms of songs or other music that you know.

You can make this 'question and answer' game more difficult by using different kinds of body rhythms. To begin with just use one length of beat . . .
2 foot taps; 2 hand claps; 2 slaps of the thighs; and so on . . .

Then let the left hand and foot make a short sound while the right hand and foot make a long sound.

You will observe that the different ways of making rhythms make different kinds of sound. You are not just making sounds or rhythms, you are making music . . . body music!

Some African tribes use simple body music to make really complicated patterns of sound . . . loud and soft; tranquil and exciting; solo and in chorus; all making the same kind of music. Sometimes different groups making different patterns can blend together. You and your child can begin to do these things together.

From rhythm . . . dancing

If you watch children, you will see how their whole bodies become part of what they are doing or feeling. Children jump with excitement. If they are painting at an easel, their whole body becomes part of that painting, not just the hand that holds the brush.

In the same way, if they are listening to a rhythm, and pick it up with the movement of a finger, that movement becomes the movement of a hand, an arm, both arms, the body swaying as it sits and then the whole body will move in answer to the continuing rhythm . . . that is dancing.

This natural answering of the body to music often becomes stilted even before it has begun. You may not be a great dancer yourself, but alone with your child it doesn't really matter. Your movements can encourage her to dance and enjoy moving to music. How this develops will depend on either continuing to help it yourself or finding other people who know how to take this natural response further.

From rhythm . . . singing

Many movements have their own rhythm, walking, swinging, skipping . . . and many work movements have their rhythms too. Think of the rhythms of polishing, scrubbing, washing a wall. Sometimes you need to keep up that rhythm longer, when you're working, than you would normally. That is where singing helps. A lot of the work on sailing ships needed that kind of encouragement, whether it was to get men pulling on a rope together, or rowing. Singing is a way of drawing people together. We have inherited a lot of work songs to do with ships.

Around the house, you can sing 'work' songs with your child, picking up the rhythms and using a song you know, or making one up yourself. For example – 'This is the way we scrub the drawer . . . ' is a way of singing 'Here we go round the mulberry bush . . . '

This may not seem to have very much to do with helping your child to play a violin for pleasure . . . but it brings music into everyday living, making it a shared enjoyment.

Radio, records, television

An orchestra playing for you while you are in a bath, a pop group singing for you while you wash up, great singers, great music . . . people to put on different records for you and all you have to do is listen! What a change in fifty years. The problem to-day is not how to get music, but how to get away from it. Our children often hear music for hours on end. With older children, the sharing of an interest in music becomes a way of being part of a group.

Sometimes people say that all this listening to music makes children lazy about making their own. But the fact is that there are more people making music now than at any time in the past, more people enjoying music, knowing about music . . . of all kinds.

On pages 88 and 89 there are ideas for you to follow in making various 'sound-makers' or instruments with which your child will be able to make music with others, including the radio, records or the television. Keep a variety of instruments in a collection – a box or a bag – and when you need a change from banging on a saucepan or washing-up bowl with a wooden spoon, you will have a variety of other things to choose from. Your child – and her friends – can pick a favourite, or try them one after the other.

Then, when the music breaks down into disorderly noise, you can collect them up again and hide them away until the next time.

Different kinds of music
Whatever kind of music you may like best yourself, why not give your child a chance to listen to various types. You probably know most of them yourself . . . How many sorts of music and different instruments have you listened to with your child, telling her what you know about them? Tick those that you hear this week:

Kinds of music		People singing	
Pop	☐	Man	☐
Rock	☐	Woman	☐
Jazz	☐	Group	☐
Brass band	☐	Choir	☐
Orchestral	☐	Children	☐
Small groups	☐	**Instruments**	
Nursery rhyme music	☐	Guitar	☐
Church music	☐	Drums	☐
Indian music	☐	Trumpet	☐
Steel band music	☐	Violin	☐

Music varies between different parts of the world, different instruments make different sounds and the ways in which songs are written differ even when written for the same instuments. The variety is endless.

Starting music with your children can lead to the sharing of learning and enjoyment.

Some books for parents

The books marked ● are general books on pre-school children; about their development and the part that parents play in these important years. Examples and observations of children give these books the freshness of reality.

● *Between Parent and Child*
Haim G. Ginott
Pan Books, 1970

● *The Magic Years*
S. H. Fraiberg
Methuen, 1968

● *The Child's World*
P. Hostler
Penguin, 1965

● *Playing, Learning, Living*
V. Roberts
A. and C. Black, 1971

● *The Significance of Children's Play*
J. Cass
Batsford, 1971

Baby and child
Penelope Leach
Michael Joseph, 1978
This book, which contains many 'activities', is highly recommended and is about babies and children up to 5 years old.

The Child, the Family and the Outside World
D. W. Winnicott
Penguin, 1964
A friendly classic about the behaviour of babies and children.

The Self-respecting Child
A. Stallibrass
Thames and Hudson, 1974
A study of children's play and development, stressing the importance of a child's environment and how the adults in a child's life can hinder or stimulate.

How to Survive Parenthood
E. J. LeShan
Penguin, 1967
This book has an interesting section on older children.

The Growth and Development of Children
C. Lee
Longman, 1969
This book gives a clear outline of the stages of development in young children, including observations which illustrate these stages.

Book of Child Care
Hugh Jolly
Allen and Unwin, 1975
A very practical book, with an emphasis on health.

Four Years Old in an Urban Community
J. and E. Newson
Penguin, 1963
This contains reports of what parents really do and think.

Children and Parents
H. A. Peine and R. Howarth
Penguin, 1975
A practical approach to dealing with behaviour problems in ways which will make parent and child feel better.

The Feeling Child
A. Janov
Simon and Schuster, 1973
This book recognises the importance of feelings in experiences of living.

Children's Minds
Margaret Donaldson
Fontana, 1978
This book describes the development of children's minds and shows how often the abilities of the pre-school child can be under-estimated.

Twins
Carola Zentner
David and Charles, 1975
If you have twins, you will find this is a very useful book which deals comprehensively with all the interesting and practical aspects of twins and their development.

The Study of Twins
Peter Mittler
Penguin, 1971
A summary of research into twins with reference to intelligence, personality, and the physical aspects of development.

● *Learning through Play*
J. Marzollo and J. Lloyd
Allen and Unwin, 1974

● *Mother's Help*
S. Dickinson (ed)
Fontana, 1975

● *Child's Play*
Septima and Margett
Dent, 1969

● *All Sorts of Everything*
M. Carrick
Heinemann, 1975

● *Look, Do and Listen*
R. Ainsworth
Heinemann, 1969

● *Pre-School Play*
K. Jameson and P. Kidd
Studio Vista, 1974

Pre-school and Infant Art
K. Jameson
Studio Vista, 1968

Play with a Purpose
E. Matterson
Penguin, 1975

Sharing Sound
D. Evans
Longman, 1977

First Art
W. Farnworth
Evans, 1973

Children and Adults
J. and L. Braga
Prentice Hall, 1976
This is a handbook of varied games and ideas for children from birth till six years old.

Literature and the Young Child
J. Cass
Longman, 1967
This is about books and the part they play in an enjoyable introduction to reading.

This Little Puffin
E. Matterson
Penguin, 1969
A collection of rhymes, songs and finger plays.

Let's Play Maths
M. Holt and Z. Dienes
Penguin, 1973
Seventy thinking games for 4-11-year-olds. Useful for bored four-year-olds and for understanding the sort of maths he may be doing later at school.

Play – Its Role in Development and Evolution
J. S. Bruner, A. Jolley and K. Sylva (eds)
Penguin, 1976
This book contains wide-ranging articles covering play for children of different ages, for different periods of time, with various animals, etc.

Chapter 4
Everyday learning

Chapter 4

Everyday learning

'You can't run before you can walk!' In the mastering of a physical skill this idea is obvious enough. A look at how one such skill is learnt helps in the understanding of the way any kind of development takes place.

Stage by stage

Imagine the many stages of development your child has to master before he can run to meet you, for example. At each stage your care will have helped him on to the next stage, by giving him encouragement and opportunity.

In the first two stages below an example has been filled in. Read through these and then fill in the next three for your own child.

Stage 1

Cradled in arms baby.

Opportunity

Giving him things to look at, showing him a wider world.

Encouragement

Talking, moving things, giving him time to look long at things that interest him.

Stage 2

Sitting up baby.

Opportunity

Giving him a variety of things to play with while he is sitting up.

Encouragement

Laughing, smiling, playing games like covering things to make them disappear.

Stage 3

Starting to crawl.

Opportunity

Encouragement

Stage 4

Standing up.

Opportunity

Encouragement

Stage 5

The first steps.

Opportunity

Encouragement

Minds develop too

In what ways is the growth of knowledge and understanding similar to the development of physical skills?

Beside the statements below are two boxes, box A for the development of physical skills and box B for the growth of knowledge and understanding. Tick the boxes that you think apply to the statements. You can tick both A and B if you wish.

A   B

● A child must have mastered one stage before he can go on to the next ☐ ☐

● The challenge offered must be one that arouses his interest ☐ ☐

● It must be offered at a time when he feels like coping with it ☐ ☐

● Encouragement, reassurance and congratulation from parents matters to a child ☐ ☐

● Development comes in spurts, with an achievement being followed by a time when no progress seems to be made ☐ ☐

● There are times when a child appears to go back to an earlier stage ☐ ☐

● You cannot expect a child to do anything he is not yet ready to do ☐ ☐

In fact, all these statements apply to both areas of development for, although the changes in physical skills are more easily seen, the growth of understanding is clear only to those who watch and listen carefully to children as they learn about the world.

Learning how to encourage the growth of a child's understanding is helped by
● observing the stages through which children's thinking develops
● supporting the child's interests and feelings
● recognising the challenges he faces so that neither too much nor too little is expected of him.

In this chapter there will be a range of activities from which you can learn more about encouraging the growth of learning.

Probably you created similar opportunities and gave similar encouragement as Kevin's parents did:

For stage 3 Kevin's dad wrote under *Opportunity* – 'Placing toys out of arm's reach so that Kevin had to move his body to reach the toy.'

Under *Encouragement* he wrote – 'Smiles, cheers all round – moving the toy a little further away and then more encouragement.'

Similarly, for stage 4 opportunities were provided by various pieces of furniture and Kevin was encouraged by getting a better view and by people saying 'clever boy'. Opportunities for the first step (stage 5) were provided by one parent holding and the other encouraging Kevin to reach the other. Encouragement took the form of a good cuddle and a hug.

Each stage is followed by a period of enjoyment and exploration as the child becomes master of the new skill.

Progress is often erratic. A child learning to walk may not bother about talking, a spurt may be followed by a lull, sometimes he may return to stages you thought he had passed.

All I get is questions

Children ask questions to find out about their world and themselves. The kind of answers we give are important because they will help or hinder the child's learning.

Questions are all different

The form of children's questions gives us a very good window on the way in which they are learning to make sense of their experience.

Some questions ask for information

| 'Ssa ?=What's that ? What ? Where ? | → | Questions they ask almost as soon as they begin to talk |

| Who ? Which ? Why ? What for ? | → | Questions which begin during the third year |

| When ? How ? | → | Questions which begin when they are nearing school age |

Some questions ask about doing and sharing

| Can I ...? Shall I ...? Will you ...? | → | These appear during the third year and are about shared activities and what is allowed |

Some questions are ideas and thinking

| Is it ...? Do you ...? What if ...? What would happen if ...? | → | These questions begin nearer school age and ask for information, want confirmation of existing ideas, and ask for help with sorting out new ideas |

Listen to some of your child's questions

Try listening to your child talking for half an hour or so, over two or three days. Have paper and pencil handy wherever you are, so that questions asked while you are working can be jotted down. Don't worry about the exact wording of each question, but try to note *how the question started* and what it was about. After two or three days look at your list and put a tick in the appropriate box for each different sort of question.

Information questions

What ?	Where ?	Who ?	Which ?	Why ?	What for ?	When ?	How ?

Doing and sharing questions

Can ...?	Shall ...?	Will ...?

Ideas and thinking questions

Is it ?	Do you ?	What if ?	What would happen if ?

Developing questions

If your child is quite young, you may have found it difficult to know whether some questions really needed a tick. You know pretty well what your child means when he says 'You want eat biscuit?' or 'Why not me go out?' but they don't follow the patterns of adult questions.

Studies of children's language development have shown that there is a regular order in which children learning English master the various types of questions. So the development of questions provides a good rough and ready guide to a child's general progress in learning language. It is usually possible to pick out four stages:

Stage 1 Two- or three-word questions made up of a 'wh' word and the thing, or person, or action being asked about. 'What that ? Where Daddy ? What doing ?'

Stage 2 Longer questions but a lot is still left out. Lift of voice still often used.

'What you doing ? Where you put it ? Me do it ?'

Stage 3 Can, shall, will are now used. 'Wh' – questions with negatives still cause difficulty.
'Can I do it ?'
'Why he don't want it ?'
'Is it raining ?'

Stage 4 All simple question-types fully formed.
'Where's my coat ?'
'When are you going ?'
'Will I be able to go too ?'
'What if it rains ?'

Look again at your list of questions and the ticks you put in the boxes, and see if these tell you anything about the stage your child has reached. You may find, for example, that you have all simple 'wh' questions (Stage 1) or that your child is using 'can' but having trouble with 'why nots' (Stage 3). You may well find that your child's questions fall into more than one 'stage'. Language development is a continuous process with no sharp divisions between one stage and the next. You just need to keep listening.

Answering questions

Your child doesn't ask questions in a vacuum, he asks *you* or any other handy person. In fact, the first question 'What's that?' didn't occur to him on his own, he learnt it from you. 'What's that?' you probably said, pointing to the light or an apple or a toy.

'Who's that?' as Daddy or a brother or sister came into the room.

'Where's it gone?' when he dropped something on the floor.

> You were urging him to find names and give you answers, so his first questions are an imitation of yours. Your questions showed him a very powerful way to find out about his world. The answers you give and the kind of questions you ask will continue to be the model for the way he uses language as his most important method of discovery and learning.

What answer is wanted?

When you ask a question of another adult you usually know what sort of answer you want. Sometimes, a single word will do; at other times you want a full and detailed explanation. The same is true for children when they ask questions, though it is not always easy to know what is the most appropriate answer to a particular question. Here is a typical example of the sort of question that arises out of an incident in the kitchen. Consider what you might have said to William.

Mother is making a jelly and William is stirring the cubes:

Mother: The jelly's melting, look!

William: Why's it starting to melt?

Mother: Because it does ... the water's very hot and it makes jelly melt when it's very hot. (6 second pause)

William: Why's it making jelly melt – when it's very hot? Why does it? (6 second pause – Mother thinking)

Mother: Well because it does, that's why. Butter melts when it's very hot.

William: It's very cold now, isn't it?

Mother: It's cooler.

William wants a full explanation and his Mother is perplexed. A scientific explanation, even if she could give it, would be inappropriate. Yet her first answer 'because it does' seems likely to dampen his enthusiasm to try to find out why things happen as they do. However, she finds a way to give a helpful answer when she tells him about something similar that also melts – butter. He can move on from here to think about the effect of heat on other substances – and of cold, too, once the jelly has set.

Helpful and unhelpful answers

There is no one way to answer children's questions. But some types of answers are likely to be more *helpful* than others. A good general guide is to start from something that you know is familiar to the child and already quite well understood, and then to relate the present, problematic situation to that. Elizabeth (aged 4) is watching her Mother shovel the wood ash from the grate into a bucket.

Elizabeth: What are you doing that for?

Mother: I'm gathering it up and putting it outside so that Daddy can put it on the garden.

Elizabeth: Why does he have to put it on the garden?

Mother: To make the compost, right?

Elizabeth: Does that make the grass grow?

Mother: Yes.

Elizabeth: Why does it?

Mother: You know how I tell you that you need to eat different things like eggs and cabbage and rice pudding to make you grow into a big girl?

Elizabeth: Yes.

Mother: Well, plants need different foods too. And ash is one of the things that's good for them.

The trouble is that a long and involved answer may sometimes be just as off-putting to a child as the uninformative answer 'because I say so'.

So the only rule is to be guided by your child. The ideal answer should be an attempt to extend a child's thinking.

Answers can be seen as a way of helping children to speculate usefully and interestingly along a path they have begun to tread. The aim is to *develop* their thinking, not simply to hand over a package of information which may close the door they have just begun to open. Try not to say just 'yes' and 'no' – tell them some more, and maybe ask a question back.

Anytime, anywhere ... questions!
Shared activities – jelly-making in the kitchen, ash-clearing from the grate – provoke questions. Sharing books is important too. Pictures can be talk-starters, question-makers.

1 Read through this topic.
2 For about an hour each day, keep a list of your child's questions and your answers, on a note pad.
3 At the end of the week, use your list to fill in the chart opposite.

Find the column along the top that you think each question fits into, and then work down the side until you find the row that best fits your answer. Tick there.

The cartoon is an example. Use this for practice – for each question and its answer

tick the appropriate space in the chart. Obviously in real life, questions and answers don't put themselves nearly so neatly into boxes. The point is to be aware of the importance to the child's thinking of his questions and your answers.

Questions, questions, questions

As we saw overleaf, the form of children's questions changes as they get older. So do their reasons for asking. Reasons for questions are related to different aspects of the world in which they are growing up. We can divide questions roughly into 3 groups: *questions about the world children share with other people; questions about the way the world works;* and – very important at this age – *questions about the world of their imagination.*

Shared activities with your child allow questions to arise naturally out of what you are doing together – or simply out of being together. Questions about the world of imagination may arise apparently out of the blue – but they need answers and reassurance too. To the child they are just as important as his more factual or sharing questions.

Questions about the world children share with other people

Children are born into family groups large or small, which they must learn to fit into. They must learn to share their thoughts and feelings and conform to rules. They ask questions to discover what is approved of and what is forbidden.
   Can I . . .?
   Shall I . . .?
   They ask questions about shared activities and people's intentions,
   Shall we . . .?
   What shall we do?
   When will we . . .?
   These questions help them to understand how they fit in with other people.

Questions about the way the world works

Children ask questions about what objects are for and what they are made of.

Why is that sharp?
Where do crisps come from?
They ask about what people are doing and who does what.
Where's Daddy gone?
What is that lady holding?

They ask about the relationship between events – what causes events to happen, and what consequences follow from actions.
What happens on my birthday?
Why did Susan fall over?
What would happen if I dropped it in the bath?

Questions about the world of their imagination

For children, the distinction between what is real and what is imaginary is blurred. In their play they act out a simulation of the adult world – mothers and fathers, doctors and nurses – and learn about it as they do so. Questions about witches and ghosts and a wide range of fantastic and improbable fictional happenings need to be treated quite as seriously as questions needing more factual explanation. They are a window into the child's inner world of feeling and imagination. They reveal both his fears and his pleasures and often, a need for reassurance about the feared thing. (See *Bathtime* in Chapter 1, pages 22–3.)
   What would happen if a wolf came out of the forest?
   What if a crab came up the plughole?

These questions are not like Elizabeth's and William's but the answers they receive will be just as important in contributing to their understanding of themselves and their world.

Answers and more answers!

The boundaries between the social physical and imaginary worlds are never clear-cut. But in our answers to children we can point out some of the differences.

What all their questions have in common is the desire to gain control over their lives by understanding how the world functions and what effects their actions can produce on it. They ask about particular objects and events in order to build up a basis of concrete examples to which they can apply general rules.

So we need to be aware of the need for both particular and general types of information in the answers that we give. Explaining general principles may be useful. For example, the principle illustrated in the cartoon is that when you go into the water you get wet, or worse. It can also be helpful to refer to something similar that is a familiar example of what you are trying to explain.

The kind of answers we give will almost certainly determine the kind of questions children ask. It is interesting to look at our answers and see how far we actually do encourage question-asking.

The 'questions and answers' activity on these pages asks you to keep a record of your attempts to encourage question-asking. There are two ways in which you can try to encourage most questions. First, whenever your child asks a question try to make your answer as appropriate as you can to the reason you believe to be behind it. Second, ask your child more questions of the kind that you wish to encourage. But make sure that they are genuine questions, not just tests of what he already knows or what he knows you know.

Questions can help the child work out an answer for himself, for example the mother in the cartoon might have asked 'Why do you think people who can't swim should keep away from water?'

Giving a helpful answer isn't always easy. No parent has the time, knowledge or skill to get it right everytime. What's important is that you encourage questions rather than dodge them.

Your answers	Child's questions		
	Shared world	Way world works	World of imagination
1 Just 'Yes' or 'No'		✓ ✓	
2 With information only			
3 By giving information and/or additional explanation or examples (specific or general)		✓	
4 By asking your child a question back, which might help him formulate an answer for himself		✓	
5 By referring to something similar as another example of what you're trying to explain	✓		
6 By trying to explain a general principle		✓	
7 By changing the subject, or some other 'dodge' – for example, 'Because I say so'			✓

● Did your child ask questions of all three broad types? If not, can you think why he didn't and how you might encourage him to do so.

● How many answers of each type did you give? Some answers may be more helpful than others (3, 4, 5, 6) – but then again sometimes only 'yes' or 'no' is required. Let your child be your guide.

● How did you cope with questions arising from your child's imaginative experience, for example reading aloud, watching TV? What do *you* find is the best means of reassurance?

Cartoon answers

First picture – the child's question is about the way the world works and the mother's answer is information only.

Second picture – the child's question is about the way the world works and the mother answers by giving information and additional explanation or examples.

Third picture – the child's question is in the same category and the mother answers by asking the child a question in return.

Fourth picture – a question is not asked here.

Fifth picture – again the child's question is about the way the world works but the mother's answer is just 'Yes'.

Sixth picture – this is 'shared world' for the child – the mother answers by referring to something similar as another example of what she is trying to explain.

Seventh picture – the child's question is 'way world works' and the mother answers by trying to explain a general principle.

Eighth picture – here the child's question is about the world of imagination and the mother answers by changing the subject.

Male and Female

'Oh well, boys will be boys.'
'She's a real tomboy – I hope she grows out of it.'
'He's mechanical – just like his Dad.'

These are comments from parents about the way they see their children in male-female terms. How do boys and girls come to be as they are? How much influence do parents really have?

Everyone knows that men and women are different. But *how* different are they? The physical sex differences are obvious and constant, but they are overlaid with a whole set of qualities - the appearance and behaviour we call masculine or feminine. And it is not so much the body which determines these characteristics as the place and times people live in.

Who does what?

Tick whether the male or female in your household mainly does the following things. If they are equally shared, tick both columns.

	M	F
cooks	☐	☐
cleans	☐	☐
decorates	☐	☐
sews	☐	☐
plays outdoor games	☐	☐
wears attractive clothes	☐	☐
uses library	☐	☐
shops	☐	☐
manages money	☐	☐
washes up	☐	☐
changes plugs	☐	☐
repairs house or car	☐	☐
looks after children	☐	☐
earns money	☐	☐

There's no physical reason why both sexes shouldn't do all these things – and most others – but in practice the division of labour in any household is usually based on child-care and jobs.

Who is what?

Tick the qualities you think describe each of you. You can again tick for both or leave a blank for neither.

	M	F
clever	☐	☐
practical	☐	☐
decisive	☐	☐
good with money	☐	☐
strong	☐	☐
loyal	☐	☐
tough	☐	☐
kind	☐	☐
patient	☐	☐
shy	☐	☐
emotional	☐	☐
good with children	☐	☐
talkative	☐	☐
soft	☐	☐

All these are human qualities, but the first seven belong to the 'typical male', the last seven to the 'typical female'. In practice again, many people cross the columns showing that the sexes have qualities in common.

News and views

Tick which of the following would annoy or please you.

	Annoy	Please
Being sent blue-for-a-boy gifts at the birth of a son	☐	☐
A neighbour's son wearing a kilt	☐	☐
Your daughter choosing to be an engineer	☐	☐
Your son choosing to be a secretary	☐	☐
A woman Prime Minister	☐	☐
The Miss World contest	☐	☐
The Equal Pay Act	☐	☐
The headline: 'No unemployment if married women banned from working'	☐	☐

While in principle you may welcome equal pay, it's another thing to encourage your son in his wish to do what is often called a woman's job. Your ticks should show whether you're pleased by 'conventional' news and views of men and women, or whether you prefer greater equality between the sexes.

Some items you may think are unimportant, but they're part of everyday life which shape your own and your children's views.

You and your children

You have your tasks, qualities and views, which may be more or less like the 'typical' man or woman's. Is your child going to copy these?

Often you give your child a model to follow saying in effect 'act like me' or at least 'do as I say'. Your demands are usually met, as your child soon learns that you have the power to enforce them. Parents also encourage children generally to act like a boy – 'boys don't cry' – or be more like a girl – 'girls don't fight'. The important thing is that demands should be matched to the child's level of thinking – you can't successfully appeal to a toddler's sense of fairness, or expect a boy to 'act like a boy' until he has some ideas of what boys in general and himself as a boy are like.

Children don't just model themselves on anyone, nor do they copy everything about one person. Obviously, parents, and especially mother, is a convenient model and is always at hand. Children of both sexes will watch their mother and copy the way she does the household chores. Also boys and girls will copy things father does, particularly interesting things like jobs around the house. The trouble is they don't always copy the things about you that you'd like them to – they copy some of your bad habits as well.

If parents lose their tempers or shout at a child or at one another, their children will often copy this in the way they in turn deal with their parents and other children. Similarly with smacking – children learn to do as they are done by. It is in a child's own family where he learns most about himself, family life, married life and male and female roles.

Q1 When your children and your friends' children were babies, did you find that (tick yes or no):

	Yes	No
(a) boys were more irritable than girls	☐	☐
(b) boys were more active and often 'naughtier'	☐	☐
(c) you cuddled boys more	☐	☐
(d) you talked to girls more	☐	☐

One of the first questions asked after the birth of a baby is 'Is it a boy or a girl?... so as to know whether to say 'she's pretty' or 'he's handsome'. Baby boys may be a little more irritable and more active than girls. But the parents' different reactions to boys or girls, in the way they handle and talk to them, and direct their attention, may turn a small inborn sex difference into a much larger learnt difference. For example, mothers tend to handle boys more, but talk to and fuss over girls more, even though they are less irritable.

Q2 Tick the 4 toys from this list your son or daughter would choose, given the chance:

	son	daughter
cooking set	☐	☐
doll	☐	☐
doll's house	☐	☐
brush and pan	☐	☐
cap gun	☐	☐
hammer and nails	☐	☐
model car	☐	☐
Meccano	☐	☐

The first four toys are 'typically' girls' choices, the last four are 'typically' boys'. Your children probably cross the columns at least occasionally. But even though a girl plays with a cap gun, she may be learning from you and her friends, the television and so on that it's really a 'boy's toy'.

Q3 Tick which of the following descriptions seem to fit mostly boys or mostly girls. If the descriptions fit both boys and girls tick both boxes:

	boys	girls
(a) get into fights	☐	☐
(b) do things with their hands	☐	☐
(c) prefer doing things with daddy	☐	☐
(d) play women in 'mother and father' games	☐	☐
(e) are talkative	☐	☐
(f) prefer helping in the home	☐	☐

Statements (a) – (c) and (d) – (f) are 'typical' expectations of what boys and girls are like. Again, they're unlikely to be true of individual children all the time – and may even be the opposite. But again, parents and others often direct children's attention to different activities, and 'draw the line' differently – for example, boys may be allowed to be rougher than girls.

Q4   Notes

(a) Ask your son/daughter how he/she knows he/she's a boy/girl.

(b) Then pick out strangers and friends and ask 'Is that person a man or woman? Why?'

(c) How does your child tell the differences between males and females – genitals, looks, clothes, behaviour – or what?

Children's interests and activities tend to get more typically 'boyish' or 'girlish' as their ideas develop about which sex they belong to and what is considered appropriate to that sex. Tests with pre-school children show in fact that their sex-labelling (man/woman) is based hardly at all on sex organs, but on qualities such as clothing, hairstyle, and what people do. So – to be male is to be 'masculine', as that is defined in the child's world.

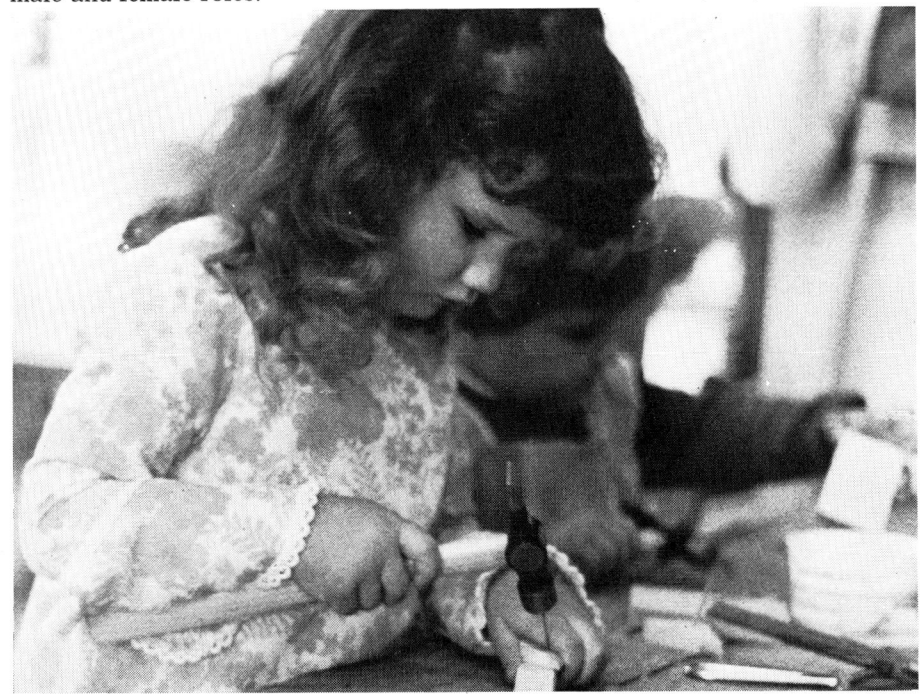

> ### Children's lib . . .
>
> So in the end, what influence do parents have? Quite a lot – depending on their power as models and their power to reward or enforce.
>
> At the same time the child is 'active' in the sense of selecting models which appeal to him, and in developing his/her own ideas about what's male and what's female. So make sure your children have contact with a wide range of adults.
>
> In today's world we can see signs of strain in both 'masculine' men and 'feminine' women. Frustrated mothers on tranquillizers, bored men tied to jobs with ulcers or killing heart diseases may be signs of the times. A straight swap wouldn't do much. More sharing and flexibility of roles might.

Tidying up

So what's 'educational' or even interesting about tidying? Nothing, you might think to begin with, but let's look at the educational interest of tidying a drawer . . . and then try doing one with your child.

First choose the drawer. The more cluttered and untidy, the more interesting the work will be. The example chosen is a kitchen drawer, but any drawer will do.

Then choose a good time. This is morning work, to be introduced when your child is fresh. This is a pleasurable and satisfying pastime, to be done when nothing else is happening.

His part

Remember what it feels like to share a piece of work with someone who can do it far better than you. You want to try to do something, but are not allowed to have a go. Your attempts are clumsy and the job is taken out of your hands and done by the expert.

If your child is to have 'job satisfaction' from this piece of work, it is worth thinking about what part he can play on his own – and what you can be doing nearby to encourage and help as needed. How much he can do depends on his age and experience and this is something you must judge from your knowledge of your child – as long as you are prepared to find that he may be able to do more, or less, than you expect.

Where do we start?

You may decide to start him off at the kitchen table while you are washing-up the breakfast things. What help and materials will he be needing during the following stages?

The sequence will show you how much your child knows or can do at this stage and gives an idea of the sort of learning that arises from such a situation. While emptying the drawer, you can discuss the names of things and what they are made of, letting your child tell you as much as he can before you help him. For instance, if 'What is that spoon made of?' gets no answer, or a wrong answer, try 'Which spoon is made of wood?' or 'Which are the spoons?'

1 **Settling him down:** a work top at a good height, for example a table with a chair drawn up sideways, so that it gives him a handrail as he stands up to work

2 **Emptying the drawer:** a tray or clear surface for the contents, put within easy reach

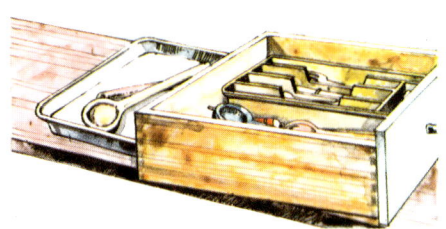

3 **Washing the drawer:** detergent, cloth or sponge, a bowl with a little water, help with the rolling up of his sleeves and an apron or cloth tied under his armpits

4 **Putting things back:** sorting advice

5 **Putting the drawer back in its place:** help in carrying it

What is learnt?

Washing the drawer calls for a number of skills like . . . squeezing a little water into the drawer, then putting in a little detergent and scrubbing around with a cloth or sponge, squeezing water out of the sponge or wringing it out of the cloth and wiping the drawer dry.

This is more than a two-year-old could manage, but is easy for a four-year-old!

Putting things back in the drawer is an opportunity for sorting and counting (see *Launder and learn* in Chapter 3 for the value of this kind of game). If you introduce counting and sorting in a variety of ways your child will have a better grasp of the meaning of numbers and the exercise of sorting.

Putting back the tidied drawer is something that a child will find satisfying. The work – or is it play – of cleaning out a drawer will enlarge his experience of his home.

See how drawer tidying goes with your child and compare progress when you do the job again in a few months.

Emptying the drawer

Does your child know the names of the different things in the drawer . . . ?
Put a cross for 'no' and a tick for 'yes'.

	Your Child	Jenny (2½)	Sarah (4)
tablespoon		X	X
desertspoon		X	X
teaspoon		X	✓
knives		✓	✓
forks		✓	✓

Does he know the names of the different materials things are made from?

metal		X	X
plastic		X	✓
wood		✓	✓

If you put spoons made of these different materials onto his cheek, when his eyes are closed, can he recognise the different materials?

metal		✓	✓
plastic		X	✓
wood		✓	✓

Can he count the number of prongs on the forks? ☐ X ✓

Can he tell the cutting edge of the knife from the blunt edge? ☐ ✓ ✓

Does he know which parts of the knife would hurt him?

the point		✓	✓
the cutting edge		✓	✓

Washing the drawer

Did he start and not get very far so that you had to finish? ☐ ✓ X

Did he do the job in such a way that you had to show him how to finish it? ☐ ✓ ✓

Did he finish the job well enough to be congratulated? ☐ X ✓

Putting things back

Did he put everything back in a muddle? ☐ X X

Did he sort things properly, for example, spoons, forks, etc. together?

partly		✓	✓
entirely		X	X

Did he sort things into sizes, for example, tablespoons, teaspoons, etc. together?

partly		✓	✓
entirely		X	X

Did he show he could count up to:

three		✓	✓
five		X	✓
eight		X	✓
ten ?		X	✓

Did he carry on until the job was completely finished? ☐ X ✓

The activity is not a test to show whether your child is 'better' or 'worse' than you might expect him to be! You will have found, by doing it, what he knows or doesn't know . . . and how a simple activity can offer many kinds of learning. Just as Sarah knew more, could do more than Jenny, you will probably find after some time, your child's knowledge and understanding will have passed through more stages. This will be reflected in the way in which he answers the same questions.

Where this can go wrong

Some parents who try this exercise will certainly find that they have failed to hold their child's interest and feel that nothing has been learnt. If the main aim of this educational exercise is finding some way for your child to be involved with you in a necessary job, however slight his contribution may be, what compromises would you suggest?

● 'Perhaps this isn't a good time to start on this job.'

● 'I'll just wipe the corners of the drawer and take a few of the untidy things away. Then we can give it a proper tidy another day.'

Perhaps the child was not interested in doing the job at the time, or there was a rival attraction, or the job proved to be more than he could cope with. This compromise lets you both off without dodging your responsibilities!

● 'Do it because I say so!'

A sure way to antagonise a child and make it unlikely that he will want to join you another time.

● 'Let's get the job finished quickly so that we can go out for a swing.'

An attitude which shows that you identify yourself with your child's feelings but manage to slip in just a little of the obligation you feel.

● '*Little* children would take half an hour to do this job. Do you think you could get it done properly in, say, a *quarter* of an hour?'

A challenge for a big child that tests his capability. Can you think of more ways in which you could draw a child in to giving a little help?

Messy and dirty?

In the course of living with young children, situations in which adult and child have different attitudes and reactions often occur. A child can only begin slowly, and after many mistakes, learn to understand adult values. He does not have the command of language that would make it possible for him to explain his attitudes and feelings – his behaviour must speak for him.

Have you noticed how your child will sometimes imitate your gestures, phrases and expressions? The way you approach tidying a drawer is just one of many examples of the events which will influence the development of your child's attitude to mess, dirt and a job of work.

Once you start child-watching, you will often see children 'dressing-up' in their parents' speech, manners and reactions in just the same way as they try on their shoes and hats.

Think about your child when he was younger – hitting or banging a lid was great fun. Hammering nails, and other simple woodwork, provides a similar kind of play, with the extra interest and challenge that 3- and 4-year-olds will enjoy. They'll be learning too, about shapes and sizes, about how to judge by eye and how to control the arm and hand.

Unlike many other sorts of play, such as drawing or water play, carpentry requires the development of definite skills in a safe and correct way. You should always be around when woodwork tools are out – don't just leave your child to get on. If you can introduce the use of tools in easy stages you'll find your child soon learns to be both skilled and safe.

All carpentry involves the eye, the hand and the arm. Let's start with hammering, the easiest, and see what skills it involves.

Hammering skills

Skill of eye: Judgement

Choosing the right length of nail for the thickness of the wood (for example, a 1″ for 1¼″ wood) and placing it in position.

Skill of hand and arm: Large movement

Gripping the hammer with the other hand and swinging it.

Skill of fingers: Fine control

Holding nail in position between the finger and thumb of one hand.

Skill of eye and hand: Co-ordination

Hitting the nail on the head.

We can use this knowledge to build up five stages of hammering which will help your child to meet with success and not a banged thumb on his first attempt.

If your child resists any attempt by you to help him you'll have to judge whether it's safe enough for him to continue on his own. However, it is always safer to keep a watchful eye on him.

Your child can work through the following stages with your help. Tick the stages he can do now, and write in, from the list above, the hand, eye and arm skills which are involved for the child at each stage.

WOODWORK

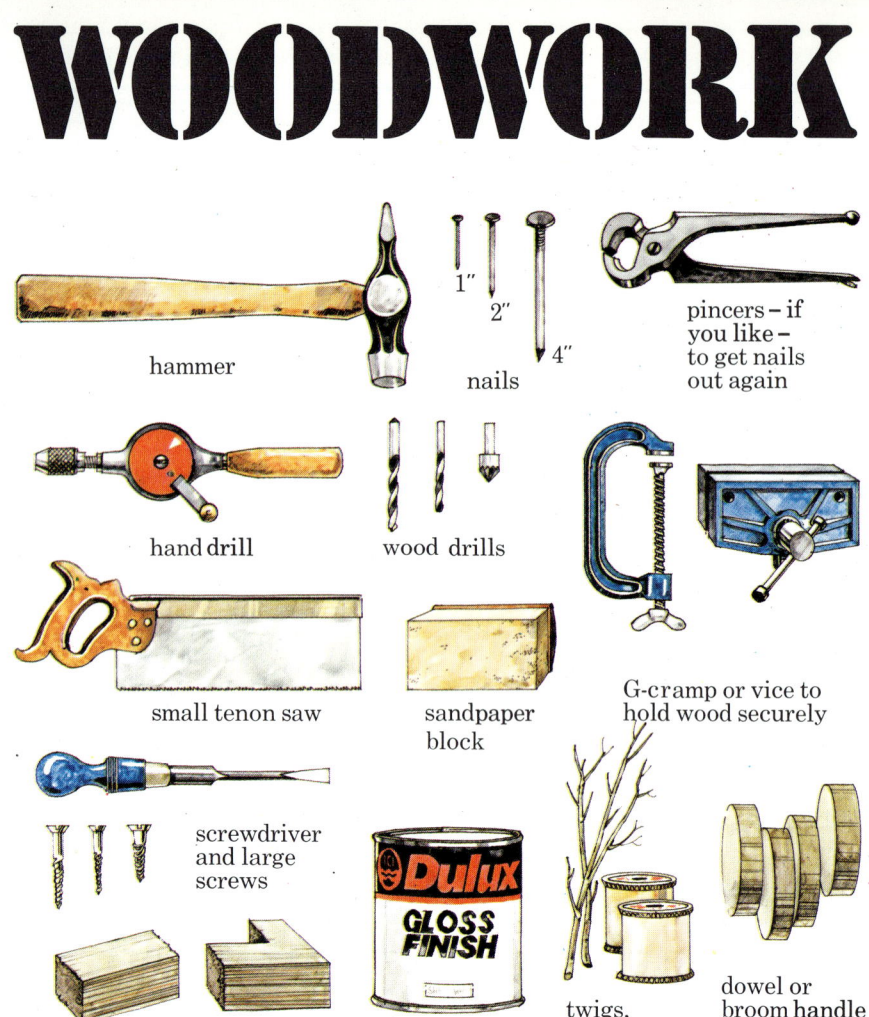

hammer

nails — 1″ 2″ 4″

pincers – if you like – to get nails out again

hand drill

wood drills

G-cramp or vice to hold wood securely

small tenon saw

sandpaper block

screwdriver and large screws

paint

twigs, cotton reels etc.

dowel or broom handle in slices for wheels

softwood offcuts

These are the basic tools and materials for your child. Tools should be 'real' – junior tool kits can be unsatisfactory and aren't really necessary.

You don't need a lot of tools or skill to make simple wooden toys.

Why not have a go yourself? Your child may like to help you, or even make them himself. Remember, though, while *you* may have the aim of a finished toy in view, your child will probably at first just be interested in the tools, and how they work.

Stage of hammering	Can your child do it?	Skills involved for child
1 *Adult* chooses and positions nail, and hammers it part way into a single piece of wood. *Child* completes hammering.		
2 *Adult* chooses, positions and holds nail. *Child* hammers it from the start.		
3 *Adult* chooses nail and positions it. *Child* holds nail and hammers it.		
4 *Child* chooses nail, positions it, holds it and hammers it into a single piece of wood.		
5 *Child* chooses *his* pieces of wood to be joined and the nail, positions, holds and hammers them together.		

Sawing

As yet there's no question of a child making anything. He is still learning to use a tool correctly, and experimenting. But when he is putting two pieces of wood together – he may name what he has made. Two pieces crossed may become an aeroplane or a sword, one piece on top of another may become a boat.

The next stage will come when he selects pieces of wood with a purpose in mind. 'I'm going to make a ship – this bit will go on the water, this is the top and this is the funnel.' Finally he will saw the wood to the shape he needs, with a picture of the finished product in his mind, but this will come only after much experimenting and experience. (Even in the early stages though your child will enjoy sanding the wood he is using and will soon recognise the difference in the feel of rough and smooth wood.)

So, sawing can be an end in itself, for the fun of it, or it can be a means to making something. Let your child decide which it's to be – but again you can help him to become safe and skilled.

Safe sawing

The three things to remember about sawing are:
● the wood should be held securely in a vice or cramp (a piece of wood held by hand is more tiring to saw and more likely to result in cut fingers)
● keep an eye on the hand that isn't sawing – though some children find it easier to use two hands on the saw
● a saw cut is started most easily by a few small backwards movements; after that the saw should cut on the forward movement only, in a steady rhythm.

Drilling

When your child can handle a hammer and saw with confidence and skill, a hand-drill and screwdriver should be easy. For drilling, the stages you guide him through are the same as for sawing (change 'saw cut' to 'drill hole' in the chart below). Turning a screw requires more skill than simply hammering, but again the stages are the same – just change 'hammer' and 'nail' to 'screwdriver' and 'screw' in the chart on the opposite page.

Stages 1 and 2 involve for your child large movement and eye-hand co-ordination. (It's harder to hammer a nail in from the start, because it may wobble until it has really got into the wood.) Stage 3 adds fine control – holding the nail – to the large movement of hand and arm and the co-ordination of hand and eye. Stage 4 adds judgement of the eye as well. Stage 5 involves the extra judgement of seeing that the nail must be long enough to go right through the first piece of wood and well into the second, to join them.

Stage of sawing	Skill involved	Tick if your child can do it
1 Finish off a started saw cut on wood chosen and cramped by an adult.	Large movement of hand and arm and hand and eye co-ordination to get saw cut through.	
2 Starts and completes own saw cut on wood chosen and cramped by adult.	As above, plus fine control to begin the saw cut.	
3 Choose wood, cramp it, and saw it.	As above, plus judgement in choosing wood and position of cut and checking securely cramped.	

As you can see in this chart, sawing involves the same sort of graded stages as hammering. As the child's skills increase, you can decrease your help.

Tick the stages your child can achieve, first with thin, narrow wood (about 1 inch wide, ½ inch thick) and then with thicker or wider wood.

WOODWORK
A child's understanding of length

A child experiences the judging of length in many ways – trying on a sweater for size, playing with different size bricks, watching you trying to fit a piece of furniture where you want it.

He also gets some confusions – even though the distance to the shops is always the same, it feels longer or shorter depending whether you walk, take the bus or drive.

It takes time for a child to become secure in his ideas about length and distance, and not to be led astray by his feelings or his eyes. Try this test – suitable for 3–7 year olds.

What to do: Find two pieces of wire (or thin string) of different lengths. For the first three questions the longer piece must be bent so that its ends are level with those of the shorter piece. For the last question, you'll need to straighten the longer piece out, as shown. Follow the instructions, filling in your child's judgements in the table opposite. Don't give clues when he's wrong – just move on to the next question. Then fill in for Andy, Brian and Carol, for comparison.

1 Ask the child: 'Are these the same length or is one longer than the other?' (Ask 'which one' if necessary.)

2 Ask the child to run his finger along the two lengths and then repeat question 1.

3 Ask the child: 'If 2 ants walked along each of these pieces which would take longer?'

4 Stretch the longer piece to its actual length and repeat question 1.

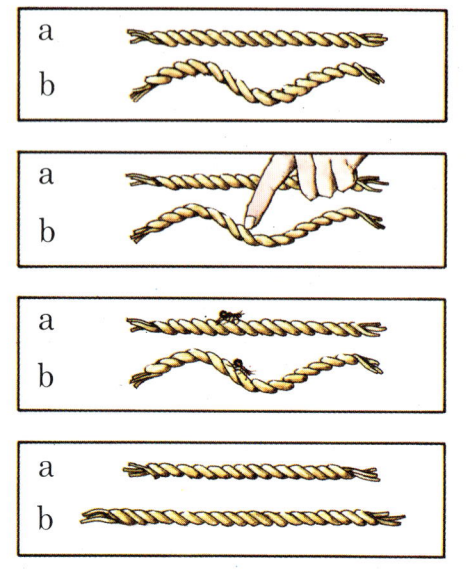
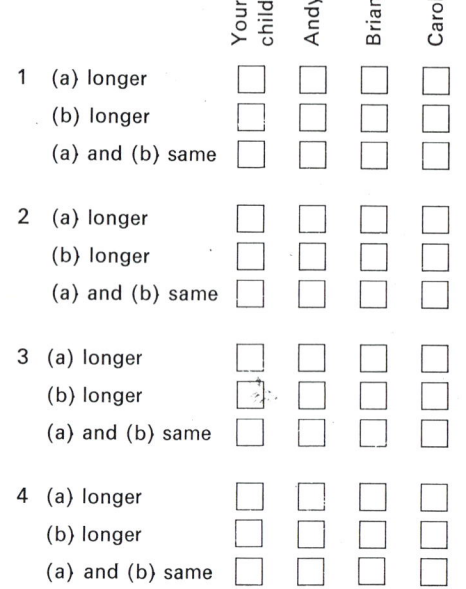

		Your child	Andy	Brian	Carol
1	(a) longer	☐	☐	☐	☐
	(b) longer	☐	☐	☐	☐
	(a) and (b) same	☐	☐	☐	☐
2	(a) longer	☐	☐	☐	☐
	(b) longer	☐	☐	☐	☐
	(a) and (b) same	☐	☐	☐	☐
3	(a) longer	☐	☐	☐	☐
	(b) longer	☐	☐	☐	☐
	(a) and (b) same	☐	☐	☐	☐
4	(a) longer	☐	☐	☐	☐
	(b) longer	☐	☐	☐	☐
	(a) and (b) same	☐	☐	☐	☐

Andy (just 4) says 'both the same' to question 1, '(b) is longer' for 2, 'it's the same for both' to question 3, and '(b) is longer' for question 4.

Brian (4½) says '(b)'s shorter because it's twisted' to questions 1 and 2, can't answer 3, but says '(b) is longer' for question 4.

Carol (5) says 'same' pointing to the level ends of (a) and (b), to question 1, but '(b)'s longer' for questions 2, 3 and 4.

The answer should be that 'b' is longer in every case but neither Andy, Brian or Carol – nor your children if they judged the lengths wrongly – are being stupid. Most children are correctly aware of the difference in length in question 4 – all they have to do is trust their eyes. Questions 1 – 3 are much harder, because they ask the child to trust his ideas, rather than his eyes. He has to work out that (b) is twisted, and therefore really the longer piece, even though the ends of (a) and (b) are level to the eye.

Andy, Brian and Carol all got question 4 right. But their answers to questions 1 – 3 show their ideas are much less secure. We learn something about the way they're thinking from their judgement (same, (a) longer, (b) longer) but this could be luck.

So the *reasons* they give for their judgements are important, too.

On question 1, Andy and Carol saw the level ends and judged (a) and (b) to be the same – Carol even pointed at the level ends. Questions 2 and 3 were meant to help the children 'stop and think'. Physically touching and then thinking about the ants seemed to help Carol, who got both these questions right. Touching helped Andy on question 2, but he couldn't use what he'd found out by touch to get the ants question right.

Brian is the least clear what it's all about. On question 1 he says '(b)'s shorter because it's twisted'. He seems to think length is to do with straightness. Touch doesn't help him discover the error, and the ants just puzzle him.

So – Andy, Brian and Carol are all developing ideas about length, but they are pretty insecure as yet. On another day Carol might be more like Andy or even Brian. If you press 'why' to get a reason for their judgement, at this age children will often change their answers – they're not sure enough of their own ideas to stick to their guns.

Ideas grow out of many practical experiences. Carpentry includes lots of measuring, judging, comparing and matching of lengths. So does playing with bricks – or sewing, or walking straight and wavy lines. Words which describe what's going on, and simple questions can help too. Children aren't stupid little adults – they need experience and encouragement to develop their ideas.

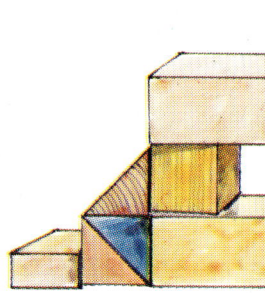

THEY PLAY, YOU PAY

Wooden toys are solid and strong and good to feel – but they're not cheap. You may be pleased with the garage or doll's house you've bought. But in the long run, is it the best play-value for your money?

These days you can also buy simple building 'shells' like the one in the picture. The building shell may not be as attractive as the dolls house to the adult eye – but it's the child's eye and imagination that matter. What do they look like from a child's point of view?

Fill in the table with a tick for 'yes' when you think a child could do the things suggested with the doll's house and/or the building shell.

	Dolls house	Building shell
Use it as a bungalow	☐	☐
Re-arrange furniture and rooms	☐	☐
Paper walls and add lights	☐	☐
Use it as a shop, or theatre	☐	☐
Use it as a garage with pumps and cars	☐	☐
Use it as a farm	☐	☐
Use it as a boat	☐	☐

You probably gave the building shell more ticks, because in fact it can be used in more varied ways than a straightforward doll's house. A house or a garage, a zoo or a farm, is designed to be just that. The child knows what it's supposed to be and plays accordingly. The shell is not so 'obvious'. It doesn't restrict play. The child can use his imagination to make it whatever he wants on a particular day – even something as improbable as a Noah's Ark – by pretending and adding whatever 'props' are needed, such as cars, or animals, or dolls. Girls may still use a shell mainly as a house, and boys mainly as a garage. But both have more choice than being put off or attracted to a toy that is traditionally 'for boys' or 'for girls'.

BUILDING BLOCKS

So, one or two building shells with 'props' can be very good play value for your money. So too can a set of wooden building blocks, for the same reasons. They don't 'tell' the child how he should play with them – they can be whatever he wants. They can be used to make things, like towers, or simply patterns. They're instantly changeable, too – one swipe of the arm and the tower's gone. And both boys and girls will play happily with them.

When you buy or make a set of bricks it helps to have the different sizes based on a standard block, as in the picture. This way your child can find out, for example, that two small square ones, or two long thin ones, make one long big one – a painless beginning to important mathematics later on at school. But if the bricks are any old size, then the child can't experiment with relationships of size and shape in this way.

Remember too that building blocks don't all have to be square-ish – if you can't find round ones, tins from the larder won't come to any harm, and will add variety.

Building block games

With a good set of building blocks your child will experiment naturally. If needed, you can help play along by introducing some new or more difficult games, such as these.

● take a standard brick and show how it can be made up from smaller bricks (see above). Then help your child to find out all the other ways he can make a shape that matches the standard brick.

● build a simple tower with all the same size bricks and ask your child to build one just like yours, with the same number of bricks. Does he match it by eye, or by counting the bricks, or both?

● when he succeeds with the simple tower, make it harder, with more bricks, of different lengths.

● build a wall, or steps, and ask him to copy it. You can count the bricks and help him with the different sizes if he gets stuck.

● make a pattern of the bricks on the floor – you copy his for a change!

COOKING

'They can't cook at this age!' They can – but it takes time and practice to learn even simple cooking skills. Hands and eyes, taste and smell, amount and time are all involved.

Your kitchen is your child's first science laboratory. What happens if . . .? How can I . . .? Why does it . . .? Talking helps your child use words, as well as actions, to find out about the world.

Can he really make a cake?

Here's a tried and tested simple recipe for apple cake, broken down into child-sized stages. First go through now and tick what you think your child can do safely and well. Then when you've got some cooking time together, work through the recipe step by step and tick what he actually can do.

You'll need:

2 eggs; weight of eggs in sugar; weight of eggs in self-raising flour; 1½ lbs cooking apples; greased 8 inch baking tin; oven at 350° (Mark 4).

Can your child . . .?:	Tick if you *think* child can	Tick if child actually can	Some ideas which may help	Comments
Ingredients				By the age of five, an experienced child can probably do just about everything. But even simple skills need time and practice to develop. The two hardest parts (apart from waiting till it's ready to eat!) are probably:
1 Get the ingredients out			**Steps 3 and 4**	
2 Count two eggs			If your child can't read the numbers, try putting a finger to mark the weight of the eggs and say the sugar and flour must make the arrow point at your finger.	● the steps which need fine control of the hands and fingers – cracking eggs, handling the knife, lightly greasing the tin. As we've seen, this sort of fine control develops later than large movements (see *Mealtimes* – Chapter 1). But you can 'grade' cutting – soft fruit like bananas, then apples, then hard carrots.
3 Weigh the eggs				
4 Weigh out the weight of the eggs in sugar and in flour (keep separate) and then weigh the apples				
5 Peel the apples			**Steps 5, 6 and 7**	
6 Core the apples			Slicing is easier (and safer) than peeling or coring, particularly if you hold the apple on a board and keep an eye on the non-cutting hand.	● weighing – this is hard for the child to understand. We'll be looking later on at young children's ideas about weight and volume, and how you can help their understanding.
7 Slice the apples into wedges				
Mixing				
8 Choose mixing bowl				Because children's skills – and often their concentration – are limited, it makes sense for you to plan ahead for joint cooking projects. Whether it's a stew, or a cake, or pastry, break it down into small steps like you've done here, and let your child help where he can. Naturally you talked while you worked together – but what happened? Do you think your answers were helpful? Did you have trouble with instructions? Talk is the most essential ingredient in cooking together, but not always the easiest one to get just right for 'quantity' and 'quality' – what you say and how you put it. In this chapter *All I get is questions* and *Instructions and explanations*, may give you some more ideas on this.
9 Crack eggs into it			**Steps 11, 12 and 15**	
10 Tip in sugar from scales			You could hold the bowl while your child beats, stirs, pours and scrapes. For general safety:	
11 Beat eggs and sugar together			● A non-slip surface to chop and stir on helps – try a damp cloth under the board or bowl.	
12 Stir in flour (mix should be sticky and smooth)			● A chair with its back to the table helps your child get safely to the right height for working.	
13 Find baking tin				
14 Lightly grease tin				
15 Pour mix into tin				
16 Wedge apple pieces in mix				
Cooking				
17 Set oven temperature			**Step 17**	
18 Place on oven shelf			Again, put your finger on the heat number and say it must go round till your finger's at the top.	
19 Judge when ready				
20 Take out of oven and eat it!				

MAKING LINKS

When your child cooks something, however simple it is, he's learning about 'cause and effect'. He's learning that his actions bring about a difference: 'When I put the chocolate in it goes brown.'

He knows he did it, but at the same time the change seems to happen almost by magic. The questions start as your child tries to find out what really happened. 'Where did the jelly go?' 'Why does it set when it's cold?'

Finding the answers that will satisfy your child isn't always easy – you just need to keep trying, like William's mother (in *All I get is questions*). Often, comparing it with something else he knows about will help, or you can try to explain what 'heat' or 'whipping', for example, do to things as a general rule. (Would it be so bad if you had to admit you really didn't know why something happens – but say you'll try and find out?)

Other questions ask for confirmation – Yes or No – with an explanation if it's needed. 'Can I take it out now?' 'Have I beaten enough?'

Still other questions arise as your child begins to use words to help him think about what will happen next. 'What if I . . .?' 'Do we do this now?' 'What would happen if we didn't put the salt in?' Here your child is trying to predict the immediate future, and is considering alternatives, drawing on what he remembers from past cooking sessions.

Food for thought

To avoid getting caught on the hop, it's worth thinking around how you could try to answer cooking questions helpfully. Listening to questions, and the 'cooking' words your child uses will give you some kind of guide as to how much your child is using words to name or ask about the 'basics' and how much to predict what will happen.

How much is your child asking:

● 'information' questions?

● 'doing' questions?

● 'ideas' questions?

Often it's not just an answer your child needs but more experience. It's only from 'doing and talking' that your child can build up general rules about the effects of heat, or see how two processes are similar, and so on. To see the complexity of cooking from your child's point of view, think about these four questions. How could you provide the experience and the words which may help your child understand the processes and the nature of the ingredients involved in cooking?

● How many ways do we use heat in cooking (for example melt, boil) to bring about different results? Can you explain them?

● How many ways is hot or cold water used (for example dilute, dissolve)? For what reasons?

● Why do some things go nicely together and some not, like sugar and beef – but what about cranberry sauce and turkey . . .? Why too is lemon juice, for instance, fine, in water but makes milk curdle?

● Some ingredients (like flour) change a lot in cooking, others stay much the same (as in a stew). How do ingredients change (for example in shape, texture, taste)? Which ones change a lot, and which stay much the same?

Ingredients and processes can be mixed to give thousands of different results – you could work from a simple cook-book to help your child explore the variety, the similarities and the differences. 'Does this recipe need butter? What are we going to do with the butter this time? Same as for the cake we made last week?' and so on.

What do we eat?

'Convenience foods' make it hard for a child to understand where food comes from, other than the shops. So it's helpful once in a while to make time to cook things right from the beginning. A stew with dirty vegetables and meat from a butcher's is a good start – and the remains can be made into soup.

It may sometimes puzzle and upset your child (expecially when he learns about milk and meat), but he'll learn it best from you. You can help him make the links when you're out and about too – even in towns you can see vegetables growing, and you can still sometimes find live chickens and cows as well.

WEIGHING IT UP

The same amount of pastry makes all the shapes in the picture – do *you* believe it?

A pound of flour, a pound of apples, and a pound of meat all look different shapes – and as you can read in the length exercises (see *Woodwork*), a child at first tends to go by his eyes, rather than trust his ideas. So how can you help your child understand that, for example, a pound of flour weighs the same as a pound of apples, even though they look different? Here are four suggestions:

Method 1 Two-pan balance scales with flour on one side, and apples on the other, allow the child to *see* that the two weights balance.

Method 2 Getting your child to hold the flour in one hand and the apples in the other helps him *feel* through his hands and arm muscles that they're the same weight. But small differences in weight, which can be important in a recipe, aren't always readily felt.

Method 3 Changing shapes. Make two identical balls of pastry. Ask your child to feel them both and agree they're the same weight. Then put one on one side for yourself, and ask him to make the other into different shapes. For each shape, ask him if he's got the same weight as in your ball, or is it more or less? Try and find the reason behind what he says. You may well get apparently silly answers like 'it's more because it's fatter', 'it's less because it's longer.' Your child's not stupid – he hasn't had enough experience to be able to disbelieve his eyes.

Try asking him to weigh the two different shapes in his hands, or get him to make his shape back into a ball just like yours and compare them again. Show him how you have to actually add or take away pastry to make the weight change – shape never affects weight. Understanding won't come overnight, and often not until around the age of seven. But early practice with weights, amounts and you in the kitchen, is likely to help.

Method 4 Eating the evidence. A biscuit broken into five pieces may 'feel' like more biscuit when you eat it and look like more biscuit on the plate, – but again, it really is only one biscuit. At snack time you could compare eating broken 'nibbles' with eating a whole one – first having shown how the broken bits fit back together again into one biscuit.

Here's a game to cheer up eating – it can be a party winner too. Besides being fun, it helps your child 'tune in' to his sense of taste and helps him find the words to describe and group together different sorts of food. It's an exercise in attention and memory too.

This first game helps your child pay attention to different tastes and find the words to describe them.

1 Put small pieces of three or four 'snack' foods (such as fruit, cheese, biscuits) each in a separate tasting bowl on the table. Get everyone – including you – to take a piece of one of the foods, for example a biscuit.

2 Tell the children (and do so yourself) to close their eyes as they eat the biscuit and be very quiet except for the sound of their chewing. Ask them to think about the biscuit – the way it tastes, the feel of it in their mouths, the sound it makes and even its smell.

3 When they've done, repeat with a contrasting bit of food, such as apple.

4 When this is done, talk about it. What was the biscuit like? How was the apple different? Follow on from their comments – if one says the apple was sweet, you could ask if the biscuit was too.

You can repeat this game with another two foods, and so on. Make it harder by choosing two that are more alike, such as apple and pear. Another day you could change to drinks (milk, fizzy, squash, chocolate).

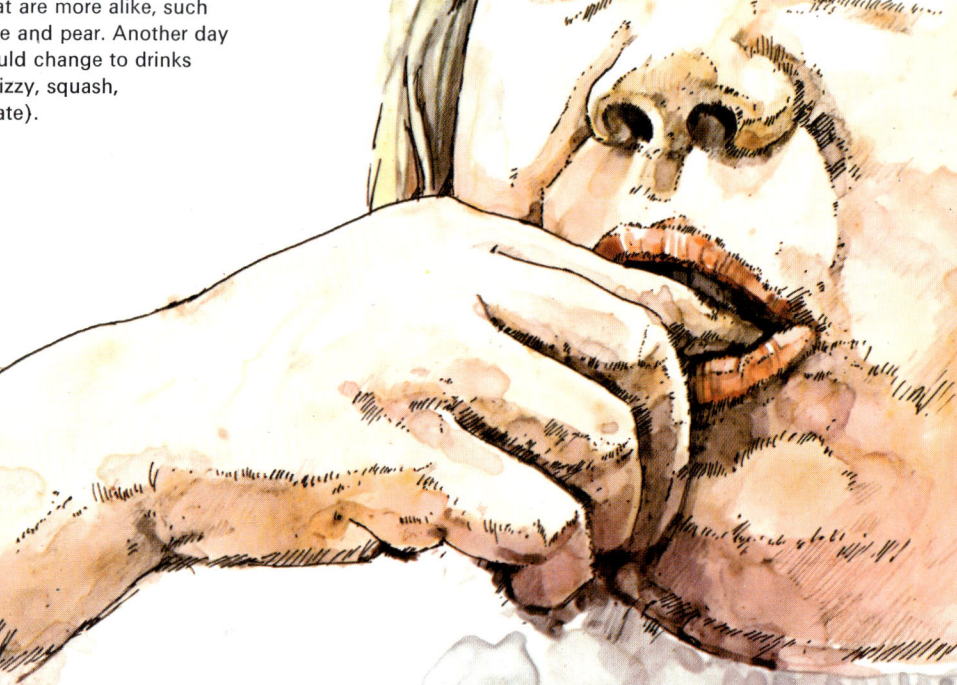

The next stage is to get the children to identify a food without seeing it. This provides practice in *recognising* something recently experienced. It helps a child to remember.

1 With the children, look at, taste, and talk about all the foods available.
2 Then close your eyes and get a child to put a piece of a food in your mouth – can you guess what it is? This shows them what to do.
3 Now you ask each child one at a time, to close their eyes while you give them a different piece of food each.
4 Ask the child each time to tell you which of the foods they have eaten. If they guess correctly – ask 'How do you know?' – and help them work out how. If they can't guess, ask questions which will rule out some alternatives and lead them nearer the answer. For example 'Was it crunchy? No? Then it can't be the apple. . . ' If they guess wrong, say 'No, it's not cheese – try another piece and tell me what it's like' – and work from there.

When the children have had some practice at this stage, make it harder again by repeating it without the first step of seeing, tasting and talking about the foods. (You could play it blindfold.) Identifying foods by taste alone, without a 'pre-taste', requires *recall* from the past, a more advanced stage in remembering.

Other variations of the game for practised children are to use bits of seasoning, or ingredients (salt, sugar, butter etc.), or to give them 'made-up' snacks (such as sandwiches) and see if they can identify all the ingredients.

MAKING THINGS

Watch a child meeting a new object. He explores it by looking at it, touching and feeling it, perhaps sucking it. He may listen to it or throw it. What is the child learning through these explorations?

By exploring in these ways, a child becomes familiar with the qualities of an object, its weight, taste, size, depth, height, texture, temperature, colour and shape. The idea is to get to know the object and all its properties. After exploration, the emphasis changes from the question of 'what does this object do?' to 'what can I do with this object?' The expression of the face changes from puzzlement and playing begins. Activities involving construction help a child to develop skills and understanding of materials.

Compare the way that two mothers and their 4-year-old children play with the same construction material:

Example 1

'I bought Carol's first Lego set as a Christmas present. She did not seem very interested in it at first. I was puzzled by it and began to fit pieces together. Carol watched for a minute or two and then began to do the same, only she discovered that you can fit the pieces corner to corner and when you do this one piece can swivel to make a door. I said I thought this was a very good idea and asked who was going through the gate and where they were going . . . she constructed a shopping area and I suggested that there should be another door for people to come out.'

Example 2

'Jane and I went to the toy shop and bought our first Lego set. I had never played with Lego before and when we got home I decided we would make a white house with a red roof. I sorted out the pieces but Jane decided to start with the windows. I told her to wait and felt irritated that my house was not progressing according to plan. Jane also wanted to put pieces in the shopping bag. I said 'No, we are building a house'. Jane lost interest and went to fetch Teddy.'

These two examples are clearly different — but in what ways are they different? Place ticks or crosses in the boxes to show what mother and child did in each example.

		1 Carol √=Yes ×=No	2 Jane √=Yes ×=No
Did the mother:			
(a)	decide to buy the Lego set?	☐	☐
(b)	start playing first?	☐	☐
(c)	decide what to make?	☐	☐
(d)	give orders?	☐	☐
(e)	make suggestions?	☐	☐
(f)	ask questions?	☐	☐
(g)	give encouragement?	☐	☐
Did the child:			
(a)	decide to buy the Lego set?	☐	☐
(b)	start playing first?	☐	☐
(c)	decide what to make?	☐	☐
(d)	make discoveries?	☐	☐
(e)	make suggestions?	☐	☐
(f)	lose interest?	☐	☐

In both examples the mothers decided to buy the Lego set – do you think that it would be better for the child to make this decision? Also in both examples the mothers started playing with it first. From here on both examples produce opposite patterns of ticks. Next time you and your child play with a construction toy, keep in your mind the checklist above and see what you do and what your child does. Children of different ages will require different kinds of support and encouragement.

What do you do?

Your role when working with a child should be to encourage conversation, and to support him in his activities without interfering. Someone has called this role 'masterly inactivity'. It is that of

- a provider, sometimes a companion
- a supporter, preventing frustration
- a conversationalist

but *not* a director. Your child will learn best by self-discovery and self-discovered mistakes. Once your child has mastered his materials he can plan their possibilities. When he reaches this stage, you will enjoy observing how he works out his own ideas. He requires concentration, use of his past experience and imagination. He needs your help when he reaches the limits of his strength, skill and understanding. He needs your appreciation even though you may not think that his boxes are the least bit like a fire engine. He will gain skills and experience from the experimenting in making things that you encourage.

Construction activities

The chart shows a variety of construction activities. Fill it in with ticks to show what skills and understanding are offered by each activity.

Activity	Hand/eye co-ordination	Use of fingers	Use of arms and legs	Selecting colours	Selecting shapes	Fitting things together	Balancing and stacking things	Solving problems
Playing with Lego								
Completing jigsaws								
Playing with bricks								
Putting lids on saucepans								
Threading cotton reels								
Stacking yoghurt pots								
Taking an old clock to pieces								
Dressing dolls								
Sticking cut out into a pattern								
Playing with a large cardboard box								
Playing with tyres, boxes, planks								

Comments

You will find that many things provide opportunities for similar skills and understanding and some activities provide more opportunities than others. Looking at your completed chart you will see that similar skills are required for completing a simple jigsaw puzzle and for fitting the right lids onto different sized saucepans. Dressing a doll is quite a complex operation which requires a great deal of hand-eye co-ordination, use of fingers in pulling and manipulating, as well as solving problems when things get stuck. It is important to provide a variety of things rather than just one and to make sure that this variety covers all areas of skill and understanding. In other parts of the book we will look in more detail at some of these activities and skills.

Watch how your child plays with all these things. You will see what kinds of skills and understanding he uses and what he is learning about materials and the way they behave. You will see, also, how your child is learning in other ways:
● building something big takes a long time
● patience and persistence will achieve more than at first seems possible – this is where your encouragement matters
● how to imagine and pretend, making exciting things out of nothing
● completion of a creation gives satisfaction

Remember the most important thing is for your child to enjoy what he is doing. If he is doing something that is a challenge and allows him to use, develop and practise his skills then he is sure to enjoy himself as well. You can stimulate his interest by supporting what he does and giving encouragement, but do not push him further than he wants to go or make him feel he has failed if he can't do something – if you do he is sure to lose interest and enjoyment in the activity.

Destructiveness

Does this worry you?
There are basically two types:
● aggressive destructiveness
● inquisitive destructiveness

Aggressive destructiveness – this is aggressive behaviour which in itself is not always easy to tell from normal inquisitive destructiveness.

A child may be very interested in the noise your china makes when it smashes on the floor (inquisitive destructiveness) and even though you will be very upset it does not mean that the child has done this deliberately to make you angry or even to attract your attention. However, there are occasions when in frustration either with the object itself or somebody (perhaps for not helping him), a child will engage in aggressive destructiveness. He may throw your china on the floor for a number of reasons. He may be frustrated by not being able to fit the lid on the teapot, he may be frustrated because he has been ignored, or he may want to 'punish' you. If this kind of destructiveness persists, the causes may go deeper: he may be jealous of a new baby, or unhappy at nursery school.

Aggressive destructiveness needs to be dealt with in an understanding way by redirecting the aggression towards an allowable aggressive action such as thumping clay, banging a drum or splashing water. The reason for this type of destruction should be looked for, especially if it goes deeper than simple frustration. The destructiveness should be stopped, definitely and calmly, especially when it adversely affects others.

Understanding and a knowledge that you have command of the situation should help him to sort out his problems.

Inquisitive destructiveness – is often an essential beginning, before constructive activity can take place. It is easier to take a clock to pieces than to put it together again; to knock a tower of bricks down before building one; to undress a doll before dressing it; to take your shoes off before putting them on.

Cut and stick

An uncluttered table, with glue, scissors, a spreader and paper on it is ready for a variety of experiences and a wealth of learning.

First exploring

The two-year-old child must start by experiencing each new item on the table. The newest and most exciting is the glue. He knows a bit about material, and scissors are fairly interesting, but glue is special! He can do with the glue what he would like to do with his custard at lunch time, but you are not too keen on that! He almost spoons it onto a piece of paper and proceeds to spread it all over. He examines his fingers now fixed to the brush. He starts on another sheet of paper, spoons it on, spreads it out, leans on the first sticky piece with his elbow and is most interested to see what happens.

He leaned on it some time ago and it did not stay on his arm! What has happened?

Perhaps this glue is different from custard . . .

No child learns to be creative overnight and the urge to try and make something may come at any time, perhaps started off by a conversation, a story, a television programme . . . or by objects themselves. Does your home encourage creativity?

Your part

You may feel tempted to instruct. With your experience, you may know what your child could make, but does this give your child a chance to learn how to make things himself?

Making a cat, but for whose benefit?

'Now today we are going to make a cat.'
'Cut around this circle James.'
'No, not across the middle – on the line.'
'Keep it straight.'
'Oh well, let me help you.'
'Now cut around that small circle.'
'Don't you want to?'
'It would make a nice cat and Daddy would enjoy seeing it.'
'Look, I'll do the head if you do some whiskers. That's right, now stick those on.'
'Oh no! Not on his body, a cat has whiskers on his face, doesn't he?'
'Of course he does!'

Eventually James has a cat, made according to adult standards, but has he achieved anything? Is he stimulated, excited, ready to move on to new activities? Or is he bored, frustrated and experiencing failures?

When standards have been set too high, he will not even try. Proceed at your child's pace, not at the pace you think he should go at.

After exploring – playing

Little by little, from successes and failures, from exploring a wide variety of materials, children find they can predict what the result will be from putting things together – what will hold, what will stick and what the shape will be.

After playing – proficiency

If a four-year-old is experienced with glue, he will most probably come to the table, gather together his materials and purposefully put the glue where he wants it and make a construction, perhaps not identifiable to the adult but satisfying to him. Experience builds confidence. One day he may cross one piece of card with another and 'Look, I've made an aeroplane'. It happened by accident, but so do many discoveries and soon he will consciously decide what he wants to make, knowing he can succeed because he can recall past success.

Is it a box or a boat?

What a joy the large cardboard box is to a child – it can be any vehicle or object imaginable including a secret place to crouch in and hide.

As you may already know, it provides hours of fun, constructive, imaginative and arduous physical play. A child can learn about the box's properties and his own capabilities with it.

After a box has been enjoyed it can safely be stamped and trampled on before being discarded and of course it is cheap and easy to replace.

Do you have basic supplies?

● **crayons:** fat ones are best, eight colours are enough
● **scissors:** blunt ends to prevent accidents and they must cut satisfactorily
● **brushes:** 2–3 about 1″ wide with short handles

● **glue:** there are various kinds – PVA adhesive is milky and dries clear and is sold under various trade names. Wallpaper paste *without poisonous fungicide*, is slightly less versatile. Both are washable.

You can make a paste from flour, blending it with cold water then cooking, stirring as it thickens.
● **paint:** dry powder paint in several bright colours
● **paper:** newspaper, computer print out, shelf paper . . . old colour supplements, magazines, etc.

Do you have a variety of extras?

Scraps of cloth
Large and small boxes
Used matchsticks
Feathers
Seaside shells
Washed sheep's wool
Bottle tops, pop tops
Cones and dried leaves
Seeds
Straws, eggshells
Packing material, straw

The list is endless. A visible and attractive assortment will have appeal for the child and he will learn to make decisions by choosing for himself.

Is the environment right?

● **Space:** a place where your child can be free to make a mess – even if only for part of the day . . . a kitchen table, playroom, bedroom, bathroom. The table must be large enough for working on.
● **Storage:** a large carton for a 'useful box', decorated with your child's drawings is always readily accessible. Or a 'keeping cupboard' if you have a spare one.
● **Display:** a place of importance for things that have been made, for example a wall to hang things on.
● **Praise:** which makes a child feel his work has been valued.

A DOLLOP OF DOUGH

'Don't touch!' How often do you say this in a day?

There are times when it is reasonable: a small hand stretched out towards the hot iron; the vegetable knife; the china ornament in a a neighbour's house. But there are many more times when we are tired, busy, anxious or all three, and the continual cry 'Don't touch!' springs from our own inner tension, rather than any real need to warn the child off.

Touch is important in all our lives. We finger materials, stroke animals, press fruit to test for ripeness, and hold out our hands in friendship. We talk about 'first-hand experience' and 'getting the feel of it', and for young children this is very important. If they don't touch, they don't 'know'.

The sort of touching that goes on from dawn to dusk makes considerable demands on anyone trying to cope with both children and daily chores. One escape from always saying 'Don't touch!' is to offer something that is *meant* to be touched and explored. Dough is simple to provide for two- to five-year-olds, and is very satisfying to handle – but forget about bits of pastry and cutters.

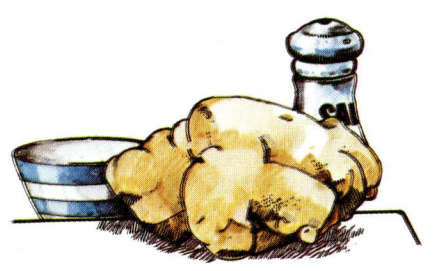

GETTING THE FEEL OF THINGS

This is what you'll need . . .

Ingredients: for a generous amount once in a while (more satisfying than 'little and often,' and still quite cheap).

Puffy dough

3lbs self-raising flour
approximately 1 pint of water

or Bitty dough

3lbs plain flour
1lb salt
approximately 1 pint water

Mixing: add the water to the flour (or flour and salt), and mix until it forms a smooth ball, like putty. It shouldn't be either very sticky or very crumbly. Think about the feel but let your child decide what *he* thinks about it.

The salty dough is easily broken into pieces, and finger holes made in it tend to stay. The saltless dough is puffier and stickier; finger holes close up when the finger is taken out.

You can easily colour the dough by adding cochineal or other food dyes to the water before mixing.

Storage Dough will keep for several days in an air-tight container in the fridge or freezer. A slightly sour smell will tell you when it's going off.

Preparing for play To avoid mess cover the floor, put an apron on your child, clear the table, and make sure he's high enough and safe enough on a chair. Or put both child and dough on a plastic tablecloth on the floor.

When you're ready, give your child the lump of dough just on its own, and leave him alone. If you can, just sit and watch a few feet away so he doesn't feel crowded. Otherwise, watch out of the corner of your eye as you do something else, or pretend to. Don't talk, but tick off what your child does on this list.

● Watch his hands. Do they:

work mainly together	☐
sometimes work alone	☐
slap pit-a-pat	☐
stroke the dough	☐
pinch	☐
punch	☐
poke holes	☐
squeeze and let go	☐
roll balls	☐
pull and stretch	☐
flatten pellets	☐

● Watch his body. Are the movements:

large and bold, using muscles in the neck and arm	☐
small and careful, using finger and thumb	☐

● Watch the face. Which of these expressions go with the use of the hands?

tongue sticks out	☐
teeth clench	☐
lips smack shut	☐
mouth opens	☐
eyes screw up	☐
eyes widen	☐
brow furrows	☐

● What do you think your child is feeling? Excitement, satisfaction, wonder...?

Do his feelings change as he plays?

What tells you if he's losing interest?

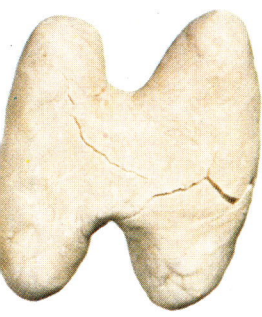

What is happening when your child plays with dough? His fingers are learning to flex and stretch and his muscles are growing stronger. His eyes and hands are learning to work together and his skin is sending messages to his brain which is storing up a library of 'feels'. Later on the 'feels' will be identified by words such as soft, rough, cold, prickly, but in the early stages of exploring a new 'feel' it is the repeated experience of touch that matters. These are best absorbed in silent concentration. If you talk too soon then part of the child's concentration is on you.

Touch and **feel** aren't quite the same. The touch of a **stroking** finger, the back of the hand, the cheek or the foot takes note of temperature and whether a surface is **smooth** and **soft,** or **hard** and **bumpy.** Feel includes what happens to the muscles too. Saltless dough is 'soft' not just to touch, but soft in the sense that it is easily pulled about and stretched.

The other senses are also at work. Dough has a smell all its own. Hearing is part of the enjoyment too: the **slapping** and the small, **sighing** sound of the mass in movement. And the eyes – **watching** what happens, puzzling, working with the hands.

Helping play along

'Do I only have to watch?' you may ask. Yes, to begin with because then it will be easier for you to judge when the time has come for you to help play along. If you step in too soon, you may just be interfering. Happiness, actions and words should be your three 'rules'.

Happiness – because the hurried, worried child can't give his full mind to what he's doing.

● Follow on from what your child says or does – don't force your own ideas or words on him,

● praise his ideas so that he feels having ideas is good, even if you have to explain sometimes why they can't be done,

● don't leap in and say 'What shall we make?' – let him decide if it's a 'making things day' or simply a 'handling day'.

Actions – because the first, long stage of 'getting to know' is through the senses. But when both types of dough have been used and your child seems ready, you could try adding the following 'extras'.

● Offer things to stick on and hide in the dough, such as buttons, fir-cones, bottle-tops, lolly sticks, spoons,

● colour the dough, putting food-dyes in the water, or powder paint mixed with flour. Or make marbled dough by sprinkling the colour on after the dough is mixed. Try black or brown as well as the ordinary plain colours.

Words – because without them your child's play gets stuck in the here-and-now. He needs words to recall what happened before, so he can work out 'What will happen if . . .' Words help what your child learns from his senses, to 'gell' in his mind as ideas.

● As you talk together naturally, name with him the feel of the dough, and the colours,

● talk as you let him help make up the dough. Questions will flow naturally 'Is it too sticky? What shall we do . . . ?',

● note when he knows what comes next. Try a different colour one day and as you open the jar, ask 'How shall we do it?' He may tell you, or he may still have to show you. If he can tell you, you know that actions and words are working together for him.

Your child's face, hands and body will tell you if he's enjoying what he's doing. If he is, you'll probably have ticked off most of the things in the lists, and maybe added more. Your child may be content at first to keep on exploring what the different doughs are like.

Next time you give him dough, mark the list again, to see if his expressions and movements are different.

At first when your child's interest wanes he's probably had enough of dough for the day. When his interest in dough alone wanes quite quickly, that is the time for you to help play along.

Look at Toby's excitement as Sam prepares to put another little lump of dough into their home-made scales. They were hanging from the shade of a lamp over the kitchen table.

To make some scales you will need:

● a length of thick wire, wood or bamboo about 15 inches long for the beam

● two discs of cereal packet card – about 6 inches across

● needle and thick thread.

Cut halfway across each disc.

Curl each disc into a cone and fix by stitching.

Hang a cone from each end of the beam by two equal lengths of thread. Stick threads to beam with sellotape to stop them slipping.

Hang the scales by a string from the centre of the beam. Balance the pans by moving the centre string too and fro until the beam rests in the horizontal position. Fix central thread with sellotape to stop it slipping.

The scales are now ready to weigh bits of dough, apples, sugar lumps, acorns . . .

Heavier or lighter – you know but your child learns! (See *Cooking* in this chapter) p 113

I can do it

'I want to help.'

'Let me do it.'

Do you hear those words often in a day?
Do you usually say yes or no?
Which of the following things would you let your child do ?

Tick the columns that are appropriate for you.

Activity	Yes alone	No never	Perhaps with help, describe conditions
Baking, for example apple pie	☐	☐	
Digging the garden	☐	☐	
Washing dishes	☐	☐	
Vacuum cleaning	☐	☐	
Washing the car	☐	☐	
Shopping in the supermarket	☐	☐	
Dressing	☐	☐	
Making a sandwich	☐	☐	
Preparing vegetables for a stew	☐	☐	
Laying the table	☐	☐	
Bathing the baby	☐	☐	
Frying sausages	☐	☐	
Paying the conductor for a bus ticket	☐	☐	
Polishing furniture	☐	☐	
Lighting the fire or bonfire	☐	☐	
Crossing the road alone	☐	☐	

Now read on bearing in mind those activities that your child does not do alone, perhaps because you think they are too difficult or dangerous.

Too hard for him?

It is only by trying to do something yourself that you learn the skills that are required in doing the job. You will know how even an adult makes a failure of a job that an expert, more skilful because more practised, can do with apparent ease. So children are often eager to try an adult job, as they dress up in adult clothes, imitate adult conversation . . . trying to understand what it is like to be a grown-up.

If a task is too difficult for a child, he will lose interest or become frustrated and will have learnt that the job is one of those that is too difficult for him. 'That's something you can do when you are a bit older' would be an encouraging reassurance. But adults often underestimate what a child can do. Each time your child shows any interest in helping, think about the activity involved. Is there any part of it that your child could help with?

Young children are eager to learn. They will let you know when they are interested. This is marvellous and should be encouraged. These situations can be used for real learning both for adult and child. 'That's all very well' you may say, 'but he wants to do things he can't do all the time'.

If your first reaction to a child's interest is to say 'No', think again. Are you *sure* your child really can't do the job he wants to? Or even some *part* of the job?

Too dangerous?

How can children learn about danger unless they meet it under the watchful eye of a wary adult? *You* know the dangers that are to be found about the house, and the best way to protect your child from them is to meet them with him as you meet them yourself in the course of living. After many encounters and warnings, your child will have the protection of wariness that you have given him, even though you are not there.

But your conciousness of danger can hinder your child's learning. A two-year-old would not have the skill to

handle a sharp, pointed knife safely, but before five, a child who has used blunt knives can learn how a sharp knife can cut a tomato, first puncturing the skin with the point and then slicing through with the sharp edge. You must judge when your child is skilful enough to meet this hazard.

Cooking or preparing food with an adult often provides excellent opportunities for working together. But first you must see the job as a *shared* one. It is no good *not really wanting* your child to help. He will know, and it may be a disastrous activity! It is better to do it when you feel you can cope. For example, let your child dress himself when you have time, but if you're in a hurry it's probably better not to get cross with him for being slow, but to help him, and explain why he's not being allowed to do it this time. It's usually a good thing to explain to your child why you are letting him do one thing and not another – for example, you may let him put the apples in the pie dish, but not cut the apples if he is very young. Children who have things explained to them are willing to accept an adult's reasons, if they are fair.

Other sandwich ideas

Here are some other ideas for the sandwich activity.

- Carrot and cheese. The carrot will need to be washed and grated.
- Hundreds and thousands or chocolate threads. These will need to be sprinkled.
- Marmite and lettuce. The marmite will have to be spread very thinly, the lettuce leaf washed and shaken dry.
- Grated apple and demerara sugar. The apple will have to be quartered and cored, grated and mixed with sugar.

Cheese and tomato sandwiches

Try making cheese and tomato sandwiches for tea, and let your child help. How can he take part?

What are the stages of the job? Tick those that you think your child will be able to manage. When you have done the job, tick the second column to see how right you were.

Stages in making a sandwich

	Part for child (aged ....)	
	You *think*	He *did*
1 Collecting things: cheese, tomato, two slices of bread, butter, a sharp knife (only if your child is able to handle a blunt knife with care and confidence), a spreading knife. 	☐	☐
2 Preparing to work, with your child *securely* standing on a chair or sitting on a stool. This is especially important if he is old enough to use the sharp knife. 	☐	☐
3 Cutting up the cheese, or grating it if you prefer.	☐	☐
4 Cutting up the tomatoes. 	☐	☐
5 Buttering the bread.	☐	☐
6 Laying cheese and tomatoes on the bread.	☐	☐
7 Putting the top slice on.	☐	☐
8 Cutting into two or four little sandwiches, putting on a plate and serving.	☐	☐

How much of the job did he manage? Before five he will be able to do it all, if he has the chance to practise.

Sometimes adults don't fancy food prepared by children. If you feel like this, your child can prepare his now, or perhaps you could make sure his hands are clean and that he doesn't drop the bread or mess up things too much. But what you MUST NOT do is let the child think that what he has made disgusts you. The sandwiches may not be perfectly tidy and may have taken him a long time to make, but they will taste all right and he has achieved something worth doing.

Encouragement while you work

Doing tasks like this with your child may be slower and the end result will probably be less perfect than if you did it by yourself. But it is important to let the child try. Only by trying can he learn what adults' work involves. We want him to see himself as somebody who *can* do things, not as someone who can't, and to see adults as people who *support* and *encourage* his activities rather than discourage them. So encourage your child to persist, and praise him for his achievements. He will get a lot out of these activities but some extra praise from you will give added satisfaction. If the result looks quite revolting, it's probably better not to go overboard with praise. Your child will notice the expression on your face, and that his sandwich doesn't look like the sandwich you've made and he won't believe you when you say 'That's the loveliest sandwich I've ever seen.' Say something encouraging like 'You've tried very hard with that sandwich. Would you like to eat it now?' That moment of congratulation and shared triumph is the reward for both of you.

Your child knows that he can make a sandwich and that is what is important to him. You know that the work has resulted not just in a sandwich, but in helping your child to realise what he can do – and that is important to you, as you help your child to learn about living.

Styles of learning

Do any of these describe your child?

'She seems to do things without thinking, grabbing the first thing she sees.'

'She takes her time to answer – I often think she doesn't know something and then she'll give me the right answer.'

'He doesn't use his eyes and guesses all the time.'

'He always says he knows, and can do things, and then finds he can't.'

'When he's playing hide and seek he's far too careful, and spends ages looking for a place to hide.'

Children learn in different ways. One difference is the way a child stops and thinks before doing and saying something and how much she acts on impulse. While it is probably true that the stop-and-think child is a better learner, there are activities like ball games where she can spend too long in making up her mind.

James is a stop-and-think child. If you ask him a question he takes his time answering. He is happy to sit still for quite a long time, but doesn't like dropping what he's doing to go out. He listens to what people say to him and takes it all in.

Susan is an impulsive child, she has lots of energy and can't sit still for a moment without fidgeting. She is always dying to get started on things before she is really ready. She often doesn't wait for the end of sentences or instructions. If you say – 'Go into the kitchen and get me a plate' – she's out in the kitchen before you've said '. . . get me . . .'

Why are these children so different?

To start with, children are born different. It's possible that that calmness or excitability, which is called temperament, is inherited from parents.

James was a quiet baby. He didn't fuss much, he liked looking at things. Susan was much livelier. She let you know she was around, making lots of noise and always demanding attention.

Partly because of these differences, James and Susan were treated differently. James's parents found him easy to amuse and weren't worn out by him demanding attention. They showed they were pleased, not only when he did things by himself, but also when he talked to them. They did not 'rush' him when he was explaining things, and, as it happened were thoughtful in their own conversation. They praised him for being independent, but were happy to help when asked. James learned that he could take his time in working things out and that adults thought this worthwhile so they would support him.

Susan's parents sometimes got fed up with her constant need for attention. 'Oh, not again' they thought and often didn't respond or did so crossly. They told her off for being noisy, for fidgeting and for always being in a hurry. She learned that adults didn't like the things she did in the way that she naturally did them. Now she is becoming more and more anxious to get rid of this dislike, so she often doesn't wait to learn what adults really want. Her attention is being diverted from thinking about a problem to the praise that comes from doing well. In this way she is getting diverted from learning.

Too hard, too easy — just right

The most useful learning occurs when a child is given material that is neither too easy nor too hard for her, but is 'matched' to her learning needs. If she can do something fairly easily, then she may get bored with it. If the task is quite a lot harder than she's used to, she may give up. The activity needs to be just a little bit of a challenge to make her want to try.

All learning needs effort on the part of the learner or it can become simply practice and repetition.

Stopping to think

How can you help an impulsive child to enjoy learning? Here are some things you could try:

1 Start off with an activity he always enjoys. *'But he's so boisterous. However can I make him stop-and-think with war games?'*
A thoughtful game can still be quite active. Set up an army camp with toy soldiers. He shuts his eyes to pretend it is night, and you capture some of his men with your commandos. He then has to discover who's missing, and how many, and send out a search party. The boisterousness is kept at a distance by the use of models.

You could also fire missiles at the camp (marbles in a cardboard tube will do), with you acting as 'spotter,' telling him where to aim. Then swap around and let him guide you.

2 Play when he's spent some of his energy – just after he's been running around. *'That's no good he takes too long to calm down.'*
Try giving him a small snack. Children usually sit still to eat, and the act of digestion slows the body down.

3 Remove all possible distractions such as extra objects and other toys.

4 Make him delay a little. If he's aged two or three, place a row of familiar objects (cup, spoon, saucer, plate) in front of him and ask him to – 'Pick up the . . . Can he wait for you to finish? Tell him how good he is when he gets the right item; when he's wrong – give him another go.

5 Break the activity down. Children often get distracted during a long and difficult activity. Instead of asking a child to build a tower just like yours, you could point to each brick in turn and ask the child to get one like it.

Let's see how Susan's mother tries these ideas. They are going to build with coloured bricks, which Susan enjoys. They have been to the park so Susan has used up some of her energy. They are going to build on a low table, but Susan's mother purposely wants Susan to have to go and get each brick, so she puts a few on a nearby chair.

Never make a child feel bad for being distracted. But whenever she shows a more thoughtful approach, let her *see* that it pleases you.

> Stop-and-think and impulsive children do not necessarily have different levels of intelligence.
>
> Most children tend to stop-and-think more as they get older but those who were more impulsive at the beginning tend to remain more that way inclined.

A little bit of a challenge

In the left-hand column of the table are a selection of activities. Tick the ones that you *know* your child will find too easy or too difficult for her. Don't bother with the two right-hand columns just yet.

Activity	Too easy	Too difficult	Made easier	Made more difficult
Ring stack			Bigger rings	Rings all the same colour. Smaller variation in size.
5 piece puzzle			Paint matching edges in the same colours.	Do blindfold; cover up design on shapes.
Screwtop jar			Paint arrow on in direction of tightening.	Two similar jars with different threads.
Cutting shapes			Mark or score the lines to cut.	More complicated design.
Threading beads (1 inch cubes or balls)			Wax the end of the string. Larger holes.	Smaller beads with more shapes.
30 piece puzzle			Do the edge pieces for the child, or 'prefabricate' the major items.	Remove the model picture.
Tracing pictures			Use thicker outline or simpler design; pin down paper.	Trace outline only and get your child to complete the picture herself.

Now have a look at the other two columns. Could the activities you have marked as 'too easy' be made more difficult to the point of being interesting and challenging once more?

Similarly, could you make items you've marked as 'too difficult' more interesting by making them easier? A lot depends on the individual child. Some will stick with a challenge longer than others and some will find the activities listed 'boring', even when the level of difficulty is just right for them. If this is the case it's time for a new activity.

Telling them what to do

Every day, and what must sometimes seem like all day, you tell your child to do things. Instructions are a very good way of finding out how much a child understands; you can tell at once when he doesn't!

Instructions are often misunderstood

Talking with young children is different from talking to adults; you have to think about what the child already knows. Some things you *know* they can understand and carry out – 'Bring me the biscuit tin and you can have a biscuit'. Sometimes you have to explain exactly *what* to do, *how* to do it and very often *why* you want it done at all. Giving careful instructions helps your child to enjoy the satisfaction of carrying them out successfully. But it is often easy, without realising it, to give children instructions which they find difficult to follow.

BRING ME YOUR TOP BLANKET DARLING. IT'S ON YOUR BED.

?

OH DEAR!!!

OH DEAR! YOU'LL HAVE TO FIND A DUSTPAN FOR THAT

HERE IT IS MUM!

The instructions for carrying out your own Instruction Test are in the first column of the chart. In the second column are seven examples of instructions. Each involves a particular skill or understanding which your child must master before she can carry out instructions of that type. The instructions are roughly in order of difficulty from 1-7. The third and fourth columns have been left blank for you to fill in while doing the Instruction Test. The last column gives further explanation of the difficulties that some children may experience.

Looking at the cartoon below—what has gone wrong? Mother is using an adult, politely indirect, form of instruction. Most children under the age of four would be confused by the use of the word *find* in this instruction but would have no problem if she said 'Oh dear! You'll have to go and sweep that up into a dustpan!' Discovering what your child does and does not understand can be funny or disastrous – but it is worth listening to yourself and your child, and noticing not only where your child goes wrong but also where you may have misled him in your instructions.

Listening to your instructions

Whenever an instruction seems to have been misunderstood, consider whether your child is ready for the kind of instruction you gave her. The chart below will give you some idea of the kind of problems she may be facing at different stages in her development.

The Instruction Test	Examples of instructions requiring different skills	
You may not have a sewing box – so make up your own Instruction Test. ● Choose a job you know you and your child will be doing together in the next day or so, for example, cooking or mending a toy. ● Beforehand, make up 7 instructions which fit the 7 categories and which you know will arise naturally, for example, for cooking: 1 – stir the mixture, 2 – find the flour from the cupboard . . . Write them in under 'Your instructions'. ● While you're doing the job, bring in each of the 7 instructions. Note in the space provided whether your child could follow the instructions or not, and what seemed to be the cause of any difficulty. If your child copes with most of your instructions you will know that he is successfully linking words and actions. If there are obvious misunderstandings, try alternative ways of giving the instructions and see which are successful. This may give you a better idea as to why he is finding the instruction difficult. It may be lack of physical skill (1); unfamiliarity with names, adjectives, action-words or words of quantity (2-5); being asked to do a number of things at a time (6) and in the right order (7). This activity should help you realise where you have been expecting too much of your child. Rather than get cross (unless you're sure it's deliberate misunderstanding) you need to simplify your instructions for the time being.	1 Does she have the physical skill to do what you ask? For example 'Pick up that piece of thread'. 2 Can she select an object from a number of different things? For example 'Get my scissors out of my sewing box'. 3 Can she select an object from a number of similar things? For example 'Find me a blue reel of cotton'. 4 Will she do what you ask? For example 'Close the lid of the sewing box'. 5 Does she show she understands 'quantity' words (number and size) by finding what you ask for? For example 'Find me two big buttons'. 6 If you ask her to do several things at a time, does she remember to do all of them? For example 'Find my needles and scissors and put them on the table'. 7 If you ask her to do several things does she do them in the right order? For example 'Find me my button box, put the scissors back in the sewing box and go and see if that was the postman at the door'.	

Instructions become explanations

More often than not instructions are followed by questions from a child which range from simply asking you to give a reason for your request:

'. . . put your boots on please.
Why must I?
Because we're going shopping . . . ,'

to questions which involve you in a careful explanation of the process involved in your instruction.

Simon: Look, it's coming off!

Mother: Yes. You have to turn it round. (the lemon) because when you've got it all off one part (the rind) you have to turn it round to get the rest off. Let me show you.

Simon: No. I can do it. (He tries to turn the grater round.)

Mother: No. You turn the lemon round, not the grater. You see, you've got it all off there, so you've got to take it off another part now.

Explaining your instructions contributes to your children's understanding of the reasons for different kinds of actions and behaviour. You can encourage them to tell you when they don't understand what you are asking them to do. The questions they ask you will give you an idea of what they are capable of doing, so that you can set them tasks which give them a good chance of success.

When an instruction turns into an explanation remember that explanations may be misunderstood in much the same way as instructions but without this being so apparent. The clues to how much has been understood can often be gleaned from what the child says in reply. As with instructions, it is important to start an explanation from what the child knows.

● When you are explaining something new, make comparisons with familiar events and ideas,

● when you are explaining something that has happened or is going to happen avoid confusion by keeping to the order in which it happens,

● if you see a blank expression creeping over your child's face go back to the beginning and explain it in more detail, checking that she understands as you go along,

● try to relate general rules to something particular that your child has experienced.

'I don't want you to play with that, it's glass.

Why not?

Do you remember what happened when Dad slammed that window? Glass breaks very easily, doesn't it?'

This kind of relaxed talk with your child helps you both to discover what can be achieved through talking and listening. Parents are not perfect though! It is one thing to understand how important it is to talk and listen to your child, to know that you can share ideas and activities by talking and discussing what you are going to do together. It's another thing to always do it. Occasionally all children need to discover that talk is an important outlet for personal feelings – yours! Take Jennifer's mother trying to cook dinner in a hurry:

Jennifer: Mummy, let me have a look what's burning.
(5 seconds pause)

Jennifer: Mummy, that egg's burning isn't it?

Mother: What?

Jennifer: That egg's burning.

Mother: Get out of my way.
(5 seconds pause)

Jennifer: Mummy, we're both going to have eggs aren't we?
(3 seconds pause)

Jennifer: I want to help you do the next one.

Mother: (shouts) I'll be a bag of nerves if you don't shut up.

More on language

● *All I get is questions*, in this chapter.
● *Talking while you work*, in Chapter 3
● *Words, words, words*, in Chapter 8.

Your instructions	Notes on your child's response	Explanatory notes
ene.		1 Very young children cannot follow instructions because they have not learnt how to relate language to actions. Even when they can, an instruction may call for a skill that they have not yet acquired, such as screwing something up or threading beads.
et the paint from the cupboard.		2 The words naming an object involved in an instruction may not be familiar enough for them to be able to select accurately, even though they may seem to understand them at other times.
Find the red pot		3 When there are several similar objects, a child will select the one you want if he understands descriptive words, such as 'red', 'wooden, and 'square'. He can still have problems even when such words are correctly understood as he may be distracted by other things around and about the object.
Beat the egg vocab.		4 If the word naming the *activity* required is not sufficiently familiar, the child cannot carry out the action required.
a little bit more.		5 A child soon understands 'more' in terms of food. But a full understanding of numbers, sizes and relative quantities takes several years. See Chapter 4, pages 110 and 111 and Chapter 1, pages 16–17 for examples.
several things		6 Instructions involving more than one action cause difficulty, because the child has to wait for you to give him the whole instruction and then has to hold all or parts of it in his memory while he does it.
ff event tasks		7 Even when he can carry a number of items in his head, the particular *order* in which he has to do them may be difficult to remember.

Tantrums and tears

The typical picture of a tantrum is a child kicking and screaming, unable to reason or to listen to reason. Anyone who has to deal with a child in this state is likely to become anxious and even panicky, especially when there are other people around.

How do you deal with tantrums?

To start off, put yourself in this position:

Your 4-year-old child wants to go out and play but his dinner is nearly ready. Rather than put his coat and boots on you say, 'Not now, have your dinner first and then go out and play'. He rushes to the back door and tries to go out. You prevent him from opening the door and repeat what you said before. He screams, kicks and throws himself on the floor in a tantrum.

What would you do now:

tick which apply

- let him go and play and put off his dinner ☐
- leave him on the floor ☐
- carry him upstairs to bed ☐
- pick him up, hold him tight in your arms and talk to him ☐
- give him a sharp smack before doing anything else ☐
- something else ☐

Before we go on to discuss what to do – think about how in the past you have handled your child's tantrums. Look at the table above right.

How have you handled tantrums in the past?			
If your child has a tantrum do you:	usually	some-times	never
a let him have what he wanted			
b ignore his tantrum and let him get on with it			
c take him upstairs and leave him to it			
d pick him up, hold him and talk to him			
e give him a sharp smack before doing anything else			

These reactions are basically – *give him what he wanted* (**a**), *ignore him* (**b** and **c**), *accept his feelings* (**d**), or *smack him* (**e**). On a particular occasion you may do one of these things or all of them. Sometimes one reaction may seem to work while at other times another reaction works. The difficulty is knowing whether one method that seems to work in stopping tantrums may be building up trouble for the future.

Ways of dealing with tantrums

Give him what he wanted

When people worry about spoiling a child they are usually concerned about letting him have his own way all the time. Although children do not start off having tantrums in order to get their own way, they may quickly learn that a tantrum is a good way to get something they want. In general, giving a child what he wanted before the tantrum is not a good way of dealing with tantrums in the long run.

Ignore him

Reacting by ignoring him avoids giving in to him but it is usually very distressing for parents. A child may hurt himself or others or do damage if he is ignored – to prevent this, parents have to take action. Taking a child to his bedroom may reduce the risk of damage but it may be a very long time before the tears and sobbing die away.

Accept his feelings

A tantrum is a cry for help which says 'Things have become more than I can bear, please help'. If we ignore him we are in effect saying, 'I don't agree that things are more than you can bear and I am not going to help'. The long term effects of this reaction will probably be to make the child withdraw his feelings and his confidence that you will help him cope with them.

By holding him close we are accepting him. By continuing to talk to him about the problem and how he feels we are accepting that he has a problem and that his feelings are real. Of course, it may be difficult; the child may struggle and hit out.

Smack him

Smacking is tricky. Nobody likes smacking but sometimes it seems to be the only thing that works.

The reason it works is probably because with all the bad feelings around it takes a sharp pain to get through to the child. The child's reaction to the smack may divert his attention from his tantrum. But the problem is that the smack might add to the bad feelings and make matters worse. It seems to depend on how surprising the smack is and how often he is smacked. You should therefore avoid letting smacking become a habit.

If you do smack your child you should still hold him close and talk to him about it, but do not give him what he wanted. The smack will not have done any harm and you have not rejected him.

Tantrums in public

If the tantrum occurs in, say, a supermarket or in front of visitors, we are likely to get even more anxious. We feel that other people are condemning us not only because our child is having a tantrum but because of the way we are handling things, but many people have, in fact, faced this situation themselves.

Put yourself in this situation.

You are busy talking to a visitor and out of boredom or jealousy your 4-year-old child keeps trying to get your attention by making a nuisance of himself. You say 'Please wait a minute' and this triggers off a tantrum.

What would you do?

If you jump up, hold him and talk to him you will be showing him that a tantrum is a good way to get your attention. Ignoring him is difficult and will embarrass your visitor, and smacking may make matters worse and will probably end up with his getting your attention. There is no right answer and perhaps the most that can be said is that when children demand attention we should try to avoid letting things get to the tantrum stage.

How can tantrums be avoided?

Go back to the first example about going outside at the top of the previous page. How might this have been avoided?

Would you:

tick which apply

a ask him to help get dinner ready (perhaps by laying the table) ☐

b give him biscuits during the morning so that he did not get hungry and cross before dinner ☐

c make sure he went out to play earlier ☐

d allow him to go out when he first asked and forget about his dinner ☐

e tell him before he asked to go out that dinner would be soon ☐

f offer a bribe, such as 'If you don't go out I will take you to the swings after dinner' ☐

If he wanted to go out because he felt bored, then giving him something interesting such as helping get dinner ready might have avoided the conflict. Accepting his feelings earlier means that you avoid the more difficult task of accepting them when they build up into a tantrum. Being hungry would make him more irritable than if he had had a snack during the morning. On the other hand he might then not be very keen on his dinner. Also if he had already spent time outside playing it is less likely that he would want to go out just before dinner.

Obviously if you are not bothered about when he has his dinner you would let him go out when he wanted, but letting a child do everything he wants irrespective of your wishes may lead to the problems of a spoilt child. If you suspected he might decide to go out you could give him a warning about dinner before he became convinced he wanted to go, you could then ask him to help. Offering a bribe might work.

These are ways of avoiding a tantrum in the short term, but a tantrum may be the result of frustration built up over minutes, hours or even days. It is sometimes difficult to realise that things are upsetting a child and causing frustration and worry and making tantrums more likely.

Why do children have tantrums?

Because there is conflict. This may be a conflict between your child and you or another child or between your child and an object, such as a toy he can't put together. Conflict is essential for testing each other's limits and for a child to come to terms with his own limits. The child who never has a tantrum may miss out on vital experience in the development of his personality. Of course if there was no conflict there would be no tantrums, but not all conflict leads to tantrums. So why does a *particular* conflict lead to a tantrum?

Before a tantrum, events may have influenced the child's feelings and motivations. A tantrum is more likely if a child is bored, tired, cold, ignored, jealous, anxious, frustrated and so on. The child may be worried and tense about things that happened earlier. These events don't cause a tantrum but they make a tantrum more likely when a conflict arises.

The more strongly a child wants to do something the more likely there will be serious conflict if he is prevented. One of the most important influences is how you have dealt with your child's feelings and tantrums in the past.

Prevention is easier than cure

Preventing a tantrum depends on you detecting when things are building up and then taking the right action to defuse the situation. If there is an issue you feel strongly about, try to avoid this coming to head when there is a tantrum around. If you find a 'vicious circle' developing where more and more often your action leads to a tantrum, remember that only you can take the initiative and try something new.

Guides for children's group-play

These are general books which provide practical details to help those working with groups of children. They describe how to plan, organise and run groups.

The Penguin Book of Playgroups
J. Lucas and McKennell
Penguin, 1974

Playgroups
H. Jarecki
Faber, 1975
This book deals with play-practice in a playgroup which involves parents.

The Playgroup Book
M. Winn and M. A. Porcher
Fontana, 1967

Publications of the Pre-school Playgroups Association (PPA)
The subjects covered in the PPA publications include: Playgroup practice; Playgroup administration; Information about the PPA; Publicity aids; Special interest publications (for example, Mother and Toddler Clubs); Playgroup philosophy; Courses. Write to the PPA for a full list containing descriptions of over 70 titles.

Being a child

The following books are about children of varying ages, and their view of the world. Some are fact, some are fiction. You will find some in the children's section of your library or bookshop, but don't let that put you off.

Look at Kids
Leila Berg
Penguin, 1972
This book contains descriptions of children caught up in the adult world of a city. The photographs and text are of compelling interest.

Dibs: In Search of Self
V. M. Axline
Penguin, 1971
A psychologist concentrates on a disturbed child.

Cider with Rosie
Laurie Lee
Penguin, 1970
Childhood in the English countryside of the 1920s, described with well-remembered detail.

The Children on the Hill
M. Deakin
Quartet, 1972
An insight into the lives of an exceptional family, describing how three children, raised in a specially child-oriented household, each developed a special ability.

Words for a Deaf Daughter
Paul West
Penguin, 1972
This is a beautifully told story of the writer's relationship with his deaf daughter and his discovery through her of a whole new world.

The Siege
C. C. Park
Penguin, 1973
A moving account of a battle to bring an autistic child into communication with the world of people.

Let the Balloon Go
Ivan Southall
Methuen, 1968, or Puffin, 1972
The book describes how a twelve-year-old spastic child is left on his own for the first time in his life. By climbing a tree he begins to understand his world.

The School That I'd Like
Edward Blishen (ed)
Penguin, 1969
This is a collection of schoolchildren's opinions, mostly about school.

Hugo, Josephine and *Hugo and Josephine*
Maria Gripe
Piccolo, 1974
Josephine, the vicar's six-year-old, is drawn into the discovery of things around her by Hugo, a seven-year-old who knows how to survive.

I am David
Anna Holm
Puffin, 1969
David is fourteen, and sets off across Europe after the Second World War to rejoin his mother.

The Goalkeeper's Revenge, and Other Stories
Bill Naughton
Puffin, 1968
Set in northern England in the 1920s, this collection of sad-happy stories is very well told.

Lord of the Flies
William Golding
Faber, 1958
This is a frightening story about a group of schoolboys who are stranded on a desert island, and forced to fend for themselves.

The Lore and Language of Schoolchildren
Iona and Peter Opie
Palladin, 1977
This is a collection of rhymes, games and other parts of school playground activities. It is interesting to see how many of the special words and phrases you know from your own childhood.

Mister God, this is Anna
Fynn
Fountain, 1977
A book about a six-year-old girl discovering God and the marvels of the world.

Stepney Words 1 and 2
Centerprise Publications, 1973
(available from Centerprise Publishing Project, 136 Kingsland High Street, London E8)
A collection of poems about Stepney, written by the children who live there.

The Gates
Leslie Mildiner and Bill House
Centerprise Publications, 1974 (see previous entry)
Written by two teenagers who are anti-school, and who are sent to all kinds of 'helpful' bodies to get them to like school again.

A Kestrel for a Knave (Kes)
Barry Hines
Penguin, 1969
Billy Caspar is a frail boy about to leave school, with little prospect of a job, except down the mines. He doesn't want to go. What he really knows about is a kestrel hawk.

Chapter 5
Going out

Chapter 5
Going out

Shopping

Children have a lot to learn about one of the most important survival skills – getting the food they eat. They have plenty of opportunity – shopping for food is usually done twice a week or more. Whether children are unwilling passengers or active helpers depends on your patience and the time you spend helping them to help you.

What's important about shopping?

Shopping is a vital part of family work. The whole activity usually involves deciding what you want before you go, selecting and paying for the goods in the shop and putting your purchases away after you get home. This is a preliminary to the business of cooking and eating the food you have bought.

Shopping expeditions are often a source of conflict between parents and pre-school children. The parents want to get the job done as quickly as possible while the child wants to examine and explore. To involve your child in helping takes some time at first but this will prove worthwhile as he begins to help rather than hinder.

Saving time is far less important than involving a child in an adult job. Having responsibility for selecting what you want for tea is quite different from merely having something served up without warning. Learning to do things which are part of the adult world makes a child feel useful and valued.

Shopping also provides many opportunities for exercising skills of identifying and choosing, as well as pre-reading, classification, arithmetic and language skills.

Preparing a shopping list

Preparing a shopping list involves:
- predicting what you need,
- checking whether you have supplies,
- deciding how much to buy.

Predicting what you need means thinking ahead for the next few days and asking whether anything special is coming up. For example, you might have a weekend with your parents staying or your child's birthday party. In addition to the special items a

standard list will be helpful. This list can be arranged in the same order as the goods in the supermarket. You and your child can check through the list, for example 'Do we need any eggs, butter, cheese, cream?' He will learn what's on the standard list and may recognize some of the words. The list can be illustrated with sketches of the items. You can rewrite the items you want with the required quantity alongside.

If you collect labels and wrappings from the items on the standard list, you and your child can go through them, sorting out those belonging to products you need. These can be taken to the supermarket and will help your child to identify the goods on the shelves.

Making a shopping list

Next time you need to go shopping sit down and write a list with your child's help.

- Ask your child what he has for breakfast, dinner and tea, remind him of his favourites if necessary.

- For each item he mentions (for example beans, honey) ask him to look and see if you have any.

- Tell him where to look if necessary.

- Ask him how many tins there are, or how full the honey jar is.

- If he is uncertain, ask him to get the tins or jar out so that you can see without getting up.

- Ask him if he thinks there is enough, and how long he thinks it will last.

- For each item which you and your child think of – or which is on your standard list – ask him to give you the information so that together you can decide if you should buy more.

- You may need to check, but do this by discussing things with him; do not imply that you do not believe him.

- Write down the items you both decide to buy and the quantity you need.

- Use labels and wrappings if they help your child.

The older your child is, the more he will be able to help. If your child hasn't helped before he may find it difficult, especially if he doesn't know where to find things or what they look like.

Help your child choose

There is a different example in each of the three cartoons. For explanations see below.

● In the first cartoon, the mother carries out the whole process but describes what she is doing.

This would be helpful for a very young child. Simply talking about your activities shows the child that you think he is able to understand at least some of what you say and do. This will encourage him to believe that *he* can do the same things when the time comes and that they are not secrets to be kept from him.

A further stage not shown in the cartoon is to ask a child to pick up an item which you point to and put it in the basket. This gives a small child some responsibility and it shows that you trust him not to drop it or knock over other items. Asking a child to choose one item out of twelve identical ones is not really much choice at all, but it again shows you trust him not to be clumsy.

● In the second cartoon the mother helps the child by asking questions. The child is allowed to act on his answers and is guided in making his selection. The mother narrows down

the choice the child faces – to make it manageable. The choice of yogurts, for example, is bewildering and unless the child is given some help he will not be able to cope with this overwhelming variety. Help does not mean doing the job for him, rather cutting it down to child-size jobs. As she approaches the yogurt shelves the mother knows she can ask 'Where are the yogurts?' with some confidence that the child will be able to see them. If she asked at the entrance of the supermarket the child would probably not know where to begin.

The question 'Where are our usual sort?' asked when they are standing near to their brand, can also be answered by the child. The questions about flavour really delegate the choice to the child. If the child chooses a particular flavour the mother will accept this. Or will she? What if the child chooses a flavour the mother knows he doesn't like – what should she do? She might say 'No, not that flavour; what about this one?' and hold up a flavour she knows her child likes.

The decision about size may be related to flavour. If the child has selected a flavour he may not like then it might be best to buy only a small portion. If the child has chosen a favourite flavour she may be prepared to accept whatever size he chooses.

● In the final cartoon the child carries out the whole process himself. He is able to break down the task into stages and to make a decision by himself at each stage. He has learnt this from his mother and can now do it for himself.

Children gradually become able to do increasingly complicated tasks:

● first by seeing the task carried out and hearing it described to them

● second by having it broken down for them into small child-size jobs which they learn to handle, and

● finally by being able to break it down for themselves and carry out all stages on their own.

Responsibility for choosing

Parents can let children have responsibility for choosing – not just in shopping but about which clothes to wear, what to eat, what outing to go on, which television programme to watch. They can safely let the child choose when they know he will make a decision within acceptable limits. If these limits are made clear—for example 'You can choose either strawberry or orange flavour' – then there is less risk but also less responsibility than if the child is allowed to choose from eight flavours.

If all possible choices are acceptable then there is no problem. But if some are unacceptable for any reason, you may have to point out the limitations on the child's freedom to choose; or risk that he won't make an unacceptable choice – only overriding if he does.

Parents can always offer choice and then retract it if the selection is not to their liking. Even if they explain the reason, doing this often will not build a child's confidence in his ability to make his own decisions. He will be put in the position of trying to guess what his parents want rather than what he wants. He will not learn to trust his own judgement. Taken to extremes this could seriously effect the child.

One of the arts of parenthood is to offer choices which you know your child can handle and where you will genuinely accept his choice.

Supermarket or local grocery shop?

Supermarkets are self-service, and shopping in them has many advantages for your child and a few disadvantages. In the traditional grocery shop there may be personal service, which has different advantages.

You could use a supermarket for helping your child to identify and choose items, and a local grocery shop to give him practice in asking for goods and handling money.

Self-service	Personal service
Goods can be handled and compared easily.	Goods cannot be handled. You have to ask for goods and details about them.
You can take as long as you like.	You may have to queue and cannot take as long as you like.
Lots of space – especially when not busy.	May be cramped.
Large range makes choice more interesting.	Smaller range of goods.
Children can choose goods but are unlikely to be able to cope with the checkout on their own.	Children can make their own purchases and may be able to take a list to the shop, give money and carry goods home on their own.
May involve travel.	May be local – on the street corner.

Child-sized shopping choices

1   You want to buy a packet of pre-wrapped Golden Delicious apples. Think about the questions and instructions which you might use to help your child choose a suitable packet.

2   You want to buy a particular variety of natural cheese. Think about questions and instructions to help your child.

3   You want to buy baked beans at the best possible value. Think about questions and instructions which may help your child with the idea of 'value for money'.

You will see situations 1 and 2 in the television programme. Compare your suggestions with how Natasha's mother handles them.

The third situation is difficult. Assuming your child does not have strong brand loyalty you will have to introduce ideas about how much the tins cost. It's probably best to avoid questions of whether it is cheaper to buy three small tins, two medium tins, or one large one. Fix on one size and then find the cheapest brand. For example:
'Which size shall we buy – small, medium or large?'
'There are four different brands, how shall we choose?'
'Let's see how much money each one costs.'
'How much does this say here?' (If he can read numbers.)
'How much is this one?'
'Which one costs more?'

Help your child choose

When you arrive in the supermarket, use the kinds of questions and instructions you worked out in the situations above to help your child choose.

Use your shopping list or labels and wrappers.
● Find the item on the list which is nearest the entrance.
● Ask your child if he can see where the items are.
● If he doesn't know, direct his attention to them.
● Ask him which brand, size, etc., you want. Take two alternatives if necessary and ask him which one – or use your labels and wrappers.
● If he can reach, ask him to select an item.
● If not, ask him which one you should get, for example, 'This one?'.
● Move on to the next item on the list and so on.
● How many items can he cope with?
● Does he pick up the idea and begin to ask the questions himself?

Putting shopping away

When you get home your child can help put away all the things you bought.

● Does he know where everything goes?
● Does he ask you rather than put them in the wrong place?
● Does he put away all the things that go in the fridge/cupboard one after the other?

● If you suggest that he groups things according to where they are kept, does it help?
● Does he stack tins to make the best use of space?
● Can he stack three small tins so that they are the same height as two medium or one large?
● Can he put the eggs into the eggrack in the fridge?

However . . .

. . . there are days when you have to get through the shopping quickly and you do not have time for your child to do anything except sit in the basket. But on other occasions when you can afford the time you and your child will enjoy sharing an important job.

Learning about reading

Children have a lot to learn *about* reading before they are ready to learn *to* read. This means acquiring ideas about the reasons for reading, the kinds of reading materials and the results of reading. These ideas help children to want to learn to read when the time comes.

The reasons for reading

Probably the best single way to prepare a child for reading is to sit him on your lap and read aloud to him the stories he enjoys, as often as he wants. The illustrated book, the comfort and security, your voice and the fascination of the story all combine to build in the child's mind the idea that books are things to be enjoyed.

If story reading is the only experience of reading that a child has it can lead to a very one-sided idea of what reading is about. Children sometimes think that books, stories and reading are all pretty much the same thing.

Book reading and more particularly story reading, is quite a small part of what most adults normally read. Reading for enjoyment is rarely their main reason for reading. Reading to see how much you have been paid, to find out what's on the television, to work out how to fix the car, to select the right ingredient for a recipe – are important reasons for reading that can lead to immediate practical results. These kinds of reasons are often essential to daily life, so much so that failure to read or mis-reading can lead to not only inconvenience but to serious accidents.

We can use the times when we are reading to introduce children to the range of reasons for reading. This will help them see reading as an important skill that will help them deal with daily life, as well as being a source of enjoyment.

Reading materials

It is surprising how many different kinds of reading materials adults come across during an average day.

Warning signs	Knitting patterns
Road signs	Catalogues
Maps	Newspapers
Bus tickets	Magazines
Shopping lists	Pamphlets
Instructions	Recipe books
Bills	Directories
Greetings cards	Dictionaries
Letters	Reference books
Leaflets	Text books

Learning about reading means that children should be able to play with and learn to handle as many different kinds of materials as possible.

The results of reading

We have already said that one result of reading can be enjoyment. Other kinds of reading lead to practical as well as emotional results. Because practical results are visible it is easy for children to see what's going on. For example, finding out what's on television could result in switching channels; fixing the car hopefully results in the car going again; the result of reading a recipe should be delicious cakes.

134

Survey your reading

The reading you do provides a model for your child and an opportunity for him to learn about reading. It's worth taking stock of this reading and looking at why you read, what you read, and the results of your reading, before thinking about what your child is learning from you.

- Either keep a record for the next 24 hours of everything you read,

- or, if you prefer, recall everything you have read in the last 24 hours.

- If you go to work or away from your child, you can ignore the reading you do then.

- Include all the reading you do when your child is about — even if he happened to be in the next room at the time.

- Lay out your notes like the example on the right.

- It is easier to note down the materials first and fill in the rest later.

- When you have your list of materials take each item and note down your reason for reading (see example).

- Next note down the result of your reading.

- In the column headed 'How important' write down 1, 2 or 3 to show whether you think the reading was (1) very important (2) quite important or (3) not at all important. Judge importance in terms of how serious it would be if you had not done the reading or if you had made a mistake in reading.

- In the column headed 'How often' write down whether you do this kind of reading (1) very often; (2) quite often or (3) not very often.

Here is the table for Mrs Sutton and her four-year-old son Jimmy

Reason for reading	Material	Result	How important	How often
To see how much the gas bill was	Gas bill	Turn thermo-stat down	2	3
To find out when Jimmy can start at the playgroup	Letter from playgroup leader	Jimmy over-joyed	1	3
To see what the invitation card said	Invitation card	Jimmy goes to a party	2	3
To find the time of the bus	Timetable	Gave up and asked someone	2	2
To see if I've won the football pools	Pools coupon and football results	I did not win	1	2
To choose new clothes for Jimmy	Mail order catalogue	Fill in order form	2	2
To make some cakes	Recipe book	Tasty cakes for tea	2	2
To see what's on TV	*Radio Times*	Switch to ITV	3	1
To knit cardigan for Jimmy	Knitting pattern	Make mistake have to unpick 20 rows	2	2
To check if I have got everything	Shopping list	Get packet of fish fingers	2	1
To relax	Story in magazine	Enjoyment	3	2

- How many of those reading activities did your child witness?

- Does he understand your reason for reading, and how this links to the material and the result?

- How can you help him to understand?

- How often does he see you reading more important reading matter?

Sharing your reasons for reading helps your child see the uses of reading. Much more can be added if you draw his attention to what you are doing — not so much a running commentary but rather say, for example — 'Now let's choose some new clothes' – 'Here's the catalogue' – or – 'What's on TV?' – 'Let's look in the *TV Times*'. If he is in the other room you might not want to interrupt what he is doing but if he was bored you could draw him into a reading activity — for example, cooking, – 'Let's make some of your favourite cakes' – 'Where's the recipe book?' – 'How much flour?' – etc.

Understanding the reasons for reading

To look at how much he understands the reasons for reading ask him questions based on your reasons, for example:

How does Mummy find the time for the bus?

How does Mummy find out what's on television?

How does Mummy know how to make cakes?

How does Mummy make sure she has got all the shopping?

How does Daddy know how to fix the car?

How does the postman know which house the letters are for?

How can you tell who a card is from?

Understanding reading materials

To see how much he understands about materials your questions could be asked round a different way:

What do you use the bus timetable for? (You need to point to it.)

What does the magazine tell you? (*TV Times*.)

What does this book tell you? (Recipe book.)

The answers will depend only partly on your child's age. Much more important is his experience, because these things are not difficult for 3- and 4-year-olds to learn if they have the opportunity.

Survey your child's 'reading'

How many different kinds of reading material does your child come across during an average day?

- Keep a record of your child's contact with reading materials.

- Again, either record for a 24 hour period or recall what happened yesterday.

- Note down each item of reading material your child attended to, and what he did with it. For example:

Material	What he did
His own books	Turned the pages and talked to himself
My library book	Drew in it
Woman's Own	Tore out a picture of a car
TV Times	Held it and said 'I want to watch *Playschool*'
Mothercare Catalogue	Looked at babies
Old birthday cards	Gave these to friends
Scrap paper with print on one side	Scribbled on it
His words, that I had written on his picture	Said something similar
My newspaper	Could not turn the pages – got angry
The book I read to him	Looked at the pages as I read
Baked bean tin	Got it out of the cupboard

The more books of all kinds, with plenty of illustrations, the better. Mail order. Green Shield and Mothercare catalogues are especially interesting because they contain many illustrations of things that are familiar to the child. Magazines and colour supplements are also interesting — newspapers are difficult to learn to handle but this is an important skill.

A particularly important category of materials for your child are greeting, birthday and invitation cards that have been sent to him. These are special not only because they have been sent to him but because they are connected with a special occasion. Collections of old cards are valuable as your child can use them again to send messages to friends.

Writing his descriptions on his drawings and painting helps make the link between speech and writing and reading. It is also special because it is his picture and his words.

The print on tins and packets will interest him, especially on those that contain his favourite foods. He doesn't, of course, recognise these by reading the print but he uses the size, shape, patterns and colours as well. Old maps interest children who have learnt that maps are important because Daddy uses them to find where he is going.

See also:

Looking at books in Chapter 2.
Your child's own books in this chapter.

Learning about reading

How much does your child know about books?

Notes

Watch him with a book he hasn't seen before:

● Does he look at it the right way up?

● Does he start at the beginning?

● Does he turn the pages one at a time?

Ask him:

● Show me which is the right way up.

● Show me the front of the book.

● Show me the back of the book.

● Where does the book/story start?

● Where does it say what the book is about.

● Show me where you read (pictures or text).

● Find me the page with the dog on it.

● Where's the top of the page?

● Where's the bottom of the page?

● Show me a word.

● Show me a long word.

● Which word do you read after this one?

Many children are perfectly happy to look at an illustrated book upside down even though when you ask which is the right way they turn the book round. Young children don't worry about starting at the beginning. Turning over one page at a time requires skilled fingers but many children master this early on. Ideas about front and back and where a book starts may take time to develop. Children are often hazy about where you actually read and may point to the pictures rather than the text. They are more likely to know where the top of a page is than the bottom – some children point to the back of the book. Adults often fail to realise that when they ask a child to look at a word the child has difficulty because he doesn't know what a word is. If he doesn't know what a word is, he's hardly likely to know which one comes next.

The task facing the child

Reading is not like riding a bicycle, where a child has a clear idea as to what it is he is trying to achieve. This is not the case in reading. Children usually have very hazy ideas about what reading is, and it is much more difficult to 'show' them. Many children believe that adults make up stories as they read and often imitate what they believe to be the case. Some children believe that you only 'read' pictures. Children who know all about story books often have little idea that reading can actually be about real life or that stories and recipes, for example, are both to do with reading.

If children can be helped to understand what reading is, what it is for and what they can get out of it, they will realise that not only can it be enjoyable but it can be *useful*. When they begin learning to read they have an idea as to what benefit this learning will bring (even though most children are taught to read with fictional story books only).

Recognising letters

Being able to recite the alphabet is not important – what is important is for children to recognise the shape of letters. But this isn't as easy as you may think. The shape of the letter does not mean anything to a child, his interest will be the colour and general size and some vague pattern. To see letter shapes as adults see them a child must become more involved in the detail by watching the letter being drawn, running his fingers over the shape, tracing or copying it.

Before children come across reading they have to get used to their toy car being the same car whatever way up it is. But this idea doesn't work for reading. Some letters are quite different if they are up the other way. For example:

d b n m
p q u w

Not only is this a problem but there are problems with which side you look – d can be b if you look at it from the other side or it can be p if you twist it round or q if you turn it over.

Children have to learn that it is important to note which way up a letter is because over half the letters in the alphabet can become one or more other letters if they are moved around. Work this out for yourself if you like – use small, not capital, letters. Children learn that b is p upside down, but what they find hard is realising that b and p are entirely different letters. After all they would think it very odd if their doll became Susan one way up and Betty as soon as it was turned round.

Not only are there 26 letter shapes to be learnt but another 17 new capital letter shapes. Making 43 shapes altogether. Also there are variations in these shapes, as well as differences of size, for example:

some of these differences in the same letter are greater than the differences between letters, for example:

hntf

Remember –
● Follow your child's interests
● Never push him beyond what he wants to do
● Never become impatient
● Never drill your child

Help your child to recognise letters

There are a number of simple ways of teaching a child to recognise the letters.

● Running fingers around cut out or moulded letters.

● Fitting moulded letters in a form board. (Mothercare produce one.)

● Talking about the shapes in alphabet books.

● Matching letters, for example 'Find me one like this.' (Two sets of Mothercare letters for this.)

● Tracing, colouring or copying letters.

● Copying the movements in writing a letter.

● Collecting different letter sizes and shapes for a scrap book.

● Drawing attention to easy to remember shapes, for example S is for snake, O is for orange.

Letters and sounds

Even though there are 26 letters there are about 44 sounds, so some letters have to be used to make more than one sound, and some sounds have more than one letter, for example ch, th, ur, aw or even ough. Also letters cannot be sounded in isolation from other letters – if they are the sound is very different from the sound they have when in a word. Therefore to teach a child – 'Kuh-a-tuh says cat' is actually not true, it is probably just as easy for the child to say – 'See-ay-tee spells cat'. You can use letter names to help your child recognise letters – for example 'Find me a "jay" for Jane.'

Words and sentences

Even when children can point to a card with a single word on it and say that this is a word they may be unable to point to that word in a text. To do this would depend on knowing that words have spaces between them and around them. This is actually more difficult than you may think; after all, spoken language does not have spaces between words so the idea that printed words do is a new one. As for sentences – very few children or adults for that matter actually talk in sentences – this is not because they are stupid or don't know their grammar but because it is not necessary to do so. It is often unnecessary to finish a sentence because the other person understands before the end and butts in. Children not only have to learn about sentences but about how they are shown in text – this involves recognising particular capital letters and full stops as well as word spaces.

It is often said that children should be taught to recognise whole words rather than try to build the word from the letters. Unfortunately the variations in letter shape make this difficult, often the shape of the same word will change more with different typefaces than the difference between two words in the same typeface.

A helping hand

If your child is interested you can write words and phrases for him to copy – don't use capitals, write the letters in the style of the sample card in the box on the right. As you write each letter say what it is. When you reach the end of a word say the word and at the end of a phrase read it back to your child pointing to each word as you say it.

Opportunities for this:

● Write on your child's drawings – 'Tell me about your picture'. Then write down what he says – do not 'correct' his words or grammar as you write.

● Write in a greetings card for your child to send to a friend.

● Write names and phrases for your child to copy.

● Write dotted letters for your child to trace, for example

a b c d e f g h i
j k l m n o p q r
s t u v w x y z

Here is a cat and a house

to Simon
love from
Angela

david
tracy
my dad
home
come and
play

derek
john
mary
my car
our house

These activities will help your child learn:

● how to draw letters,

● that the order of letters is important,

● that words are made up of letters,

● that words mean something,

● that there is a link between written words and speech,

● that the order of words is important,

● that there is a left to right sequence for words,

● that there is a top to bottom sequence for lines of words.

Helping children learn about reading is of great value but anxious parents drilling their children is a harmful practice. Let a child be in situations that stimulate him, with materials that fascinate him. Help him understand the reasons for reading and he will be well on the way to becoming a successful reader.

138

Your child's own books

By the time he is five your child already has a library. It will be an odd assortment – the remnants of baby books, old comics and catalogues, a mixture of hardbacks and paperbacks, presents and loans. Some are seldom looked at, others are referred to daily. All have one thing in common – they belong to your child.

Making a library together

Specialist children's book shops are few and far between. Most people rely on what they can find in the local stationers or post office. Some supermarkets and chain stores sell children's books but these are usually limited to a range of cheap paperbacks and annuals. Among these there are some good bargains to be found. For example:

● The Ladybird range for the under fives includes basic picture books for the very young; *Talkabout* books for the two- to three-year-old; and an excellent new series *Learning with Traditional Rhymes* which spans the two to five age range and reminds you of rhymes you have forgotten and lots you never knew. Look also for information books like Macdonald's *Starters* series, on almost every topic for the four- to five-year-old who wants to know everything from how a fire is put out to all about the sea shore.

● Collins' *Colour Cubs* are smaller versions of the big Richard Scarry books where funny little animals do busy everyday human things from cleaning their teeth to building a house. Children like them because they can recognise the details on every page;

older children still pore over them, as they begin to understand the processes the drawings describe.

More books you can afford

Don't wait for Christmas or birthdays, especially if you don't have a handy shop; look out for books all the time. After all they are much more nourishing than sweets and last a lot longer! You will have little trouble finding the books that have been mentioned so far.

There has been an enormous increase in the variety of cheap children's paperback story books. A wide choice of excitingly illustrated, well told stories is now available.

Look out for the *Picture Puffins* series – *Where the Wild Things Are*, *Rosie's Walk*, *The Fat Cat*, *The Very Hungry Caterpillar* are just a few. Look out also for the *Picture Piccolos*, *Picture Lions* and *Colour Knights* series. You probably won't find them in supermarkets yet but they are being much more widely distributed. On pages 32 and 64 of this book we give some ideas for books to borrow or buy which under-fives may enjoy listening to or looking at.

Are comics just a load of rubbish?

All children will read comics sooner or later. Whether you want to spend eight to ten pence a week on a pre-reading child depends on the value you think they may have. For some children they are good pre-reading material. (See *Learning about reading* in this chapter.) The words follow the pictures closely and they will soon recognise that the writing tells in words what is happening in the picture above. Once they have had the fairly simple stories read to them they don't find it difficult to relate explicit pictures to what they remember of the story and can get a lot of pleasure out of 'reading' their comic just like you read your newspaper or magazine. It can be a weekly event to look forward to and has the advantage of being something they are allowed to colour and draw on! Comics for young children, like books, are very varied in their content. Some of the stories are based on familiar television series that have been seen just once (see *Television and books* overleaf). Some of the stories are fairly unimagi-. native tales of 'naughty' children, 'wicked' wizards and 'funny' animals. The sort of world that is presented to children in print is looked at overleaf – and you may feel these questions apply to comics too, (see *Choosing a book for your child* – questions 5–7). Some comics can be quite frightening or confusing for under-fives and – if read at all – are best read together.

Choosing a book for your child

Which of the following would you consider important in selecting a book for your child? Tick the appropriate column according to how important you think each reason is.

Reason	Very important	Quite important	Not very important
1 The price	☐	☐	☐
2 The size of the book and the print	☐	☐	☐
3 The relationship of the pictures to the story, their originality and attractiveness	☐	☐	☐
4 The length and interest of the story	☐	☐	☐
5 The way the book describes the appearance and behaviour of imaginary people	☐	☐	☐
6 The way the book describes events from real life	☐	☐	☐
7 The way the book describes how little boys and girls behave	☐	☐	☐
8 The language of the story	☐	☐	☐
9 The quality of the book – whether it is clearly printed on good paper and so on	☐	☐	☐
10 Your child's reaction to the book when you have looked at it together	☐	☐	☐

1 is related to how much money you want to spend – but also to how you feel about the book.

2 is not very important since your child can't read and both small and large books can be equally satisfying.

3 is vital since children need the support of the illustrations. Look for pictures which appeal directly to you and your child – and which he can understand.

4 is clearly very important. What really interests your child is something you can't be sure about – some books become interesting when they are familiar. If the story is too short your four-year-old may feel disappointed, but if the story is too complicated for your child to follow then length should be a consideration.

5, 6 and 7 are often considered very important. The descriptions of books help children build up a picture of the world, and what people are like. But often books for children are very simplistic. Things are presented in a 'black and white' fashion: people are silly or clever,

all nice or nasty, good always beats bad. Many books show girls (or girl animals) wearing pretty dresses, helping at home and playing with dolls – even though in real life women and girls do many other things. When you give a book, you give ideas. So when choosing – ask yourself if you find the ideas and descriptions acceptable things to be giving your child.

8 is very important. It is up to you to look out for clumsy writing, or authors who write down to the child. Children can understand different vocabulary; they should not be made to accept language which is deliberately child-like.

9 is quite important. Print and pictures should be clear, not blurred – but childhood books are to be used and enjoyed, not collected for sheer quality.

10 is obviously the most important and you can forget all the rest of your reasons for liking or disliking the book if your child feels strongly one way or the other!

Television and books

Many children spend much more time watching television than listening to stories with their parents. Try to notice what stories are being offered on programmes for pre-school children.

If you and your child enjoy a particular story look out for it when you are shopping or on a visit to the library. Young children need to see things repeatedly and are unlikely

to have made much of a single experience of a story, however well it is presented on television. But it may have provided a good introduction to a slower and richer savouring of a book in your company. There is nothing wrong with television but for small children the images flicker past quickly while the page of a book can be looked at again and again for as long as you like.

Different ages and stages

Two to three

At two your child still enjoys taking part in nursery rhymes and finger games such as: 'Rock-a-bye Baby', 'This is the Way the Farmer Rides', 'Ring a Ring o' Roses', 'One, Two, Three, Four, Five, Once I Caught a Fish Alive'. He enjoys looking at books with illustrations which are as lively as his response. By two-and-a-half to three he is joining in more complicated rhymes and stories that build up verse by verse like 'The House that Jack Built', stories like the old woman and her pig:

'Stick, stick, beat dog!
Dog won't bite pig;
Pig won't get over the style,
And I shan't get home tonight.'

The repetitive rhythms which you find in nursery rhymes and folk tales are something to look out for in the stories you read to them. Many books

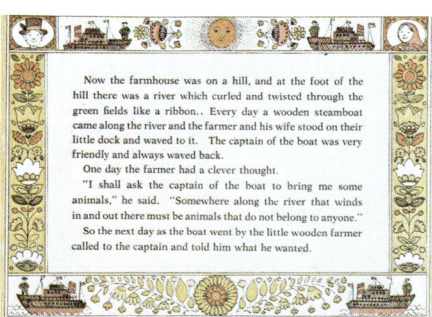

for the very young retell old stories like The Three Bears, The Three Little Pigs, The Little Red Hen. Modern stories take these old tales as a model, using the same sort of repetition, which children enjoy. Books like *Mr Gumpy's Motor Car* (illustrated above) and *Mog the Forgetful Cat* are modern stories where the authors understand a child's need to join in.

Three to four

During this period your child will listen to longer and more complicated stories. He will still need the support of pictures on every page to hold his attention and to help him interpret the words he hears. (Consider how difficult the words of the story shown at the bottom of the previous column might be without its accompanying picture.)

The stories you read help him understand his growing experience of the world. It is a good idea to look for books about things you know he is interested in or worried about. So many things are happening for the first time. These can be explained in a straightforward factual way or often more effectively as a story about an imaginary child or animal who starts at playgroup or has a new sister. Books about going to the doctor or the dentist or into hospital, like Blackie's *Topsy and Tim* books and the Dinosaur books by Althea, can be reassuring.

Four to five

By now your child has met a lot of different books, some at home, some at playgroup and some he will have borrowed from the library. He is much more likely, and able, to say what he wants to read. He still needs stories read to him because they confirm and strengthen the way he feels about many new and puzzling experiences. He will be aware of school looming up soon, possibly with mixed feelings. He wants stability and may return to familiar stories for reassurance.

During this period children become less dependent on pictures as props. They can listen to longer stories like Leila Berg's *Little Car*. Or collections of short stories, like Dorothy Edward's *My Naughty Little Sister* or David Harrison's *Book of Giant Stories* (illustrated below) are ideal. Don't hurry them away from picture books – they will need them for a long time.

Finally he snatched up the witch herself.

"Are you ready to behave yourself?" he rumbled.

"Oh, all right," she snapped. "You win. Put me down and I'll remove the spell." And she did.

After that, the giant and the little boy often took long walks together up and down the valley. The giant's thundering footsteps still made the ground shake.

As their experience of the world outside home grows they want books about their new interests; aeroplanes, fishing, cookery, castles, lighthouses, dinosaurs. Books on these topics may seem a bit difficult but *you* need them, for your own sanity! 'Where does lightning come from?' 'Who was the Black Prince?' Look for Ladybird, Macdonald and Pan *Piccolo* simple information books.

Going to the library

Some of the books in your child's collection will probably be library books. Depending on where you live, you may be lucky and have well stocked libraries with good children's sections complete with their own librarian. Or you may have to rely on infrequent visits to a mobile library which doesn't park particularly nearby and isn't much fun on a wet day.

However, visiting any kind of library is an exciting experience for pre-school children. The librarian should be able to help by giving detailed information on new books for your child's age group and taking an interest in helping you both to make a choice. Larger libraries will have all sorts of activities for younger children from story-telling mornings, visits to and from playgroups, to puppets and painting during the holidays. Ideally a trip to the library should be unhurried and relaxed: a time when you and your child can browse through books which are different and an opportunity to experiment with books, to discover what there is and what you like. It is a chance to have expensive books about the place for free, to decide whether you do really want to ask Gran to buy one of them for a Christmas or a birthday present.

Looking after their books

Books soon begin to look tatty if they do not have a permanent home so encourage your children to look after them. Think about ways of storing and caring for your child's expanding library – but first consider these statements.

Put a tick or a cross beside each one to show whether you agree or disagree.

	Agree √	Disagree X
1 Books need to be seen and reached easily.	☐	☐
2 Books must be kept clean.	☐	☐
3 Books look untidy and should be kept out of sight.	☐	☐
4 A torn page should be mended immediately.	☐	☐
5 Children should not be left alone with books.	☐	☐
6 Children enjoy sorting books of different shapes and sizes.	☐	☐
7 Books must be treated carefully.	☐	☐
8 Children care for books when they have learned to enjoy them.	☐	☐

Children care for things they like – and enjoyment of books comes from a variety of experiences. Torn pages will frustrate them more than dirt will; but adult views and warnings can put them off books. So we would agree only with statements 1, 4, 6 and 8.

A special storage place encourages care of books. Try a painted box, or make a rack from a piece of hardboard with wood strips and curtain wire to keep the books in place.

Young children seem to have an endless supply of energy. They revel in movement, particularly when they have confidence in what they can do. You can help your children build up their physical skills – which doesn't mean exercises, or olympic-champion-type training sessions! It means just finding ways to help your child explore movement enjoyably.

Running, jumping and standing still

The 'normal' rate of growth illustrated in baby books is usually the average for any particular age-group. But it's perfectly normal for children of the same age to vary widely around this average – for example, compare the two two-year-olds in the photo above, born within weeks of each other.

When looking at the development of physical skill, it's not age that is important. What's important is being able to recognise the *stage* of growth and development your child has reached, so that you know what you can reasonably expect and encourage her to do.

Different types of movement

Movements fall into two main groups:

Controlling the body –
  in one place (balance) –
  moving from one place to another

Controlling objects –
  Carrying –
  throwing –
  catching

Examples of each group are listed in the chart (right). Many of them are common to everyone – standing, walking, running, sitting, kneeling and so on. Other movement activities depend on the opportunities open to the child.

They vary from town to countryside, or from country to country. For example, city children are more likely to have the chance to climb steps, roller-skate or ice-skate; country children are more likely to ride horses and have grassy slopes to climb and roll down. Rough-and-tumble play is often encouraged in English boys; Asian girls are often encouraged to dance in their own country's style.

Stages in learning

Each time your child learns a new movement skill you may be able to see three stages:

Stage 1: first attempts – and a lot of 'failures' (remember those first faltering steps – and all those bumps and falls?). Your child knows what she wants to do, but doesn't really know how to do it.

Failing is all part of learning, but for a child it can be very frustrating not to be able to do what she wants, or what her parents want her to do, or even just what her friends can do. If she can't do something, don't make a thing of it: simply reassure her that she will be able to do it soon. With encouragement from you she'll feel happier working through Stages 2 and 3 in her own time.

Stage 2: organised experiments – and increasing success as your child tries out different ways to see which are the most successful. In this stage your child is concentrating hard on what she's doing, and often watches the parts of her body most involved in the action.

Stage 3: automatic actions – gradually your child can make the movement she wants to so successfully that she can take her mind off it. The movement becomes 'automatic' and her attention is free to do something else at the same time – for example walk and talk, or carry a toy and walk. She couldn't do this in Stage 2.

Look at the chart again. The movement activities are grouped in five bands. The five bands, and the movements within each band, are listed in the order in which they are usually mastered by children. But children don't go neatly through the three stages of one movement before going on to the next. Look at the example of Gary in the chart. His pattern of ticks gives a 'snapshot' of what his development was like at one point. *Within each band* there is an upwards diagonal line of ticks – most of the easier movements at the top of each band are 'automatic', while the harder movements further down each band are only just being tried or still being experimented with. Gary is having a go at all the movements listed. But if you compare the five bands overall, you can see that, when this chart was drawn up, his body control movements were better developed than his control of objects. In particular he's only just beginning to master the hardest two bands – throwing and catching objects.

Using the chart

To find out your own child's stage of development, tick each movement in the chart according to the stage your child has reached. You might like to do it twice – once now and then again in 6-12 months' time to see what changes have taken place.

Broadly speaking you're likely to see the same sort of pattern as Gary's – upwards diagonals within the bands, and more automatic actions in the upper bands of the chart. But your child is an individual, and it's a question of 'learning when the body's time is right'. Your child may not be physically ready to even try some of the more difficult movements. It's perfectly normal for children of the same age to vary quite widely in physical skill. And because children have different play experiences, your child may have had more opportunity to practise some skills more than others. So don't expect to have neat lines of ticks! But you can ask yourself – is my child getting the chance to try all these movements, when she's ready?

Doing things their own way

Look at this child throwing. Do you throw a ball in the way a child does? Almost certainly you don't. Children need to do things differently from adults because:

● they find balance more difficult,

● they're less strong,

● their arms and legs are shorter in relation to their bodies,

● they're not ready yet to carry out complicated movements (such as throwing) which involve many parts of the body.

Only a few of the pre-school child's movements are at the 'automatic' stage. Many are very crude and vary each time they are performed. It's important to help a child do things her way – that is, in ways she is currently physically capable of. There's no way she can achieve an adult pattern – so don't impose your way of doing things on her. If you're not convinced there's a great difference between what you and your child can do – compare the pictures of adult and child kicking patterns on these pages. The adult pattern is smooth and economical. The child (rising two years of age) takes a short run, nudges the ball with her left foot and then makes a push kick movement with her right foot. No footballer yet! . . .

A checklist showing Gary's stage of performance in various activities

	Example: Gary			Your child		
	Stage 1 first attempts	Stage 2 organised experiment	Stage 3 automatic actions	Stage 1 first attempts	Stage 2 organised experiments	Stage 3 automatic actions
1 Controlling the body						
1A In one place: balance						
sit			✓			
stand			✓			
kneel			✓			
bend and stretch		✓				
turn round		✓				
twist round		✓				
swing arms		✓				
stand on one leg	✓					
swing while hanging	✓					
1B Moving from one place to another						
crawl			✓			
climb			✓			
walk			✓			
run			✓			
jump		✓				
hop	✓					
skip	✓					
2 Controlling objects						
2A Carrying						
grasp			✓			
push			✓			
pull			✓			
lift		✓				
carry		✓				
2B Throwing						
throw		✓				
kick		✓				
hit	✓					
2C Catching						
trap ball against body			✓			
stop large ball with foot or hand		✓				
catch large ball		✓				

Learning to catch

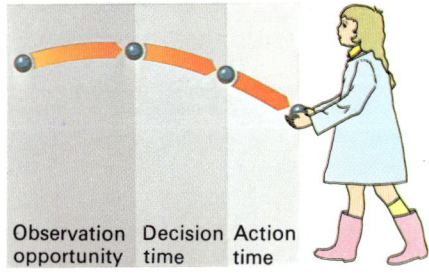

Observation opportunity | **Decision time** | **Action time**

Correct decision and timing

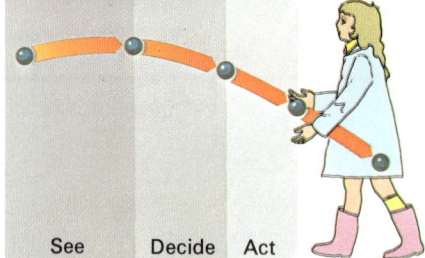

See | Decide | Act

Timing right but decision wrong

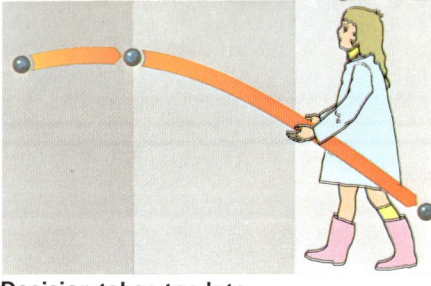

Decision taken too late

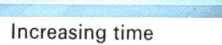

Increasing time

Games like tennis and football involve complex combinations of actions – throwing, kicking, catching, hitting and so on – as well as rules and teamwork. The young child's limited ability to cope with rules and teamwork is fairly obvious if you've ever tried to organise games for pre-schoolers. What's not so obvious is how complicated even one of these movements can be for young children. Take catching as an example.

In catching the child has to look at the ball and be able to:

● *see* how fast it's coming, and where from, to be able to

● *decide* where, how and when to place her hands in order to

● *act* in time to catch the ball.

Catching is very difficult for young children because they cannot judge speed accurately. (Many road accidents are caused by this.) Nor can they predict the arrived flight of the ball. Even if they could do these two things, they may take too long in deciding what to do to allow them to act before the ball passes them by. The diagrams show in 'slow-motion' a successful catch; as well as what happens when the wrong decision is taken, or the child doesn't act in time.

In general, *see/decide/act* is a good way of breaking down, in your own mind, any skill your child is having difficulty with. You may be able to help her – or you may realise that she's just not ready to do it.

Children's games

First and foremost, games should be fun. So what games can pre-schoolers cope happily with?

Games can be divided into three types, according to whether they depend on *physical skill*, *strategy*, or *chance*. Many games combine two or all of these things. Games can also be divided into those that are played *alone*; and those that are *co-operative*, or *competitive* (large team games are both).

Younger children play games which are fore-runners of adult games. They cope best when only one or two basic physical skills are involved. Strategy – deciding what they can see, when and how to use the relevant physical (or mental) skill – needs to be simple. So do the rules – even waiting to take turns in a game can be hard for a four-year-old. (Children will often make up and change the rules as they go along.) Competition is often best avoided at this age.

Children also play games that fall into two other groups: *central person* games, when one person is put temporarily in a position of power (for example, tag, or 'king of the castle');

Physical skills	Strategies – plans of when and how to use the physical skills in games to:
Running	Chase
Turning (swerving or dodging)	Avoid
	Detain
Jumping	Escape
Balancing	Protect people
Moving body while stationary	Avoid people
Catching objects	Protect areas
Carrying (pushing and pulling objects)	Invade areas
Throwing, hitting and kicking objects	
Rhythmic movement in unison	

and non-competitive games which have a lot in common with dance, drama and song and where things must be done 'just so', the same way each time (for example, ring a roses; oranges and lemons).

The table above summarises the physical skills and strategies children use most often in their games.

Children need a chance to climb, jump, balance, swing, creep and crawl . . . . .

In the chart are some examples of adults' and children's games. Complete the chart by ticking what the game depends on (it may be more than one thing) and how it is played (whether alone, competitively, cooperatively, central person.) The first two are completed for you as examples.

Game	Does it depend on:			How is it played?
	Physical skill	Strategy	Chance	
Patience		✓	✓	Alone
Darts	✓			Competitive
Dominoes				
Chess				
Football				
Tiddlywinks				
Hide-and-seek				
Hopscotch				
Tag				

It's not always easy to see exactly what a game involves — some suggested answers are given below. Some games, like proper football, are obviously too complicated for pre-schoolers. But what the table doesn't show is the level of physical skill and strategy required. Some of the games in the table require physical and mental skills (darts and chess, for example) that are far beyond the pre-school child.

The questions to ask yourself if a game isn't going well are:
● is the strategy too difficult to understand,
● are the skills too difficult (or too many skills having to be combined, as in cricket),
● is co-operation or competition causing problems?

Answers
Dominoes (strategy, chance/competitive), Chess (strategy/competitive), Football (physical skill/strategy/co-operation and competitive), Tiddlywinks (physical skill/competitive), Hide and seek and tag (physical skill, strategy/competitive and central person), Hopscotch (physical skill, strategy/alone or competitive).

Children's skills and strategies

Consider two children's games – tag and hopscotch. Try to write down in the chart exactly what's involved for the players.

	Skills	Strategies
Tag:		
Hop-scotch:		

In hopscotch, the child may not be able to sustain her strategy of *invading areas* by throwing the stone into the squares one after the other. Or her physical skills of *throwing, jumping* and *balancing* may not be well enough developed to keep her feet and the stone within the lines. In either case a competitive version of the game with a better player would almost certainly lead to trouble.

In tag, a child may be caught because she failed to see where the 'he' was and so made a wrong strategy decision about where to go to *avoid* or *escape* him. Or she may have carried out her physical skills – *running* and *turning*—too slowly. Failure of the 'he' to catch anyone may be a failure of strategy (for example, unable to make up his mind who to *chase*) or physical skill (*running* or *turning* too slowly) or both (for example, choosing to chase a runner he can't keep up with).

Running, jumping and standing still

Developing children's skills

Providing enjoyable opportunities for your child to develop her physical skills means you need to consider these four things:
- the nature of the play *space* available;
- the nature of the play *apparatus* available;
- whether your child is ready to share apparatus and games with other children; and above all:
- what your child enjoys – there's no sense in forcing her.

Children's readiness to share play with others is a long slow development that is only just beginning in the third year. It's discussed in Chapter 7.

We'll be looking at the opportunities your child has and enjoys, along with ideas for games to play and apparatus to make. But start by looking at play space in your home, and what play apparatus can offer.

Play space

Different abilities are needed to cope with different types of play space. So some play spaces are more suitable for certain stages of development than others. There are four basic types of play space, as described below. Each one makes different demands on the child's skill. Of course, the same physical space can quickly change from being one sort of play space to another: for example, you may get extra chairs for the living room, or the playgroup hall may become a combination of the last two types on a chaotic morning.

Check your play space

1   Make a rough plan of the room where your child is playing at the moment.
2   Count the number of stationary obstacles and the number of moving ones, including people and animals. Enter these numbers in the table.
3   Moving obstacles are harder for the child to cope with than stationary ones, so multiply the number of moving obstacles by two. Add your two sub-totals together to make the obstacle-score for your room.
4   Check your child's age and your obstacle-score in the table provided. Do they roughly line up opposite each other? Or is the room very easy for your child to cope with (low score, high age) or too hard (high score, low age)?

Example: Mrs. Smith's sitting room: a suitable environment for Linda, aged 2?

Mrs Smith's obstacle score		Your obstacle score	
Static	Moving	Static	Moving
9	2		
	×2		×2
	4		
Total	13	Total	....

Obstacle score		Age of child
Simple	0	
	6	1
	12	2
	18	3
	24	4
Complex	30	5

Age only gives a very rough indication of developmental stage. We've used it here for simplicity – but you may rightly feel that even though your child's age and obstacle-score match, that the space is too easy or hard for her to cope with. This exercise is only a beginning – you need to watch how your child is coping in any particular play space. Roughly, the more obstacles and movement, the harder it is for a child to cope and concentrate on developing her own skills.

You might like to assess in this way the play space in your other rooms, or the balcony/yard/garden, or even your local playgroup hall. Remember – complex surroundings are likely to bewilder a young child, while an older child enjoys the greater complexity because she's learnt to ignore what she's not interested in. Familiarity makes a difference too – the younger child copes better in familiar complex space, where she's learnt about the obstacles, than in an unfamiliar place.

Types of playspace

Clear space with no objects for example, a bare room or open grass.

The child is free to concentrate on her own body and her control of its movements.

Clear space with one moving object for example a large ball, an animal or another child.

The child can watch the object, try to judge its movements and learn to move herself accordingly.

Crowded space with a number of objects for example, a room full of furniture and ornaments, or a playground full of climbing apparatus.

The child can explore the properties of a wide variety of unmoving objects in terms of her own skills.

Crowded 'moving' space for example, a room full of running children.

The child learns to be aware of the movements around her, to avoid being knocked over.

Play apparatus

A child needs somewhere to play which meets the needs of her imagination as well as her body. It may be part of the 'natural environment' – a demolition site or a country copse. Or it may be a planned play area. These vary enormously, from a few fixed swings to real adventure playgrounds. (See *Opportunities for older children* in Chapter 8.) Planned areas are often safest for young children – but they can be very dull. A lot depends on the apparatus.

Good apparatus, indoors or outdoors, is an item which:

● *is usable by more than one child at a time* (or by children in quick succession). This way children get more opportunities to use different items. Many small pieces may be better than one large piece.

● *is adaptable to different activities* Children may get bored with one type of movement, so apparatus should provide opportunities for more than one activity. Again, small, movable items which can be re-arranged to present new challenges are often better than one large, fixed piece.

● *encourages imaginative play* If the apparatus is not obviously one thing or another, children are free to use their imagination to make it what they want. A rocking horse is a rocking horse – but a box on wheels can be any sort of vehicle the child wants it to be. When apparatus can 'change roles', then different activities will appear with each new role, and children are likely to use the apparatus more often.

Compare the opportunities offered by each of these four types of apparatus by filling in the chart below.

Opportunities offered by:	Climbing frame	Large boxes	Swing	Train
How many children can use it at any one time?				
It is adaptable to different activities?				
What changing roles can it have to encourage imaginative play?				

On all three counts the frame and boxes are likely to come out better. Here are some of the things you might have put down:

Number of children—swing 1, train 1 or 2, frame and boxes many.
Activities—swing 1, train—sitting, pushing, pulling; frames and boxes many (for example, lifting, climbing, push-pull for boxes, swinging for frame).
Roles—swing 1, train 1, frame and boxes many (for example, house/den/tower/ship; box—car, fire engine, etc.).

There's still a place, obviously, for items such as swings, and trains—as long as you are aware of their limitations.

● Why not take a closer look at the apparatus you have at home, in your neighbourhood, at the playgroup, to see how it measures up in terms of the numbers of children, the activities and roles it allows in play?

What chance has your child got...

Keep a record for a week of the movement opportunities your child has, indoors and out. Various activities are listed in the chart below. For each day this week, tick those your child has had a reasonable length of time to do and put an E by those she seemed to enjoy most, regardless of her stage of skill.

At the end of the week, take stock. If you haven't many ticks or Es, don't make excuses about the weather! Instead, have a think about the opportunities your child could get at home or in her neighbourhood to try out those areas of experience she hasn't had this week. Could you make something for the backyard or garden? Could the playgroup look again at its apparatus? Try some of the suggestions for developing skills, below.

Outdoor play

Outdoor play *can* be dangerous. Play facilities often leave a lot to be desired.

Apparatus and landing ground should always be checked to see that it is safe to use. Some pieces such as swings and trampettes should always have an adult standing by if used by very young children. Even playgrounds designed for young children can have neglected, unsafe equipment. Don't assume they must be safe...

But going out to play isn't just about developing physical skill—it can be a chance for parents and children to meet others. See also:

● *Safety outside the home* in this chapter.

● *Hello stranger* in Chapter 6.

● *Playing together* in Chapter 7.

● *Opportunities for older children* in Chapter 8.

Activity	Mon	Tues	Wed	Thur	Fri	Sat	Sun
In a large space, usually outdoors:							
Run as fast as possible							
Chase as far as possible							
Roll							
Throw as hard as possible							
Kick as hard as possible							
Hit as hard as possible							
Catch							
On apparatus, indoors or out:							
Climb up, down, along, around, inside							
Jump down, over, onto							
Balance on moving apparatus							
Balance along narrow surfaces							
Swing under, around							
Creep and crawl along, inside							
Slide down straight or curved slopes							

Developing skills used in games

The movement skills used in games can themselves each be turned into a solo or shared game. Here are some ideas to get you started:

Movement	What you need and what to do...
Body control – alone:	
Running	Room to run varying distances on varying surfaces.
Turning	Obstacles to run round and poles to turn or swing around on.
Jumping	Obstacles to jump over, onto and off.
Balancing	Lines or raised planks to walk along, wobbly things to try to balance on.
Body movement while stationary	Touching body parts games like 'do this, do that'. Bending, stretching and twisting the whole body. Getting through small spaces, filling large spaces.
Body control – groups:	
Moving games	Skipping and galloping, singing and clapping games such as 'ring a roses' or 'the big ship' or 'oranges and lemons'. Stop-and-start games such as 'statues' or 'musical chairs'
Control of objects, alone or together:	
Carrying	Boxes, blocks, balls. Places for carrying to and from. Holding and grasping, lifting and lowering, pushing and pulling games you invent.
Throwing	Bean bags, soft balls, large and small balls.
(throwing, striking, kicking)	Use large balls for kicking and small balls for throwing. Young children should not be expected to aim. Throwing for distance will cause them to improve by progressing to the next stage of throwing. If striking with an implement, have the ball static on the floor or suspended on string, don't throw it at first.
Catching	Bean bags, soft balls, large and small balls.
(and stopping)	Make this easier by rolling balls along the floor or on a raised surface. Large balls are 'caught' by trapping them against the body.

Sand

Sand provides a rather different sort of outdoor play. Dough is an easy material for the under-five indoors at home. (See *A dollop of dough* in Chapter 4.) It's softer than clay and less messy than sand. But sand in the park, the playgroup or the garden offers a different type of touch.

When you next have the chance, watch a child playing with sand, and make a list, like the one for dough, of what the child is doing. Watch the hands, the body, the face. And remember, the 'rules' of play are the same:

● First let them feel with their hands. Wet sand is for thumping and shaping. Dry sand, a three-year-old said, is 'like dry water' – it trickles and pours through the fingers.

● Sometime later, offer 'tools' – not always buckets and spades. With dry sand, try sieves, or flowerpots with holes. Wet sand builds a world – see what happens with feathers, sticks, stones, racing cars (plastic ones don't rust). If there's water near dry sand, does the child put the two together?

● Talk about what's happening when the child invites you to do so by word or gesture – but be careful not to spoil the fun.

Pets

The care of a pet can be an important part of growing up. The relationship can give a child a new dimension to life and a loyal and lifelong friend. Choosing a pet and learning to live together requires great care. Remember some children are allergic to animals . . .

It is important to think about the difficulties involved in owning a pet *before* your child asks to have one. Once a pet has been taken into a home it becomes entirely dependent on the family for all its needs. The care of a pet is a complete responsibility and your child may not realise this. Your example in carrying out this responsibility will provide a model for your child, which will help her to gradually take on more of this responsibility herself.

What about the neighbours?

Councils and landlords often have restrictions on keeping pets in their property in order to avoid their becoming a nuisance to the neighbours. In selecting a pet you should bear in mind the possible nuisance to both yourself and your neighbours – this is especially important if you wish to keep a dog. In general the smaller the pet the less nuisance it is likely to cause.

A pet for a bored child?

You should not buy a pet to solve the problem of a lonely, irritable or bored child unless you have looked carefully at the reasons for the problem. Inviting other children to your home, or taking your child to a playgroup might be better ways of tackling these problems.

A pet won't live forever

The death of a pet should be handled with sensitivity. You should explain to your child before a pet dies that pets, like everyone else, eventually die. It is surprising how the ritual of a funeral can provide comfort for a child – but remember to put the pet in a sealed bottle or box to avoid the disaster of another animal digging up the once beloved pet.

Strange animals are not always friendly

A child who has grown up with a pet must not expect other animals to behave in the same friendly way. The young child who is used to stroking his own dog must realise that a strange dog, however friendly in appearance, may not be cooperative and may be dangerous.

Other ways of learning about animals

Remember that owning a pet is not the only way that a child can see and learn about animals. Friends' pets, pet shops, zoos, shows, game parks, farms and the countryside generally provide opportunities for seeing animals. Also children's television programmes and documentaries often feature animals.

However, these rarely provide opportunities for actually handling animals, and owning a pet is often the only way of doing this. Owning, and caring for a pet does provide a good opportunity for a child to learn how to cope with important responsibilities.

Which pet?

It isn't possible to give you details of every pet but below are some of the questions you should consider when thinking about owning a pet. Some of the pets you and your child might be thinking about are listed below. Select three of them and then run through the questions to get an idea of some of the problems. If you and your child decide that none of the pets you have chosen are suitable, then select another pet and run through the questions again.

If you do not know the answer to the questions and wish to know more, you can find out from your local library, the RSPCA, pet shops and friends.

Pets:

horse	mice
large dog	gerbil
small dog	fish
cat	budgie
rabbit	tortoise
guinea pig	stick insect
hamster	

Questions

1 How much does the pet cost to buy?

2 How much does the pet's bed/cage/tank cost to buy and maintain?

3 What does the pet eat?

4 How much does the pet's food cost?

5 What health care does the pet need? (jabs, pills, sterilisation)

6 Where will the pet be kept? (indoors/outdoors)

7 Can arrangements be made for the pet when you go away? (for example, shopping, visiting, on holiday)

8 How often does the pet require attention? (cleaning, feeding, exercising)

9 Can your child prepare the pet's food?

10 Can your child clean out the pet's bed/cage/tank?

11 Can your child control the pet?

12 Can your child exercise the pet?

13 How long will the pet live?

14 Will the pet breed? What will happen to the offspring?

15 If you already have a pet will another pet cause trouble?

After you have thought about the costs, arrangements, opportunities and difficulties that different pets involve, you are ready for discussions with your child about the kind of pet she would like. During these discussions which may happen over a number of days or even weeks you will be able to point out what having a pet will involve for her and for the rest of the family.

You can change the inside of your home to make it safer for your child, but, apart from your garden, there is very little you can do to the outside. So it's even more important that you and your child know what's dangerous outside your home and how to avoid getting hurt.

Parents' awareness of dangers

Are you, as a parent, aware of the possible dangers to your child outside your home? Above is a RoSPA poster. Look for as many accident risks as you can find.

A list of some of the risks is given below. You should have found many more, as there are about fifty altogether.

1 Playing ball against wall
2 Running into road
3 Dog in road
4 Stone throwing
5 Ladder hazards
6 Gate open
7 Paraffin on bonfire
8 Water hazards
9 Teasing cows
10 Toys on step
11 Upturned rake and fork
12 Pond unguarded
13 Riding on tractor tow-bar
14 Firing arrows
15 Riding tricycle on pavement

Dangers outside your house

Now go outside and do the exercise again, only this time for real. Note down the accident risks you can see.

Hopefully there won't be as many as there are on the poster but there are bound to be a few. You should take steps to reduce the dangers you find in your own garden.

Talking to your child about safety outside the home

As there is very little you can do about reducing the dangers beyond your garden, it's important that your child learns to recognise these accident risks.

Talk to your child about the dangers in the picture. Refer to *Safety in the home,* Chapter 3, where some types of questions you can ask your child are listed.

From your discussion with your child you should have found out some of the things he doesn't know about or understand. Next time you see these particular hazards when you are out you can talk about them with him.

Many children don't live near water so are less likely to know about water safety than, say, road safety. So make a point of walking by water so that you can talk about the dangers and how to avoid them.

Learning all the time

Many parents feel that there's no point in talking about and demonstrating safety rules when their child is so young. But the beginnings of learning about safety start as soon as your baby is old enough to sit up in the pram and take notice. You may talk to him about the cars going fast and he may sense your apprehension when trying to cross a busy street. So even while he is safely in his pram he is using you as a model. By the time he is able to walk he already has some idea of what is safe and what is dangerous.

You probably take your child out most days, so make it part of everyday life to show him how to cope with the hazards outside. It's one thing for parents to be aware of dangers, but this awareness must be passed on to their child. It's no good grabbing his hand before you cross the road if you don't explain why. Talk to your child frequently, not only about what is dangerous, but why it is dangerous, and how to keep safe.

Children's playgrounds

You probably take your child to the local playground – is it safe?

Although they are designed as areas for children to play in, some of the apparatus can be quite dangerous. Older children are more likely to anticipate a swing going backwards and forwards, or the speed of the roundabout, or the dangers of the slide. However, most of the apparatus is too dangerous for a pre-schooler to play on unless someone is with him.

Road Safety

As traffic hazards are the most common dangers outside the home, we will look at these more closely.

On your normal trips out to the shops, playschool, the park, visiting – you and your child will probably have to walk along a busy street, cross the road, and avoid traffic hazards. How you behave in dangerous traffic situations will be copied by your child. So always do what you would like your child to do. For instance, always use the zebra crossing.

The Green Cross Code

You may have been brought up on the 'look right, look left, look right again' rule. Unfortunately, some of the children drilled in this rule thought that as long as this ritual was performed it would make the cars stay away by magic. The *Green Cross Code* was introduced to give children more understanding of the dangers. It gives a list of instructions in words and pictures on how to cross the road safely. Here is a summary of it:

1 *Find a safe place to cross.* It gives examples such as zebra crossings, traffic and police patrols, subways, etc.

2 *Stand on the pavement near the kerb.* The precise position is described.

3 *Look all round for traffic and listen.*

Be sure your child is safe on the roads. Use this leaflet to teach...

A LESSON FOR LIFE

4 *If traffic is coming, let it pass.* Look all round again.

5 *If it's clear walk straight across.*

6 *Keep looking and listening for traffic while you cross.*

How do you think your pre-schooler would cope with this code? As it stands it may not mean much to him. But are you putting into effect what the code says when you help him to cross the road? His understanding of road safety comes gradually over the months and years you and he are out together coping with traffic dangers.

The Tufty Club

Tufty Clubs are usually run by the local Road Safety Officers. They aim to help younger children to become aware of the dangers outside their home. Ask at your local police station for the name of your local Road Safety Officer.

Road Safety Officers often go into playgroups to tell children about the Tufty Club and road safety. They usually tell stories about animals who act out normal everyday situations in the street. Children usually enjoy these stories, but do you think the make believe world of animals crossing the road will have much effect on the way children cross the road in real life? The greatest influence on the child will be his everyday experiences of how you and he cope with traffic dangers.

All this awareness of traffic dangers and how to cope is preparation for the time when your child will have to cross the road by himself. Parents often think their child can cope better than they actually can. There are two activities below which will help you to check your child's understanding. If he doesn't understand, he's unlikely to be able to cross the road safely. But just because he does understand does not guarantee he'll be able to do it properly.

> See also:
> ● *Safety in the home* in Chapter 3.
> ● *Running, jumping and standing still* this chapter.
> ● *Opportunities for older children* in Chapter 8.

Talking about crossing the road

In this activity you can find out what your child knows and understands.

In the chart are eight questions about road safety that you can ask your child. Fill in his answers on the chart. Also on the chart are the answers given by two other pre-schoolers. You will be able to compare them.

Although the age of the child will affect his knowledge and understanding of road safety, the way parents teach their children about road safety has an important influence. Perhaps Paula's parents have not talked to her about it as much as David's parents. Unlike David's answers, Paula's tend to show a dependence on her mum doing it for her.

They both seem to understand why they have to be careful crossing the road in their answers to Question 2. But their answers to 7 and 8 show that neither of them seem to be aware of the many distractions, such as running after a ball, seeing a friend on the other side, which make it difficult for a child to cross the road safely.

How do your child's answers compare with Paula's and David's?

I can take my mummy across the road

The activity at the bottom of the page is about your child's knowledge and understanding, now let's see if he can put it into practice. Ask him to take *you* across the road. He's bound to make small mistakes but you are there to prompt him. His mistakes will provide talking points for helping him learn.

Before he goes to school, he is not ready to take the responsibility of crossing any road by himself. Even if you live on a quiet road with little traffic you must still be there in the background to make sure he's OK.

Questions	Your child's answers	Paula's answers	David's answers
1 Tell me how you cross the road?		'Looking which way and stopping.'	'Look and listen.'
2 Why do you have to be very careful?		Else a car will come and knock me over.'	'Might get run over.'
3 Where is it safe to cross?		'Mummy says by Caroline's house.'	'Zebra crossing.'
4 What is a zebra crossing for?		'Don't know.'	'For cars stopping.'
5 Where is it dangerous to cross?		'By shopping.'	'Where you can't see.'
6 Do you run or walk?		'You must cross over walking.'	'Walk.'
7 Do you think it's hard to cross the road safely?		'I hold Mummy's hand.'	'No.'
8 Do you sometimes forget to cross the road properly?		'No.'	'No.'

Unspoken words

People communicate with each other partly through words and partly through the gestures, tone of voice and mannerisms that together make up body language. What sense do young children make of body language? Can they understand these unspoken messages? Can parents help to make these messages clearer?

Today there is a lot of interest in how gesture, facial expression and tone of voice can communicate feelings. It's not just a question of sending out these unspoken messages but also of how other people make sense of these messages. Body language, the name given to unspoken communication can be quite complicated. We may send messages about more than one thing at a time or the messages we send may contradict each other. For example someone can seem relaxed because he's smiling but you may notice that his hands are twitching or playing nervously with his tie or ring.

Just as we often choose our words with care or even stay silent to avoid saying the wrong thing, so we can, up to a point, choose and control our body language. But our ability to send only the messages we choose is limited. We often send messages without realising that we have done so and are very surprised when people react to what we considered to be our most inner thoughts. At any one moment you may reveal through your body language your present mood – for example:

● your current feelings about life

● your feelings on what you are talking about

● your feelings about the person or people you are with or talking to

● your feelings about what you expect to happen soon.

Message received

The person receiving your message has a 'decoding' job to do to get the picture straight.

The list just given shows that it may need a good deal of understanding to guess more or less what a person may be feeling and what the feeling is about. Someone you are talking to may look irritated and upset or may look far away and lost in their own thoughts.

Without words to help, you are left guessing whether he is irritated over something you may have done, has had something important to him go wrong or is expecting some frustration to come his way in the near future.

How good are you at sending accurate messages and 'decoding' other people's messages? There will need to be two of you to do the following activities. One of you is to be the 'sender' of messages and one of you the 'receiver'.

Tone of voice

The 'sender' should choose a simple statement which would mean little when spoken in a flat voice, for example – 'I've had a hell-of-a-day' – or – 'I stayed at home yesterday.' The 'sender' should now repeat this statement a few times, in a particular mood or feeling. The 'receiver' should try and guess what mood or feeling is being expressed. The 'receiver' should also note down what gestures or movements the 'sender' makes to help express this feeling – these may be facial gestures or total body movements. Use the table for your results. Some suggestions for the 'sender' are:

depression   delight
amusement   sadness
anger   frustration
embarrassment excitement

Take turns to be 'sender' and 'receiver' and afterwards discuss how you got on.

Facial gestures/ body movements noticed	What feeling is being conveyed?	Did you guess correctly?

Were there any feelings that were guessed incorrectly? If so this does not necessarily mean that the 'receiver' failed to understand; it may have been that the 'sender' wasn't accurate in his message. People rarely send clear precise messages. Discuss those you didn't agree on and see if you can work out where communications broke down.

Perhaps when doing this activity the 'sender' was a bit self-conscious. If so, his body movements may have been more rigid than normally.

Things you may have noticed

Hands are used to emphasise meaning particularly when trying to express strong feelings

Eyes are open more fully/eyebrows raised when a positive feeling is being expressed and closed or turned down with depressed or sorrowful feelings. The same is often true of the mouth and cheeks.

Body position varies quite a lot. The body tends to hunch up with head sagging and legs close together when negative feelings are being expressed. The back is straight, shoulders back and relaxed, the head up, legs relaxed and move apart if positive feelings are being expressed. When excited or angry a person may sit forward on his seat quite tense or move the upper part of his body forward as he speaks.

Gestures only

Now have a go at a harder version of this activity. Swap roles so that the 'receiver' is now the 'sender' and vice versa. Repeat the activity, only this time no words are to be used. The 'sender' must convey his feeling only by the way he's sitting and his facial expression. You will hopefully become aware of how many complex and unpredictable aspects there are to body language.

Children as decoders

Do the activity with your child using gestures only. Use easy examples – feeling happy or sad, angry or afraid – and ask your child to guess how you're feeling by the faces you make. When he gets the idea ask your child to have a go at acting feelings for you to guess. If he finds it difficult at first, give him some simple choices – for example 'be afraid or be surprised'.

Children enjoy miming games and once they get going will have lots of their own ideas – try it with a small group of children. This is a good way of helping children to give names to and talk about their feelings – that is what makes them feel happy, sad, annoyed, etc?

Points of view

Decoding involves not just the 'sender's' feelings but the 'receiver's' feelings too. Whenever someone is feeling uncertain, fearful or angry his own capacity to put himself in another person's shoes seems to be decreased. At such times we tend to think that the feelings shown by another person have something to do with ourselves; we therefore often distort the messages they are sending in body language or even get them quite wrong.

Children are more sensitive to body language than we might think. They seem able to recognise unspoken messages and react to them strongly. Young children not only notice these messages but also tend to think that feelings shown by the other person are something to do with them. It is always important to remember this when dealing with children.

Until they are about four or even older all children find it difficult, even at the best of times, to see things from another person's point of view. The result is that they tend to take everything very personally. When the other person seems happy then the child may well feel he has something to do with the happiness and it will be shared. Should the other person be angry then the child may well feel that they are angry with him. One of the messages that children pick up very clearly is anything that they feel means 'I don't want you around just now'. They also pick up easily the message that suggests 'I like you and what you are doing just now'.

For a young child the unspoken messages he receives are often more important than the words he hears. Facial expressions, attitudes and words that express alarm, uncertainty or fear seem to be picked up especially easily and children tend to react by becoming alarmed themselves. It almost seems as though these emotions are in some way infectious. Where feelings are concerned children are never too young to notice, though they may not be able to understand the whole picture, how an adult may be feeling.

Children have feelings

Understanding the meaning of any form of communication is a two-way affair. So how a child may be feeling will be important to how he reacts to his parents' and other adult messages. Do you notice any particular messages your child sends when he's in different moods?

How does he behave towards you when he's:

● happy, confident

● lonely, bored

● hungry, tired

● uncertain, unconfident?

When a child is feeling happy, confident and absorbed in his own affairs he is less likely to notice messages unless they are for him or are of a kind that alarms him.

When he's feeling that he would like some company because he is getting slightly bored or hungry and tired or frustrated, he is in a very different mood. Now he usually needs to be sure that someone is at hand who will help him to find something interesting to do or feel alright again. Once a child in this mood begins to notice that helpful people, like his parents, are around he will become much more sensitive to any messages they are sending. A message that increases his feelings of discomfort will soon make him feel he wants his own needs dealt with. He'll become clinging and 'mummyish' if the adult does not include a message that means 'I like you and want to be near you'.

A sign that a child may be feeling wary or unsure is for him to be uncertain whether he wants something or not. Children in this state come to people or start doing something and then stop, retreat, maybe do something else and then come back to the original person or activity.

Loud and clear

You can't always get it right. Sometimes your messages will go astray. Sometimes you'll read the wrong things into other people's messages. With children this doesn't matter too much providing you can send the following spoken and unspoken messages clearly and consistently to your child:

'*I love you and always will.*'

'*I am not alarmed by you.*'

'*I like to have you around even when you are angry.*'

'*We are both able to work together to find ways in which you can avoid doing things that are dangerous or hurtful to yourself or to other people.*'

You can do this quite easily when what you say is what you really believe. It's the kind of communication that goes a long way to building confidence and security for your young child.

Most adults find it difficult and often painful to think about death. All kinds of uncomfortable feelings are aroused and we find ourselves facing questions which have no definite answers. Small wonder we are frequently tongue tied when trying to answer children's questions.

In this topic we will look at the range of experiences that lead to children's ideas about death – how parents can answer children's questions – how children react when someone dear to them dies – and how best to console them.

Children's understanding of death

Children's understanding of death, like their understanding of other ideas, grows out of a range of experiences. What they see, do and talk about, slowly builds up into more and more powerful ideas. For example, a four-year-old was cutting an orange and said 'I'm killing the orange. I'm cutting it – that's killing it isn't it?' Another four-year-old thought that everyone turned into statues when they died because he'd met Queen Victoria as a statue in Kensington Gardens and was told that she had been dead for a long time!

Because the idea of death is complicated and because adults often try to avoid talking about it, it is very easy for children to get the wrong idea. To avoid this we can help them acquire ideas by talking to them as often as the opportunity arises naturally.

Children's experience of death

Which of the following has your child experienced and talked about?

dead flowers	☐
dead plants	☐
dead trees	☐
dead insects (flies, wasps etc)	☐
dead birds	☐
dead wild animals	☐
dead meat	☐
butchers shops	☐
dead fish	☐
fish shops	☐
funerals	☐
coffins	☐
graves	☐
undertakers shops	☐
death of animals in books	☐
death of people in books	☐
death of people on television	☐
death of animals on television	☐
death in cartoons on television	☐
playing cowboys and indians	☐
playing soldiers	☐
playing cops and robbers	☐
playing hospitals	☐
death of a pet	☐
death of someone known to the child	☐
death of someone dear to the child	☐

It's surprising how many experiences of death children have. They see flowers and plants die, they see dead birds and animals, they eat meat and fish that is bought from butchers or fish shops. Funerals and graves are often seen by children. Television and books frequently show and mention death. Children's games involve death. They seem to use play to grapple with the idea of death in the same way that they come to grips with other ideas. It's only the last group of items that rarely happen to a child. The death of a pet is rare and the death of people known to the child occurs less often than people moving away. Finally, the death of someone dear to a child is the most disturbing experience of death.

How the experiences are explained to children and how other people react to them are crucial in the growth of the child's understanding of death.

In grasping ideas a child is limited by:

● what he has already seen and learnt

● the stage his thinking has reached

● how well he can use language

● the stage his ideas about time have reached.

With an idea as complicated as death children need to work it out over many years. It is not until the age of seven that some children seem to grasp the idea that death means not living and that it is not reversible. Very young children see death as sleep and are not able to give it any other meaning. Between three and five many children see all events as being caused by someone doing something to someone (or to something). As a result many children think that to be dead is the same as being killed or murdered. Another common idea children have is that a dead person becomes a baby.

Although pre-school children are hazy about what being dead means they are aware that death means separation. For the young child who does not know the difference between next week, next year and forever – going away for a long time is the same as dying. It is important, therefore, to talk to the child about absent parents and friends and help him to realise that they will return, whereas dead people will not.

Answering children's questions

To answer a child's questions we come face to face with our own beliefs and feelings about death. It is useful to clarify these in advance:

● what you believe about life after death,

● what you will tell your child about your beliefs,

● how you feel about death.

The answer to these questions must, of course, depend upon your own beliefs. But it is important to be truthful about the fact that whatever has happened, the person who has died cannot come back to everyday life. We can distinguish between having them with us as a memory and having them around as a person.

Your child will be interested and curious and will not be upset by talking about death. But he will be very sensitive to how you feel about it. If he picks up that you are frightened and sad he is likely to feel that death is frightening and saddening. On the other hand if you show respect and acceptance that death is not over-whelming, though it usually brings sorrow and pain, these ideas will get across.

You may find it helpful to think of how you would answer the following questions from your child.

How do you die?

Do you wake up when you are dead?

Will Mummy die one day?

Will I die?

Why don't we see Gran anymore?

Did Daddy have a daddy?

Will Gran and Grandad be able to talk to each other now they are both dead?

Can hospital make you come alive again?

Why do flowers die?

Is the cowboy really dead?

It is important to talk with the child who asks these questions and answer in a way that is as correct as possible. Avoid long explanations which he may not understand and may give him a mistaken idea. Do not hesitate to say 'I don't know' or 'No one really knows the answer to that, but we believe . . .' Saying 'I don't know' is important and helps the child to understand that some things are truly unknown.

Children's reactions to separation

Adults react by mourning, after the death of close friends and relatives. An important part of mourning is searching for what we have lost. Once children, who have been separated from someone dear to them, notice that that person is missing they begin to search. First by asking where the person is and then by becoming more desperate as they search.

After some hours of searching the picture changes and the child becomes sad, listless and withdrawn. Then the searching begins again and it seems as though feelings that it is worth making an effort to find what he wants alternate with feelings of sadness and despair.

After a day or so the child appears to settle but he is no longer curious, eager or spontaneous. Should the person who has gone away now come back, he treats them with some reserve, which can be very upsetting to the person concerned.

Throughout this time the child will be trying to make sense of the confusion. He may do this by coming to conclusions that are frightening and may be mistaken. For example, he may reason like this: 'Mummy has gone away. I was angry with Mummy for not doing what I wanted – I sent her away, now I can't find her.' At this point the child will feel hurt and angry with Mummy for going away, angry with himself and guilty because he has sent her away.

How can I console a bereaved child?

Keep a bereaved child as far as possible in touch with people and places he knows, as well as his personal belong-ings and familiar routines. Stay around and comfort him by letting him ask questions and by answering them gently, patiently, tactfully, but within his understanding. It is a great tempta-tion to try to cheer up the child and help him forget, for no-one enjoys seeing a grief-stricken child. The quickest and most effective way to console a child is to let him work through his grief. You can show the child by the way you speak and the tone of your voice, that although you are sad too, you know that, in time, you will find consolation.

Giving consolation also means show-ing the child you understand how he feels. Stay quietly on the side lines until he gives the signal that he is ready to take his mind off what has happened to him. This will be when he stops searching for a while and begins to take an interest in other things for longer and longer periods.

People who want to console the child have to stay around, for it will not help if yet another person in whom the child has begun to trust, vanishes. Consoling children is not easy and it is not a sign of weakness to seek help.

Consoling a child who has lost some-one dear to him is especially demand-ing. But pets are also important and provoke the same kind of reactions, though not as strongly as a person who is particularly dear. The same guide lines apply and in addition children seem to gain consolation from carrying out the ritual that goes with a respectful burial.

One of the thoughts to ponder is that in helping a child work out what death means we are helping him to come to understand that pain can be survived and there is a difference between sometime and never. Both are of immense help to him in growing up and the rest of his life.

Days in bed

Children accustomed to good health cannot understand what is happening to their bodies when they become ill. In their bewilderment, they look for someone they are sure of, who knows more than they do.

An adult encountering a new illness is not so different. They would go to their doctor, looking for someone who knows what is wrong and who is

● reassuring, not anxious

● sympathetic, not harsh

● calm, not irritated.

Your child reacts in much the same way. He looks to you!

At first you notice a change in his behaviour. He may become listless and tearful, or angry and irritable. Often he will become more babyish, perhaps

wetting himself when he was dry, becoming less independent, wanting your company.

At this stage, there is no telling how the ailment will develop. It may be

● a passing minor infection that will get better by itself, like most of the feverish ailments of childhood,

● an infection from which the child will recover much more quickly if treated with an antibiotic,

● one of the infectious diseases which most children get sooner or later which give them a lifetime's immunity,

● an emotional disturbance.

What the child needs is loving care, which you communicate mostly without speaking, by the way you touch, hold, and are available. No one gets priorities right all the time, but a sick child needs to come high on the list.

Judgement born of experience – your own, your friends, neighbours, etc. will help you in deciding when to call the doctor. You know your child when he is well therefore you know how unwell he is. Usually, after a day or two, you know whether he is getting better or not and by this time any symptoms would have developed. By these, the illness can be diagnosed and treatment prescribed.

Prepare for new experiences

If there is the prospect of a visit to the surgery or a call from the doctor, it is important to prepare the child for what he will meet. A doll can be the patient and the teddy the doctor. Perhaps you can do the talking for the doctor who makes the doll laugh with a tickle from his cold stethoscope. Laughter is a splendid tonic, easing anxiety and preparing the child to meet the doctor in a relaxed mood. Playing with 'people' toys allows the child to 'act out' feelings of fear and anxiety too big and frightening to talk about directly. Sometimes children feel their

illness is a punishment because they have been naughty. They may fear that the doctor will give them pain. Fears of this kind can often be acted out, and if you are there, you can, by reassuring the anxious doll, reassure your child.

A full description helps your doctor to help you. A clear account of your child's condition helps him to judge the urgency of the call.

When you last called your doctor, how much of the information (right) were you able to give him? Tick the relevant boxes if you gave the information.

Whether the child was hot and feverish	☐
How long he had been ill	☐
Whether he was in pain	☐
If so where	☐
Whether he had been sick	☐
Whether he had a rash	☐
If so where	☐
Whether his breathing was normal	☐

Play for the sick child

What a sick child needs most is company and it is often possible to arrange that the child can be nursed in the living room so that he is not shut away from family life. Keeping company with him gives you a chance to catch up on those odd jobs! To meet the other need, for rest, the parent must observe with sensitivity so that a tired child is not kept awake by either company or the television.

In either living room or bedroom, the child will need plenty of satisfying things to do. Since illness nearly always comes as a surprise, it is a good idea to have a secret store of oddments that can be brought out in an emergency for this because your freedom to go out shopping is reduced. A packet of gummed paper or sticky shapes, a small packet of fresh crayons or felts, a bubble pipe . . . being able to produce these as if by magic will bring a lift in the child's spirits. The kind of playing will match the stages of the child's illness.

Look at the interests of four-year-old Janet when she had measles. If your child is ill, perhaps you would be interested to look back on his needs and how you met them when the crisis is over.

Interests of child	Stage of illness		
	Sickening	Unwell	Recovering
Mother	√	√	√
people toys	√	√	√
puppets	√	√	–
books	–	√	√
mobile	–	√	–
kaleidoscope	–	–	√
bubbles	–	√	√
dough	–	–	√
plasticine	–	–	√
crayons and felts	–	–	√
records/tapes	–	√	√
television	–	√	√
radio	–	√	√
construction toys	–	–	√
scissors	–	–	√
jigsaws	–	–	√

Look down that list and see whether there is anything that you could stock up with in your secret store. Remember the 'going back' from present activities in illness – you may want things that you thought your child had grown out of.

To begin with, in that initial bewilderment, you mean everything; the loss of interest in play is one of the things that will have alerted you to something being wrong.

Toys can help too!

As you can't be everything to your child, you will be glad to have, as fellow-comforters, one or two of the favourite people toys, and that special cuddly toy that may be important to your child.

After this comes a time when, in addition to the discomfort of the body, the child is resentful at his loss of freedom. Most children can be expected to go back to an earlier phase of play, enjoying simple puzzles and familiar playthings to begin with. As with the appetite for food, 'little and often' is the way to meet a child's returning interest in play. And, just as you would take trouble to make the little bits of food tempting, so it is worth while taking trouble to make the little bits of play tempting.

This is where your secret store will be helpful: a saucer of gummed shapes and a circle of coloured paper served on a tray will be a delight if it comes unexpectedly. One of the regressions you will notice is that in a still-recovering child, the ability to concentrate is probably less than usual, hence the need for a variety of activities, broken by periods of rest and relaxation.

Footnote for working mothers

It is often impossible, sometimes difficult, to judge first thing in the morning if you are going out whether a child is unwell or just tired at the usual getting-up time. Children are more often ill in their early years as their bodies build up a natural resistance as infectious diseases are encountered. Later on, mothers begin to matter less, and past experiences of illness prepare the child to know what it feels like to be unwell and that recovery will follow.

If you are at work, emergency plans need to be thought out in advance. The ideal, from your child's point of view, is for you to be able to put your work in second place whenever sickness strikes, to be accessible all the time so that if a morning tiredness develops into a temperature, you can be called and give the child the company that he needs. The alternative from your child's point of view is that the person looking after him has those vital qualities of warmth and understanding, and the freedom from the demands of others that would allow her to give him the special attention he needs.

Slowly back again

The recovering child, without much previous experience of illness, will be eager to get back to a full life as soon as possible. He is not to know that his recovering body will need a little more rest than usual and that is where your greater knowledge can help him. A snuggle with a book in the middle of the morning, in the early afternoon and going to bed early – these are the things that will help the natural recovery. The telling of stories and the reading of books are important skills for you to foster. Both give the child that most important thing – your company.

Sorting things out

Most people collect something – stamps, books, old furniture, or just things they simply can't bear to throw away. Collections are special objects over which you have total control – you can sort, group, order, add to or take away from them as you like. On a rainy day, a collection of buttons and caps can keep your child happy for hours.

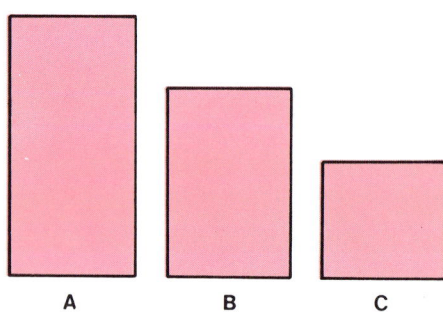

A place for everything

As a collector, you enjoy arranging your things as you want them. You may also find it satisfying to make a chaotic room neat and tidy again. It's nice to know that there's 'a place for everything' – whether or not everything's in its place!

Much of everyday life is spent grouping and ordering the things around us. We make sense of the world by seeing similarities and differences between things. Imagine how difficult life would be if every single object had to be treated as unique and we couldn't say to ourselves, for example – 'Yes, this is a book, like other books, it has a cover, pages and print'.

This all sounds very obvious – but to a young child it's not. The groupings and orderings adults use aren't written large on objects. They are ways of thinking about the world, dividing it up and linking parts of it, and they have to be learned. Much of this learning takes place naturally at home as you talk to your child and he helps you round the house (see Chapters 3 and 4). A collection of objects offers a special chance for your child to try out as many ways of grouping and ordering as he's interested in. There are no rights and wrongs with what he does with these objects. He's in control of them and he can use them to practise his new-found sorting skills.

Ways of sorting things

There are fewer ways of grouping things than there are things to be grouped. This is just as well – otherwise grouping wouldn't help us very much in our attempts to sort the world into a manageable number of categories.

It is possible to sort things out by what they do, what they are used for, or simply whether we like them. Similar things can often be sub-divided into groups by shape, size or colour.

As children learn to identify shapes and colours – something that takes time – they are able to cope quite happily with sorting all the *round* buttons or all the *blue* buttons. *Round and blue* they find more difficult because they have to keep two qualities in mind. And *round and blue and four holed buttons* is even harder.

Children need to keep in mind what they've decided is important. This isn't always easy. Watch a child sort out round-and-blue. He can get distracted because some are large and some small, and so can switch to sorting *large and blue*. Sometimes a child may also try to sort everything in the collection into groups. It's easy to sort out *green ones* from 'the rest'. Keeping several colours, shapes, or colours-and-shapes grouped in his mind is much harder.

Making comparisons

Children also have to grasp the idea that size is relative – John is smaller than Daddy but bigger than Robert his friend next door – and they need to be sure about what it is that makes something 'bigger than'. Here a collection really helps, because you can take objects that are identical in colour and shape and feel, and concentrate on the difference in size. These are the simplest comparisons for your child to make – he can't be led into thinking that it's a difference of colour, or shape, or texture that makes things 'bigger'.

Even when he begins to understand size and amounts – same, bigger, smaller, more, less – your child will find ordering three things hard. He has to change his vocabulary to include 'biggest, largest, smallest'. He also has to change his thinking. Two things can be compared directly, one to the other, but three things involve three direct comparisons and then the drawing of a conclusion:

A	B	C

● A is bigger than B (direct comparison)

● A is bigger than C (direct comparison)

● B is bigger than C (direct comparison)

● Conclusion: A is bigger than B and C, but B is also bigger than C, therefore A is the biggest and C the smallest.

Putting things in order is often a very useful way of sorting out the world. But it's really quite hard for the under-fives. They need to be very secure in their ideas of sameness and comparisons with two objects before they're ready for the next step. The story of 'Goldilocks and the Three Bears' is one good way of helping children to form ideas about orders of size!

Play with buttons Buttons and caps

1 Make up a collection of buttons or caps for a rainy day – ideas for what you need are given on this page.

2 Go through them yourself one evening, before your child plays with them, just to see how many sorting and grouping possibilities you can see. How many groups of buttons or caps can you make, which are the same:

		Numbers of groups
1	size	☐
2	shape	☐
3	colour	☐
4	colour and shape	☐
5	colour and size	☐
6	shape and size	☐
7	colour, shape and size	☐

With a reasonable collection you should be able to make at least one group of objects for each of the ways of sorting, and preferably two or more groups for sorting by size or shape or colour. Groups that contain items of the same colour and shape but different sizes are useful for making comparisons of size or putting into order. If you can only make a few groups, get rid of the single left-overs in the collection and add more 'alike' items to give a greater number of groups.

3 When you've experimented yourself, choose a good time to introduce your child to the collection. Spill the things out onto a tray or clear table, with the sort of flourish that magicians use when pulling rabbits out of hats. Then see what happens ...
Your child may start playing by himself – if so hang back and watch. When you notice his interest waning, suggest one of the easier sorting games you have tried yourself. Begin it yourself and when he joins in play alongside for a time taking less and less part in the play until you can withdraw altogether.
When your child is interested, notice the way he investigates the things and tick the relevant boxes. Does he use:

eyes	– looking at them from all angles	☐
nose	– sniffing them	☐
mouth	– feel with lips and tongue	☐
fingers	– feel shapes and textures	☑

● How does he sort them?

● Does he do other things than sorting, for example use them in 'pretend' games?

● How long does he play before he loses interest?

Children are different – compare the way your child plays with a collection, with the way other children play. Children at different ages and stages will play in different ways and for different lengths of time. Over a period of time you can compare the way your child plays as he gets older and gains experience.

A collection of buttons or plastic caps can provide hours of enjoyment and learning for your child. Here are some ideas to start you off. Sorting and grouping and ordering are fun–but there are often other equally valuable possibilities. Buttons can become pretend food; plastic caps can turn into families of little people. They're 'good' play materials simply because your child can use them in so many ways, at a level of difficulty or imagination that fits his mood on any particular day.

If your child enjoys buttons or caps you may find he wants to start his own collection – of stones, toy cars, feathers or grasses. The possibilities are endless. You can help him find a variety when you're out shopping, or going on walks. If you don't want to bring things home, you can always play 'I Spy!'

A collection of plastic caps

It may take some weeks to build up a good collection, but take a look round and start today.

What to do ...

● Collect plastic caps from bottles and tubes of all kinds – detergent, polish, shampoo, ketchup, toothpaste, deodorant, scent, etc.

● Make sure the caps are well washed, too tough to be broken if bitten and too large to be swallowed, stuck up noses or put in ears.

● Keep the collection together in a bag or screw-top jar.

Some ideas for sorting and grouping

● How many can you use to build a tower?

● Sort them by size/shape/colour/texture, or any combination of these.

● How many 'twins' are there?

● How many can you fit under the biggest one?

Some other uses

● Sing while you play – 'Ten bottle tops sitting on a wall . . . ' makes a good falling game, each cap being pushed down when its cue comes.

● Make the caps into little people – add plasticine heads, buttons can be hats, milk bottle tops crowns, pieces of cloth for cloaks. Have a procession or a wedding.

A collection of buttons

The earlier a collection is started, the more interesting and valuable it will become as time goes by.

What to do ...

● Save spare buttons when you buy a set.

● Cut the buttons off clothes that are to be thrown out.

● Collect buttons from jumble sale leftovers.

● Buy sample buttons from discontinued lines.

● Keep the collection in a tin.

Some ideas for sorting and grouping

● Sort the ones that are identical except for size into 'big' and 'small' – and then gradually into order of size.

● Sort the two-holers from the four-holers.

● Sort according to the material they are made of – metal, plastic, cloth, etc.

Some other uses

● Talk about the buttons – 'This is one from a pretty striped jersey that Alice knitted for you when you were three!'

● Shut your eyes and guess by feeling how many holes there are – or feel through them all to search for one in particular, for example 'a square, wooden one'.

● Arrange the buttons in patterns and shapes.

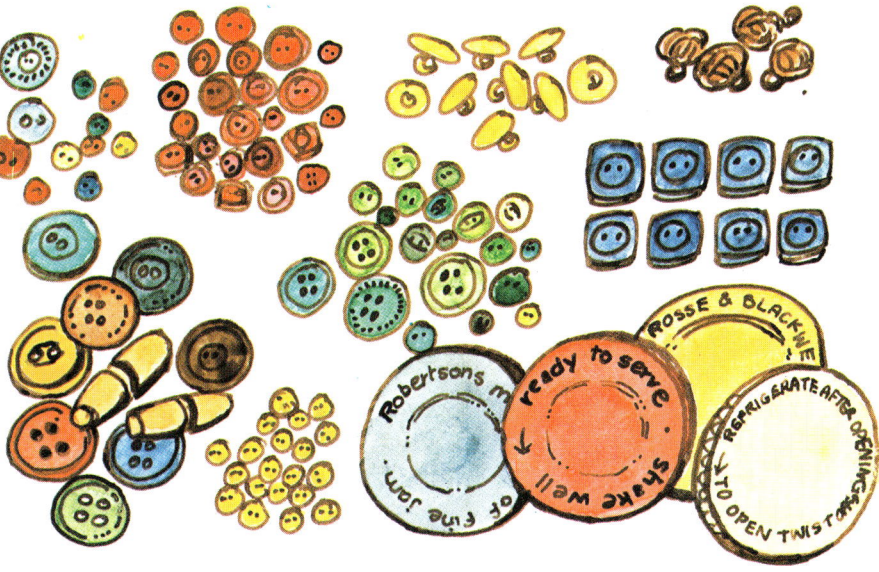

Some books for parents

The world outside your home affects your growing child. If you become aware of what can be done, you are part of the way towards doing something about it.

Discovering with Young Children
B. Ash, A. Winn and K. Hutchinson
Elek, 1971
This book gives ideas for developing a child's perception of the world around him.

Playgrounds

Playgrounds and Recreation Spaces
A. Lederman and A. Trachsel
Architectural Press, 1969
This book contains photographs and plans to inspire dissatisfaction with most playgrounds.

Planning for Play
M. Allen, Lady Allen of Hurtwood
Thames and Hudson, 1965
This describes playgrounds which are inviting to children in search of play.

Environmental Planning for Children's Play
A. Bengtsson
Crosby Lockwood, 1970
This book describes playgrounds which offer variety, both in design and in the use of different materials.

Do It Yourself Playgrounds
P. Friedberg
Architectural Press, 1976
This book contains constructional details for making interesting equipment from simple materials.

Adventure Playgrounds
J. Lambert and J. Pearson
Penguin, 1974
This is mostly about the need of older children for freedom to play.

Hospitals

Young Children in Hospital
J. Robertson
Tavistock Publications, 1970
This is about the effect on a child of separation from his mother; and about children's needs for play provision.

Play in Hospital
S. Harvey and A. Hales-Tooke
Faber, 1972
This is a helpful book to those who are taking a special interest in this subject.

The Empty Hours
M. Oswin
Penguin, 1971
This book is based on observations of children from a variety of institutions. It demonstrates with sympathy and clarity how a more informed and humane policy is needed to help these children take a part in the world outside.

NAWCH publications
7 Exton Street, London SE1 8VE
The National Association for the Welfare of Children in Hospital produces advisory leaflets providing information and advice on where to find hospitals with totally free visiting, beds for overnight stay of parents, playworkers who stimulate activity on the wards, etc.

About sex

These are books which set education about sex in the wider context of loving relationships.

Sex in the Childhood Years
I. Rubin and L. A. Kirkendall
Fontana, 1971

Teach Your Child About Sex
J. Dawkins
Pearson, 1964

The Needs of Children
M. Kellmer Pringle
Hutchinson, 1975
This is a survey of the present understanding of children and what can be done to help them.

All Our Children: Pre-school Services in a Changing Society
J. Tizard, P. Moss, and J. Perry
Temple Smith/New Society, 1976
This book contains descriptions and statistics of the provision of pre-school facilities throughout Europe.

Education, the Child and Society
Willem van der Eyken
Penguin, 1976
This is a scrapbook of writings which have influenced the development and understanding of pre-school education.

Escape from Childhood: The Needs and Rights of Children
J. Holt
Penguin, 1974
Children are people: and this is a book about their place in society.

Time for School
C. Mitchell
Penguin, 1973
This book explains what infant schools and modern infant education are like – and how parents can help their children to get the most from their first years at school.

Double Shift
B. Toner
Arrow, 1976
This is a practical guide for mothers who are thinking of going back to work. It covers research findings, jobs and alternative ways of looking after children.

Maternal Deprivation Re-assessed
M. Rutter
Penguin, 1972
This is a study of the effect of alternatives to the total care of a child by his mother.

The Captive Wife
H. Gavron
Pelican, 1970
How much do children tie mothers to the home and limit independence? This book discusses the future of the mother's role.

Early Experience: Myth and Evidence
A. M. Clarke and A. D. B. Clarke
Open Books, 1976
A re-examination of the influences of a child's early years on his later life.

The Playgroup Movement
B. Crowe
Allen and Unwin, 1973
A description of the growth of the playgroup idea and its incidental benefits.

Two Worlds of Childhood: US and USSR
U. Bronfenbrenner
Penguin, 1974
This book studies attitudes in contrasting societies towards children and their need.

Parents and Mentally Handicapped Children
C. Hannam
Penguin, 1975
A short account, using interviews, of what life can be like for a family with a mentally handicapped child. It highlights the needs of both the parents and the child and suggests what sort of help is needed.

Right from the Start
Bernie Spain and Guy Wigley
MENCAP (17 Pembridge Square, London), 1975
A practical discussion of the problems and needs of a mentally handicapped child and his parents. Includes a section on parents' feelings.

Chapter 6
Meeting people

Chapter 6

Meeting people

Going places

Where do you go with your child?
Is there much variety or do you usually
go to the same places? Can you introduce
more variety? Can you and your child
get more out of the
outings you
do make?

Settings

Most children go out to the shops, the park, the playgroup and other peoples' houses. These are just a few examples of the different kinds of settings your child finds himself in. Each setting is a mixture of five things. This is explained in the chart.

On the next page we are going to examine the range of settings young children find themselves in. Then we will go on to look at what you can do to get more out of outings.

		Explanation	Examples
1	The place	Where your child is.	Shops, park, playgroup.
2	The time	When you can go to this place.	Shop 9 – 6 Monday – Saturday. Playgroup 9 – 12 Monday and Wednesday.
3	The people	Types of people your child comes into contact with in this place.	Shop-assistants, customers. Playgroup – helpers, children.
4	The things	Things your child comes into contact with in this place.	Shop – items being sold. Playgroup – play materials.
5	Activities	What your child does in this place.	Shop – helps choosing and finding, buying. Playgroup – plays, mixes with other children.

Anne's day

Let's look at a typical day for Mrs Smith and Anne, aged 4. The chart opposite shows how Anne was in several different settings during the day. A 'setting' is a combination of five factors: *place*, *time*, *people*, *things* and *activities*. But some settings are so alike that though they're different, they're not really providing variety. Roughly, where three of the five factors in two settings are the same or similar, the settings are counted as one.

Anne seems to have been in several settings during the day. To find out just how much variety there was for her, we have looked at what she did in terms of the five factors. Her visits to the bakers and the newsagents have been counted as one setting as they are similar in opening *time*, the types of *people* Anne is likely to meet, and the sorts of *activities* she is likely to do there. So, although it seems that Anne went to five different settings, in fact there was slightly less variety – just four settings on that day.

Anne's chart:

Place	Time	People	Things	Activities
Own house	Anytime	Mum and Dad and anyone who calls	Most things in the house, own toys, equipment for cooking and housework	Eat, sleep, play and help
Church hall	9-12 Monday, Tuesday and Friday.	Helpers and other children	Playgroup toys	Play, talk and listen to story
Local park	Daytime	Casually, other people and children	Trees, grass, flowers, water, ducks, swings	Physical activities, feed ducks
Bakers	9-6 Monday-Saturday	Assistants, other customers	Bread, cakes	Buying, chatting
Newsagents	9-6 Monday-Saturday	Assistants, other customers	Papers, sweets, cigarettes, etc.	Buying, chatting

Your child's 'Going-out Chart'

Make a list of all the places you and your child went to last week. Use the chart of activities in *Routines of the day and week* in Chapter 1, the 'going out' column, to help you. Try to work out how many different settings this involved. Fill in the place, time, people, things and activities, then see how many different settings there are.

Place	Time	People	Things	Activities

Is there enough variety?

You probably won't have many more than six different settings in any one week. Is this enough variety for your child? Have you both got into a rut? The same old activities in the same old places at the same old time with the same old people and things? Travel – or when you're with a pre-schooler, simply getting out and about – broadens the mind, but only if you're seeking new settings and not just more of the old ones. There's a lot to be said for some kind of routine, but not for a rut full of old experiences, nor, on the other hand, a sudden rush of new ones.

Whether you are able to find a completely new setting for your child will depend on where you live and what's available to you. The bigger the place you live in, the more facilities there are and the greater the number and variety of settings. But is this the most important consideration for your child? There are positive advantages to living in a small town. One study has shown that:

● children from large towns spend a little time in a large number and variety of settings, while children from small towns spend more time in fewer settings;

● both groups of children spend the same amount of time with adults, but children from small towns meet many adults casually, while children from large towns spend most of their time with only a few adults.

Involvement

It is not just a matter of a variety of settings but ensuring that a child is involved in the settings he is in.

The small-town-child's experience may be more restricted and repetitive, but as a result, his sense of community – people, places, events – is clearer and more secure than that of a child from a large town who spends his time in many different places, but who doesn't meet many adults casually.

Our sprawling old cities or big modern estates, don't usually provide a 'small town' feel of involvement and knowledge about what's going on. Involvement seems to be the key to helping a child get more out of his outings. You may have read in Chapter 5 how a child *can* get much more out of a shopping expedition. Similarly in the same book the way to help your child enjoy a trip to the library was described. By applying what you have learnt in these topics to everyday outings, you can help your child to become more involved in the different settings he finds himself in.

There are ways you can help your child learn about and adjust to the outside world, both by preparation before an outing and by talk and play activities afterwards.

Walking on a wall may be more interesting than a country house.

Preparation for outings

With most first-time trips, talking about it in advance is not enough; children cannot visualise the unknown. So before a trip to the zoo, a farm, etc. visit the library or search your own bookshelves. Show your child pictures of different animals and talk about what they eat and how they live. Don't let your child believe that the natural place for animals is a cage! Talk about the people who look after them and their daily routine. When talking about a new animal compare it to one your child already knows.

Most other children's outings can be prepared in the same way, with 'research' done by you and your child.

Preliminary visits

Other visits can, and sometimes need to be, prepared for by going to 'look and see' before actually going on the outing. A first visit to a swimming bath can be very frightening. Think about it from a 3-year-old's point of view – a huge, noisy, echoing place with a funny smell. Many baths now have pleasant viewing galleries and even a café. So perhaps a first visit could just be to watch, to see that other people are 'having fun' and to feel a twinge of envy because you can't go in. This is surely a better introduction than an immediate plunge even if it is at the shallow end.

Similarly visits to playgroup or school should be possible from the 'side-lines', just watching children in the school playground from quite an early age can give a school a familiar feel, aided by your pointing out familiar faces of children from your neighbourhood.

Less pleasant outings

Watching from the 'side lines' at the dentist's and the doctor's is often possible. Most dentists and some doctors are prepared to have 'watchers' in their consulting rooms, knowing that this pays dividends when it is the child's turn for a visit.

Preparation for 'adult outings'

These are trips when you have a sneaking feeling that your child will be bored stiff! For instance a visit to your maiden aunt or to a museum. But these visits can be just as valuable 'learning situations' for a child as a trip designed to please him. He can learn about other people, their homes and their way of life. By discussing it beforehand you can increase the child's understanding and curiosity about what or who he is going to see, and, by continuing to 'work' a bit on arrival, you can maintain his interest for a time. But be prepared for his interest to flag or be diverted in odd directions. Auntie's cat is more interesting than Auntie and the 'best' exhibit in the museum may well be the collecting box at the door! Be ready to provide a diversion before boredom strikes, a picture book or small toy produced from your bag or pocket will work wonders. It could be relevant to the trip. A catalogue of exhibits may be more interesting than the 'real thing' and is good for 're-membering' games afterwards.

Taking one or more of your child's friends enriches the experience for everyone. The children will be able to talk about what interests *them* in their own language. Listen and *you* will learn. You can all look back and talk about this shared experience later.

Parties

There is a tendency to think children will enjoy parties because they are supposed to! But it is always useful if you can find out a bit about the party before so that you can tell them what to expect. Going to a birthday party for six children is a very different event from the Christmas party held at Daddy's works, and yet children will often set out with the same expectation of each. Meeting a be-whiskered Father Christmas at the normally familiar play-group hall can be very upsetting without prior warning.

Travelling with young children

Children get fed-up and restless very quickly when travelling. There are many ways in which you can help. Some of them arise as you go along, others need preparation before the journey.

Different journeys give rise to differing activities. Let's look first at activities suitable for car travel and then at any additions or alterations needed for other forms of travel.

Travelling by car

Before the journey pack an 'entertainments bag' this could include:

A favourite cuddly toy.

A doll for dressing.

Some paper, crayons and a board to lean on.

Some picture books.

Some I-spy or Ladybird observation books.

Some homemade observation cards (see below).

A first geography lesson

Draw a simple map for your child before you go with the main towns you will pass through, and the rivers and railways you will cross marked on it. Go through it with him before you leave, then give him the home-made map to keep by him in the car and let him cross off the places marked as he comes to them. This way he will begin to understand the difficult concept of distance and what the words country, county, town and village mean.

Things to do on the way

● *Singing and story telling* Both of these can involve physical action too to get inactive muscles moving, for example, Pat-a-cake, Old MacDonald, Simon says, This Little Pig, etc. You could make a special cassette with a varied programme of nursery rhymes, stories and so on.

● *Observation games* 'I spy something blue' can be started as soon as a child is moderately accurate at naming colours. Remember – vision from the back seat of a car is restricted so make sure your child's safety seat is fitted as high up as possible so that he can see out of the window. If he has safety straps, sit him on a cushion so that he can see more. Count the cars of a particular colour, spot cars like your own, guess the colour of the next one to overtake.

Make a pack of road signs, either draw your own or cut them out of an old *Highway Code*. Share the cards out and then put them in a central spot when they are spotted. Explain what they mean.

Similarly make up a pack of observation cards showing familiar road-side sights, for example a letterbox, a cow, a church, etc.

● *Word and memory games* When the view becomes boring, as on endless miles of motorway, then this is the time for more 'internal games':

Rhymes – You say 'I am thinking of something that rhymes with cat'. Hopefully your child will guess something appropriate! for example hat, mat.

Shopping list game – Each person adds something to a shopping list but has to repeat the whole list first.

What's in the bag? – Use a paper bag. Put in small items one at a time, for example a key, a lipstick, a penny, and try to identify them by feel.

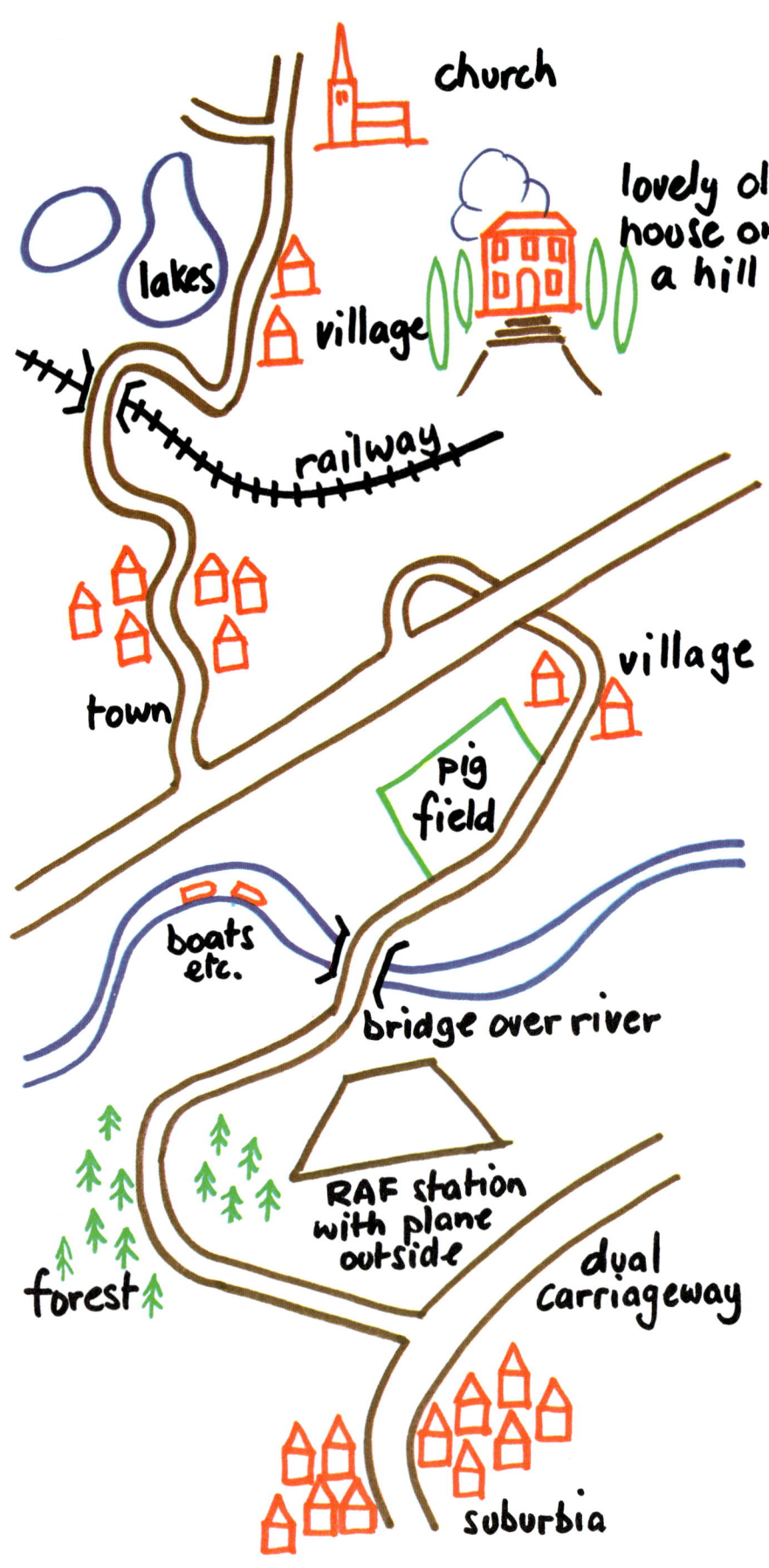

Travelling other ways

● Buses – The view is much better than a car especially if you can climb up to the upper deck. All the observation games can be played. Singing may be out, but not storytelling.

● Trains – A bit more room here but you cannot endlessly run up and down to the toilet and buffet.

● Walking – You can collect things as you go – flowers, twigs, etc. Jumping the cracks in the pavement are all good walking games. This is a good time for storytelling and for listening, for example machine sounds, bird sounds, bells, voices, etc.

At home again

Perhaps some trips are best forgotten, there are always those times when everything went wrong and you just do not want to remember them! But in the main there is a need to reinforce what has been seen, so that the event becomes a part of your child's 'total experience', to be considered at leisure and 'used' again when similar situations occur. In fact he may even want to re-live the 'nasty times' too in play and so make them more tolerable to himself.

We can help in this reinforcing by providing games and activities as well as by simply talking about the experience.

● *Imaginative play* You can't *make* your child play imaginatively but you can provide simple 'props' that will help him recall outings and situations:

an old clothes horse – could be an animal cage,

a large cloth over the table – could be a tent,

two cloths on the washing line – could be the curtains of a stage,

dressing up clothes, homemade or cast-off from home or a jumble sale – provide items for re-enacting visits.

● *Collecting* There are some obvious collections to make when you are out and about, shells and stones, leaves and wild flowers – taking the opportunity at the same time to start teaching the country code so that future generations will not strip the country of every available specimen.

Some collections involve slight expenditure, but can be valuable to a child now and later on when he goes to school. Most 'places of interest' sell postcards and for a few pence you can start a collection that will interest your child for years. Keep cards together in a box or book and look at them together and talk about the places that they represent. Another cheap collectors' item is a button badge, most children like wearing any type of badge for a few days, but then they get lost! Try instead sticking them into a large scale map stuck on the children's wall. (Cheap maps are available at most garages, or use the one you made for the travelling games.)

● *Memory games* These can even start on the journey home, simply listing the things that you have seen; an elaboration of this could be to describe something that you have seen and then ask the children to guess what you are talking about.

● *Scrapbook* Get the scrapbook habit, but let your child do the sticking and only when he wants. It's easy to be obsessive about books like this and to want them to be tidy, but initially just let the child stick in things that are reminiscent of his holiday or some other occasion.

● *Photographs* These are valuable aids to memory, especially if you are prepared to sit down and really talk about them.

● *Books and toys* Many of the things you already have at home will have more relevance once your child has more experience. The farm set, the toy train will be viewed with renewed interest once he really knows what the machines do and how the animals move and sound.

● *Repeated visits* Recall things you saw before and compare them with similar situations. 'On this beach there are only pebbles, last year we saw sand and played in the dunes.'

● *Television and radio* These are good providers of material for your child to remember as long as he accepts that the programme will be interrupted while you discuss it with him.

Helping children to 'see' the world is rewarding work. Not only will it increase the variety of your child's settings, but also involve him in the ever widening world. The rewards are not just in the child's increased knowledge but also in your own increased awareness. Looking at things afresh is good for everyone.

Hello stranger

How do you get to know strangers? And how does your child get to know them? What sort of help can you give him in getting to know strangers?

Making contact

Imagine you're at a party and find yourself next to a stranger. How do you get to know each other? First, you must both show a *willingness to be acquainted* – usually by giving each other friendly looks. Then one of you makes an *opening move* – asks a question, smiles, waits for an answer. If the other wants to go ahead, he or she will reply, and return the friendly look. Opening moves can be offputting if you don't take care:

'Doesn't that redhead look as if she has a temper'
'My wife is a redhead'
'Oh, well, I meant that one over there'
'That *is* my wife'.

But once you have a *good* opening, the acquaintance can be kept up, perhaps by finding out what you have in common. All our meetings with others involve complicated rules which we usually notice no more than we notice our breathing. For instance, there are rules about looking at people: you don't stare hard at someone as you approach in the street; if he is a stranger, you alter your gaze as you get closer. Whether or not to shake hands, how long to hold out your hand, how warmly to greet someone, whether to use christian names – these all involve rules which cause embarrassment to everyone if they are ignored or misunderstood.

But what happens when child meets child? Are the rules the same? Take a good look – you may be surprised by what you see.

Child meets child

Choose a time when you're not too busy to watch – on a trip to a park or a recreation ground, or indoors when there are several children together. Find a place where you can watch for a few minutes without being noticed. But first a word about watching. It's the easiest thing in the world to sit and watch – and then very quickly forget what you have seen. So

● try to give a running commentary to yourself – silently, in your head, telling yourself what is going on

● even better, make notes very quickly on a piece of paper, or keep a pencil and small notebook handy for this purpose

● keep to what you *see* happening, not what you *think* the children are feeling. For example, 'Sam takes two steps towards the other child, holding out his arms and smiling. The other child backs away, watching'; *not* 'Sam makes friends with other child who isn't interested'.

Observation guidelines

Where is it?

home territory	☐
familiar place but not own home	☐
strange place	☐
indoors	☐
outdoors	☐

Who's there?

strange children

	older	same age	younger
One			
Several			
Many			

familiar children

	older	same age	younger
One			
Several			
Many			

What happens?

(What happens depends in part on whether the child you are watching meets a familiar friend or a strange child.)

Who looks at what?

. . . .

Who makes the first approach?

. . . .

How long does he wait before approaching?

. . . .

Does your child first approach:
a child? a grown up? a toy? another object?

☐ ☐ ☐ ☐

Does he wait for you to encourage him before he leaves you?   Yes/No

How does he respond to others?

smiles	☐
turns away shyly	☐
hides behind you	☐
hits out	☐

Once he's established contact with another child, does he move away from you?   ☐

How long does he stay with other children before returning?

Few seconds	Minute or more	Doesn't want to come back
☐	☐	☐

Comment

You will probably notice that the 'rules' for children getting to know each other are very different from those of adults. Shaking hands, saying 'hello' or 'how do you do', are much rarer among children. Adults find out about each other by asking questions—it seems rather rude to start a conversation by saying something about yourself. But pre-school children frequently start a conversation by saying things like 'I've got a toy car' or 'We've got jelly for tea'. And perhaps this is important. Have you ever heard a conversation like this?

Two three year olds meet for the first time. Silence for about one minute
'I've got a *Mr Men* book'
'So've I'
'I've got Mr Strong'
'I've got Mr Dizzy. Do you want to see it?'

This looks like a simple chat, but notice that both children start by saying something about *themselves*. The first question and friendly move come at the end of the conversation with 'Do you want to see it?' By that time, each has shown he is the proud owner of a *Mr Men* book, so honour has been satisfied! A three-year-old has learnt far more about himself than he has about others of his own age – so when he is not sure of his ground (such as when he meets a stranger) he starts from what he knows best. Maybe it's also a way of showing his own colours – after all, he doesn't know whether the other child is friend or foe. Hitting out may not really be aggressive. Touching someone, either gently or hard, is a very direct and easy way of making contact with them.

Have you met my dwarf?

Six hundred years ago, noblemen kept midgets at court, and thought it very funny when these tiny creatures behaved like normal-sized people. They also used them as waiters when it was important to impress visitors. In the same way, parents today often set great store by introducing their children to other adults, and can feel embarrassed if a child doesn't want to meet them. It's worth asking yourself how *you* feel when your child fails to 'impress the visitors'. It's one thing to feel proud of a child and quite another to treat him as a showpiece. Does your child think of himself as a showpiece? Do you ever treat him like those dwarfs?

The two cartoon strips show Mrs James and Jane meeting two of Mrs James' friends. In the cartoon above the child becomes shy at the meeting; the adults are literally looking down on her. But in the second strip, the meeting is different for Jane. Why?

First, notice that Jane had something to talk about – her dolly. Her mother's friend – Mrs Clark – used the doll to take attention away from Jane herself. (Dolls and teddies are often a child's friends, and can be usefully taken along to share the embarrassment of meeting strange adults.) What's more, she uses the 'child-like' technique of saying something about herself first – in this case her own daughter – something Jane could readily understand and find interesting. Then she crouched down so that Jane could talk to her face-to-face, instead of face-to-kneecap. Mrs James probably isn't really offended. She knows she'll get her turn, and is pleased to see Jane warming towards another adult, instead of becoming shy.

What makes for friendly meetings?

We can sum this up in four basic points:

Don't expect too much
Don't make demands the child can't meet. Don't expect two year olds to carry on lengthy conversations with strangers. Don't be surprised if three year olds take time to make friends. Don't expect all adults to know how to talk to children.

Practise beforehand
Practise what to do and say on potentially scaring occasions in a very relaxed way and well in advance. The three year old often enjoys make-believe games of shopping, meeting people, imaginary telephone calls. A child may get lost in a crowded store, and it could be helpful if he knew his name and address by heart, so that he could give this information even under stress. Explain and discuss what adults mean when they say 'How do you do?' and what to do when they say 'Shake hands'. Sayings like this can be puzzling when your child meets them for the first time: How do you do *what*? Did he say *shake* my hands? Practise answering the questions you know grandma and her friends will ask, this can make a tea-party easier for a shy child.

Don't increase embarrassment
If your child is shy, don't rush him, or make him more worried by trying to force or persuade him. Beware of answering for him all the time or criticising him openly in front of others. If you let him take his time, he'll gradually make his own advances. It's usually better to start gradually by offering him opportunities for contacting others, such as sharing out sweets, showing a toy, or handing the biscuits around. He may still do this in silence, but at least he'll have the chance to feel he's making some contact. Above all, don't remind him about bad contacts, for example on his last visit to the doctor, he cried when he saw the white-coated stranger. You can help the strange to become familiar to your child: one bedtime story about doctors and what they do is worth a dozen pep-talks on how to be brave.

The older the better
A child's readiness to get to know strange adults usually grows with age and experience. The following summary gives a rough guide, to which you will be able to add particular details for your own child. His reactions partly will depend on how strange the stranger is, see overleaf.

Two-year-olds may
● be friendly with familiar adults, but often refuse to talk to strange adults
● just watch solemnly
● run to mum

Three-year-olds may
● sometimes respond shyly to adult's greeting
● approach familiar adults and start conversations

Four-year-olds may
● often seem confident, even talkative
● volunteer own name, age and introduce other members of the family
● still become shy if the situation is unusual
● sometimes talk about their embarrassment and get over it

How strange is a stranger?

What kinds of adults does a pre-school child meet? Can you add others to the list?

Friends and neighbours of parents
Note:
Your child may know your friends and neighbours, but do they know him?

Friendly strangers
(Playgroup leaders, relatives whom you don't often see)
Note:
They may wish to meet your child, but does he wish to meet them? He will usually take his parents' advice. Children's judgements of physical attractiveness often differ from adults! Elderly people may inspire awe, fear or repulsion. Be prepared to cope with your child's personal remarks.

Local strangers
(Bus conductors, shopkeepers etc.)
Note:
Let your child do something here like asking for something, or paying.

Formal strangers
(Doctor, dentist, health visitor)
Note:
Watch out for uniforms and white coats; these people seem to have authority. Does your child think that *you* are nervous? Do you and your child dress more carefully than usual?

Dangerous strangers
Most of the strangers whom young children meet will be friendly or neutral. Some may be hostile and a tiny minority might be dangerous. You need to help young children in limiting how much they trust strangers.

If you *never* speak to strangers yourself, you cannot teach your child how to speak to them. If you do speak to strangers, he will learn from you how conversations are started and he will recognize the reserved tone of your voice.

After such conversations you can talk to him about meeting strangers. You can limit his natural friendliness in whatever way is necessary, depending on where you live. Perhaps a good rule is that he doesn't speak to strangers unless you are with him. This gives him freedom within certain limits that you may feel you need to impose.

Imagine you're a stranger

Imagine that you're a stranger in the place where you are living now . . . or perhaps you are and there is no need to imagine! Where would you be able to get to know people and what sort of opening moves would you make?

Few people have the self-confidence to knock at all the doors in the street and say 'I am Josie Maloney and I have come to live in Number 16'. Few people have the confidence to approach a stranger in the street and invite them in for a cup of coffee. It's often easier to make friends by joining a club or group where you go to *do* something, where you have a reason for going other than making friends – to play games, or dance, or take the children. Parents of young children often find that it is easiest to make friends with other parents. Days run to the same routines, you are facing similar problems.

Joining a group is itself a way of saying that you want to get to know people. Whether or not you are welcomed will make a great difference to your life and that of your family. You should remember this when you have lived in a place long enough to see the arrival of more new people. Can you give them the welcome you received – or the one you wished you'd got?

Opening moves
Walking down a High Street and not knowing anyone can be a depressing business. If you're depressed, your child must surely realise this (See *Unspoken words* in Chapter 5.) If there is no one for you to talk to, your child will have no chance to learn how friendly people greet each other. An outing in which you meet friends is more interesting for both of you and gives your child a feeling of security, an assurance that outside the immediate family circle there are more friendly people. If you are ready to make friends, your face can speak for you.

Which of these opening moves have you tried recently with a stranger?

- [ ] smiling at an adult
- [ ] smiling at a child
- [ ] asking or answering a question
- [ ] giving or asking for help
- [ ] giving or receiving sympathy
- [ ] admiring something done by a child
- [ ] showing interest in something held by a child
- [ ] showing something to a child

If you haven't made a friendly gesture to a stranger recently, you could try doing one of these things and see what comes of it. Sometimes you will meet a rebuff, more often from an adult than from a child. Perhaps you have noticed how, if you smile at a child, he will often check with his mother to see whether it is all right for him to smile back? If she doesn't smile back at you, his response will stop. If she smiles at you, he feels that he can continue the communication which began with your first smile. Exchanges of this kind help to give children a feeling that there is a friendly world outside the small group of people he knows well at home.

'Wait for me!'

Moving house can be a tremendous upheaval for any family. The pre-school child's home is his world and as long as he has Mummy and Daddy and his 'things' about him he should not mind where home is – or should he?

Do you remember moving house at an early age? The chances are that if you do there was something 'nasty' about it, a favourite toy forgotten, the garden swing left standing.

Preparing

Talk about the move to your child, bring him into your conversations. Don't let him half-hear, half understand adult talk.

● Introduce play and stories about moving. He will enjoy packing and unpacking his toys and your kitchen equipment. There are a surprising number of children and animals in story books who are 'on the move'.

● When out shopping look out for other people's removal vans and for sale signs, and show him that moving is a common occurrence.

● Buy or make a house-warming surprise present to greet him in his new room.

● You know that you are going to miss the familiar faces, shops and everyday life in your old neighbourhood. Your child will miss his friends too, but how much he misses them will depend on you. Try and avoid the 'Oh we shall miss you' conversations with friends and neighbours. They make life hard for everyone. If possible take him to the new house before you move, let him think he is choosing his own room or corner.

● Visit the new area and point out shops selling his favourite things. Pick out anything familiar.

● Find out in advance about local playgroups, mother and toddler clubs or nursery schools.

Not all of the 'preparation plan' will, or need, be achieved. Above all treat the whole thing in a matter-of-fact way, don't make a great issue of it. To a great extent *he won't understand anyway*, but after the event you will find that time spent in preparation has helped your child to take the move in his stride.

It may help to take time to make a list of what you used to do with your child.

There will be replacements for some of those you have left behind. Look for them!

What was enjoyable	Meeting people	Other things
shops		
friends		
park/recreation ground		
library		
clinic		
mother and toddler club		
playgroup/nursery		
church		
club		

Moving day

Whether you are pleased or sorry about leaving, the removal day itself can be awful! Whether you choose to start packing weeks in advance or leave it to the last moment, you must plan for the child in advance. Will you:

Park him out before, during and after the event? Simplest from your point of view and may be best for him. Provided he is used to being away from home and enjoys it, and he understands what is going on and won't feel that he may be left behind for ever. If you are desperately unhappy about the move this way would probably be the best idea; seeing you in tears for days on end will do nothing for his security!

Park him out on removal day? Again fine if he is used to it. Will you be able to pop in for lunch? Will he be able to see 'his' furniture going in the van? This could be fun, but might be very distressing.

Keep him with you? Are you prepared to cuddle him if he's miserable, cope with activities when he gets underfoot, and with food when he's hungry? He may enjoy all the fun of emptying rooms, even seeing his own things go, but he may be horrified. Whatever the reaction, you can be sure

he won't be 'good', and sit in a corner and watch it all happen!

Only you can assess what his reactions may be. Even you may be wrong but at least you will have the consolation of having thought about it!

Settling in

After all the upheaval and consequent straightening out everything may suddenly go quite blank. It can be quite a time of panic and to a certain extent everything is left to you. Friendly help from neighbours makes an enormous difference at this stage— remember this when you see someone else unpacking a removal van!

Child's eye view

Once you've moved you may be feeling desperate and trapped in your new but probably lonely house, but your child may not feel the same way. He may be more prepared to accept the situation than you are. He has got you and his 'things' safe in his own world again. But he may not be quite ready to start stepping out from this new world.

Don't feel you must rush out to find friends for him. Give him time to settle at home first and then to start digesting the simple things on the list. Trips to the shops, the library and the park are undemanding and fairly impersonal. This may delay your meeting people for a week or two but giving him these situations first will make it easier to settle into more demanding social situations later on. Too much change too quickly will bewilder a small child. He needs time to feel secure and established in his new world before exploring further. This is especially important if moving has meant that somebody special has dropped out of your child's life. If he doesn't understand why he's lost that person, he will make up his own explanations. His questions take time to form in his mind and he needs the opportunity to ask them. Giving him the time, especially at bedtime, is the most important part of settling him into his new world.

171

Parents have many faces

"BOBBY, I'VE TOLD YER TO COME HERE TWICE. NOW YOU'RE FOR IT!"

"ROBERT DARLING, COME NOW AND WE WILL WALK HOME WITH THE VICAR"

Do you change when you are out with your child? Parents are always advised to be consistent in their behaviour and attitudes towards their children. If you change, are you consistent? Take a look at yourself!

Have you ever thought about the many people you are? A list of different people could include:

wife/husband   customer   patient
daughter/son   employee   employer
mother/father   stranger   friend
housekeeper   neighbour   cook

Depending on the life you lead, you may be able to add to this list. To all the people you meet you are a 'different' person because you react differently to them and to the situations in which you meet them.

Your pre-school child is usually with you when you meet other people. What does he think about the many-faced person with whom he spends his days? How can he adjust to your constantly changing self?

A day can go like this....

Breakfast time

Often a hurried time. Not much time for affection, more likely a row over the burnt toast or an unironed shirt. You probably won't start throwing things, but a small child will register slammed doors and cross voices. A knock at the door and there is the postman with a parcel. Suddenly you are all smiles and cheerful – 'Good morning' – and – 'Thank you'. Daddy did not get a kind word but this stranger did. How do you sort that out when you are only three?

Visitors arrive

Milly pops in for tea. This friend has children of her own and is prepared to let you interrupt the chat to find a bit of jigsaw or endlessly to put on and take off coat and boots. Everyone is happy and relaxed. But later Mrs Bates calls. Her children were brought up on 'seen and not heard' principle. Suddenly you expect your child to behave as she says hers should. 'Play quietly in your room.' 'You'll have a good smack if you are naughty.' You withdraw from a cuddle. 'Find it yourself' – you say when the jigsaw piece is lost. 'Put it on yourself . . .' if help is needed with a coat. Think about your child's feelings in these situations. Is he supposed to know how you react to your friends and act in a way that matches *your* behaviour?

Here are some situations that you might meet with your child. You may meet them in company with people like:
Milly – your kind, tolerant friend, Mrs Bates – the neighbour whose children were brought up to be seen and not heard, and . . . your own mother-in-law. Would you react to your child in the same way as you would have done if you had been on your own? First, consider each situation and then write in how you would react if you were alone. Now put a tick if you think your behaviour would remain unchanged.

Situation	With Milly	With Mrs Bates	With mother-in-law
You want your child to come off the swings before he is ready because you are cold and bored.			
He falls over and grazes his knee but makes more fuss than seems necessary.			
He spills his squash in your lap when you're in the café.			
He climbs higher up a tree than you really would like.			
He stays with his nose glued to the toy-shop window while you still need to get to the baker, and it is nearly time for the bus.			

Do you find that you are most consistent when you are with people like yourself? The more unlike you they are, the more you change your reactions. From your reactions, your child is learning about different sorts of people – different values and ways of talking.

Off to the shops

Depending on your mood and that of the people you meet, shopping can be fun or unpleasant for both of you. You may discuss what you are going to buy, let him 'choose' the packets, hand in the money . . . or you may strap him firmly in the push chair and say 'Don't touch!' a dozen times, and chat endlessly to a friend. Often what you do will depend on the people you meet, the friendly grocer or the horrid assistant, the old friend from school or someone who always seems to have something to complain about. How is a three-year-old going to understand all these varying situations?

Out for lunch

The opportunities for trouble at mealtimes are endless! Your child may be a bit fussy and at home you let this pass by giving him things that you know he will eat. But when you are at your friend's house and her two are happily tucking into a dish that is unpopular with your child things are different. It's so easy to side with your friend, whose opinion you value, by saying that your child is just being fussy, trying to force him to eat, and then being ashamed of him because he makes a fuss. How unfair! He knows he does not have to eat it at home so why has he got to eat it now? This means that your action could certainly cause some reaction in him, maybe a sense of betrayal.

To the playground

You want him to be tough when there are onlookers, to be a brave boy if he falls, to be a clever, confident climber, good with a ball and friendly to everyone.

But how often, when you are on your own with him, do you say – 'Be careful, dear, you will fall! Don't do that, it is dangerous!'

Home for tea

A time when Daddy is home. He is tired and irritable because the management of his shop has changed and he is worried about the future of his job . . . You are kind and thoughtful towards him. But is your reaction to an irritable husband always the same?

Tick the boxes below if your reaction would be the same if the cause of his irritation were that:

● he couldn't find the screw-driver you'd used to fix a plug ☐

● you'd invited some friends he didn't like very much to supper ☐

● there are children's toys all over the house ☐

● you'd had a quarrel the night before because you were too tired to make love ☐

What does your child make of your different reactions to the same man?

Getting him settled in bed

You know a baby-sitter is coming. You want to impress her with your model child who never wakes – to such an extent that you may be disloyal to the child who wakes and finds himself in the charge of a stranger.

So within one fairly normal day, the number of different 'you's' has been many and varied. How consistent have you been with your child?

The majority of the examples so far have been of the kind of situation in which parents draw away from their children, almost disowning them. There are also situations in which parents become puzzling, kind, tolerant and pushingly possessive . . .

You and your child

You meet a friend who does not like to be interrupted when she is talking. You let your child get away with outrageous behaviour because you don't 'want a fuss'. In this case, a child may become very resentful, even thinking – 'She doesn't love me any more!' His reactions then may vary, but they all have one object, to get your attention. He may whine and tug, become aggressive and kick either you or your friend. Or he may just sit still and be quiet, withdrawing into his own world entirely. He does not really want a cross Mum, but any sort of Mum is better than a withdrawn, indifferent one.

He will test himself against you to a point, when even he will be alarmed by his reactions. He will be crying out to be stopped. If he isn't he will again feel that you don't care and feel insecure.

Over protection

You over-protect because you fear the criticism of others and defend him against all comers. How can he learn not to be clinging and timid?

Showing him off

You ask him to 'do his act', something he can do rather well, like an imitation that will amuse or impress. How can he feel that he matters to you just because he is himself rather than because he can amuse your friends for you?

Being dependable

How can your child learn what standards are expected and acceptable?

If you allow your own relationships with others to alter your natural behaviour with your child too much he will become insecure and unhappy in unfamiliar surroundings and with other people. Your own changeability will result in your child having difficulty with his own social development. This sounds alarming . . . does it mean that parents should always be the same?

No! They still need to be individuals as well as parents. They cannot be expected to bury their personalities in order to make the way smooth for their children. Apart from the fact that it would be impossible, it would also be undesirable. So how is it possible to make sure that both children and parents get a fair deal?

Being 'consistent' sounds a bit dull, perhaps to be 'dependable' or 'reliable' would be better. If you can be depended upon when it is important, your child will find it easier to accept that people behave in different ways at different times.

Soon he will be playing the many-faced game himself; to his teacher he will be one child, to his classmates another. Having many faces is part of being human and your job is to teach your child how to live with it.

HE'S PERFECTLY ALRIGHT MOTHER DON'T FUSS

COME DOWN DARLING YOU'LL FALL

For their own good

Even by the age of four, children are usually quite skilled at fighting for their own interests, and parents on the whole allow them to do this. So there's the possibility of conflict at every turn in a child's life. He has a continuous choice between behaving in a way acceptable to his parents – or not. You, as a parent, have the choice of trying to be boss, or working things out between you.

Imagine each of the following ten situations has occurred with your pre-school child. (For convenience, the quiz has been written for mothers about sons, but obviously it can apply to fathers and daughters, too.) There are no right or wrong answers.

● Choose *one* answer which most nearly matches what you would try first if the situation arose.

● Work through quickly, being honest.

● When you have finished, circle the solutions you chose in the summary answer chart at the end.

1 You think it's bedtime, but your child starts to cry because he wants to watch something on television. Would you :

  a march him straight up to bed regardless ;

  b tell him he'll be tired in the morning if he goes on watching ;

  c remind him there's a bedtime rule in your family – and it's to be kept ;

  d let him stay, knowing he'll go off on his own accord quite soon.

2 Your child isn't watching what he's doing, and spills his drink all over the table. Would you :

  a tell him big children don't spill their drinks ;

  b give him a smack/tell him off ;

  c tell him to get down from the table until he can pay attention ;

  d explain to him how to hold his beaker so that he won't spill it again.

3 Your husband promises to take your child out to a favourite place at the weekend, and then has to dash off to do something else. Your child sulks all day, and won't talk to him. Do you say :

  a daddy's sorry he had to go, and you're making him even more unhappy ;

  b it can't be helped so stop making a fuss about it ;

  c how would you like it if daddy didn't talk to you ? ;

  d children shouldn't behave like that to their daddies.

4 Your child's done something naughty, but when you find out about it, he says he hasn't done it. Would you :

  a tell him off, to try to prevent him from lying again ;

  b ignore it, feeling children of that age don't really know the difference between lies and truth ;

  c explain to him you know he's lying and it makes you unhappy.

5 Your child brings you flowers – and you realise he's got them from your neighbour's garden ! Do you tell him that :

  a children should never take things that don't belong to them ; .

  b the neighbour will be upset because he has taken her flowers ;

  c he must go without a treat because he's been naughty.

6 Your child's been going to a playgroup quite happily for two months. Then, one day, he says he doesn't want to go. He's not ill or anything, but won't tell you why when you ask him, however hard you try. In the end do you say :

  a but you always go to playgroup ;

  b don't be so silly, you're going to go ;

  c if you don't go, you won't see your friends ;

  d the playgroup leader will wonder where you are.

7 You've been out shopping. When you get home you find your child has picked up some little thing from one of the counters without you noticing. Would you :

  a go back with him to the shop and explain with him what happened ;

  b feel you can't do much at this age, because they don't really understand the difference between right and wrong ;

  c give him a really good telling off ;

  d explain that he mustn't take things that belong to the shop keeper without paying.

8 You ask your child to do something for you, like fetch in the milk, or help tidy up, and he says – 'I can't do it now I'm too busy'. Would you :

  a feel he should help you right away, and insist that he does ;

  b feel he should help you right away, but allow time before you insist ;

  c do it yourself, feeling he's as much right to think he's busy as you have ;

  d do it yourself, but feel disapproval that he won't help you, when you help him.

9 Your child is playing at being a shop-keeper, or an engine driver, and could do with someone to be a customer, or a passenger. Do you :

  a feel that you can let your hair down and join in at his level ;

  b feel more at home with other kinds of play such as puzzles or drawings ;

  c tell him to go and play with another child, or on his own.

10 You've been doing something together quite happily you think, but suddenly your child turns round and says – 'Stop telling me what to do all the time !' Would you feel :

  a that he has a right to tell you off sometimes too ;

  b that it's time for what you're doing to stop ;

  c that he shouldn't behave that way towards you.

Answer chart – ring your answers here and add up the numbers of rings in each group.

	Style 1	Style 2	Style 3
Q1	a	c	b or d
Q2	b or c	a	d
Q3	b	d	a or c
Q4	a	b	c
Q5	c	a	b
Q6	b	a	c or d
Q7	c	b	a or d
Q8	a	b or d	c
Q9	c	b	a
Q10	b	c	a
Totals :	1	3	6

Answers to the quiz

The possible answers you can choose fall into three main 'styles' of control or discipline that parents use with their children. Research shows that most parents use all three styles – but that they also tend to prefer a particular one which they use most often. Is this true of you? Did you:

● choose answers from all three styles? This is natural. What you say or do in a problem situation depends on not just you and your child, but on the situation itself – how serious it is, how often it happens, who's involved.

● find that, nonetheless, most of your answers fell into one 'style' – for example, six or more in style 3; or five in style 1, four in style 2 and only one in style 3?

● find it hard to restrict yourself to only one answer per question? You were asked to pick what would be your 'first choice' answer if these situations had actually occurred – but in real life what you want to do doesn't always work. So for example you may start by being reasonable and gradually become more abrupt and give your child orders.

What the styles involve

Style 1 – is very direct and sometimes punishing. For example:

● it can't be helped, so stop making a fuss about it;

● march him straight up to bed regardless;

● he must go without a treat because he's been naughty.

Style 2 – is concerned with family rulings about what children may/should do. For example:

● remind him there's a bedtime rule in your family – and it's to be kept;

● big children don't spill their drinks;

● feel he should help you right away, but allow time before you insist.

Style 3 – is explanatory, with more give-and-take between parent and child. For example:

● explain to him how to hold his beaker so that he won't spill it again;

● Daddy's sorry he had to go, and you're making him even more unhappy;

● feel that your child has a right to tell you off sometimes too;

● let him stay up, knowing he'll go off on his own accord quite soon.

Care beyond reason

All parents intend that what they say and do to control their children should be effective in the long-term, for the good of the child. Parents feel responsible for the actions of their children. They worry – if only to themselves – about possible long-term wrong they could do by not controlling behaviour early on: 'Suppose she gets to fifteen and is still lying/too shy to talk to people/wetting her bed/not reading...' The phrases parents use also show how they feel their child's behaviour reflects their own: 'a pride and joy', 'he lets me down in public', 'she showed me up the other day'.

So parents give their children 'care beyond reason', going to great lengths for them – a thing they would not do if they were not their own children. Care beyond reason can take many forms. For example: accepting the bedtime ritual a child dictates, allowing behaviour at home that wouldn't be allowed in public, letting a child dominate family life in times of need (like a four-year-old who has night terrors).

Care beyond reason means being concerned to meet your children's needs effectively, both in the short-term and the long-term. Perhaps a child's greatest need is to grow up with a sense of personal value and their own worth, together with a sense of the needs of others.

Let's take a closer look at the styles of parental control in these terms. How does a parent see this 'job' – and what effect do their actions have on the child? In the quiz, ten isolated, imaginary incidents are considered. However, in real life what's important is the ongoing patterns of understandings – and misunderstandings – between parent and child in control situations. All styles of control are intended by a parent, to be effective. But what do children actually learn from their parents' style of control? We can make some reasonable guesses:

Style 1 Adult authority

Here, the parents feel they have a natural authority as adults. They should command, and children should obey. They direct their children, physically or with orders, giving little or no explanation. The child is expected to obey, or be punished. The adult sees himself as 'the gaffer', and the child learns to expect control to come from above. He's not expected to control himself or to give or receive explanations.

Style 2 Position in life

Here the parents have definitive views about what children of different sexes and ages should or shouldn't do, or be able to do. So the explanations they offer the child are in terms of what they see as his position in life: 'You are too old for that', 'big boys don't cry'. They treat the child as a child, not as a partner or equal. For the child's part, he gets some 'feedback' on what he's doing, but it's very generalised. For example: 'big boys don't cry' doesn't really explain to him why he shouldn't be crying at that moment, given the situation as he sees it. It's unlikely that he really knows why he should follow his parents' rules.

Style 3 Personal give and take

Here the parents view their child more as a junior partner in the business of being a family. He has his rights and responsibilities. His parents want him to learn to work out the rules of a situation for himself. The explanations they give are personal to the child, to his skills and characteristics, and to the situation concerned. They try to help him understand why he's done something 'wrong'; how he can avoid it in the future; and how other people feel as a result of his behaviour. In the end parents are still in control but a child is treated more as an individual, a person of value. He is helped to understand and take responsibility for his actions, and their effect on others.

Choosing your style

To some extent you need to vary your style to fit different situations. A long explanation when your child's about to slice himself with the breadknife is obviously out. But the situation might not have arisen if you had already introduced knives to him and explained how they must be used. The stage your child has reached also matters. In general, two-year-olds are much less open to reason and less able to think of things from another's point of view than are four- or five-year-olds. In the short-term a 'no' or 'children aren't allowed to' is probably simpler for you, and may seem quite effective at the time. But in the long run, personal explanations seem most likely to make the child more sensitive to the consequences of his behaviour on people and things, and more able to control himself from within.

No parent is perfect. It would be impossible to be so all the time anyway! What matters is being 'good enough' to give your child the chance to learn from this kind of approach.

For their own good

Language and control

The three styles of control involve words in different ways: orders, 'position' statements or personal instructions and explanations. Finding the right sort of explanation for your child isn't always easy (see the sections on language in Chapter 4). But every time you do this, you're showing your child that words can be a useful 'bargaining tool' in sorting out situations. Whether you're prepared to do this depends on your control style, but also on how important you think words are generally. Try answering the following questions:

1 Which of the following things would be *much more* difficult to do with pre-school children if you couldn't speak:

1 teach them everyday tasks, like dressing ☐

2 help them to make things ☐

3 draw their attention to different shapes and colours ☐

4 show them how things work ☐

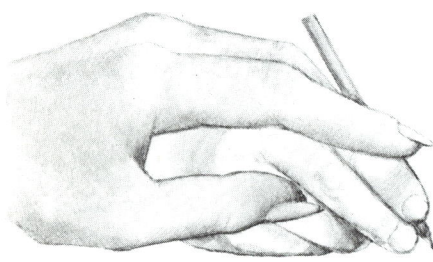

5 discipline them ☐

6 show them what's right and wrong ☐

7 help them work things out for themselves ☐

8 let them know your views ☐

2 Here are some reasons for talking to people. How often do you talk for each reason (often/sometimes/rarely)?

Reason	often	sometimes	rarely
1 To be friendly	☐	☐	☐
2 To show your feelings	☐	☐	☐
3 To find out what others think of you	☐	☐	☐
4 To increase the number of people you know	☐	☐	☐
5 To exchange ideas	☐	☐	☐
6 To question the world about you	☐	☐	☐
7 To increase your knowledge of the world	☐	☐	☐
8 To find out more about people	☐	☐	☐

3 Have you ever told your child any of the following things:

               Yes No

1 That babies come from Father Christmas, under gooseberry bushes, or somewhere equally impossible

2 That a policeman (or another frightening figure) will come and get him

3 That you'll send him away if he's naughty

4 That his nose will fall off if he picks it (or something similar)

5 That you'll punish him some way (but then you don't)

Probably control and reasoning (items 5–8 in Question 1) would be harder without words. But as we've seen it's a question of what you say. Items 1–4 relate to the teaching of skills, but 4 is a general 'thinking principal' whereas 1–3 are concerned only with specific skills. Your answers to Question 2 may show you how interested you are in words for thinking things through (items 5–8) in contrast to using words for social/emotional purposes. Question 3 asks you – how truthful are you and your words? Most parents at some time distort the truth by telling their child such things. But if it happens often, your child may gradually learn that it doesn't matter if words aren't honest, and that the things you threatened rarely come to pass. Why then should he trust you?

Home and school

A personal style of control involves reasoning and explaining with words. Parents who use this style are most often those to whom words are important, not just for control, but for thinking things through, explaining how and why things happen – and for finding the truth. Their style of control, and the importance they place on reasoning with words helps their children to do these things too.

What happens at home seems to spill over into other areas of the child's life. At age eleven, children's level of reasoning with words seems to be linked in part with the parent's personal style of control. Even earlier, such children are perhaps more likely to be at an advantage when they start playgroup or primary school. They're more likely to see adults as helpers than 'controllers'; to direct their own play and learning of skills; and to establish their own social place in the group, rather than wait for a 'position' or orders to be imposed upon them.

A time when words won't do

The parent who *never* smacks their child is a rare one – though many won't admit to others that they smack their children. The question perhaps is not whether to smack but how often and why you do it. The little girl who turned on her mother one day and said 'how dare you do that' has a fair point – but sometimes it's the only way to get through to a young child. (Equally, they may feel that hitting you is the only way to draw your attention to what they're feeling, but can't say.) There's a world of difference between the occasional smack that relieves your feelings, hauls the child up sharp and allows you both to start afresh and say sorry, and the smacking habit – a regular flick of the hand, without explanation which applies in all sorts of situations. You may smack because you believe in the long-term it will help your child learn control. But the pre-school child's memory is short and he may not see what he's doing as naughty at all. As far as he's concerned, it seems much more likely that smacks just come and go as an unexplained part of life. And as their 'surprise value' goes down, so does even their short-term effectiveness.

In every family there comes a time when words won't do – but if it happens to you, ask yourself: is my child learning anything from being smacked regularly, except that I see fit to hit him? Punishment is always negative – it may stop a particular behaviour, but it doesn't show the child an acceptable alternative. But explanations may prevent situations arising again. Or you can describe the alternatives and re-direct the child's attention, without punishment.

Talking about sex

'Little children have no idea about sex so, thank goodness I don't have to worry about that for some years yet!' So some parents think . . . are they right or wrong?

Children are born male or female. You don't think of them as a person until you know their sex. In the course of living with them you are teaching them about sex, not by words but by the way you react to your husband or wife, other adults and children. They learn from the way you touch not only theirs but each other's bodies. Before they understand words, they learn about the expression of love or rejection, anger or tenderness by the expression on your face.

Often the snigger, the shrugged shoulder, the strained look and hushed voice . . . is all many children meet when they try to find out about sex, something that seems to be important and interesting. Giving sex education to your children cannot be avoided, the question is what sort of education are you giving? Children learn more from what you do and are than from what you say.

Education in sex isn't just relating the 'facts of life' in one short talk. Children need to learn how babies are made but they also need to learn that love is about the giving and receiving of happiness through the body. Children are born needing to be stroked, touched gently and held tenderly as well as to be fed and kept clean. The giving of love and responding to it are part of the sex education that you are giving.

The attitudes of parents in the first years of their child's life becomes the basis of future feelings about the enjoyment of sex. Anxieties, misunderstandings, fears and feelings of guilt that arise in the minds of young children can interfere with adult enjoyment of sex, making problems that can only be corrected with difficulty.

In learning about how children grow, it is important for parents to understand what is happening, to accept each stage as a step in their childrens' growth towards maturity. It would be very strange if the awareness, acceptance and understanding of parents had a part to play in every kind of development except that of sex.

Boy and girl differences

Sooner or later, children notice that girls do not have a penis and may decide that girls may have lost theirs – and this can cause boys to fear that they may lose theirs too. This fear is deepened if people say that a penis will drop off if it is played with. Children work out their problems in a very logical way, using the knowledge they have. If their knowledge does not answer their problem, they will make up an answer that seems to them to make sense.

Their own explanations

The explanations that children make up for themselves can become something very frightening (see *Day's end* in Chapter 1). If they are given all the information they are looking for, there is no need for them to have these fears.

It is not enough to say that the only difference is that girls don't have a penis. It is at this stage that both boys and girls can begin to learn that little girls have a womb or uterus and a vagina, with as much detail and explanation as they are interested in.

Something like this might be useful: 'Girls have a kind of strong balloon inside their tummies which is shaped like this . . .'

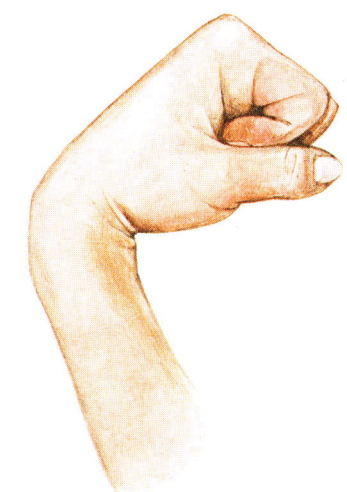

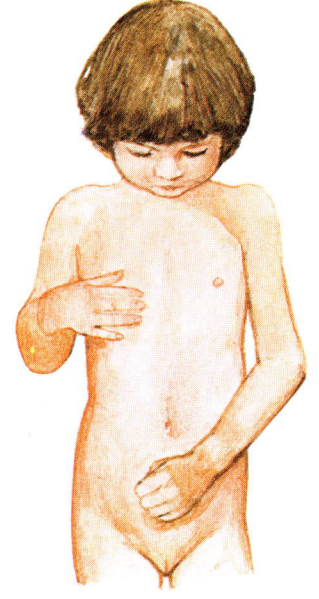

'Just about here . . .'
'. . . just as important as Peter's penis, but inside where no one can see it! It's where babies grow.'
'The balloon has a tiny opening between the legs just behind the place where wee comes out. That is called the vagina.'

You can't give children a calm, unembarrassed attitude about sex unless you have it yourself. If your little children are accustomed to seeing you naked in the privacy of your own home they will not be embarrassed. They will be helped to understand the difference between private and public behaviour, how some freedoms are especially for enjoyment at home. Later on they will change, without you teaching them, to become sensitive about nakedness. Often the problem involved in speaking freely is a difficulty in being able to use the words you need if you are to explain. It helps if you practice the words for all the parts of the body as you are bathing, drying or undressing. Use the names that come naturally to you. If you don't know names you may like to use those that you would meet in books.

177

Feelings about sex

Most parents find themselves uncertain about how to react when their children show an interest in sex. What do you think children feel when their parents react in situations like the following? Would they be linking sex with good feelings, interest, excitement, tenderness, the pleasure of giving and receiving . . . or bad feelings like shame, guilt, secrecy, rejection and fear? Try to decide in each of the examples below.

● **Philip**   I went upstairs this afternoon and found my neighbour's little girl had got her knickers down and was asking to see my son's willy. I told her it was time for her to go home. I don't think we should ask her in again.

Good feelings ☐   Bad feelings ☐

Philip's reaction told both children that they were doing something naughty. They would have been puzzled. Why was it that he was very pleased if they were interested and curious about what happened to bath water when it went down the plug hole, but was shocked and embarrassed when they were finding out about each other's bodies?

If children are able to satisfy their natural curiosity, their interest will soon move on to something different. If they find out that this kind of playing upsets their parents, they may go on in the hope of discovering just what it is that makes it so special, and come back to sex play time and time again. Therefore it is often easier to react to a discovery of this kind of play by acceptance. Let it go on for a bit and then be ready with a suggestion for something else – or the information that the children are looking for.

● **Helen**   When I bathed Johnny one night, his penis stood up and he said – 'That's nice'. He's only two . . . I was really embarrassed and told him not to be naughty!

Good feelings ☐   Bad feelings ☐

Helen just hadn't realised that all this meant was that Johnny's penis was in good working order. When his appetite was in good working order and he ate up all his beans and said – 'I like them' Helen showed that she was pleased. But when he had a nice feeling when his penis stood up and said so . . . she said he was naughty! What is a child to make of that? Perhaps Helen could have smiled or laughed and just said – 'That's what's meant to happen now and then' – and left it at that. If he asked any questions she should have answered them because unsatisfied curiosity is the basis on which a child can build fantasies that may be very frightening.

● **Sue**   My four-year-old gave me a hug last night and said he didn't like his Daddy and was going to marry me himself when he grew up. I hugged him back and said that his Dad would be glad to know he loved me and we could see what he felt like about marrying me when the time came.

Good feelings ☐   Bad Feelings ☐

Little boys often go through a stage of loving their mothers deeply, resenting the intrusion of their fathers into the relationship. Sue's loving acceptance shows that she understands how her son is feeling, but keeps him gently but firmly in touch with reality. He needs the loving of both his mother and father. This will have been a reassurance to the child and was all that was needed.

● **Jenny**   My friend's daughter was clean at eighteen months but our Beth is nearly two and still dirties her knickers. I think she is being naughty. I think it's disgusting and have warned her that I will spank her next time it happens.

Good feelings ☐   Bad feelings ☐

Jenny's attitude to her daughter's failure to live up to the competition next door is just due to lack of knowledge about the ways in which children differ. Her reactions of disgust at the workings of nature is very likely to spill over into other natural performances. You can't hurry along development by threats. Fears and anxieties about emptying bowels can become fears and anxieties about sex.

The variety of feelings aroused by the emptyings of bowels and bladders were described in *Clean and dry* in Chapter 1. Children often find that similar kinds of feelings are connected with sex . . . there are mysteries not understood, and grown-ups seem to think that there is something different and special about both.

● **John**   My daughter who is nearly five wanted to bath with me. I think she is too old now for that sort of thing and told her she would have to wait until I had finished.

Good feelings ☐   Bad feelings ☐

John's daughter would begin to get the message that naked adult bodies were not to be seen, even in the privacy of the bathroom at home. Also John lost an opportunity of letting his daughter learn something more about a man's body. Children learn in slow stages, not much at a time. If he had welcomed her to the intimate relaxation of a shared bath, he might have had the opportunity of answering questions she had not yet asked. What was he worrying about? Long before adolescence, children naturally develop their own sense of privacy without being taught. John's refusal begins to make a mystery of the body, making sexual curiosity a different thing from any other kind of curiosity.

● **Betty**   My mother-in-law noticed that my girl of three had put her hand into her knickers and was wriggling her bottom. She said – 'Stop doing that, it's nasty.' I couldn't say anything then, but that night, when I was drying her vulva after her bath, I said – 'That's a lovely place, I don't mind you touching it but it's better not to do it when other people are around.'

Granny's scolding:
Good feelings ☐   Bad feelings ☐

Betty's reassurance:
Good feelings ☐   Bad feelings ☐

Wasn't Betty sensible? Mothers often get caught in a situation when they are torn between two or more loyalties. Her mother-in-law might not be willing to learn other attitudes. Betty did not accept her mother-in-law's standards. Before the scolding became too deeply overlaid by many more experiences, she made an opportunity to speak about it. She showed that she accepted her daughter's enjoyment but also how important it was to be responsible about other people's feelings.

The idea that playing with sex parts will lead to later dangers and uncontrollable sex practices is quite wrong. But the anxieties started by adult reactions can lead to the very things that are feared. To a healthy child whose home provides plenty of interest, playing with genitals sets its own limits of pleasure. It is soon forgotten for the time being because there are plenty of other things to do. If your child begins to learn that responsibility, enjoyment and your acceptance are all part of sex education, you will have made a good beginning.

● **Edward and Jane** usually lock their bedroom door at night but one night they left it open by mistake. Four-year-old Simon woke up with a bad dream and went to look for comfort only to find his parents making love. 'Go back to bed', said his father, 'It's not time to get up yet!'

Good feelings ☐   Bad feelings ☐

Poor Simon. He could be learning that behind the door that was usually locked at night, his parents were fighting and when they were fighting they didn't want him. A door that is usually left open means that there is nothing to hide. A child who knows the pleasure of a cuddle himself will recognise love-making as a kind of cuddle, especially if he is drawn in to share in the love, rather than being driven away.

If you are able to speak naturally to your child about sex, you will be helping to break the unnecessary flowing of fears about sex from one generation to another. Often the reactions of parents like Philip, Helen, Jenny, John, Granny and Edward are based on things that happened in their own childhood that have been forgotten. The fears are still there and are brought back by what their children are doing. Only Sue and Betty rate 'good feelings' ticks! If you understand the workings of your bodies and pass this understanding on to your children with love, you will be helping them to enjoy sex free of needless fears.

All about babies

Most children ask where babies come from sooner or later. 'Out of mummy's tummy' is a standard answer. The photograph is of a model in the Edinburgh Museum of Childhood which show one meaning these words could have. Your child will put his own interpretation on what you say.

Children's questions about sex can come at any time and they may catch you at an inopportune moment, perhaps when you have some visitors or when you see a pregnant woman on a bus. If you want to *choose* the first time for talking about a subject that you may feel uncertain about, it is a good idea to find a book to help you.

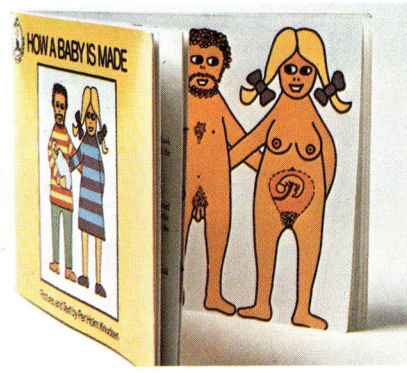

If you leave one of these lying around, it is certain to arouse curiosity, especially if you are to be found looking at it yourself! You can read it with your child just as you would any other book.

Sometimes, these books give only the 'bare facts' and you may find that you want to add details yourself from your own experience. You will probably find it easier to do that than by starting from scratch. Using books helps to open the subject for discussion. Without a helpful starter you may find that your child picks up the idea from friends that the whole subject of babies is something secret, that only is talked about in whispers, amidst nudges, winks and sniggers.

Attitudes towards sexuality in children have changed a lot in this century. Most people were shocked when it was first suggested that children had sexual feelings and were interested in sex. Children were thought to be 'innocent' until adolescence, when sex suddenly became very important. Even now, the only sex education that some girls get from their mothers is the warning at the time of their first period – 'Now you can have a baby so don't go and get pregnant'. Attitudes are still changing so that parents and grandparents will seldom think about sex in the same way. In simple societies, where families lived in one room, children grew up knowing about how adults make love so there was never the same need for explanation. With separate bedrooms, it has become necessary to explain what was previously known . . . and this can be a long and gradual business.

Learning by repetition

Education is never a once-and-for-all business in any subject. It is a continuing, developing process which is not confined to any age or stage. Learning about babies is something that comes a bit at a time. In looking through a book one or two pictures or phrases will be interesting and stick in the mind for a bit – and then be forgotten. After many tellings of the most frank, straight forward and simple kind, your child may still, suddenly and unexpectedly show that he has still not grasped an idea that you thought you had made very clear. Take Peter, whose friend said with pride that his mummy had a baby in her tummy. 'Well, my mummy had got a crocodile in hers!' Don't think you've failed, if your child has not learnt things that you think you have taught him. The chances are that he will remember something of the explanation, even if it is only that if ever he wants to know something about babies, he can always come and ask you.

Enough is enough

In answering questions about sex and babies, it is a good idea to resist being carried away into long explanations when one simple fact was asked for. If your answer provokes another question you can go on but usually children just want information on the subject of their question. When that is answered, their interest will go on to something else.

Curiosity about the bodies of the opposite sex is something to be expected. The more they feel that it is something naughty to do, the more they will want to keep playing to find just why this kind of playing is so naughty. If you met such curiosity would you be able to overlook the bare bottoms and say something quite unrelated in a most ordinary voice, 'Goodness, what a mess these toys have got into. Can you get dressed quickly and help me tidy up?'
or
'Time to be going out soon . . . can you get dressed?'

Afterwards, before the memory is overlaid by too many new experiences, you might like to talk to each on their own, asking what they wanted to know, but not making a big issue of it if they don't want to talk. Perhaps they had found out all they were curious about and that was that.

Be prepared

It is a good idea to think out beforehand the kind of answer you would give to unexpected questions. A group of mothers of older children will probably be able to supply you with plenty of examples. When you have thought out your answers, practice saying them out loud, listening to your voice to see if it sounds the same as it does when you are answering an ordinary question like 'What's for pudding?' If at each conversation you are being honest without embarrassment, you are making a good job of giving your child part of his education in sex.

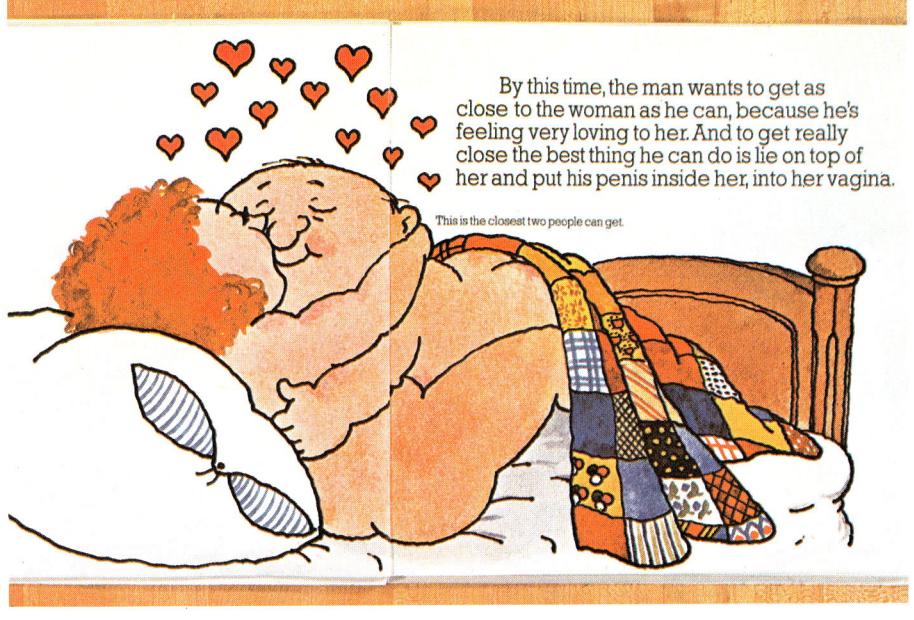

By this time, the man wants to get as close to the woman as he can, because he's feeling very loving to her. And to get really close the best thing he can do is lie on top of her and put his penis inside her, into her vagina.

This is the closest two people can get.

Ways of thinking

The Lord of the Jungle swung down from his bunk bed. He was free – free of civilisation. For four years, his toes had struggled against bootees, slippers, socks and leather. Free! He could wriggle his toes, so of course he was Tarzan. Tarzan had bare feet, hadn't he? 'But darling, that's not why we call him Tarzan. He's called that because – well, because he's big and strong and all the animals are his friends'. 'Well, I'm Tarzan 'cos I've got bare feet.'

For Jonathan, bare feet were much more important than big muscles and a girl-friend called Jane. What sounds a 'silly' answer to us is chosen by him because he *sees* Tarzan differently. Tarzan was a hero to Jonathan because he didn't wear shoes! When a child uses the word 'because', it does not mean that he is using it in the way that an adult would.

What's straight about thinking?

'Giving good reasons' for what we do is something we take for granted. We all think we know what it means. We all like to believe we can 'think straight' if we have to, and most parents would say it was something they wanted for their children. Clear-thinking people are usually respected; they get O-levels and good jobs. Yet what does it *really* mean to 'think straight'? Do children reason things out as we do, or differently? Are good reasoners born or made?

Putting thoughts together

A new-born child seems to have little idea of what's happening around him. He doesn't really seem to notice whether something is happening inside or outside his body. But when he can reach or touch, it's a different matter. He soon finds out that if he hits at a hanging toy in his pram, it swings. Later, he learns that if he lets go the bars of his playpen, then he falls down. If, as a two-year-old, he builds his brick towers too high, then they also fall down. 'If . . . then.' He may not actually know these words, but he has

begun to realise that some happenings lead to others.

As he approaches school age, he learns to ask which happenings go together by using 'why?' and expecting the answer 'because', driving you crazy with his questions! But don't be misled. While he may be *asking* 'why', and expecting 'because', he has by no means sorted out all his ideas. He may not really be thinking in an organised way at all. His picture of the world, and of why things happen, may not look like the adult picture.

Ask your child

● Why do boats float and stones sink?
● Why do birds fly?
● Why do the stars come out at night?

Now leave the questions for a day or two and ask them again. This time, listen carefully to their answers, and ask other questions to follow up. You might get a conversation like this:

First time
Q Why do birds fly?
A Because they're strong.

Second time
Q Why do birds fly?
A Because they can make their wings go very fast.
Q Why does that help them to fly?
A Because they've got feathers and a tail.
Q And why do feathers and a tail help them to fly?
A Because they're clever.
What do you notice about the answers?

The second answer to the question 'Why do birds fly?' is different. What's more, the replies to the follow-up questions do not really give a satisfactory answer. The reasons for birds flight are not linked. But there is another reason for the above questions. While it's true that many parents give answers to their *children's* questions, they only rarely show curiosity *themselves*. An inquiring mind can be encouraged by an inquiring parent.

The logic of blind man's buff

Here's a game to develop reasoning. Blindfold a child, and hand him an object. He has to identify it by touch, describing it as he examines it. 'It's long and thin. It's flat. It's smooth. It bends a bit. It's hard. It's a ruler.' You can improve the game by making it a competition, and by introducing a question master, who sums up what has been described so far. This helps to train the child in pulling his thoughts together.

Missing pieces

It's easy to assume that all reasoning is done with words, but this is not always so. Children need to reason with shapes and pictures just as often. Jigsaws are a good way to build up this kind of thinking with the eyes – but do make sure you've chosen one that isn't too hard or too easy. Jigsaws done with mum or dad can give a lot of training in the use of five of the most important 'thinking' words. They are – and; or; but; if and then.

Something to talk about

Age 3

Magnet will pick up pins – and paper clips – but not everything.

Cut out fish shapes from cereal packet cardboard and slip paper clip on to the head. Go fishing over the side of a chair with a magnet on a piece of string.

'I can't find any piece that goes here.'

'Well, let's look at the colours next to it. What have we got?'

'It's red here, *and* green here, *and* black on this bit.'

'Can you see any bits with those colours?'

(Looks) 'Yes, I've got two.

'Good. So it's either that *or* this one. Try them.'

(both pieces seem to fit)

'Well, this one's the right colour, *but* it's got the wrong shape on it. *And* this one's fitting *but* the red looks different.'

'*If* you take the first one *and* turn it round, *then* the shape would be different wouldn't it?'

What really matters here is that the child is being 'talked through' the problem, and is learning to use 'thinking words' in a natural way.

> 'Fine. So he'll grow to be a jigsaw genius. But he'll not make any great discoveries that way, will he?'

No, he won't make a discovery simply by finding the right answers to puzzles or problems. But he needs to think clearly *before* he thinks creatively, or he won't be able to make his new ideas work. If he learns to use thinking words in conversation, puzzles or play, there is a strong chance he will lay his own foundations for later work in school.

Age 3

Work out from *outside*, which window belongs to which room. Put teddy on window sill if a clue is needed.

If you live in a flat, hang something out of the window so that you can recognise it from outside.

Age 3

Fill a bowl with hot water – Put a wooden spoon and large metal spoon in and after a minute feel the handles.

Age 4

In autumn plant a hyacinth on top of a glass jar full of water. Leave in a dark place until nearly Christmas. Then bring out and watch it grow.

Age 3 Magic water

Take three bowls and put them on a table so: with cold, warm and hand-hot water:

Put one hand in cold water, one in hot at the same time. After about a minute, put both in the warm water. The same water feels different to the hands.

Age 4

Take three foil boxes. Fold a piece of kitchen paper to cover the bottom. Wet two of them. Sow sawdust or sand in one of these, mustard or cress seeds in the other and also in the dry box. Keep the wet boxes damp and look at them all, most days for a fortnight.

Dry paper and seeds	Wet paper and seeds	Wet paper and sawdust or sand

PS Other things grow – acorns, conkers, beans, grass seed.

Age 4

Dissolving – watch and taste.

This is a time to talk about poisons that give tummy aches.

Water	Water and Salt	Water and Sugar	Water and Lentils

Ways of thinking

Thinking clearly and thinking creatively are not really so far apart. You can play quite exciting 'just suppose' games by using *if* and *then*. But this time, the *mood* is different. Instead of being careful and precise, be playful, and let their imaginations go. Simply think of unlikely or impossible (but not frightening) events and try them out on your child and his friends, when they are chatty and relaxed, but not too boisterous. Here are a few ideas to get you going:

What would happen if . . .

clouds had strings on them like balloons?

suddenly all children became giants and all grown-ups became small?

trees became soft and tasted like chocolate?

cars could fly and you could drive one?

If you can, avoid the traditional fairy-tale situations such as magic carpets and talking animals. Choose ideas which you think will surprise them, but which they can still understand. Follow up the answers in a gentle way. Would you tie strings together and make one big bunch of clouds? Would you pull the clouds down and into the house? What would that do? This might well lead to a factual question on what clouds are made of, which is fine. The basic rules are not to *block* any questions, and not to be too sensible! Most children enjoy listening afterwards to a tape-recording of the game, so you might like to try that. It is also a good way to invent a new story.

It's not in the story

Both children and adults often take events and ideas for granted. We all *know* Humpty Dumpty sat on a wall. Have you ever stopped to wonder why? What was he trying to see? Who was he trying to get away from? Who robbed Mother Hubbard? And just why did someone send three mice in dark glasses to attack a farmer's wife? Nursery rhymes, like other stories, leave out what is not important. But sometimes, asking a question about something everyone takes for granted can make the story more interesting and exciting, as well as leading children to ask 'why?'.

Find a book of nursery rhymes and think up similar questions.

. . . clouds had strings on them like balloons

YOU'VE PULLED OUT THE PLUG!

CLOUD GARAGE

1   Make a picture using cotton wool, paste and thread.

2   Paint cloud shapes on balloons with strings.

3   Pretend to pull a cloud down on a string till you are covered by it. What would it be like?

. . . suddenly all children were giants

1   Make pipe-cleaner giants and matchstick adults.

2   Play a game with children standing on chairs and adults kneeling (giants have to look after the adults).

3   How would the adults sit at the giants table?

4   How would you talk to a grown-up now you're a giant?

. . . trees became s

1   Make a tree out

2   What would we m

3   What would happe

tasted like chocolate

ke and cotton wool.

les and chairs from.

e sat on chocolate chairs?

What does he think you're doing?

Children gain many of their thinking habits from their parents. The question is whether they pick up good or bad habits. After all, if you yourself are bad at putting thoughts together, it is much harder to blame your child for being muddle-headed. Try these questions yourself:

	always	sometimes	never
1 Do you try hard to find the *right* answer to a problem?			
2 Do you get cross if you are proved wrong?			
3 Do you get annoyed when asked to explain why you are doing something?			
4 When planning something, do you enjoy playing around with different ideas?			
5 When going out, do you tell your child:			
a where you are going?			
b why you are going?			

1 – 2 There is evidence that some people find it very difficult to put up with more than one answer to a question. They enjoy being accurate, and can become irritated with such questions as: how many uses can you think of for a brick? Pre-school children are much more at home with such questions if left to themselves, but may be led to copy adults.

3 Children can be hard on human nature. There is a risk, though, that irritated replies to a child's questions could train him the wrong way, and make him think that it was impolite to ask for explanations.

4 This is really the reverse of Question 1. Most children will join in happily when discussing different choices, but do make sure you let them know what the *final* decision is!

5 With two-year-olds, it is probably less important to give detailed explanations, but it could save tantrums with older children, who may have their own shopping to do!

... cars could fly and you could drive one

1 Make a car with wings from Lego or plasticine.

2 What would you do if you ran out of petrol when you were in the air?

3 Where would you fly to?

Wiggle a finger in the air and a baby will watch its movements. Play peep-bo over the edge of a cot or pram, popping a finger up and down and you will have given the simplest puppet show.

Make believe and pretend

In their ordinary play, young children will use what happens to be handy for whatever they need. Any lack of skill will be overcome by 'pretending' so any limitations with finger puppets will not bother the young child. The advantages of the glove or hand type are that they can handle 'props' such as a ball, bell or a brush. These puppets will sweep, fill and carry a basket, ring a bell, and play hide and seek. This is the natural step that follows peep-bo.

The stick or rod puppet has its own possibilities – and limits. A picnic-plate face stuck to a long wooden stick with a cloak can be made to fly about.

Self expression

While playing with puppets (maybe hiding behind some kind of make-do stage) young children express themselves freely and reveal much of what is in their minds concerning their feelings about relationships in and around the family. They are not concerned about audiences, their puppet-play is an extension of their ordinary play. They may play alone or with others. In a playgroup centre the older children *may* give short 'shows' to each other (quite possibly with interruptions from those watching), but it is not an adult's concern to produce 'performers' among the under-fives.

Making puppets is easy!

A glove or hand puppet can be just a sock pulled over the hand, with four fingers in the foot and the thumb in the heel to give jaw movements.

A *finger puppet* can be made from felt, and worn on the finger. A whole range of characters, both human and animal, can be invented. Small faces drawn on card can be stuck to glove finger-tips or made with stitches.

Puppets as teachers

Puppets are ideal for teaching. Children will always watch and listen to a puppet and have vivid memories of what happens on the puppet stage.

Puppets are used:

● in road safety and safety-in-the-home plays,

● in children's wards in hospitals, to ease the anxiety of being away from home and perhaps an approaching operation.

● in photographic studios to divert children from the camera.

Dolls and puppets

A doll, like a teddy or some other stuffed creature, is for *private* play. A puppet play is for an audience. This, however, is a difference that young children ignore when they play with puppets themselves. A doll or teddy may be used as a puppet; a puppet may be put in the doll's pram along with the dolls.

If a child can't find the character he needs he will quite happily use a matchbox, thimble or other object as a stand-in for that character.

Adults too use objects to stand in for puppets. This is sometimes a technique used in television commercials, tins, cartons, potatoes are seen to come to life.

Puppet plays and story-telling

Unlike story-telling which needs children to use their own imagination, the puppet play is *here and now*. Puppets are real creatures. They can be touched, have conversations with each other and with the audience. Young children spontaneously call out to puppet characters . . . 'No, not there, over *there*!' And as in all Punch and Judy shows – 'Oh *yes* you *did*!' to Punch's 'Oh no I *didn't*!'

Hide-and-seek

For the under-fives – moving on from simple 'peep-bo games', hide-and-seek is a favourite activity for puppet characters, both in the adult performance and in the children's own puppet play.

It's easy to use furniture as props so that the game can be improvised anywhere – using simple glove or rod puppets.

Children's puppets

What their own puppets mean to young children is seen in two (of numerous) incidents.

The first is in a reception class. Children in the school hall watching a show, their own matchbox puppets on their hands becoming part of the audience.

The second, after a demonstration of simple puppet-making for five-year-olds. After watching a show and having returned to their classrooms, they come surging back into the hall later, armed with socks made into creatures, and head for the stage chanting – 'I'm a snake!' – 'I'm a monster!' – 'I'm a witch!' On the stage, solid with children, the puppets pop out everywhere, through doorways, out of windows, shouting in sheer delight. There is always the need for immediacy; puppets are for use and must be created as quickly as possible.

Adult group shows

Simple take-around shows can be developed by small groups of adults, the Parent/Teacher Association, Young Mothers' Club, Women's Institute, playgroup leaders. 'We are putting over ideas through puppets, which is better for the children than sitting in front of the television.'

Books

Many textbooks on puppet-making have been published. One of the most inspirational for beginners is The Know How Book of Puppets, part of a general Know How series by Usborne's. It has coloured illustrations and diagrams and clear instructions. The best way to begin is to start gradually – with one or two leaflets about basic starting points produced by the Educational Puppetry Association (see page 192).

Family puppetry

Those who start 'puppetting' in the pre-school period may well go on to performing as infants and juniors. Many well-known professional puppeteers began in their childhood. Older children in the family may already be 'doing' puppets at school. Fond aunts and grannies can become involved, and baby-sitters, for example will find puppets invaluable. Puppet-shows have become very popular at birthday parties – and for the youngest age group they need only be short and simple.

A stick or rod puppet can be made by pushing the handle of a washing-up mop through a perforated plastic ball, which then becomes the head and the mop the hair. The hand holding the stick can be hidden by wrap-around material or by poking the stick through a central hole in a handkerchief or duster.

A technical point

Technically it is important to have comfortable puppets. Glove puppets (like your own clothes) should fit and allow free movement for the handling of 'props' (a ball, bell, basket, etc.). A grown-up's glove puppet on a young child's hand will flop about and a child-sized puppet will be too small for an adult's hand.

Children in hospital

Almost half the children in this country will be admitted to hospital by the age of seven. If careful arrangements are not made this can be a disturbing experience. Many hospitals now allow parents to visit at any time and provide beds for mothers to stay with their children.

Preparation just in case

More than half the children's admissions to hospital are emergencies, so learning about hospital should be part of a child's early education.

Take advantage of the many opportunities in everyday life when you can talk to your child about hospital. For instance, she may hear an ambulance siren or someone she knows may have to go to hospital.

There are some good picture books and stories about hospital now available (see page 64), which would spark off lots of interest and questions. They help a child to find out about the difference between life in hospital and life at home.

You may be able to arrange for you and your child to visit your local hospital and have a look round the children's ward.

Children enjoy playing hospitals. Doctor's and nurse's clothes and equipment are all useful play materials and a hospital play setting can usually be arranged using dolls and furniture. Help your child to familiarise herself with hospital life by giving her new information and developing her play into new areas without upsetting her game. She may even want you to be part of her game which means you are right there to sort out problems and give new information.

Being sent to hospital should never be made a threat. A child should accept that the doctors and nurses there will help them to get better if they have an accident or are ill. And sometimes there's a bed for Mummy too, or if she can't stay, she will be able to visit a great deal.

If a young child has to go into hospital suddenly, it won't seem quite so frightening if she has been well prepared.

Getting ready for hospital

A child must know the facts. For instance don't pretend it won't hurt if you know it will. You may be able to arrange a visit to the children's ward beforehand and a chat with the ward sister about what will happen. Afterwards you can play through the expected experience with your child.

The lady in the white coat is pricking Anne's finger. She squeezes out a little drop of blood, so she can test it. Anne says "ouch!"

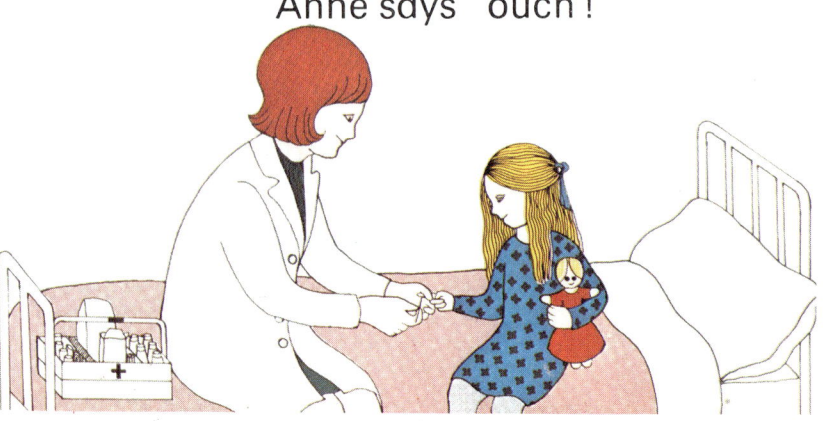

Planning for a stay in hospital

The only certain way of making sure a young child is happy and well cared for in hospital is for a parent to stay in the hospital with her. The next best thing, is for parents to be there with the child as often as possible.

If your GP is arranging for your child to go into hospital there are three questions you must ask him and three answers you will want to hear.

Q Can I be with my child as often as possible?

A Yes, parents can visit at any time.

Q Can I live in?

A Yes, mothers of young children can live in. (Even if you are unable to live in it shows the hospital is sympathetic to your child's needs.)

Q Can I visit on the day of the operation?

A Yes, this is very necessary and is allowed both before and after the operation.

If you're not satisfied with the answers you get, here is what to do:

● Ask the hospital consultant or your own GP to press for the arrangements you want.

● If the hospital will not agree ask your GP to send you to another hospital.

● If you still cannot find a satisfactory hospital, then ask the National Association for the Welfare of Children in Hospital to help.

Going into hospital

Let your child take her favourite toy or cuddly plus anything else she wants to take, within reason. The ward sister will need to know any particular likes or dislikes, special names for things, etc. If you can be with your child as much as possible it will help her to cope with all the new experiences in hospital. The nursing staff will appreciate your co-operation and the practical help you can give in caring for your child.

Parent's rights

The need for parents to be with a child in hospital has long been accepted and recommended by the Department of Health. Parents have the right to visit their children in hospital whenever they like and now the opportunity for them to do so exists in many hospitals. But:

● one-fifth of hospitals still have limited visiting

● one-third of hospitals have no accommodation for parents to stay

● many hospitals still do not allow visiting on the day of operation

So if you want to be with your child:

1 find out what the visiting hours are before she goes into hospital and whether parents can stay in. Contact the children's wards in all the hospitals in your area;

2 when your child has to be admitted try to arrange for her to go to the hospital with the best arrangements, or

3 persuade your local hospital to change its rules. The Community Health Council will help you and you can also get together with other mothers to lobby for change. Try some publicity through the press, pointing out the Department of Health's recommendations over the past few years.

Children in hospital for a long time

If at all possible, children are allowed out of hospital to carry on being nursed at home. But a few children have to be cared for in hospital, and may have to stay for several weeks or months. Because they are separated from home and those near to them, these children can easily become depressed and withdrawn. This can be helped a great deal if they have confidence that their home still exists and also if they have plenty of stimulation and varied opportunities.

Play is a vital factor in the mental, emotional and social development of all children. This must be continued in hospital. Some hospitals have a play worker to organise play in the ward for children fit enough to take part.

It is essential to maintain links with home. Frequent visiting by the family, talking about home, cards and letters from friends, all remind a child that home is still there waiting for her.

You may be able to arrange for her to come home at the week-end if she is having tests which cannot be done during this time.

A child needs her parents more than anyone else – so see that you are with her as much as possible and are able to take an active part in her care.

What sort of parent could harm a child?

Try to answer the following questions:

● Parents who injure their children are usually mentally abnormal   Yes/No

● Men are more likely to act violently towards children than women   Yes/No

● Children are more likely to be seriously deprived or neglected if their mothers go out to work or spend time with neighbours   Yes/No

● Violence towards children has increased in recent years   Yes/No

Almost any parent could, under stress, hurt a child in ways that might affect its whole future

Research shows that answers to the above questions are almost certainly 'No'. The large majority of parental actions that cause harm to children are done when anger gets out of control, and most of them are intended to punish 'naughty' behaviour.

Could you harm your child?

In this topic we shall look at some of the things that can go wrong and their causes, their possible long-term effects on the child, and at some of the things that can be done to reduce the risks.

How do you treat your child?

BE VERY HONEST: A tick for 'yes', a cross for 'no'. Fill every square – write in details.

In the last month (one tick for each occasion)

	Have you done it?	Have you come near to it?	Have you thought of it?
Hit your child unnecessarily hard?			
Shaken him or pushed him away violently?			
Used any kind of *object* to teach him a lesson? (for example rolling pins, hot stoves etc.)			
Refused him needed food, warmth or comfort?			
Left him alone, dirty or messy, or 'crying it out'?			
Told him you 'couldn't stand him' (or similar)?			
Yelled, nagged or been coldly sarcastic?			
Picked on one child against another unjustly?			
Drawn a child into a parental quarrel?			

This isn't one of these 'tests' where you can count the ticks; and if there are more than so many in the first column you should see a doctor. But obviously if there are a good many ticks in the first two columns you need to do some stocktaking and make a few changes for the future. If you have put crosses all the way down the last column and none anywhere else you must be superhuman. Perhaps you had better check through again!

You may have noticed that the questions were given in three groups of three questions each, roughly corresponding to 1 physical harm, 2 deprivation, and 3 emotional harm, but all these things overlap. Further, since severe punishment damages the child it is likely to worsen the situation rather than improve it, and so lead to even more severe measures. There are many more and crueller ways of abusing children than are suggested in the few questions in 'How do you treat your child?'

Some long-term effects

In the box you will find summarised a few of the long-term effects that parental actions can produce. Although these refer to severe ill treatment, scaled down they still show the risks that parents take when they allow a disturbed relationship to develop unchecked.

Some physical effects of ill treatment

Blows in anger (especially to the head); vigorous shaking; shoving or throwing so that the child falls:
Direct results may be: deafness, bone malformations, injury to brain and central nervous system, spasticity.
Long-term effects: mental backwardness, poor physical control, and aggressiveness and other behaviour problems in later life.

Some effects on growth of deprivation or neglect

A child frequently deprived of food or warmth may 'fail to thrive'. He becomes undernourished and has low resistance to disease. Malnutrition can cause stunted growth and mental backwardness. Being deprived of comfort can make a child listless and emotionally unresponsive.

Some effects of emotional ill treatment

Children who are emotionally rejected may grow up anxious and incapable of loving. Children exposed to shouting, persistent nagging or quarrelling may become withdrawn and watchful, or turn into calculating little 'pseudo-adults' before their time.

Children alternately fussed over and rejected may themselves become emotionally unstable.

Perhaps the saddest outcome of bad treatment during childhood arises from the way children easily model themselves on their parents. After all, they are the only adults they know well. Parents who misuse their children must expect to see their grandchildren treated in the same way.

What makes some people harm their own children?

You already have part of the answer to this question. Unless some very strong influence from outside the home intervenes, parents follow the only close model they have for bringing up children: their own parents. Sometimes they know they are wrong, particularly if there are visible signs like bruises or thin, peaky faces to remind them that their children must look ill-treated to the neighbours. But they feel trapped, they can't break the pattern, because they have no experience of other methods of child-rearing. People like Tom's mother (see below) are even less fortunate. They feel sure they are right. Tom's mother will often tell you that she has high standards and is proud of them.

Other factors, however, do play a part, and some of these, once understood, are more easily changed. Others are not. Here are only a few of them:

'Ideal parenthood'

To have a child of one's own, to love and care for and enjoy – that is the dream of many young people. Surely, when the new baby comes there will be a new beginning for the parents. Just having the baby will somehow transform its parents and their lives – and all for the better. All the right feelings will come naturally and they will know instinctively all the right things to do.

But that's all a dream. Babies can be 'all work', and there's no time to enjoy them. They scream and you're tired out all day, and they cost a lot of money and never say 'thank you'. In the dream they brought parents closer together; in life they can come between them. Coping is a drudgery. Parenthood has let them down and turned them into failures. At this point, many feel helpless and guilty and it's easy to blame the child. The important thing to realise is that twentieth century parenthood is something that has to be learned – even feelings have to be learned. It can take a long time, particularly if you have started on the wrong lines. Good friends and books can help with the techniques, but if you feel really low and the child is suffering, you need professional help. That false dream can explode into an unending nightmare unless it is replaced by an acceptance of reality: a child who is human and demanding (like his parents) but who, just because he is real, is in the long run much more fascinating and rewarding than a dream.

Environmental stresses

Isolated mothers are more likely to hurt their children than those with many social contacts. When a mother spends everyday alone with her child or children she often gets depressed and irritable. Something must be done to break the isolation and bring her new interests. A playgroup can help if one can be found or formed. So can a part-time job, even if it only pays for the fees of a good child minder. Either can provide a break for both mother and child.

Poverty and unsuitable housing are environmental stresses that are harder to break out from. They make life stressful for a great many families . . .

A case study

This is a story illustrating the risks attached to what may seem a mild form of deprivation:

Read it and consider what longer-term effects would you expect for
● Tom's mother
● Tom?

Tom is four years old, physically normal and healthy. His mother believes in using food as a disciplinary tool. If Tom misbehaves she says: 'That's IT! Now you'll get no pudding for dinner!' Dinnertime may be three hours away. By the time it comes Tom is very hungry and says so, but he is given his usual, well-calculated ration of meat, potatoes and greens. Tom loathes greens (he'd prefer his vitamin C in orange juice) but Mum invariably insists on a clean plate because a child must learn that food isn't provided just to be wasted, so he manages to control his heaving tummy, finishes quickly, and says 'What's for pudding?' 'Nothing for you', says his mother tucking into her apple pie, 'have you forgotten?'

Tom has, of course. His memory, like all small children's, can be short, but he does remember that he was extraordinarily good about the greens. Unappreciated, frustrated and still hungry, Tom settles for a tantrum.

Comments

Tom's mother: Looking at Tom's mother's later behaviour (this is a true story) suggests that she is now fully confirmed in her conviction that she is unlucky in having given birth to a child who is always unreasonable and bad-tempered. She feels she will have to be even 'firmer' in future.

Tom: To Tom the meal table seems a natural battleground. This means that he may develop chronic indigestion and also lose his native instinct to select for himself the foods that are good for him.

He is also becoming convinced that his mother (and hence possibly all women) is an unreasonable, cold-hearted person. He doesn't think she can possibly love him, whatever she says at other times, if she punishes him when he is good by frustrating his most important needs.

particularly when the parents are young or there is only one parent. Many happy families are raised, of course, in very poor homes, by brave, loving parents who can settle, at least temporarily, for a low material standard of life.

It isn't easy to advise parents who feel that intolerable conditions are pushing them to take it out on their children. They must try to locate their real enemies, and their real allies.

Great expectations

Parents long for a perfect, trouble-free child but if they haven't had much close experience of young children they may have unrealistic ideas about what they can expect. It is impossible for a three-month old child to show love and gratitude, but some romantic young mothers want this. On the other hand, some children are still wetting their beds at the age of seven and their parents don't worry. They should – or rather, they should worry just long enough to see a doctor – because with such children there may be something wrong, either physically, emotionally or in the method of training. Children vary a great deal but it is important to set limits on expectations and get advice when outside those limits. The first line of advice is usually a health visitor.

Mothers, as well as children, are welcomed by many playgroups

Lapses in love

No, not all parents love their children deeply, at least not all of the time. It may be hard to love a child who, say, came when it was least wanted, or who (because of illness in parent or child) had to be separated from the mother for some time immediately after birth. Those first weeks were the time when he was most wanted, when the strongest bonds are normally formed. Learning to love can be a long and difficult process. Such parents need a lot of help.

> If you have read this topic and wondered at any point 'could I be harming my child?' apply this test: Go back to 'How do you treat your child?' and for every tick in the first two columns ask yourself: did the child or the relationship improve in any way as a result of this action? If you cannot be sure that the answer is 'Yes' (in the light of the rest of the topic) then you must try to re-arrange your life to prevent such actions happening again.

When everything gets too much, remember there are people who can help

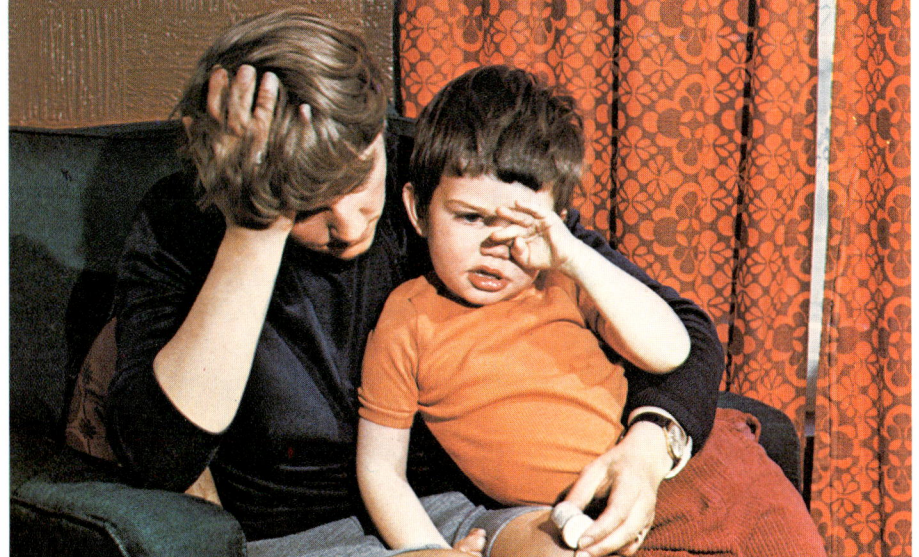

Getting help

Asking for help is very hard for some people. We all like to think we can solve our own problems. Isn't seeking help an admission of failure – and anyway who else could really understand?

But successful parenthood is a highly skilled, very difficult job which people enter untrained, unprepared and often under unsuitable conditions. It is only too easy to fall into a pattern of child-rearing which could prove unsatisfactory for both parent and child. No-one would expect to re-train for any other skilled job without expert guidance. Most people in this situation need advice and help.

● *Family doctors and health visitors* know that they are expected to help and advise.

● The NSPCC is a *voluntary body* and has local branches with trained and experienced social workers whose first job is to prevent things going wrong, not as some think to prosecute wrong-doers.

● *The Samaritans* are another source of help if a crisis arises, their telephone number is always in the telephone book; they will respond to any kind of acute distress.

● The local *Marriage Guidance Council* can often help if things are not going well in a marriage (a frequent cause of stress on a child). The earlier advice is sought the easier it is to put a disturbed relationship right.

● The Government is aware of the need for help and advice and all local authorities are required by law to provide a service for parents and children through their *Department of Social Service*.

The important thing from the parents' point of view is to find someone from one of these agencies with whom he or she can be completely honest and whom they can trust. This is partly a matter of matching personalities.

If you already have a doctor to whom you can speak freely, start there. Don't be put off with comforting words but insist on a full discussion of your problem.

If you aren't satisfied by the other agencies that have been suggested, keep on trying until you feel you have found someone who can really help you. But don't expect immediate easy solutions.

Getting your relationship with your child on to the right lines is so important for both of you. You must be prepared to persist in seeking advice at all costs until you feel sure that things will go better in the future.

Play and Education

Child's Play (formerly Children and Youth Action Group Ltd), Victoria Chambers, 16/20 Strutton Ground, London SW1.

This is 'an information and resources agency for those involved in play provision for children between the ages of five and fifteen'. Within this area the library holds material and answers enquiries on aspects such as adventure playgrounds, holiday playschemes and clubs, children's houses, play ideas and equipment as well as more technical aspects of adventure play such as insurance, fencing, surfacing, etc. There is, at present, no membership scheme, nor are there any regional branches. The group publishes a monthly magazine *It's Child's Play*.

Fair Play for Children Campaign, 237 Pentonville Road, London N1.

The Campaign's basic aim is to make play provision for children a higher priority in society. It is involved with the play needs of children of all ages, and is made up largely of voluntary organisations concerned with children's play, though individuals and local authorities can be mailing members. Encouragement and support are given to play councils/associations which operate on a district or neighbourhood basis, bringing together those concerned with play in their areas to exchange ideas and information, to share resources and examine community needs. The Campaign publishes a news bulletin, pamphlets and discussion papers, and *Play Fact Sheets*, the latter in conjunction with Child's Play, the National Playing Fields Association and the Pre-School Playgroups Association.

National Playbus Association, c/o Mr D. Denton, Stone Ville, 42 Ashfordby Road, Melton Mowbray, Leicestershire.

An association formed by those working with playbuses who found the need for discussion on the particular difficulties, challenges and opportunities in providing play facilities in buses. Experience accumulated over several years in widely differing areas is available through this association to others thinking about starting playbus schemes.

National Playing Fields Association (NPFA), 25 Ovington Square, London SW3.

Its aims are to encourage the provision of recreational facilities for all age groups and it specialises in the play needs of children and young people, and encourages playleadership. It provides technical advice and information and carries out research to further these aims. It raises funds and makes grants, and organises holiday playschemes. It employs regional play advisors who are responsible for visiting established playschemes, new schemes and individuals or groups interested in starting schemes. There are local offices in many counties. It would be useful to know what is being done locally by the representatives of the Association and to bear in mind that they may be able to help.

Pre-School Playgroups Association (PPA), Alford House, Aveline Street, London SE11 5DJ *and* 7 Royal Terrace, Glasgow G3 7NT.

'The PPA exists to help parents to understand and provide for the needs of their young children. It aims to promote community situations in which parents can with growing enjoyment and confidence make the best uses of their own knowledge and resources in the development of their children and themselves.' The PPA was formed to encour-

age mothers to establish their own playgroups. It provides advice, help and encouragement to all affiliated playgroups, either directly, through a local branch or an Area Organiser, or by means of its publications. These include *Contact*, which is monthly (except December and August), and free to members; and *Under 5*, which is quarterly, for playgroup parents, and sold through groups or PPA branches.

The interests of members, branches and the Association itself have broadened to include many aspects of living with children. Local branches are often an introduction to people actively interested in a wide variety of subjects related to children in the community. In many areas, there are:
● courses planned in collaboration with Further Education Departments or the Workers' Educational Association (WEA);
● meetings and conferences that cover a wide variety of subjects of special and general interest.

Involvement can make people aware of the great variety of young children's needs, the work that is being done and the resources that are available for meeting these needs and help them learn how to make the best use of inadequate resources.

Education

Advisory Centre for Education (ACE), 32 Trumpington Street, Cambridge CB2 1QY.

The Centre aims to offer independent and unbiased information on education to parents and others, to encourage greater co-operation between home and school and to stimulate the discussion of educational issues. It publishes *Where: The Education Magazine for Parents*. This is a monthly magazine which often includes articles relating to the pre-school age-group. Some of these have been collected together to form a book: *The Best of 'Where' on Pre-schooling*, Cambridge, Advisory Centre for Education, 1976.

Educational Puppetry Association, The Puppet Centre, Battersea Town Hall, Lavender Hill, London SW11 5TJ.

This provides a source of speakers and information about courses and publications.

Federation of Children's Book Groups, 17 Andrew Close, Ailsworth, Peterborough PE5 7AD.

The Federation is concerned to increase interest (particularly of parents) in children's books, and to improve book services. Activities range from meetings to discuss children's books or listen to speakers to organising exhibitions, selling books and organising 'National Tell a Story Weeks'. It publishes *Books for Your Children*, booklists and information leaflets. There are local branches throughout the country.

National Association for Gifted Children, 27 John Adam Street, London WC2N 6HX.

The Association is concerned with the education of gifted children and aims to provide parents, and others involved in this, with advice and assistance and to promote, encourage and finance relevant research. There are regional centres staffed and run by voluntary workers. Through these centres meetings are arranged for educationalists, parents and specialists. Informal social evenings are organised for parents to meet each other, and parents are helped to contact the relevant local authorities.

Chapter 7
Getting together

Chapter 7
Getting together

Working mothers

The decision to go out to work can be agonizing for
mothers of pre-school children. Jobs can offer
mothers fulfilment, or badly needed money, or a solution to
loneliness or depression. Yet in the balance with their needs
are those of their children, and of the family as a whole.
And there are the practical difficulties of finding
a job and suitable alternative care for the children.

Life in day nurseries

Should I work?

Mothers first need to come to terms
with their doubts about leaving their
children. Some of these doubts stem
from within themselves, or from things
they have read or heard about. There
are outside pressures too. The lack of
early child-care facilities for children
in this country is partly a reflection of
the widely-held belief that a mother's
place is at home, not at work.

The evidence

There is little evidence so far that
children whose mothers work differ
greatly from children whose mothers
do not. This seems particularly true
when the mother is happy about
working and has found a suitable
alternative care for her child. But
there have been few large-scale or
long-term studies, and it's a difficult,
emotionally-charged area to research.

The findings of the experts often seem
to disagree. In part this is because two
types of study have sometimes been
confused. There is a world of difference
between *being deprived of a mother* (or
an alternative mother-figure) for long
periods of time—for example children
in institutions—and *being separated
from the mother* for part of each day

when the mother works. Yet evidence
of the ill-effects of deprivation of
mother has sometimes been taken to
suggest equal dangers when mother
and child are separated on a short but
regular basis.

Working mothers have often heard
the name of John Bowlby. In 1951 he
published a study of children deprived
of a mother and raised in institutions.
He concluded:

> What is believed to be essential to
> mental health is that the infant and
> young should experience a warm,
> intimate and continuous relation-
> ship with its mother (or permanent
> mother substitute) in which both
> find satisfaction and enjoyment.

Most experts would agree with
Bowlby that young children need this
sort of relationship and that children
in institutions may be deprived of it.
But it doesn't mean that a child must
have 24-hour-a-day care at home by
his mother. Twenty years on, Michael
Rutter writes:

> Bowlby's writings have often been
> used wrongly to support the notion
> that only 24-hour-care day in day
> out by the same person is good
> enough. Thus it is claimed that
> proper mothering is only possible if
> the mother does not go out to work.

Rutter's view is that children of
working mothers do not suffer—
provided that the child has a stable,
continuous and happy relationship
with the person who cares for him
during his mother's absence. Other
recent studies have stressed the importance of the mother's attitude:
satisfied, contented mothers, whether
working or not, produce 'well-adjusted'
children.

In this country, the National Children's Bureau is following the development of several thousand children
born in 1958. In a summary of recent
findings that noted that:

● The physical health of children
whose mothers work is at least as good
as the health of children whose
mothers do not.
● At seven, children whose mothers
take jobs once the children start
school are slightly less well adjusted
than those whose mothers took jobs
earlier.
● School performance does not differ
between children of working and non-
working mothers.
● Children of working mothers seem
no more likely to be delinquents.

The summary again noted the importance of the mother's attitudes and
the quality of the alternative care.

Working mothers

To work or not?

Research findings are generalisations. You and your child are individuals — so what is commonly found may not be true for you.

Each mother has to find what she believes to be the right compromise between her own needs and those of her child. To help you judge your own case, consider those of Mrs Brown, Mrs Green and Miss White in the next column. Weigh up the pros and cons of them working under the following headings. Score points out of 10 for the importance of each issue for and against.

For	Brown	Green	White
● Extra income			
● Company of other adults			
● Interest of having a job as well as being a 'wife and mother'			
● Better family life			
● Change of surroundings			
Against			
● Loss of time with children			
● Can't control what happens to children			
● Tiredness			
● Mother feels guilty			
● Lack of support from husband			

What sort of care?

Suppose Mrs Brown, Mrs Green and Miss White all decide to work. What arrangements could they make for alternative care for their children?

Finding alternative care isn't easy. Child-care facilities for working mothers in this country are limited. On the next page we look at alternatives in terms of the needs of children. Here we are simply looking at alternatives in practical terms of opening hours, age range taken, who gets priority, and so on.

● Turn to the topics on *Pre-school groups* and *Other people's children* in this chapter and read through the descriptions there of the various forms of child care. For the purposes of this exercise, assume the following options are open to these three mothers: nursery school, nursery class, day nursery, hall playgroup, mother and toddler club, child-minders.

● Re-read the descriptions above of the mother's family circumstances and the jobs they have in mind.

● Tick in the chart (right) which form of provision you think would best meet their practical needs. Mrs Brown has two children — should they have different arrangements?

Mrs Brown

Two children aged two and four. Husband's income covers rent, food and household bills, but no extras. Lives on the sixth floor of inner-city council block. Flat offers little privacy or space for children to play. Does not know neighbours. Rarely sees her family who live in the north. Suffers from depression and has treatment for it. Feels trapped, lonely and frustrated. Has been offered part-time job in shop.

Mrs Green

One child aged three. Husband is civil servant. Family lives in own semi-detached suburban house. Gave up job as a beautician on birth of child. Resents loss of independence, feels stifled by domesticity and lack of money. Wants to start work from home on freelance basis, with the child cared for away from home while she works. Husband not enthusiastic though agrees money would help.

Miss White

On her own with one baby aged twenty months. Lives in bed-sitting room and shares bathroom. Conditions very cramped but cannot afford to move. Lives on supplementary benefit so cannot afford baby sitters for occasional relief. Has no contact with her family or former friends. Stopped working as a teacher to care for baby but feels exhausted, isolated and unhappy about the future. Feels that full-time work is her only way to change.

Comment

In our view, Miss White would stand the best chance of a day nursery place. However, these are so scarce that there might be a long waiting list in her area or no places at all. Mother-and-toddler clubs are the only other group that caters for the age-range she needs, but they are not the sort of provision she would need as a working mother. Her only other option is a child-minder.

Mrs Green's intention to work freelance from home implies very flexible hours. If this is what she wants, then nursery or play-group provision is unlikely to meet her needs. Nor is she likely to be a 'priority' applicant. Her most likely option is a child-minder — or she might consider having someone in to mind the child at home.

Provision	Brown 2 years	Brown 4 years	Green 3 years	White 20 months
Nursery school				
Nursery class				
Day nursery				
Hall playgroup				
Mother and toddler club				
Child-minders				

Comment

This exercise touches on only a few issues. You may have felt for example, that company was very important for Mrs Brown — perhaps to be weighed against guilt and worry about leaving the children, or that Miss White should weigh the freedom of money against tiredness in a full-time job. The information given doesn't really allow you to make a decision for them. But if you are thinking of working, you may find it helps to set out clearly in your own mind what your family position is, and make your own full list of pros and cons.

If you give yourself, or the mothers in these case-studies, more points against than for, ask yourself: could some of the items in the 'for' column be found in more flexible alternatives than paid work? For many women it is important to feel — and to be seen — as someone in their own right as well as being someone else's wife, or mother. A job can give a woman this separate 'identity'; but it may also come from other interests and responsibilities. For example:

● *Company and interest* Helping in the local playgroup, going to an evening class, doing volunteer work, studying at home. The growing number of mother-and-toddler clubs and playgroups suggests that for some mothers these groups provide a separate identity, responsibility and interest.

● *Family life* Living with young children can be stifling for both sides: taking turns with a friend to have all the children gives them variety and you some time off for your own needs.

In a way, Mrs Brown has a double problem, given the age difference between her children. Having been together so much, they might support each other by being cared for together. However, the four-year-old, nearing school age, would probably benefit from the experience of playing with children the same age; the two-year-old is barely ready to share play with strangers. (See *Playing together* in this chapter.) The options most likely to be open seem either to be the same minder for both children, or, probably preferable, a minder for the two-year-old and a place at nursery school or class for the four-year-old. Nursery provision often suits part-time work better than full-time, but there is the problem of school holidays both now and after five. The minder might be able to help here. There is little local authority provision for this, although in some areas there are holiday and after-school schemes.

The needs of children

The quality of care your child receives is vital to his—and your—happiness with the arrangement. You need to consider a place at a nursery or with a minder in terms of the needs of your child as well as the hours of opening, and the arrangements for physical care—eating, sleeping and exercise.

Emotional needs

All children need to feel loved and secure with the person looking after them. Babies under a year old thrive on a happy one-to-one relationship with an adult, though clearly in families with more than one child they do not get the total attention of their mothers. It is a matter of degree. If there are any doubts about the amount of individual care a small baby might get there may be a good case for delaying work until the baby is older.

Children aged between one and two years are thought to have greater difficulty adapting to an additional mother figure. They are more aware of their surroundings and more suspicious of change. But again, children vary by temperament, and according to how used they are to being with other adults. A one-to-one relationship becomes less important as the child grows older. But security in the form of a regular—though not rigid—routine remains a good idea for all pre-schoolers.

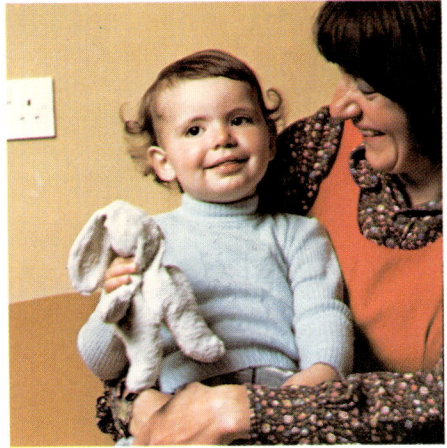

Social needs

The child under two will play some types of games with his parents and sometimes older children, but these very much depend on the other person joining in the baby's interests. Sharing play with other children of the same age is a development that takes many years, but from two or three onwards children do begin to take an interest in and enjoy, this sort of play opportunity.

Interest needs

Even young babies need interesting things to look at and handle, as well as people to talk to. As your toddler becomes more mobile, and more talkative, the need for interesting things to do and talk about increases. But under-twos can get easily frustrated by both people and things, and this needs to be understood and accepted. In the pre-school years, practical experiences of many kinds lay the foundations for later ideas and skills, as you can see elsewhere in the course.

The best sort of care

Determining the quality of care offered by a nursery or minder isn't easy. It helps if you can watch them at work. Obviously it helps too if you can work out what your own requirements are in terms of the needs of your children. For example, Miss White's priorities for her 20-month-old might be:
● Hygienic surroundings with good facilities for eating and sleeping
● A stable routine
● A warm family atmosphere.

On the other hand, Mrs Brown's priorities for her four-year old are likely to be rather different. For example, she might emphasize:
● Company of other children
● Adult conversation
● Toys and books

From the sections above, and what you know of your child, you should be able to draw up your own list of priorities, bearing in mind that needs change as children grow older. Whether an arrangement works or not is best judged by the child's reactions to it. The child may show open signs of stress. But the unnaturally quiet well-behaved child may also be depressed and under stress. If the child is bright and content, there's probably little cause for worry.

Taking care of yourself

Mothers who work need a high degree of organization and a certain amount of co-operation in their domestic life if they're to cope successfully with being a worker, wife and mother.

In the panel opposite is a list of things that you could do in addition to working. Before reading on, work through the list ticking the items according to whether you think they are essential, important or not important. Ring those from 1–8 that you get help with – from your husband, your children, or paid help.

We think . . .

Items 1–4 are essential to keep a household running, but so are items 9 and 10, if family life is not to suffer in personal terms. Items 5–8 are important once in a while – how often depends on your standards. But are they really essential? It's probably more important that you should have ticked at least one of the items 13–16 as essential, or that you have some kind of relaxing interest. It's not lazy to put television before polishing – in terms of your crowded life it's sensible.

Tick these items according to whether you feel they are:	Essential	Important	Not important
1 Basic cooking for family			
2 Day-to-day washing of clothes			
3 Housework – barest essentials, e.g. washing up, hoovering			
4 Shopping – basic needs			
5 Special cooking involving more time			
6 Washing blankets, curtains			
7 Housework – polishing, dusting, etc.			
8 Shopping – clothes, special purchases			
9 Time with children			
10 Time alone with husband			
11 Treats for husband or children			
12 Going to bed early because you're tired			
13 Seeing friends			
14 Going out to pub, film etc.			
15 Watching television, reading			
16 Making things – sewing, knitting etc.			

Is it working out?

Your answers to items 11 and 12 may show how well you and your family are adapting to your job. Quite apart from finding suitable employment and child care, working mothers are often hindered by guilt, a nagging feeling that they are not fulfilling their functions as child-minder, house-keeper and wife. Consistently feeling tired enough to consider going to bed early or guilty enough to consider special treats as essential or even important, suggests things aren't working out too well. You need to take another look at your priorities. And you do need help or cooperation with items 1–8. Your family needs to recognise that you have your own individual needs as well as you serving their needs.

Success and pleasure in being a working mother don't always come easily. But if

● the care arrangement for your children is a good one;

● you yourself are happier working than not;

● your family accept the routine required by your working; then hopefully you will have few problems.

'Going to work' means everything and nothing to small children. It means everything because for part of each day they are separated from their parents; and it means nothing because they find it hard to imagine what this 'work' thing is.

Parents at work

Most children are aware from a very young age that their father goes to work each day. Before they have any idea of what work is, they are aware that his absences are part of the family routine. The daily separation is rarely disturbing. As they grow older, they realise that most other children's fathers go to work too, so it must be alright.

It is more difficult to ensure that children whose mothers work as well are not disturbed by the separation. It is vital that their lives away from home, with childminders or in day nurseries, are stable and happy. And it's also important that the separation is treated as normal. (See *Working mothers* in this chapter.) Even so, as the child of a working mother becomes aware that not all mothers work, resentment can develop. She may learn from books, television programmes, or with her friends that there are mothers who stay at home all day with their children. She may absorb the generally expressed feeling that mothers who don't work are more normal than those who do.

Understanding work

When a child asks 'Why are you going to work?' she doesn't want a lecture on household economics. You can explain in shops 'We can buy this because I get given money when I go to work.' But what your child is really asking is 'Why choose work when you could stay with me?' She doesn't want to feel second best in your life. You need to reassure her that while you need a job, you also wanted a child, and that you're very pleased to have both.

Knowing more about parent's work can help avoid concern or resentment at either parent spending so much time away. But explanations need to be in the child's terms. And making time to be together shows your child that, although you work, she too is special enough to have part of your day all to herself.

Going to work: children's views

Susan's father leaves for work each day at 8 am while she is still eating her breakfast. He wears a suit and carries a brief case. She knows he is going to the office. At 9.30, Susan goes to Aunty Jan while her mother goes to work at the hospital. Her mother also wears smart clothes when she goes to work and she is usually in a hurry to leave in the morning.

Susan is three. If you were her parents, how would you explain to her where you hurry off to each morning and what you do? Tick the four methods that you think would be the best explanation at her age, from the list below:

1 tell her stories, about people who do all sorts of different jobs ☐

2 tell her you'd all have nothing to eat if you didn't work ☐

3 tell her you like to be away from home – just like she likes being at aunty's or the playgroup ☐

4 ask her to describe what she thinks you do at work, and then talk about it ☐

5 show her pictures of offices and hospitals ☐

6 take her to similar places (for example to visit a sick friend; to collect something from the Town Hall) ☐

7 let her spend an hour or two with you at work ☐

8 help her make her own 'work' corner or game at home, where she can play at being you ☐

As with most 'mysteries' in the child's world, some explanations are more helpful than others (see *All I get is questions*, and *Instructions and explanations* in Chapter 4). Generalised explanations about people at work (1) are only helpful when she has begun to understand about the place of *your* particular job in her life. Implying that you like to be away from her (3), or that she'd starve if you didn't go (2) may be true, but can be very threatening. Perhaps you'll decide not to come back one day? Or if you're ill, what would happen to her? Asking her about your work (4) may be revealing, but simple talk at this age won't help her very much. Young children need something 'real' to link words to – for example, pictures (5) and visits (6) accompanied by simple explanations related to the child's life – 'At the hospital, doctors and nurses help people who hurt themselves, like when your friend Mary broke her arm.' If it is possible to take your child to your place of work, to see her 'parent-in-action' for an hour or so (7), this can be very helpful. (Don't assume your employer will say 'no'.)

From these sorts of experiences your child learns enough to be able to learn more through playing at being you (8) – see *Playing mothers and fathers* in Chapter 2. He also develops important attitudes towards activities called 'work'.

Spending time together

A consistent routine helps children feel secure. But within the framework of coming home – teatime – bedtime it's important too to allow time for the child to be with her parents, to play, or to talk or to cuddle. The child needs this time to develop the special bonds with her parents that are vital to her well adjustment and development. Whether only one parent goes out to work, or both, the child may feel a sense of loss or rejection. But this can be overcome by an expectation of the regular time you spend together.

Within a shared routine, the needs of both parent and child should be considered. For example, the child can wait until father's taken off his jacket, washed and had five minutes with mum – or the newspaper – before expecting him to read to her. Definite signals to the child that it's *her* time – 'after tea' – 'when I sit down in the sitting room' – may help. Time spent with the child in the day, or early evening is more likely to result in peaceful nights – the child goes to bed content.

An ideal routine is one that is secure but flexible. The child should be confident that her 'shared time' will happen, so that daddy being home half-an-hour late won't cause a tantrum. It does mean finding a compromise between your own and your children's needs – but providing you've planned ahead, you should be able to work this out between you.

Much of the above applies also to parents at home. Family work takes time and effort, and you can't always respond to your child when she wants. With four-year-olds particularly, part of the compromise can be to involve your child with you in the family work that has to be done. You won't want to do it all day and every day – but there are suggestions you can try in Chapters 3 and 4. And you can try to encourage more self-sufficient play while you get on with jobs on your own (see *Family work* in Chapter 3).

Family routine

Susan and her mother get home at 4.15. Susan's father gets home at 6.15. Between 4.15 and Susan's bed-time at 7, she must be fed and bathed. Susan's mother must prepare tea for Susan and supper for her husband and herself. She must also attend to urgent domestic chores.

Draw up a routine for the family which includes shared time for Susan with both her parents.

Time	What Susan, mother and father could do:
4.15	Susan and her mother arrive home
4.30	
4.45	
5.00	
5.15	
5.30	
5.45	
6.00	
6.15	Father arrives home
6.30	
6.45	
7.00	Susan goes to bed

A possible routine for Susan and her parents might be like the one below which builds in the essentials – food, bath and time with both parents. But obviously, the time spent on each can vary from family to family and from day to day – a routine should not mean rigid clock-watching.

4.15 Quiet time – drink and cuddles

4.30 Play together – with things that are easy to set up, for example drawing, puzzles, bricks

5.00 Susan helps her mother get her tea

5.30 Susan has tea in kitchen while her mother prepares supper

6.00 Susan has her bath and gets into her pyjamas

6.30 Father talks to Susan and reads her a story giving mother time to cook or tidy – or put her feet up

● With more than one child life becomes more complex. How would you adapt this routine if Susan had an older brother, Mark, who is collected from school by his mother and Susan, and goes to bed at 7.30?

Long absences from home

If parents' jobs take them away from home for several days or more, the child may find the break in the normal family routine difficult. As has been seen in other topics a child's sense of the future is limited: how is she to understand that daddy or mummy will come back in a given number of days or weeks? You can try explaining the length of time in terms of the number of 'sleeps' without the other parent, or by crossing off days on a calendar – but there's still the problem of what to do in the meantime, if the child is upset by the absence.

The danger for parents trying to reassure children is that they will over-react, either by ignoring the child's worries, or by compensating with a new, exclusive routine. Telling the child not to fuss won't make her worries go away, while creating a new routine makes it difficult for family life to resume as normal as the diagram shows.

Keeping life normal

What a child needs is for life to be as normal as possible. In a way it is easier if absences are a regular feature of life – the child becomes aware of a pattern of absence always followed by a return. Even so, she may be upset by changes in routine. So you need to ensure that the regular balance of family life remains, as far as possible, the same.

Don't do too many special things 'because daddy is away'. (This includes taking the child into your bed – it's asking for night-time trouble when he returns.) Father might phone, or send postcards to be read, at the time he would normally be with the child. The child could make drawings to send to daddy, or to keep for when he comes home. Both parties could keep a scrap book of what they've been doing, and swap them and talk about them when you're all together again. You could plan a surprise for daddy's return, or talk about what he's doing now this minute.

Keeping life as normal as possible, and finding practical ways to reassure your child that the absent parent is alive and well and coming home sometime, are the best precautions you can take against long absences affecting your child.

Father away

Child is bewildered at loss of father and does not understand when she will see him again

Exclusion of father from family life

Mother adapts family routine to the absence of father

Father returns, and intrudes on the new routine

Child is resentful, first because father went away, now because he demands mother's attention. Shows signs of jealousy and rejection

Father senses exclusion and is hurt by child's attitude

Mother is torn by the demands for her attention from both child and father

Feeling low

It is known that as many as two-thirds of mothers at home with pre-school children experience a peak-period of dissatisfaction, and that nearly a half experience periods of severe depression.

Most people experience a feeling of depression at some time or other. Often it can be lifted by a good night's sleep, but sometimes it can grow and may begin to affect the whole family.

The change in life

A recent study found that two-thirds of young mothers had very romantic expectations of what it would be like to have children. Many women feel depressed when life doesn't live up to their expectations and they feel guilty because they don't enjoy looking after their children as much as they'd expected. These feelings of low self-worth and loss of identity are some of the main reasons that many women feel depressed when they are at home all day with young children. It reflects the low status that society gives this kind of work, as well as the difficulties women have in finding suitable jobs when they want to return to work.

Housing and housework

Inadequate housing is one of the most common causes of depression in women. Those living in inadequate accommodation are more likely to find things getting on top of them, than women with larger houses that have more space and garden for children to play in. The need for a higher family income is also one of the main reasons many women are forced to find paid employment outside the home.

Nowadays, with so many household gadgets and labour-saving machines, housework can be less time-consuming. Ironically all these modern conveniences have not reduced the number

Is it just me?

No, you are not the only person who feels depressed. Below are extracts from conversations with mothers who have experienced depression. They describe how they felt at the time. We have placed each quote beneath the reason why they felt that way. Tick which of these feelings you too have experienced.

● Finding themselves unprepared for the total change in their way of life.

'Very, very depressed, very inexperienced. I didn't know what was expected of me as a mother, parent or anything, and it's changed my life completely.' ☐

● Feeling imprisoned in the home, having lost the feeling of identity which they had experienced as a working person; losing the interest, satisfaction, sense of achievement; lack of adult company, loneliness.

'I still feel I'm just tied to the house, to the family, to the children, I don't feel a person in my own right.' ☐

● Finding housework boring.

'I get extremely depressed by the housework because it's never-ending.' ☐

● Finding housing inadequate.

'We lived in a 2-bedroomed house which I found very difficult to manage, because it meant Cathy couldn't go into her room to play because the twins were in there sleeping.' ☐

● Finding the demands of small children exhausting and irritating, always feeling tired.

'I thought everything was going to be wonderful – but if you have a good baby you're lucky; if you've got a little terror, you've had it.' ☐

● Not getting help from husband or husband not understanding cause of depression; husband spends too much time with the baby; not having own money.

'It's just handed down from family to family – you have to do what my mother did, and they don't realise times have really changed.' ☐

Perhaps you are surprised to find that other people feel as you do, that many of the troubles that you had felt were your own peculiar problem are in fact also the problems of others.

of hours the average woman spends on housework. One recent survey found that three-quarters of the women interviewed thought housework was monotonous. They also gave the lack of contact with other people, and isolation as reasons for their dissatisfaction.

Helping husbands

One of the main factors that can prevent women feeling low during this period is the amount of support they get from their husbands. 'You just can't take it all by yourself. And to have a wonderful husband who can take care of the kids, to me is ideal.' This doesn't just mean help with the housework and looking after the children, but emotional support – having someone willing to talk and listen and help with the problems.

Although it's becoming more common to find men helping at home, they are still only a minority of the population. A recent survey found that about 15 per cent of them actually took a fair share of household tasks.

There are still parts of the country where the traditional roles have changed very little in recent years – the woman's place is still thought to be in the home and her main role in life is to look after her husband and their children. Sometimes women share this view. 'Several of them round here – they hate to see a man pick up a dish or anything. I think the women have got to be changed as much as the men in encouraging the men to help.'

The greatest social changes have occurred in the large cities where a larger proportion of the population have been to college and university.

Young and middle class men are more likely to help. Those who were brought up to play a part in the running of the household are more likely to do so for the rest of their lives. Your experiences as a child – the way you saw your own father behave – are very important influences on your behaviour. So what are you doing as parents to prepare your son for his future relationships; or what expectations are you giving your daughter?

Most mothers have strong feelings of responsibility for the care and happiness of their children. However, a depressed mother can have a bad effect on her children and on the whole family. For example research has shown that the children of depressed women are very much more prone to accidents than other children. 'If things start to get on top of you, you get edgy, you get depressed and you tend to shout and hit out.'

Simply lasting out

Stages of childhood pass . . . and so do stages of mothering! If people are not subjected to more strain than they can bear – and this varies from person to person – they will survive until life changes. But the responsibility of raising a family lasts for many years and simply lasting out without help from husband and friends is more than most mothers can manage.

So what can help?

What do people do when everything gets them down? The mothers we talked to had this list of suggestions to give. These are ways they adapted to the changes in their lives. Which have helped you – or could do so?

Adapting to the change	You
Simply lasting out	☐
Getting pills from the doctor	☐
Returning to work	☐
Getting help from husband	☐
Getting help from friend	☐
Becoming a child minder	☐
Having children in to play	☐
Leaving child with friends	☐
Getting used to lower standards of housekeeping	☐
Meeting people, for example at playgroup, book group, Housewife's Register . . .	☐
Going out	☐
Working in a playgroup	☐
Doing other voluntary work	☐

Pills from the doctor

There is an increasing use of tranquillisers and anti-depressants by mothers of young children. Pills reduce the amount of worry but do not alter the facts of living.

What is a doctor able to do for a mother who complains about feeling low? It is possible to prescribe pills which may help a mother through a bad patch. However these often only provide a short-term solution. It is not possible to prescribe helpful supporting friends . . . and it is not always easy to find them yourself.

Returning to work

It has been found that there is less depression among mothers of young children who are out at work. Many factors contribute to this:
● having more money and the satisfaction of earning it;
● being financially independent;
● getting out of the house and away from the children;
● having an identity separate from that which they have at home;
● the interest of the work itself;
● meeting people.
But there are the complications and the cost of providing for the children when you are at work. This subject is discussed in the first topic in this chapter, *Working mothers*.

Playing together

Development from simple to more complicated forms of social play is gradual. Given the chance, most children between the ages of two and five learn how to play together in groups; but the extent of their involvement does not always depend on their 'stage' of development.

Types of play

Children need to work through several stages of learning to play together before they enjoy the give and take of playing in a group. Once a child has become confident about playing with others she will still sometimes want to enjoy playing alone or alongside other children as well as playing with them.

In very broad terms, we can identify half a dozen different kinds of social play. Each type of play shows more involvement between children, and more ability to relate to, and communicate with, others.

Solitary play . . . playing alone

Playing can take up all of a child's attention. There is much to explore in the world . . . shape, texture (rough, smooth, or slippery); consistency (hard or soft); colour; tastes . . . all need to be explored, felt, smelt and tasted. That is what playing is about to begin with and another child is of no greater interest than a ball, a doll or a cat.

Parallel play . . . playing alongside others

Even before showing an interest in the play of others, a child will probably be content to spend much of her playing time in their company, without making any real effort to make contacts with them. She is at ease just playing alongside them, in 'parallel'. She is busily intent on her own activity, and at most might defend her toys or the attempts of others to take something away from another child. So, although there may be a few occasional tussles and stern looks and words, these are short exchanges and don't develop into anything.

Looking-on play . . . watching from the edge of the group

A big change happens when a child begins to show an interest in the activities of other children. At first, this interest may seem rather passive. Long spells are spent merely watching another child or group at play. You will notice, however, that this behaviour is very different from aimless wandering or unfocused attention because the child is quite clearly absorbed in his or her observations.

Joining in play . . . playing with others within the group

Early moves towards joining-in play may be smooth or stormy, depending on the children in the group and on the individual who wishes to join it. At all events, relationships within a group are likely to be formed quickly, broken off perhaps just as rapidly, and as often as not, resumed within a few minutes or hours.

There are two characteristic kinds of joining-in play. The first involves doing the same thing as everybody else in the group, merely for the sake of being the same – or perhaps, as a way of becoming a group member. A common example would be a small group of children running around together, perhaps shouting a catch phrase to each other like 'We're the first train in the station' – or making Tarzan calls.

The second kind arises where group members may be engaged on the same activity (for example, crayoning or sitting at a table doing puzzles) but where the main thing they are interested in is talking to one another. The subject matter of their talk may range far beyond the immediate activity and include exchanges of information about parents, possessions, family relationships and special events, such as outings and parties. The crayoning and puzzles may be mentioned, but again this will often be in a much wider context of what they like or dislike in general, or about what each is doing.

Co-operative play

At some point, the interest of the group shifts back from the swapping of ideas to the game they are playing. In co-operative play, belonging to the group becomes very important. The child has a definite place in the group, which is quite different from that with the emphasis on *individual* activity found in solitary and parallel play, and also with the simple *socialising* shown in joining-in play.

Co-operative play can be the simple sharing of a task (for example three children building bricks together).

Simple co-operative . . .

Complex co-operative . . .

In this type of play, children divide roles, taking the part of someone not themselves. They act the part that they have been given, playing 'Let's pretend' games (like hospitals) and games with complicated rules. Particular make-believe roles such as 'mothers and babies', 'big girls with pet dogs', etc. may be acted for days, or even weeks on end, with varying degrees of elaboration and interruptions from competing interests. A particular child may tend to lead the group more often than falling in with the plans made by other would-be leaders.

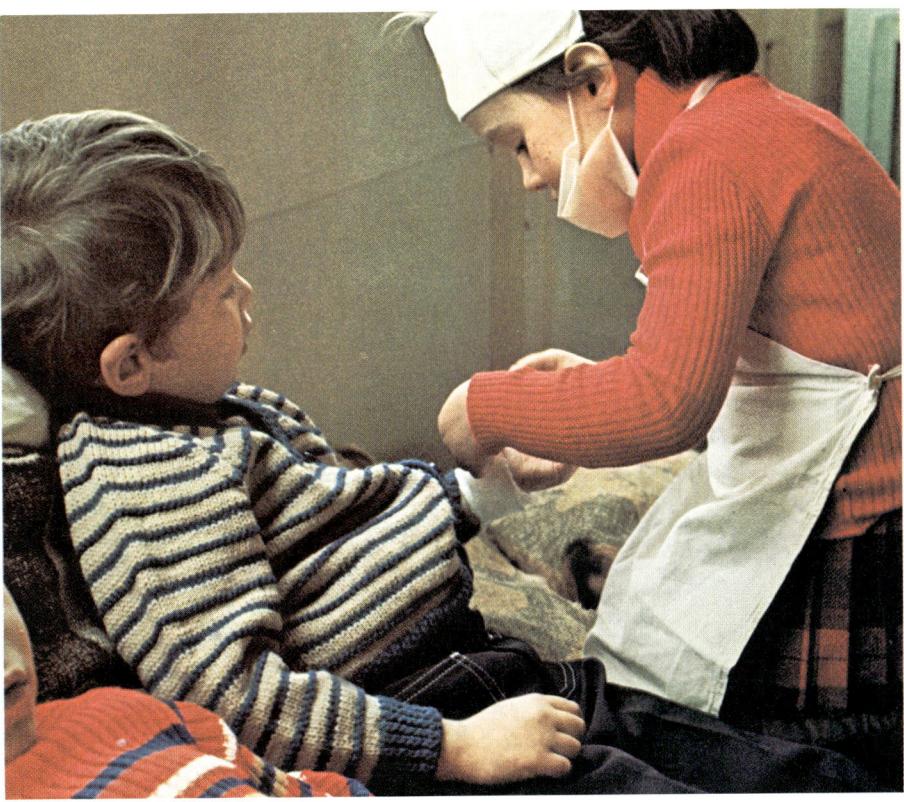

Solitary
Absorbed in own play apart from other children, showing no interest in their activity. Plays with different things. Often silent, talks to herself sometimes.

Parallel
All playing the same part, or with the same things. No sharing or taking turns. Talk is not usually directed to anyone in particular or the play may be silent.

Looking-on
Shows interest in other's activity but remains alone. Other children are much more important than playthings even if there is no conversation between them.

Spot the play

Using the summaries above as a guide, can you identify the following kinds of play, putting ticks under the appropriate headings? Conversation will give you another clue.

● Is the child saying anything at all?
● Is she speaking to herself?
● Is the talk related to the playing?
● Is the child speaking as herself or is she pretending to be someone else?
● Are questions answered in a way that makes sense? Or do they only sound as if they are making sense? Answers to these questions will help you in deciding what name to give to each kind of playing. For instance:
● if the children are talking to themselves or their plaything, the words may be in sentences or may just be repetitive, the play would be called . . . **Solitary**
● if the children, are playing beside each other in silence or with little unrelated chat, the play would be called . . . **Parallel or looking on**
● if the children are talking to others about all sorts of things, which are not especially related to what their hands are doing, the play would be called . . . **Joining in**
● if the children are talking as themselves to others about what they are doing, answering real questions with appropriate answers, the play would be called . . . **Simple co-operative**
● if the children are talking, acting out the parts of people they are pretending to be, the play would be called . . . **Complex co-operative**

'I am a dalek'

1 Three children are marching round the room in a group all chanting 'I am a dalek'. Nobody else takes much notice. They sometimes point at each other and at other people with their arms outstretched, chanting and intermittently laughing together. One says – 'Are you my best friend today?' – the other just laughs.

2 One child points outstretched arms at another and says – 'I am a dalek. I am going to exterminate you'. Ah-ah-ah-ah-ah. The second child pretends to fall down dead.

3 One child points outstretched arms chanting – 'I am a dalek' – over and over to thin air. Nobody reacts. Nobody else is playing at daleks.

4 One child organises her fellows into two groups and orders the 'daleks' to enter an 'enemy hide-out' and 'round up' the enemy. She threatens that the enemy 'will be exterminated' if they resist. She orders her daleks to lead the enemy away.

5 Three children are sitting at a table drawing with crayons. One says to himself, rather than anyone else in particular, 'I am a dalek, I am a dalek. I'm drawing a dalek, a dalek, a dalek'. The other two children carry on with their own crayoning and don't appear to hear him.

Solitary	Parallel	Looking-on	Joining in	simple	complex
				Co-operative	
☑	☑	☐	☑	☐	☐
☐	☐	☐	☐	☑	☐
☑	☐	☑	☐	☐	☐
☐	☐	☐	☑	☐	☑
☐	☑	☐	☐	☐	☐

(Answers are given on p. 206.)

So what?

In a family, younger children become drawn into co-operative play earlier then they would if they were just playing with other children. They are given the passive roles – the dog that is taken for a walk, the patient that is being treated by nurse and doctor. If they enjoy it, their play and talk often develops ahead of other children of their own age.

If you watch your child's play from time to time in this way, you will notice developments and changes in your child's interests and in the patterns of her play relationships that you might otherwise have missed. Also it might be interesting to look back at this activity after a year or so and see what pattern of playing you notice then.

This understanding of the development of social play helps a lot in the practical business of living with young children – for example:

● you will know that a birthday party with a lot of two-year-olds will not be a social success! By the third birthday, some children will be ready for joining in play but others will still be at the solitary or parallel play stage;

● when children are ill, or feeling insecure, their playing will 'return' to a simpler stage and they will play as they did six months or a year ago – and this should be expected and provided for;

● if your two-year-old runs upstairs when your friend comes with her child don't fear that she is going to grow up unfriendly! Two-year-olds are like that;

● most children accustomed to playing alone will take time to work through the various stages of learning to play in a group. You cannot expect them to enjoy the group unless they have had a chance to learn at their own pace. This kind of learning takes place most naturally and easily in the years before school. Pushing children away with – 'Go and play with those children' – presents them with a problem. They cannot do it if they are not ready.

together

Joining in
Trying to join in the group play of others, either to be accepted as a group member. A little talking, sometimes in imitation.

Simple co-operative
Taking part in shared activity, doing the same things. Shares toys, takes turns, works with others. Talk is mostly related to playing.

Complex co-operative
Complicated pretending games with other children taking agreed parts. Talk is mostly concerned with the parts being played.

While the older children will, from time to time, play alone or in conjunction with others, two-year-olds do not play in a co-operative way. Social play is learnt as children discover how to communicate with each other in speech.

In general:

● one-year-olds play mostly alone, barely interested in others;

● two-year-olds are interested to watch other children at play but do not play very much or for very long. Others are often rivals, and when in trouble they look for their mother;

● three-year-olds begin to want to join in other children's games and are often made happy by being accepted into a group;

● four-year-olds will sometimes play quite complicated acting games, but they also play in ways that would be called simple co-operative, joining in, parallel, solitary . . . as well. They enjoy all kinds of play.

The learning of new kinds of playing is like learning new words. As the vocabulary grows children are able to express themselves more clearly, and more accurately. As they learn to play more complicated games with other children, they do not lose the enjoyment of, and the need for, the kinds of play from their younger days.

The learning of social play is a gradual process, and passes through stages like other kinds of learning. Children learn at different rates and will sometimes regress, as in other kinds of learning, for example a four-year-old feeling unwell will not be interested in group play. Children learn best if they are allowed to go at their own pace with your support, if you are needed, and your encouragement.

Before they reach the age of five, most children, given the chance to play among others of their own age, will learn the give-and-take of living with a variety of other children. This learning comes naturally at this age and is sometimes more difficult if left until later. It certainly seems to add to the enjoyment of living for both the children and their mothers. Look back to *Choosing a group* if you want to think more about this.

Building together with bricks is simple cooperative play. As building progresses a third boy joins in the play.

How can you help?

First by giving your child the chance to grow through these stages of learning to play with other children. Once in the group, what is the play-leading part of the mother and of other adults?

● Supporter: the mother settling her child into the group being prepared to accept the advice of experience in choosing the time to withdraw. Ensuring the child is ready to encounter new experiences.

● Introducer: the suggestion of new ideas, always being prepared to be spurned if the child is intent upon following a chosen course of action.

● Stimulator of conversation: sometimes conversation will spring naturally enough from playing, leading the children's thinking away from the here and now.

● Giver of advice: judging carefully when the child will be able to learn from experience or when it would be better to step in.

● Comforter: the acceptance of alternatives to mother is a stage in the development of independence.

● Referee: making judgements that sort out or prevent clashes of will.

● Part of the play: accepting whatever part is given in the course of playing a complicated game.

● Helper of a child in difficulty: when a task is beyond him.

Keep a playchart

Make a few notes next time your child is playing with other children. You will probably be able to pick out the types of social play she is enjoying quite quickly. Note down on the left hand side of the chart what your child is doing, for example playing ball, see-sawing, playing 'mothers and fathers'. Check the descriptions of the different types of play and tick under the heading in the chart the one that describes your child's play.

If you are uncertain tick two columns.

After following your child through several spells of play, a pattern may emerge that will show the kind of play she is enjoying at the moment.

Watch a group of children playing for five or ten minutes and repeat your observations with an older and a younger child.

Watching Ian

Ian has just joined a playgroup. He is a little unsure of himself. His mother stays for the second session, watching him out of the corner of her eye as she writes her shopping list. His behaviour, which is described in the chart, shows her that he is beginning to settle.

Answers to 'I am a dalek'

1 Joining in
2 Simple co-operative
3 Solitary
4 Complex co-operative
5 Parallel

Imaginative play is supported by the provision of a few simple 'props'.

Play incident	Solitary	Parallel	Looking on	Joining in	Simple Co-operative	Complex
1 Name *Ian* Age *3yrs*						
1 Riding on trundle car	☐	☐	☐	☐	☐	☐
2 Leaves car to climb frame	☐	☐	☐	☐	☐	☐
3 Watches from vantage point	☐	☐	☐	☐	☐	☐
4 Slides down to join others at dough table	☐	☐	☐	☐	☐	☐
5 Says, 'This is my pudding'	☐	☐	☐	☐	☐	☐
Name Age						
2	☐	☐	☐	☐	☐	☐
	☐	☐	☐	☐	☐	☐
	☐	☐	☐	☐	☐	☐
	☐	☐	☐	☐	☐	☐
	☐	☐	☐	☐	☐	☐
Name Age						
3	☐	☐	☐	☐	☐	☐
	☐	☐	☐	☐	☐	☐
	☐	☐	☐	☐	☐	☐
	☐	☐	☐	☐	☐	☐
	☐	☐	☐	☐	☐	☐

Children's quarrels

Put two or more pre-schoolers together, and sooner or later there'll be a fight or a quarrel. Why does it happen and what do you do about it?

What do you do when children quarrel?

For each situation below, ring the *one* answer that most nearly matches what you would do or say as your first line of action.

1 You go to the park on a fine day. Lots of other parents are there with their children too. Your child wants to go on the swings. When he sees they are all taken he screams and stamps and yells 'get off'. Would you:

(a) Try to explain to him about waiting and taking turns?

(b) Smack him or tell him off loudly to show you're in charge?

(c) Tell him he's being childish?

(d) Let him get on with it?

2 Your child comes running in from play to say that a playmate has hit him, but he's obviously not hurt. Would you:

(a) Go out and work out with them what the quarrel was about?

(b) Say 'Well, go and hit him then'?

(c) Tell him he's big enough to look after himself?

(d) Tell him you don't want to hear tales?

3 Your child is squabbling with a brother/ sister over a toy. Would you:

(a) Try to arrange for them to share?

(b) Remove the offending toy?

(c) Say they ought to know better?

(d) Leave them to sort it out for themselves?

Answers of types (a), (b) and (c) are based on the different styles of control that are discussed in *For their own good* in Chapter 6. In each case an (a) answer suggests a personal, explanatory style — you're prepared to be drawn into the situation and to act as some kind of 'arbitrator'. With (b) answers you use your authority as an adult to command or direct the child and the situation. With (c) answers you give the child comments on his behaviour as not being in keeping with his age/size/family — his 'position in life'. Answers of type (d) are rather different — you're refusing to be drawn into the situation at all.

Reasons for what you do

Quite probably your answers to these questions weren't all of the same type. What you do in any given situation does depend on who's involved – strangers, friends or family – and the seriousness of the quarrel. Particularly you may not want to 'fall out over the kids' with neighbours, as this could cause trouble. But the problem with staying out of the situation is that your child has to fend for himself. You may feel he's got to learn the world is tough – but does he learn best how to cope with it by himself?

What your child learns

When you do take part, it does seem that children learn different things from what you do. Direct commands or actions, or comments on what they ought to do in their 'position' give them little help in sorting the situation out for themselves. True, words don't always help, but the 'arbitrator' role of the adults gives children a chance to explain themselves and their grievances, and become involved in working out what the solution should be.

Why do children quarrel?

Personality differences are part of the reason – some children seem to be naturally more aggressive than others. But for all children quarrelling and fighting are part of learning to play together. When you're three, or even four, you're still fairly absorbed in yourself and what you are doing. You're curious about the activities of other children but you're uncertain whether you want to join in, or how to do so. If someone tries to join in your play, you can do four things: ignore him, withdraw, push him out of the way or attempt to share.

Property

It can take a long time for children to learn to share. Mary Richards found this out when she took her daughter, Lindsay, three and a half, to play with her friends across the road.

'When Lindsay goes to play with the others she grabs their toys as if she never had any of her own in the whole world. But when they come here to play she won't let them touch her toys and screams the place down if any of the children tries to play with them. I don't know what my friends must think I'm like with her at home.'

Parents do get embarrassed about such behaviour from their children as they feel it's a reflection of the example they are setting. Mary can't understand where Lindsay's 'It's mine – don't touch' attitude comes from. She and her husband Pete spend a lot of time sharing and doing things with Lindsay at home.

Young children take for granted the sharing of a home and love but sharing of possessions is something else. Apart from food, children have limited experience of sharing things with others, and it takes time for them to learn that they've nothing to lose by it.

They need the experience of seeing their parents involved with and sharing with others as well as with themselves. On the other hand, having rights over one's own possessions is an aspect of privacy which children can learn if there's mutual respect in the household.

It can help if each member of the family has some private place that no one goes to without permission – a toybox, a desk, or a workbox. The contents may be valuable, or sentimental or dangerous or merely personal in the sense of 'I'll share anything and everything with you – but that is mine and you must ask first.'

Pre-school groups

What is the difference between a nursery school and a day nursery? Between a crèche and a playgroup? There is a great deal of variety and some important differences that are well worth knowing.

All forms of caring for other people's children, whether singly or in groups, are legally the responsibility of at least one department of your local authority—the County, City or Borough Council. These departments may be the providers and have full responsibility, financial and practical, or their responsibility may be limited to overseeing what others are doing. There are many local variations in provision, sometimes only in the names used. This guide gives a description of the groups, schools, and nurseries that are commonly met.

Key to symbols used

 Babies and children under the age of 3

 Three- and four-year-olds

 Mainly four-year-olds

 Buildings

 Staff – nearly all are women; recently a few men have begun to work in nurseries. They are especially valuable in day nurseries where they may be the only men in the lives of fatherless children.

 Times of opening

 Parents – their role and responsibilities in the group

 How financed

 Department of local authority which has responsibility.

Nursery schools

 Under-threes only in special circumstances.

 Usually have purpose-built premises with outside playground.

 Trained teachers and nursery nurses with the head teacher fully trained in the special field of nursery education. One adult to every ten or twelve children – local variations.

 Monday to Friday, 9.00 to 3.30, during normal school terms. Most children attend only morning or afternoon sessions.

 No fees to parents other than a small charge for snacks or the school's funds. Cost for one child to attend for one year is over £500.

 Some schools involve parents a lot, others only a little.

Education department

Children who attend nursery schools don't have to live in its immediate area. Some schools have long waiting lists and have to select children. Some take children in strict order of application, others select on the basis of individual or family need. Nursery schools don't deliberately teach children how to read and count. They provide many kinds of play activities so that children can learn in their own way and develop as individuals at their own speed.

There have been local-authority nursery schools in Britain since the early part of this century. To begin with they were opened to meet the physical needs of children in the poorest parts of big cities. More schools were started in areas with plenty of employment and where factories needed women's labour. Now, however, nursery schools are found in most counties.

Education Acts in 1944 (England and Wales) and 1946 (Scotland) enabled local authorities to provide nursery schools. This development was halted in 1960 but in 1972 a large expansion was planned, to be completed by 1982. Some classes were started before large scale cutbacks in education halted further development.

Nursery teachers have a three-year training which is related to children from three to seven. Sometimes teachers of older children take a special short course to qualify them to teach younger children but it may be difficult for them to adjust to the different needs of the under-fives. Nursery nurses train for two years to work with children from birth until the age of five, in nursery schools, day nurseries, creches and in private work.

Trained teachers do not encourage children to master the three Rs too quickly. They provide varied and stimulating play that is appropriate for the under fives.

Nursery classes

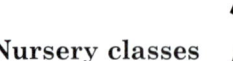

Children usually attend only in the year before compulsory schooling at five.

 Part of an infant or nursery school.

 Teacher not always nursery-trained. Overall responsibility held by head of the whole school.

 As for nursery schools.

 As for nursery schools, but marginally cheaper to run since administrative expenses are shared with the larger school.

 Education department.

Nursery classes tend to be smaller units than nursery schools, usually taking around 20 four-year-olds at one time, becoming a downwards extension of the regular school pattern. Usually only children living in the area are admitted, and there is rarely accommodation for three-year-olds.

Day nurseries

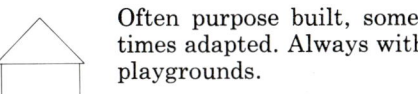
Often purpose built, sometimes adapted. Always with playgrounds.

Matron is likely to be trained as either a nurse or a nursery nurse. Other staff are nursery nurses and aides. Sometimes there are trained teachers.

Normally 7.30 to 5.30 closing only for public holidays.

Parents pay according to their means.

It is difficult for parents to be involved because children only attend if their families are undergoing stress of one kind or another.

Social services department (England and Wales), social work department (Scotland).

Selection for the very limited number of places in day nurseries is based upon the families' needs. On the whole, they cater for the children of single parents, mothers who must work or families undergoing short- or long-term stress. Children may attend for varying periods, some for short spells – as when their mother goes into hospital – while others attend throughout their pre-school years.

Traditionally, day nurseries have had to put greater emphasis on physical and social rather than educational care since they have the whole responsibility for most of the children's waking hours. They may have no teacher-trained staff and are usually not as well equipped as nursery schools and classes, even though the needs of the children are usually greater since their homes are also often lacking things that stimulate interest.

Children's centres

Purpose-built premises for a new type of group that aims to combine the best features of both nursery school and day nursery. Normally it is run by both education and social work services departments.

Trained teachers and nursery nurses.

Open from about 8.00 to 5.30, closing only for public holidays though less accommodation may be available in school holidays.

Charges sometimes made for day-care accommodation but not for school hours accommodation only, apart from charges for food.

Most children's centres make special efforts to involve parents in the work of the centre.

Variable: sometimes education, sometimes shared between education and social services.

Like the nursery school, day centres often accept children whose families are not in any particular social difficulty. These centres have only recently been built and there are not many of them.

Local authority provision

The scale of local authority provision varies in different parts of the country. Many people are unaware of the work that is being done in some areas, of its value and the extent to which it falls short of the need. Elsewhere there is none.

Choose an area around your home, neighbourhood, town, borough or county according to your interest. Find out as much as you can about the work being done for pre-school children. You can get information at your public library, from teachers in your nursery and lower schools, and from town, city and county halls.

How many kinds of local authority provision can you fill in? If there is no provision, say so.

It is not easy to get an accurate figure for the number of pre-schoolers but your librarian may be able to help. Then try to find out how much community and private groups are contributing. Your Pre-school Playgroups Association branch or playgroup adviser may be able to help, or the Social Services (Social Work Services in Scotland).

Try to share the collecting of this information with others.

One o'clock clubs
(but only if accompanied by an adult)

Huts or permanent buildings in parks.

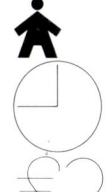
Playleaders who have undergone related training.

From 12.00 to 3.00, weekdays throughout the year.

No charge.

Parks department which has the responsibility of staffing and equipping the club.

The first One o'clock clubs were started in London in 1962 to encourage mothers with young children to use the open spaces of city parks. Some of the activities found in nursery schools are provided – painting, puzzles, clay, etc.

Play buses

In some places where there is no suitable accommodation, old, but still serviceable, buses have been adapted and equipped as mobile play centres. Although local education or social services departments are usually responsible, they are often equipped by volunteers.

Total number of children under five

Nursery schools
number
total number of places
total number of children,
(both full- and part-time)

Nursery classes
number
total number of places
total number of children

Day nurseries
number
number of places

Children's centre
number of places
number of children attending

Mother and toddler clubs
number

Hall playgroups
number
total number of places
total number of children

House playgroups and childminders
number
total number of places

Pre-school groups

Other groups of children

Under the Nurseries and Child-minders Act of 1948, those who take care of other people's children for two hours or more for gain are required to register with the local authority. These groups go by various names but the names themselves are no guide at all to the nature of the group. The name, and the alternatives 'nursery school' or 'playschool', may mean almost anything in England and Wales. In Scotland, the term playgroup usually applies to a parent-run group in a hall; it sometimes does in England and Wales. Some characteristics of these groups are described in the following sections.

House playgroups

Playgroup leaders who may have appropriate qualifications, but may also have attended playgroup courses, or have neither qualifications nor course experience. One adult to every eight children.

Commonly from 9—12, sometimes not every morning, sometimes all day, perhaps for different children in morning and afternoon.

Fees paid by parents are used at the discretion of the playgroup leader. Sometimes fees of children in need are paid by the social services department.

Few house playgroups involve parents.

Must register with social services departments.

Community groups
Mother-and-toddler clubs

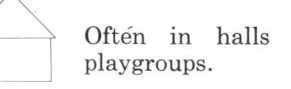
Often in halls used by playgroups.

Often they are self-helping organisations with no one person in charge. Sometimes one person, with or without her own children is asked to take on the role of hostess.

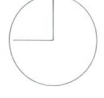
Usually afternoons from 2.00 to 4.00 p.m.

Usually only mothers are free to come, but sometimes fathers on shift work bring their children.

Fees are charged to cover the cost of renting the premises, for equipment and refreshments.

There is no legal requirement for authorities to recognise the existence of these clubs since the mothers remain with the children. They have emerged on a wide scale only since the late sixties. Mothers often bring children over three if they also have babies or toddlers. The clubs are often formed for the younger brothers and sisters of playgroup children but sometimes the opposite happens and a mother-and-toddler club gives rise to a playgroup as the children get older, and are happy to play without their mothers. When this happens the playgroup must be registered with the local authority as described earlier.

Sometimes the groups of mothers drawn together plan a programme of speakers and events, but usually the afternoon is just a welcome chance to sit down and talk. The children gradually begin to explore a world that is wider than the home, playing with toys that they find there and gradually becoming interested in other children, the ideal introduction to playing together.

Hall playgroups

(Unless four-year-olds go to local nursery classes, in which case there are only threes).

Church, community, village and other public halls, shared with other users. Sometimes schools or buildings owned by the playgroup offer unshared accommodation.

As for house playgroups. Parents serve on committee, they appoint staff, help in sessions.

Fees paid by parents are determined by either a private individual or company, or an elected committee of parents.

Must register with social services departments.

The way money is spent is decided by either the 'owner' of the group or by the committee of parents. There have long been private nursery schools but the idea of the community playgroup only emerged during the sixties. In these playgroups, parents are often closely involved in all aspects of the work and many find that the playgroup is an introduction to a friendly community. Most playgroups have to find all their income, though in some areas of need they receive grant aid. Playgroups aim to give children the same kind of variety of activities as those found in local authority nursery schools. Many playgroups belong to the Pre-school Playgroups Association (see page 192). When local authorities open free nursery schools or classes, the fee-charging, parent-involving playgroups may lose so many children that they must close. Sometimes, however, the playgroups continue, perhaps on a smaller scale to meet the continuing needs of under-fives and their parents.

Family centres

Just beginning to emerge are a few family centres. They are the voluntary or self-help equivalent to local-authority children's centres. They can be run by a committee that includes representatives from PPA, Gingerbread, Community Relations Councils and other groups interested in the overall provision for young children.

Such centres could provide flexible facilities, meeting the needs of the community as they reveal themselves, often using the same premises for more than one purpose, e.g. one hall to house, in succession, a playgroup, mother-and-toddler club, after-school centre for children of working mothers, and an opportunity class for handicapped children.

Private nursery schools

Many are like private playgroups, giving the children an experience of learning through play in the way that is followed by LA nursery schools. In others, often to meet parental pressures, or to acquire a reputation, a start is made on reading, writing and maths, sometimes inappropriately. The result of a premature introduction to, say, multiplication, confuses a child's mind so that his first teachers in school have to try to clear the confusion before the child can begin to learn.

Other schools

'Kindergarten' was a name introduced by Froebel for the school for young children that he founded in 1840. The term is still used for some nursery schools. The idea of learning through play is shared with local-authority nursery schools. Montessori and Steiner schools are often characterised by a greater control and direction than is found in most nurseries. There is less emphasis on and encouragement of freely creative work, more on the learning skills and self-mastery.

Crèches

This name is given to places that care for children of mothers who are working for instance in factories, offices, adult-education centres, colleges, hospitals. It's also used for places that care for children while mothers are temporarily away, e.g. shopping or using the facilities of a leisure centre.

The ages of children cared for are determined by the facilities and staff available. The younger the children, the more demanding are the regulations about provision and staffing.

They are a service that is created by persistent demand or is offered as an extra attraction. The organisation, financing and quality vary a great deal.

Child minders

Sometimes child-minders are able to get registration to look after a group of children for a few hours in addition to the children they mind for longer periods. This then could be called a 'house playgroup'.

Check your knowledge

As a final check on whether you are now familiar with the main features of different kinds of pre-school group, could you complete the following table? There will, of course be local variations, but on the basis of the facts given and more information that you may have found, complete the table with ticks to show where the answer would be 'Yes', crosses for 'No' and question marks for doubts.

	nursery school	nursery class	day nursery	children's centre	one o'clock club	house playgroup	private hall playgroup	community playgroup	crèche	mother-and-toddler club
Takes children under 3 usually	☐	☐	☐	☐	☐	☐	☐	☐	☐	☐
Takes children from 3–5	☐	☐	☐	☐	☐	☐	☐	☐	☐	☐
Takes children from 0–5	☐	☐	☐	☐	☐	☐	☐	☐	☐	☐
Mothers must stay	☐	☐	☐	☐	☐	☐	☐	☐	☐	☐
Run by local authority	☐	☐	☐	☐	☐	☐	☐	☐	☐	☐
Staff must have recognised qualifications	☐	☐	☐	☐	☐	☐	☐	☐	☐	☐
A free service	☐	☐	☐	☐	☐	☐	☐	☐	☐	☐
Teach reading	☐	☐	☐	☐	☐	☐	☐	☐	☐	☐
Children attend five sessions a week	☐	☐	☐	☐	☐	☐	☐	☐	☐	☐
Parents have responsibility, make decisions	☐	☐	☐	☐	☐	☐	☐	☐	☐	☐

Comment

You will see that there are many different ways in which the needs of children can be met. You will see also how difficult it is to get an overall picture or to find out what is available for a particular need that you may have.

In some places, people are drawing together to collect local information and to make it available to families in some widely-publicised centre. Through this opportunities to lobby for provision that is lacking can often be opened up.

Answers to check tables

Takes children under 3	X	X	√	√	√	X	X	X	√	√
Takes children from 3–5	√	√	√	√	√	√	√	√	√	√
Takes children from 0–5	X	X	√	√	√	X	X	X	√	√
Mothers must stay	X	X	X	X	√	X	X	X	X	√
Run by local authority	√	√	√	√	√	X	X	X	X	X
Qualifications required	√	√	√	√	X	X	X	X	X	X
Free service	√	√	X	√	√	X	X	X	?	X
Teach reading	X	X	X	X	X	?	?	?	X	X
5 sessions per week	√	√	√	√	X	?	?	X	X	X
Parents have responsibility	X	X	X	X	X	X	X	√	X	√

What's in a name

Different groups operate in different ways, offering different services for various age groups. One thing, however, can never be clear from a name, *is the group good of its kind*? There are many excellent nursery schools, there are some that are very poor. The same is true of playgroups and day nurseries, indeed of every kind of pre-school group. They depend very much on the quality of the people working there, and as people come and go, the nature of the group can change.

For this reason, it is important not to be misled by a name, nor to assume that a name guarantees quality. Very few areas will offer all kinds of pre-school group and very few parents really get the chance to choose. But it is still important for parents to get the opportunity to know what they want for their children. When they approach the kind of group that they think they would like at any stage of their children's development, it's helpful if they are able to assess whether the group is likely to satisfy the needs of themselves and their children.

Choosing a group

Not so long ago, most children had little chance to learn and play regularly with other children in organised groups until they went to school at five. Now, for many, things are different.

Many parents can make real choices for their pre-school children but most, when they make their choice, are not really sure what they should be looking for. In *Pre-school groups*, there was a sorting out of names and their meanings. With this background information, parents can begin to make their choice.

Do you want a group at all?

Parents are free to choose for themselves. Compulsory education begins at five and before that, parents can choose whether or not to take their children anywhere. Parents of four out of every five children aged three and four want some kind of pre-school group for their children, and they are encouraged in this by most teachers, health visitors and doctors. But even the most ardent supporters of pre-school education have no wish to see it made compulsory. Parents know their own children, they know what they want for them and for themselves. Should you listen to the opinions of your family, friends and professional people? Of course! But make up your *own* mind – the choice is yours!

Listen to two health visitors talking:

Mrs Cooper and Miss Davidson work in Deefield. Mrs Cooper is a strong supporter of pre-school education and does everything she can to encourage parents to use the local nursery school or playgroup. Miss Davidson on the other hand believes that five is young enough for children to attend any kind of group on a regular basis and she

sometimes feels mothers take their children to these groups just because it seems the thing to do.

Peter and Jane Duncan have just come to live in Deefield. They have three children aged nine, seven and three. None of the children has ever attended a pre-school group. Jane isn't particularly keen to take Peter, her three-year-old, to either the nursery school or the playgroup, but Mrs Cooper is trying hard to persuade her. Here Mrs Cooper and Miss Davidson are discussing the family.

Mrs Cooper I wish I could persuade Jane Duncan to take Peter to the playgroup or the nursery school.

Miss Davidson Why, if she doesn't want to? She can't think the other two missed anything.

Mrs Cooper But Peter is on his own now that the other children are at school and there are no other children of his age living near them.

Miss Davidson He has Jane. She's good with him and she takes time to play with him.

Mrs Cooper But that's the point. She feels he's her baby, and she wants to keep him that way.

Miss Davidson They're a very happy family and all the children get on well together. Why should Peter leave home before it's time for school?

Although it's difficult to judge from this sparse evidence, on balance do you think you would try to persuade Jane Duncan to take Peter to a pre-school group?

Why look for a group?

If Peter and his mother are happy together at home, the only question that needs to be asked is whether he will enjoy starting school at five without having been away from mum before. We have seen how all kinds of development are gradual processes, with stages that are passed through usually in a predictable pattern.

The weaning from home and mother to school is another such development. Going now and then to a group outside the home is the natural introduction to a community outside the home, especially if the group is one that welcomes the mother to stay for as long as the child needs her. If Peter grows to enjoy independence in a playgroup or nursery school he will probably take to school like a duck to water, and that will be a happy continuation of his education.

In *Playing together* we saw how important stages of the social development of children take place naturally between the ages of two and five if the opportunity is there. A child who plays alone until five often finds it difficult to join in with the play of his own age group, especially if the others have already been accustomed to playing together. He has to pass through those stages that the others have already passed before he can be one of the group.

In playing alone at home, he will have missed out on many pleasures that only happen when little children have a chance to play together – there will be chances ahead, but they are different from the kind of co-operative play that is enjoyed by pre-schoolers.

So if the chance is there for Peter to go what is lost? His mother may be left lonely: she may need him more than he needs her. This is the kind of situation in which the mother is helped if the group welcomes her, needing her for the help she can give. Groups can help mothers to wean themselves gradually from their children just as they can help children gain independence from their mothers.

What's best for everybody?

The choice should meet the needs not only of the child but also of the mother and the circumstances of the family. Few families have the freedom of choosing which primary school they should use, but in the pre-school years parents may have the privilege of choosing. When their first children are young, parents often do not know a great deal about early childhood education and the choice is often made, if it is there, upon feelings rather than knowledge.

If you've lived in a small community for some time, you probably know through your friends where the groups are and something about them. If you've lived in a town, it's unlikely that you are aware of the full range: there's probably a lot more going on than you might think.

Finding out

Generally it is unlikely that any one individual or department will know all the provision that is available. Few parents will be interested in every kind of group for their own purposes, but all these are parts of the pre-school world and each had its role to play. Sometimes one will affect others, sometimes services can be developed that are useful to all, but these cannot happen if all operate completely independently, without knowledge of or interest in the other.

You may start your search with some idea of what you want for your child, but be prepared to modify your ideals! Once you have decided what kind of group you want, check on those available in your area, where and when they meet. Choose those that particularly interest you and contact the group leader. Ask to see the group in action. If you simply go along to the group without first making contact, try to go at the end of a session so that you do not interrupt what is going on and be prepared to go back at a mutually convenient time.

What matters to you?

In some areas you may have a choice. The choice may, however, be limited for one reason or another. Some groups may be too far away, too expensive, or ask too little or too much of you! In some you may just feel that your child would not be happy, an instinct you should not ignore.

If there is a choice, you may want to consider the sort of questions listed below to help you make up your mind.

● How long will it take you to get there?

● Are their hours convenient for you?

● Are there fees?

● Does the group need your help?

● Will you have responsibility in the group?

● Do the neighbours' children go there?

● Will your child eventually go to school with children from the group?

● Is there a variety of equipment?

● Is there plenty of talking?

● Can children play quietly?

● Are children free to move from one activity to another?

● Is the first impression . . .

   friendly
   happy
   fresh
   noisy
   grubby?

● Are there a variety of activities, for example:

   sand
   water
   painting
   dressing-up
   jigsaws
   carpentry?

You may wish to decide in your own mind how important you feel some of these questions really are. You may feel it is more important for your child to learn to play with other children by attending a group that is local but not well equipped for example, rather than attend a play-group which is ideal but farther away, or not attend one at all because it does not come up to your expectations.

Choosing . . .

Children, parents and groups are all so different that it is not possible to give advice in the choosing of a group; this is a personal matter.

Sending your child to a group will make a great difference to your life. If you choose to work you will find yourself freer to do so. If you choose to take part in your child's group you will find that they have newsletters that need compiling, bazaars that need organising and posters that need designing.

However, you may choose to stay at home and leave your child to attend a group on his own and participate in this by hearing about all the fun he's had when he comes home.

The best choice for everyone

What is best for the family? This is the difficult one. A child may be ready for only one or two short play sessions a week, but the mother would like him to attend every morning because she has other commitments at home which could be easier if he were not there, or she might begin a part time job. Other mothers may react the other way, wanting their children to attend as seldom as possible because they themselves are dependent on their children for company. Sometimes, whether or not the parents themselves are aware of it, interests conflict. This is where advice can be useful: interests and needs have to fit each other. The group that suits you both best is the one which helps you to enjoy each others company even more at home!

> A child attending a pre-school group part-day, five days a week still spends 90 per cent of his waking life away from the group in his own home.
> A group that encourages the experience of the hours spent in the group to spill out into that 90 per cent will make the greatest difference to all the family.

What if there's no group?

There are still areas where mothers can't make any of these choices because no group exists. For those who want a group, the choice is either to sit back and do nothing, or to do what many others have done – pool resources with other mothers and set up a community playgroup.

First assess the interest. A postcard in a shop window is all that is needed. You can decide what to do next by the response it provokes. Just one or two supporters may mean that the community does not really need a large playgroup. It may be best to start in a house, with a few children. With a lively response, you can think bigger. From the beginning share responsibilities as widely as possible. The decision could go something like this: you need people, either fathers or mothers, to:

● Get information from the National Pre-School Playgroups Association and make contacts with other playgroups and the nearest PPA branch. Many pioneering mistakes can be avoided by listening to the advice of others who have been through these early stages.

● Get details of premises.

● Contact social service departments to find what help and advice is available locally.

● Start to plan money raising.

● Plan publicity.

There are many rewards, hard work and disappointments for those who start on this work but you will learn a lot and make friends as you work with others to provide a playgroup for your children.

Look for the results

It is always difficult to know whether pre-school groups are successful but, if you decide to take your child to a group, ask yourself these questions after a few months:

● Is my child more able to do things by himself?

● Can he communicate better?

● Is he more interested in stories and books, and in what is going on around him?

● Is he more confident than he was?

● Is he more willing to play with other children?

● Have I more confidence in dealing with him?

● Is life more fun for both of us, especially when we are together?

If you can answer yes to the majority of these questions, especially the last, you have found a really good group!

Joining a group

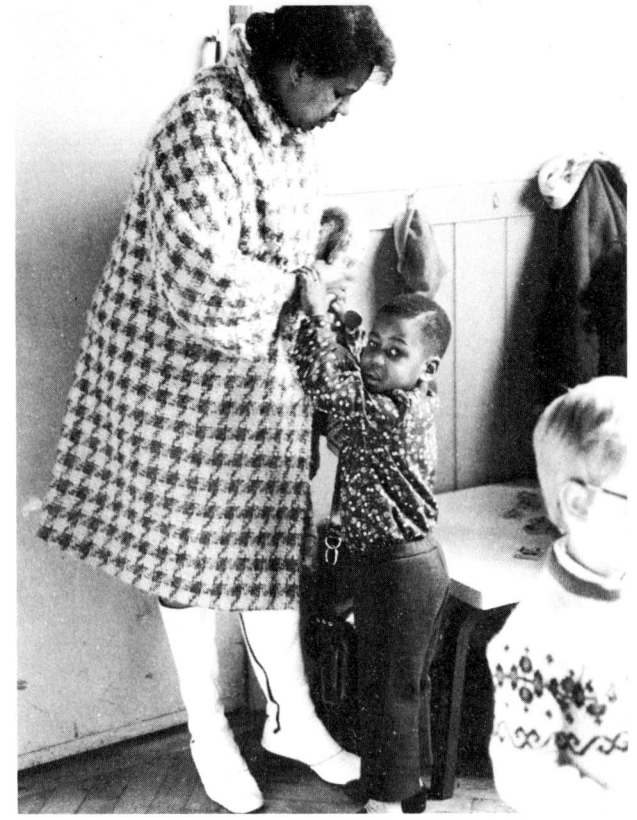

Children vary in the age at which they are ready to leave their mother. Your child may be happy to spend an hour with a neighbour or granny but going to nursery or playgroup is different.

Is your child ready to allow other adults to care for him, would he be happy in a strange large place, furnished differently with strange sounds and lots of children? Does he want to go? If his experiences away from you have been short, happy ones he will be fairly sure that you will return – and he must be sure of that before he can relax and enjoy himself. If he is ready to be left, is he ready to stay?

Are you ready?

How do you feel about someone else being in charge of your child? Do you trust them? Your child takes his emotional cues from you. The more matter-of-fact you can be, the more relaxed he will be. It is your responsibility to smooth the way.

Much depends on why a mother and father want their three-year-old to join a group and on what they expect from it. If you feel you 'can't cope', and 'they' are going to 'sort him out', he will sense it is not going to be much fun – whatever you say.

You can help

● You can try to provide short absences and happy reunions.

● You can make sure your child really believes that he is left on his own for just a short time and that you will return.

● You can encourage play where you pretend to 'act out' separations and returns. Playing peep-bo, when you hide your face behind a cushion and then pop out again, is a game that helps children to believe that people still exist even though they are out of sight. A three-year-old can play more complicated games with you and his toys. Perhaps you can let a teddy be

the child going to playgroup and a doll be the mummy. They will go to the playgroup, perhaps a space under a table, together. There the teddy will play with toys until the mummy doll comes to collect him back again.

● You can try to take him to the playgroup the term before. Ask if you can both call sometimes for up to half an hour. Ask if you can spend a few full mornings there with him before he really starts. Have a talk with the

leader, ask her about the group and tell her all that she needs to know about your child. It is important that she should know something about the child's skills and about your home. It will help if they know about a new baby, or Dad being out of work, or Granny coming to live or the older children being at school. This kind of information may help the staff to understand how the child feels about joining the group.

Is he ready to join a group?

Look down this list bearing your three-year-old in mind (or think of another child if yours is much younger or older). Make your judgements about whether Peter and Paula, are ready to join a group and then decide about your own known child.

Has the child:	Peter	Paula	Your child
stayed happily alone with a neighbour?	yes	no	☐
had a baby born in the family recently?	two months ago	two weeks ago	☐
visited a group?	twice	no	☐
talked about a group?	plenty	no	☐
been able to manage trousers/panties?	yes	yes	☐
been able to wipe own bottom	yes	yes	☐
been able to ask for the toilet?	yes	no	☐
been able to recognise coat and shoes?	yes	yes	☐
wanted to play with more things than there are at home?	yes	yes	☐
Do you think they are ready?			
Yes	☐	☐	☐
No	☐	☐	☐
Worth a try	☐	☐	☐

Peter is capable and ready to explore a wider world with confidence. Paula is not so secure. She would probably survive starting but, as she is not yet self reliant, it would be better for her to wait a bit. In a few months time she will probably be more confident and sure of herself, and ready to enjoy her indepedence.

Is the time right?

How secure is he feeling? Have there been any recent changes? Moving to a new house may have made so many changes in his life that it would be wise to wait until he feels his home is secure before he moves off into a new world without you. If you need more time for a new baby, don't let him hear you saying so, he may feel that he is being driven away. Better to wait a little until he finds the company of others at the playgroup can be more fun than just being at home.

Talk about it now and then

A three-year-old can't anticipate, plan or reassure himself that mother will return. He can't tell the time, and 'soon', 'presently' or 'in an hour' all mean one thing . . . not *now*! He doesn't know what questions to ask that will tell him about what he will be doing and who he will meet. His parents have to think what he needs to know and help him to ask the right questions. In the course of talking, make sure that he knows the answers to questions like . . .
- 'Can you stay, Mummy?'
- 'How long will you be gone?'
- 'Do they know that I sometimes need help to wipe my bottom?'
- 'Can I go into the little house without asking anyone?'

The first day

Joining a group is a big change but if you have been preparing for it the first day is just another step. Allow plenty of time – for breakfast, toilet and putting on outdoor clothes. Enjoy the walk or ride and talk about what your child chooses. When you can, steer the conversation towards cheerful topics like – 'Remember the sandpit? – rather than frightening ones like – 'There will be big noisy boys.' Avoid nonsense threats like – 'If you're not good, the leader won't let you stay!' If there is anxiety, talk about it, reassure him without making a big thing of it, but don't suggest that it is silly. Talk about the time after the playgroup – tell him what is for dinner or what you will be doing in the afternoon. You may be feeling anxious and unsure of yourself but don't let your feelings show.

The teacher or leader will have her own welcoming routine. This may include expecting you to stay for all or part of the first few sessions. As well as helping your child to settle, spending time in the group will give you a better idea of what happens during the session, of the aims and methods used. Your child will be less likely to feel that his home and the group are two separate worlds.

Handing over

Another part of your help is to gradually pass responsibility for your child to the teacher or leader. Try to be just an observer, if necessary an interpreter, allowing your child's interest to centre on the leader and the activities she is guiding. If she suggests that you take a seat and watch or get on with your knitting, rather than follow your child around, she is helping you to retire for a while from your child's world so that others can enter. If you stay in one place, he can find you immediately if and when he needs you.

The exception

Some children settle quickly; others don't. Some settle better when father brings them, or other mothers, or a member of staff. Some are happy if they stay only half a morning at first. The teacher/leader will have settled other children and will have ideas if your child is not happy. There is no hurry.

Some children take a long time to settle; even half a term or more. If your child does not settle at all, the problems are really:
- how much does it matter?
- would he be better off at home till he does settle?
- can I, or do I want to stay every time until he does settle?

Each child is an individual. His inability to settle may be his only way of showing that he needs more time with his mother. Some children who find the group too large can be helped by the introduction of some regular arrangement like an exchange with a friend's child, going to a childminder or to a playgroup in a house.

The answers depend on you, the child, the group – and there is no one right answer. We aren't all 'joiners' and perhaps you can give most of what the group would give to your child, at home. If your child indicates that he is not ready, and you are able to delay his move into the bigger world, remember he is your child and the decision belongs to you and your husband or wife as the parents, not the group, and certainly not the neighbours.

You remember how weaning to solid foods was a gradual business? Here is another weaning which usually comes gradually and naturally when a child's growing ability to be independent shows that he is ready to leave you.

If the group will allow you to persevere, the big gain is that in the event of an emergency, your child has learnt to accept care from other people. He has also learnt that he can be happy away from you. He has begun to learn how to get on with others in a group and when he goes to school he will settle with confidence.

Is he ready to stay in a group?

Make your judgements about whether Rachel and Simon are ready to stay in a group and then decide about your own child. Should Simon be hurried into accepting his independence before he is ready? Will Rachel be glad to be left on her own, to grow up a little in company?

Has the child:	Rachel	Simon	Your child
been with mother to the toilet?	yes	yes	☐
learnt the teacher/playleader's name?	yes	no	☐
realised the teacher/playleader knows his/her name?	yes	yes	☐
felt free to play with clay and water?	yes	no	☐
started painting?	no	yes	☐
enjoyed the sand?	yes	yes	☐
smiled from the other side of the room?	yes	no	☐
understood that mother has shopping to do?	yes	yes	☐
felt happy to be left?	yes	no	☐
Do you think they are ready?			
Yes	☐	☐	☐
No	☐	☐	☐
Worth a try	☐	☐	☐

'You can go now!' If this is suggested, be sure to say – 'Good-bye' – to your child, explain that you won't be long . . . and *go*! If your child is not happy when you come back, he has at least learnt that you do come back. Trust and confidence will grow as the experiment is repeated. If all goes well, the absence can be lengthened next time and soon he will be running in each morning with the minimum of good-byes.

Coming together again

So he's joined the group. What does he feel about it? How can you know? Can you share his new experience? You can if you let him in his own way and in his own time.

Even if later on you and your neighbours share the collecting, try to collect him yourself to begin with. It is important to be on time, to be found by your child's searching eyes among the first group of mothers. Greeting him warmly will show that you missed him. Accept what he wants to tell you. Think of ways of showing him you're glad to be together again, like a cuddle on the bus, or a special bit of home information . . . 'What do you think the cat or dog did this morning?' Remember that he may be tired and hungry and his greatest need may be just to be quiet.

Go easy on the questions. It is better to let his impressions pour or trickle out at his pace rather than asking him a lot of questions that need thinking about. The really important things may come out much later in the day.

'Did you have a good morning?'
'Did anything special happen?'
'Who was there this morning?'

. . . could open up the conversation if they are asked in a casual way. He may just need a companionable silence. His most important feeling may be one of anger at having been left and until he has had a chance to be reassured he may find it difficult to talk about other things. It is important that you reflect his interest shown by the way he talks: if he is enthusiastic about something, it must be important to him even though it may seem trivial to you. Remember that a conventional greeting question can become as meaningless as 'How do you do?'

Sometimes he may bring home something that he has made or a picture that he's painted. If it is similar to everyone else's you will know that most of the thinking and perhaps of the making too will have been done by adults. If the playgroup or nursery encourages children to think for themselves, he may bring home something that may seem strange or messy to you. Whatever it is, it should be treated with respect and interest.

Or he may bring nothing. It may be that his morning has been spent 'just playing' and that he has learnt.

● how to hop,
● how to fill a bottle through a funnel of the right size,

● the kind of sounds that come from the collection of sound-makers that the playgroup has collected.

This kind of learning calls for respect but it would not have an end-product that he could hand over.

Sometimes playgroups or nursery schools feel under pressure from parents to provide some evidence that the children have been 'working' and not 'just playing'. If they respond to this pressure they will often find that they have to direct a child's activity so that he will live up to their expectations. Almost inevitably, the amount of adult help will increase, perhaps without the parents being aware of it. Then, when the child goes to school and shows his parents work that is all his own, they will think that it is not as 'good' as the work he did at the nursery.

Home again

Most newly joined children are tired after a morning in the group. Children show tiredness in different ways. You know your own child—watch for his tiredness signals.

Is he hungry, more demanding, more boisterous? Does he withdraw with a repetitive soothing game? Sit in a chair with a comforter or cuddly? Dig a hole in the garden? Or what?

Your morning may have been quieter than usual, but *his* has been full of new impressions – now he'll need to relax and absorb them, assure himself that his home world is still intact.

You can expect that you will need:
● to give extra attention for a time upon return;
● to provide a meal fairly promptly;
● to allow for a quiet recovery time after the meal.

For your child food has always been a practical expression of mother's care and provision. Following the morning's physical and emotional expenditure of energy, especially in the first few mornings, he will literally need 're-fuelling'. Eating with mother in the familiar surroundings of home reinforces the warmth of reunion, helps him relax in the security of affection and physical wellbeing. If he doesn't have a large appetite, it may be that he is just too tired. Perhaps a light snack, followed by an early and satisfying 'tea' would be better on playgroup days.

A winding-down time

After a morning away from them, he may need time to *check on familiar things*—his toys, his bed, the garden . . . Like the child who has been ill, he may need a chance to regress a little, to be a 'baby' and play in a younger way than recently with undemanding items from his playbox.

● You know your child: will it be a favourite picture book, small cars, wooden blocks, the dolls, pots and pans?

● He may unwind as he plays and want you to listen – can you work quietly within sight and sound, giving him the opportunity? In any case, your bodily presence will be comforting.

● If your daily pattern has in the past allowed for 'a special time' for expressed affection and playing together earlier on, why not set a new pattern of an *after dinner* cuddle with a book or a story? Does he choose the book, or do you provide a surprise?

The baby - is it a rival?

It is at this sort of time that a child is most resentful of the rival demands of a baby. He feels the need of your attention after his absence and, if you are aware of this, you can sometimes plan things so that he can claim first attention for a while. It is often in these quiet moments of relaxation

that the important talking happens. The incident that he had forgotten about in the whirl of getting home comes bobbing back into his memory. He may need to tell you one thing or ask you to explain another.

It takes time for the ideas to take the shape of words. Those moments of leisure at critical periods in the child's day are often the time when the most important things are said – and if you are too busy, you miss them.

Settling back

If there are special tasks around the home that he enjoys doing with you, *can these be saved for the afternoon*?

● preparing the evening meal together (shell peas, dice carrots, roll pastry, make jelly . . . ?)

● grooming the dog or cat;

● cleaning the budgie or goldfish bowl;

● watering the pot plants;

● defrosting the fridge;

● winding the bobbin of the sewing machine;

● making a shopping list;

● putting the box of groceries away;

● folding the washing;

● polishing the door knob.

The familiarity of these tasks and the easy affectionate companionship, may trigger off some confidence about 'the group'. The chief thing is that you're together and available—a useful pattern for later homecomings.

New kinds of play

By now he may be talking more readily about the group, and what he does and doesn't like doing, and the other children. Some children spend most of their time at the group doing what they never do at home. They may be glad to play with other children, boys may welcome the chance to play with dolls. Messy finger painting and big building blocks may be special nursery things, reserving puzzles for home. Others use the quiet equipment more often at the group and move about more at home. Much depends on the size, resources and situation at home.

Friends

At first he may not be interested in having other children to play on group days. But later on, most children enjoy the different play possible with one, two or three others in the home of one of them – especially on days when the group does not meet. Making friends, visiting other people's homes and receiving visitors are important parts of adult life. It all begins here with children coming in to play or have a meal. The children may like to repeat some of the group activities, especially imaginative play generated by 'Home corner' or bricks and cars.

Linking the two worlds of home and group

It is a help to your child if there can be some continuity between the separate parts of his world.

Think of ways in which you can make continuity in your child's world, building bridges between home and group by introducing new ideas from his playgroup. What equivalent can you provide for the following?

Have you been able to offer these at home in the last two weeks? Tick if you have!

Group activity

Home corner	☐
Dressing up	☐
Junk table	☐
Construction toys	☐
Paint	☐
Crayons	☐
Collage	☐
Climbing opportunity	☐
Book corner	☐

Do you know the songs and rhymes and finger plays they use in the group? Why not try them out at home, say at bath time? Be ready to enjoy the rhymes he brings home. Sometimes only a part will be remembered: what a surprise it would be if you complete the rhyme, showing that you knew something about the other part of his world. Perhaps the rhyme was part of your childhood too and you can recall that.

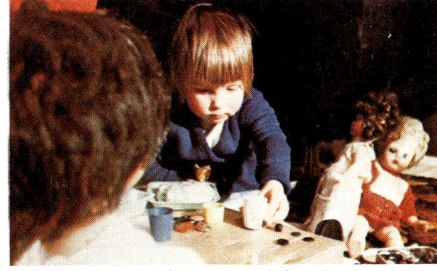

Can you sometimes spend time in the group when he is there? This makes the best link of all. Many schools and most playgroups welcome mothers and helpers. Sharing your child's group experience in this way ensures that you know what takes place there and what is valued – you know the daily pattern, the other children and some of the incidents he has enjoyed, or perhaps disliked? He sees you and the teacher/leader united in your caring. You will see other children alongside your own, and other people working and playing with them and with your child. This can be very helpful – you see your child as a separate person. When they see their child playing among others, many mothers are relieved to discover that he is not unusually shy or boisterous, bossy or quiet. They may find however, that on the days that they are helping, that their child is clinging, calling for attention and resentful of having to share them with all the others. In a group where helping is a tradition, this kind of behaviour is recognised as normal. It will probably pass after one or two helping sessions.

Taking part in the group will help you and the other adults in your shared task of making the most of the years before school. For the children, the group will be a happy extension of home.

Other people's children

Local-authority day nurseries meet no more than a small part of the need for day care. Child-minding can be satisfying for mother, child and minder.

Little children gain a sense of security from being looked after by a small number of familiar people. It is very difficult to ensure this in a day nursery that looks after many children. With lunch breaks, holidays, illnesses, day releases for staff in training, and changes of staff, it is difficult to achieve this.

Could there be other solutions to the problem of day care for the children of parents who must provide for their children while they go out to work? Meet two child-minders:

Mrs P lives in a Victorian terrace in an inner-city area. She left school early, but is bright and receptive to new ideas. She is a warm, welcoming, mature person who loves children but is not possessive. She reads widely, and has developed a keen interest in child development.

Mrs P started minding to help a friend. Her own children have grown up and left home. She organises her housework so that she has plenty of time to spare with the children. She looks after three. She provides a variety of stimulating play, singing with them, telling stories, reading to them. Each day she makes a point of taking them out. She behaves as a 'good mother'. She would probably enjoy a course that would broaden her awareness of children's play needs but she has one overwhelming asset as a childminder—a good relationship with the parents. She is straightforward and honest, sensitive to a young mother's uncertainties about leaving her children with another woman. She always tries to co-operate with the mother. She goes out of her way to talk over things she may have noticed during the day, perhaps a new achievement or the first signs of behaviour that might develop into something worrying, perhaps a slight squint or a food fad.

Mrs E lives in a modern house on a new but cheerless estate. Technically she is a 'child-minder', though she thinks of herself as supervising a 'home playgroup'. Her husband, a shift worker, shares her interest in young children. Each day, they transform their ordinary living room into an exciting place for under-fives. They have also built on a sun room for painting and 'messy play' and woodwork. The garden has been safely enclosed and has a sand pit, climbing frame and paddling pool. The children are encouraged to keep pets and are taken to local parks. In the summer they go on outings.

Mrs E has benefited from two playgroup courses and is now a tutor. She began minding because she had trained as a nursery nurse, and she wanted company for her own son when he was little. The experience in those early years had made her feel that what she and her husband have to offer is of real value to working mothers and their children. In co-operation with the social services, she sees herself doing a highly professional job.

Becoming a minder

Perhaps, like Mrs E, you have found that you really enjoy little children and regret the fact that your youngest is alone, when his brothers and sister go back to school after the holiday. Perhaps you want to be at home with your children and want or need to be earning money, or perhaps you feel, like Mrs P, that you have been left high and dry after your children have started school. Why not think of child-minding? It would give you a chance to meet families and the satisfaction of doing important work as well as earning a little money.

First you will have to register with the social services department (social work department in Scotland) of your local council. The department sends someone who will visit you to look over the house from the point of view of fire risk and toilet provision. On the basis of this and the space that you can offer, the number of children that you can take is decided. The regulations have been introduced to protect children, to give parents confidence and also to give recognition to those child-minders who are doing a good job.

Experience of playgroup work and courses about child care will be helpful in looking after other people's children. If you haven't experience of either enquire about local evening classes. You may also find, or perhaps form, a local group of childminders. (See page 224.)

Some local authorities value the work done by child-minders so much that they lend equipment, open centres where minders can drop in for a chat, arrange courses or talks to help them in their work. Sometimes they will advise on standard rates of pay and recommend minders to parents who are looking for a place for their children.

Children with two homes

Whether a child-minding arrangement is a success depends mostly upon two things:

● are minder and parents interested in each other, do they like and understand each other? This is the beginning of that vital co-operation between parents and other adults that will be so important in later education.

● is the minder's home an extension of the child's own home, with the same, or better, standards of caring? Very different sets of rules and values will confuse, but small differences will be an enrichment of living, making the child more able to adapt to new people and places.

Ideally, there should be a gentle and gradual introduction to the idea of visiting another home and staying without you – see 'Joining the Group' in this chapter. Allow plenty of time for questions to form in the child's mind and come out in conversation or play. It is important for your child to understand what you will be doing when you are away from him, for him to be quite sure that you are going to be coming back and will be looking forward to doing something nice when you are together again.

Information exchange

When the young child's world is split up, it is important that information is shared between the people who look after him. Look back at the way in which Mrs P went out of her way to talk with the mother about the things she may have noticed during the day. With this sort of information, the mother can talk to the child about the happenings of the day with interest, building bridges between the two parts of the child's world.

Some information must pass between parent and minder to make sure that both have the same basis of agreement. This would include:

● terms of care, for example fees, hours, overtime fees, payment during holidays, illnesses;

● information about parents, for example home address, place of work, work telephone number, name and address of child's doctor, expected time of return;

● information about the child.

It would never be possible to give all the important information about a child in one go. But day by day, bits of news can be passed on. The more chat that passes, the more there will be for both parent and minder to talk to the child about. You could include things like:

● news about the people in the family at home;

● special likes and dislikes, so that they can be talked about even if they must be ignored!

Risks of having two homes

Falling between two stools In a caring concern for the child, it will be important to make sure that the child does not lose out because both parent and minder think the other is doing or giving something. This would be so in any part of the shared responsibility but perhaps especially in such matters as:

● nutrition—that between the homes the child is receiving a balanced diet

● fresh air and exercises—particularly in winter when the child may not be in his own home in daylight, this responsibility must rest with the minder

● play of all sorts—stories, rhymes, books, songs, meetings with other children. Do both minder and parent feed the child with these?

Double standards Will differences between the two homes make a confusion in a mind that is beginning to sort out the experience of living? If something is acceptable and encouraged in one home but is frowned upon in the other there is bound to be confusion unless the matter is talked about. Children are ready to accept sensible explanations. Perhaps the minder will always insist that toys are put away immediately after they have been finished with. This may be very necessary if there is to be room for two or three children to play freely, though at home you may not insist until it is time for the big tidy up.

At present, the overall picture of child-minding is not good, with few minders choosing the work because of an interest in children. Many minders look after more than the recommended three children and offer them no chance to play in yard, garden or playground. Many have poor toys and no books. Many do not play with their children, or read to them. Most do not allow 'messy play' with sand, water or paint. However our real life examples show what is being achieved by some.

Benefits

The more minder and parent respect each other as people, the more thoughtfulness and consideration they show for each other, the more secure the child will feel in his world with two homes.

With understanding and acceptance, the widening of the child's experience of places and people can prove to be an enrichment of living for all—minder, parents and child.

Other people's children
An attractive 84-page booklet, published by the BBC has been distributed free to many registered child-minders through local authority social service departments (social-work services in Scotland). It has many tips, packed in with help and advice—just one advantage of registering as a child-minder!

Children with a difference

This course is about individual children, your child, and the children he plays and learns with. Perhaps the most challenging thing about children is that they are all different. If your child is very different in some way you may begin to wonder whether he could be handicapped. The earlier you get help the easier it is to make sure that whatever his difficulty he will be able to go on developing in the best way for him.

A child's potential

Every baby born has the built-in potential for developing in an enormous number of different ways. He also has built-in limitations. Some of these inborn talents and limitations are specific to the individual child. A child born blind, for example, may become a great musician (many have) or a craftsman but he is very unlikely to succeed as a portrait painter.

But *all* children, including the blind child, are far more like other children than they are different. No human child will ever fly like a bird or creep through the ground like an earthworm. They all grow and they all learn; and the child's potential abilities that develop most fully depend upon the particular opportunities his early life presents.

A good parent is always a kind of talent-spotter watching for the things the child seems to do well and offering encouragement, but leaving it to the child to decide when he wants to try something new. Parents should not be time-and-motion experts with one eye on the stop-watch and the other on the progress chart of the child next door.

Development and learning

Children develop at different rates, some are generally slow to learn, a lucky few quickly 'pick up everything'. Some shoot ahead in one area but perhaps because of an inborn handicap make little progress in others. Comparing an individual child's pattern of progress with average progress is one way of spotting areas where he might benefit from special medical or educational help.

Progress check

Opposite is a table drawn up from observations of a very large number of children. Before you start checking your own child's progress you should bear two things in mind:
1 Probably only a very small number of children of a particular age fit exactly all the squares in their age column. Very advanced children will be ahead in some or all the areas while slower children will be behind. But this does not mean that there is necessarily something 'wrong' with children who vary from the average.
2 *All* the activities described depend both upon natural growth of inborn potential *and* upon opportunities to learn. Don't expect any two-year-old to feed himself with a spoon if he hasn't ever been given one, helped to use it and allowed to practise. Similarly, young children will often use both hands and both legs equally; don't impose a 'handedness', give them opportunities to develop in their own way.

What to do:

In the table opposite each column represents the age by which half the children in the sample had acquired the skills listed. The child is expected to acquire these skills sometime during the previous year. If he is less than six months through a year, take his last birthday. If he is six months or more then take his next birthday. For example, if he is three years five months count his age as three years; if he is three years seven months count his age as four years.

Select the appropriate column and tick those skills that apply to your child. If your child can't do some of the things in the column for his age, go back a year. Can he do everything? If he can't, go back another year.

If your child is different

If your child differs clearly from the average, either in a particular area, or overall, he may have a specific handicap which could be relieved or compensated for with professional help. One year behind on more than half the items *provided he has had every chance to learn*, or two years behind on two or more items, would be a guide that professional advice should be sought, even though in most cases there is probably nothing wrong at all. Some children grow smoothly, others have fast and slow rhythms of growth. Never keep a worry to yourself — pass it on quickly to your health visitor or doctor and worry them until you are really satisfied that either, everything is all right, or, the best treatment is being given. They are paid to worry. You aren't.

There is a variety of handicapping conditions from which a child may suffer. This course is not for medical students and medical labels have very little value in everyday life. (See page 224).

In general, many physically handicapped children and those with sensory defects become dull *because* of their inability to walk or to hear. These handicaps deprive them of essential experience unless special steps are taken early in the pre-school period to compensate. Many of the ideas in this book can be applied to enrich the experience of handicapped children. Brain damage is different of course and more difficult to cope with.

A detailed programme of psychological care is more important for most handicaps than a programme of physical care.

Activity	At the end of: 1 year	2 years	3 years	4 years	5 years
Getting around	Crawls	Walks	Using alternate feet going upstairs	Use pedals properly on tricycle	Goes up and down stairs using alternate feet
Feeding	Drinks from cup with help	Feeds himself with spoon	Drinks from ordinary cup, no spilling	Uses knife to spread jam	Uses knife and fork well
Toileting	Shows some regularity – will sometimes use potty when put on it	Lets you know when wants potty – bladder control by day	Toilet trained, few accidents	Toilet trained completely, can go to toilet alone	Toilet trained completely
Cleanliness	Helps by holding out hands for washing	Washes hands without much help	Washes and dries hands	Brushes teeth	Washes by himself
Dressing	Helps by holding arm out, etc.	Helps by trying to put on things	Takes off and puts on simple things	Needs help with difficult fastenings	Dresses and undresses with very little help
Independence	Will go and explore if parents are in sight	Will amuse himself while you are busy	Will play in protected area outside alone but needs constant watching	Can be trusted to play outside alone or with other children	Looks forward to starting school
Drawing	Will use pencil to scribble	Can copy a line	Can draw a circle and sometimes a cross or kiss	Draws a man, sometimes with detail	Can draw simple pictures, houses, cars, people, etc.
Playing with others	Cooperates playing pat-a-cake	Begins to let other children play with toys	Joins in play with other children	Plays cooperatively with other children and will take turns	Will invent and keep to the rules in games
Pretend play	Pushes small car along	Some pretend play, for example putting teddy to bed	Pretends lot of time with toys	Complicated pretend games with other children	Plays complicated role playing games
Grammar and vocabulary	Babbles 1 clear word	50 clear words 2 together	Uses plurals	Talks sentences; leaves words out	Correct grammar most of time; fluent
Using language	Makes noises for things he wants	Asks for things he wants by name	Simple conversation of what's happened	Always asking why, what, how, etc.	Asks 'What if . . .?' and 'When . . .?' questions

Parents' reactions to handicap

Parents who learn that their child may be mentally or physically handicapped for life react in a number of ways. Some of them are quite unhelpful to both child and parent, but helpful or not they need to be understood.

Let's look at some of the reactions that have been experienced and consider why they happen (if, in fact, they do). A typical sequence is given below in four stages: shock followed by grieving; feeling different and alone; spending all their time and energy caring for the handicapped child and coming to a balanced solution.

Stage 1

Shock followed by grieving

Emotional reactions might be described as *natural*, shock is a natural response to the unexpected. Recovery occurs when more is learnt about what can reasonably be expected in the new situation. Grieving is more complex. It often accompanies a sense of loss. But the child who has just been labelled 'handicapped' is still there, the same little boy that he was before. All that has happened is that his parents should now be able to understand better some things that were worrying them about him.

Why does grieving happen? Perhaps it is something to do with the false values of a competitive society which lays great stress on 'being a success'. If and when parents come to realise that even the most handicapped child can be a success *in his own terms* they will stop grieving. One of the most rewarding experiences for any parent is the pride and joy that comes from watching their child progress and master new skills, with their patient help. This may be even more true for a handicapped child, whose achievement in some areas may be slow and difficult, than for the child to whom most things come with little effort.

Stage 2

Feeling different and alone

It would really be necessary to look at the real situation to decide whether or not these feelings are based on fact. Some (a few) parents who accept the social values of always being a success may feel ashamed of their child, and that is a 'difference' – but one they share with some parents of non-handicapped children. It is difficult, too, for some parents to believe that they are not different when other people behave towards them as if they are different. For example, some people pick parents with a handicapped child out for pity, or uninvited advice, and others will chat to them about other 'cases' they have known and ignore the real child who would like to be smiled at just like other children. And then there are 'friends' who seem embarrassed and start to avoid the family. Real help often begins with positive action by other parents. All crises teach us to know our true friends. They are the ones who accept us for what we are and offer the help we really need. This is so often practical, because handicapped children often mean extra work and more demands on the pocket.

In reading the following case history pick out the part that others played in (a) helping Maureen, Paul's mother, feel different and (b) helping her to overcome the feeling.

Paul

When Paul was eight-months-old it was discovered that he couldn't see very well. We come in on his case study when the health visitor introduced him and his mother to another mother with a handicapped child who helped run a group. His case study is written by the other mother.

'Poor Maureen, his mother, was very upset, she thought she had a nice normal little boy. It was her first baby and she didn't know what babies should be doing at certain times. Paul used to smile at her and turn his head when she talked to him, she thought he was all right, he didn't play with toys, just kept touching his fingers and he wasn't happy about sitting up.

The Health Visitor became worried about him and he went up to the hospital. Tests showed that Maureen probably had German Measles when she was carrying him. They say he can see dark and light, but not shapes very well.

At first Maureen didn't want to come to our group, the Health Visitor brought her, but later she told us it saved her sanity. She didn't mind telling us her worries and problems, she knew we'd understand because we had them too. Soon she was as eager as the rest of us to help these handicapped children and we all set about forming a proper Opportunity Group.'

Stage 3

Spending all their time and energy caring for the handicapped child

Handicapped children can be very demanding, and it is very difficult to say that a particular parent who behaves like this is 'over-reacting'. But there are real dangers in such a situation, and a mother can reach the point where a family feels neglected and resentful and her burden is increased still further. It is better to take stock early, decide how much she can manage alone and ask frankly for help both inside and outside the family.

The following case study shows what can happen when priorities are not sorted out:

David

We take up David's case study when he and his mother join a Mother and Toddler Club. It is written by the leader of the club.

'David's muscles of his right leg and arm are tight, he can just walk but he drags his foot and he holds his arm bent and his hand in a fist and doesn't use it. David's mother, Ann, told us that he had a difficult birth and the doctors were not sure if he was going to be all right or not, they couldn't tell at first. It was awful, she said, not knowing if he was a normal child or not, she didn't know quite how to treat him, he'd been in an incubator and she hadn't really seen him for several weeks. He'd been a stranger, she said, and then when she did get him home he had done nothing but cry. He was difficult to feed, too. David was older than the others but he soon settled in.

Poor Ann got very upset when they suggested David went to a special school, she's so wrapped up in David, she's rather drifted away from her husband, he's away so much on business. As Ann says, "I'd feel quite lost if David was taken away – what else can I live for, my life has become centred around David and I do everything for him".'

Stage 4

Coming to a balanced solution.

Here the child is warmly accepted, his needs understood and met, and the family takes its natural place with others in the community. No need to comment here. This is obviously the ideal solution. It is, however, usually reached only after initiatives from both inside and outside the family. The following account shows how this stage can be reached quite quickly by loving and sensible parents, supported by really wise professional advisers, and normal (not nosey or pushing) good neighbours.

Jenny

Jenny suffered from spina bifida from birth. We come in on Jenny's case when she was a month old and ready to leave the hospital. It is written by her mother.

'We both went to fetch her home, she looked lovely, just like any other baby, perhaps it was because I'd always wanted a girl or perhaps it was because she looked like Fred or perhaps I just had time to get to know her on my daily visits to hospital, but I took to her and loved her from the start. She was an easy baby, but she soon let us know when she wanted feeding.

At first I was frightened of the scar in her back and whether I should touch her head where the tube was, but the hospital were so helpful. I soon stopped worrying about it. At first I felt shy about going out with her, but Fred and I had to take her back several times to the hospital for check-ups. They explained that a check must be kept on her waterworks as one of the nerves going to the bladder might be damaged and it might not work. Also they said if she became drowsy or very irritable, it might mean that her head tube was blocked and we were to come straight to hospital. They introduced us to some other parents of another little girl with spina bifida who lives quite near us and we became friends. Soon we had a regular coffee morning in each other's houses, our next door neighbour had a baby the same age as Jenny and she was feeling so depressed we asked her along too (her baby's not handicapped) and before we knew what happened, we'd started up a Mothers and Toddlers Club. Another lady up the road used to be a physiotherapist and she came with her baby and could tell us what to do with Jenny's legs, one seems quite strong. Not all the muscles work and she can't feel anything so she can get splinters and blisters and not know it.'

The real needs of parents

Some authorities argue that parents with handicapped children receive too little help with their emotional relationships within the family. They therefore recommend the personal counselling that the family's doctor, social worker, health visitor or child specialist can provide. Many parents, however, argue that in general personal relationships would sort themselves out if parents were given the practical means to support their child. These include: information, practical advice, financial help, housing assistance, child-minding help, short term relief from providing full-time care, laundry assistance and assistance with transport. A recent government report said:

'Most parents are devoted to their handicapped children and wish to care for them and help them develop to their full potential. About 80 per cent of severely handicapped children and a higher proportion of the more mildly handicapped live at home. Their families need advice and many forms of help, most of which at present are rarely available.'

Too little care and support is being provided for the handicapped child and family in their own home, neighbourhood and community; even though 'community care' has been government policy since 1961. This lack of practical support may be the root of the emotional and isolating experiences of families. For example, taking a child on outings is more dependent on whether parents have a car or not than on how severe his handicap is. Similarly, inadequacy of housing or even laundry arrangements may on occasions make the tasks faced by the parents overwhelming. Simple help with transport, babysitting, washing may help any parent cope with the problems of caring for their child.

Welfare of children and parents

Child Poverty Action Group, 1 Macklin Street, London WC2B 5NH

The Child Poverty Action Group aims to promote action for the relief of poverty among children and families with children. It researches into and publishes facts about family poverty in Britain, investigates methods of preventing poverty, and provides information on existing benefits, including appeal machinery, to social workers and others. It publishes a periodical called *Poverty*.

Family Welfare Association, 501 Kingsland Road, London E8 4AW

This association promotes family welfare by establishing centres for advice and guidance. To find out if there is a centre near you, contact the above address.

Gingerbread, 35 Wellington Street, London WC2

A self-help group for single parents with many branches throughout the country.

National Association for the Welfare of Children in Hospital (NAWCH), 7 Exton Street, London SE1 8VE

It aims to improve understanding of the special needs of children in hospitals and promote their welfare; to ensure that new hospitals have adequate accommodation for mothers to live in with young children; and to encourage the home care of sick children whenever possible. It assists parents by providing details of visiting facilities throughout the country, and works towards the improvement of these facilities. There are branches throughout the country. Its London office provides an information service. NAWCH produces various publications including comics and painting books that help a child understand what hospital is all about.

National Childminding Association, The Hon. Secretary, Camric, Brasted, Westerham, Kent TN16 1HS

This association provides support for childminding groups throughout the country. It has an information and advisory service for childminders who want to set up local groups.

National Council for One Parent Families, 255 Kentish Town Road, London NW5 2LX

The Council is concerned with one-parent families and watches over legislation and administration on their behalf, offering a service to parents and the social workers who advise and help them. It is working for a more informed public opinion sympathetic to the needs of one-parent families. (In Scotland approach Scottish Council for Single Parents, 44 Albany Street, Edinburgh EH1 3QR.)

National Society for the Prevention of Cruelty to Children (NSPCC), 1–3 Riding House, London W1P 8AA

The NSPCC is concerned with the prevention of private and public wrongs to children. It provides advice and help to parents, mostly by visiting families in their homes. The Society works to keep the family together wherever possible.

Royal Society for the Prevention of Accidents (RoSPA), 1 Grosvenor Street, London SW1

RoSPA aims to prevent accidents, including accidents in the home, on the roads and in leisure pursuits, by educational means. It runs training courses, conferences and national publicity campaigns, and produces posters and leaflets as well as maintaining a film library.

Save the Children Fund, 157 Clapham Road, London SW9 0PT

Its aims are to promote child welfare and to raise the standards of child care all over the world. It runs playgroups for children in need in inner-city areas and hospitals.

Handicapped children and parents

Centre on Environment for the Handicapped, 126 Albert Street, London NW1 7HF

The centre has a register of facilities, e.g. playgrounds adapted for the handicapped. Information about the register and other related matters can be obtained by contacting the centre.

Handicapped Adventure Playgrounds, 3 Oakley Gardens, London SW3

This organisation provides and administers adventure playgrounds, which have been specially designed and equipped, for handicapped children and young people.

National Deaf Children's Society, 31 Gloucester Place, London W1H 4EA

It aims to promote the welfare of deaf children and to increase public understanding. There are regional associations throughout the country.

National Society for Mentally Handicapped Children (MENCAP), Pembridge Hall, 17 Pembridge Square, London WC2 4EP

MENCAP is concerned exclusively with the mentally handicapped and their families. It aims to increase public knowledge and understanding of the problems they face, and by so doing to secure better provision. The Society provides a wide range of services for parents and professionals, as well as publishing books, reports, pamphlets and journals for both these groups. There are affiliated local societies throughout the country, some of which run playgroups of 'opportunity' classes. (In Scotland approach Scottish Society for Mentally Handicapped Children, 69 West Regent Street, Glasgow G2 2AN.)

Royal National Institute for the Blind (RNIB), 224–8 Great Portland Street, London W1N 6AA

The RNIB provides an Education Advisory Service for the parents of young blind children and social workers, maintains the Sunshine Home Nursery Schools (usually for children of not less than three years), and has produced a leaflet *Hints for Blind Mothers*. These are the services that are of particular relevance to this course but the RNIB does offer a much wider range of services.

Spastics Society, 12 Park Crescent, London W1N 4EQ

The Spastics Society aims to promote facilities for the treatment, education and vocational training of spastics, and to co-ordinate and advise on all activities for spastics. There are many local groups and affiliated organisations. It has established schools, residential homes, assessment centres, training centres and holiday homes among other things. (In Scotland approach **Scottish Council for the Care of Spastics,** Corstophine Road, Edinburgh EH12 6HP.)

Toy Libraries Association, Seabrook House, Wyllyotts Manor, Darkes Lane, Potters Bar, Herts EN6 2HL

The Association can supply addresses of toy libraries for handicapped children throughout the country. These libraries will lend toys which have been specially selected and sometimes specially made.

Chapter 8
Widening world

Chapter 8

Widening World

A review

The topics in this book invite you to take stock of your life now, and to look towards the future. Start with all the things you have read, watched, listened to and done so far. What have you learned? Where can you go from here?

Types of development

Textbooks on child development are often divided up into different sections. Five common ones are the child's emotional, physical, intellectual, language and social development. But *life* isn't divided into such sections. So we have tried to build this book around the everyday experiences of families with young children, using them to show different kinds of development when appropriate.

Most of the topics are based on familiar situations and events. But within these 'settings' you are asked to do one or more of the following things:

● to look at your own views and feelings;

● to find out, by observation, what young children can understand or do, or feel;

● to apply what you have learned from reading and observing, by trying out new activities or new ways of doing things with children.

The following five photographs and questions recap on the book in these terms. For a change, these have been chosen to illustrate a specific kind of development.

● The young child's development is shaped by the experiences he gains living day to day with his parents. You cannot mould a child to be exactly what you want. But your feelings, your understanding of him and the experiences you offer him are very important influences.

Physical development

Physical development means growth in size, strength and skill of the body. Each body 'matures' at its own rate. But you encourage development with the food and exercise you provide, and – just as important – the experiences and help you give your child.

● Girls differ from boys in the size and strength they grow to. Some of this difference is inborn. But strength also seems to depend in part on the opportunities they have for physical play. Would you give boys and girls the same opportunities for physical exercise and 'rough-and-tumble' play? (See *Male and female*, Chapter 4.)

● Large movements and simple movements are achieved successfully before fine control of the fingers or difficult sequences of movements. At roughly what age would you expect a child to be able to: pull on a hat? handle a fork? catch a ball? (See *Dressing* and *Mealtimes* in Chapter 1; *Running, jumping and standing still* in Chapter 5.)

● Hands are used very often every day. Can you think of two times yesterday when you encouraged or helped your child to become just a little bit more skilful with his or her hands?

Emotional development

Emotional development is about feelings – feelings about oneself and other people, about the experiences one has, and about things. Your child is building up in his mind 'pictures' of himself, of the world about him, of the people in that world, and the way they see him. Imagination plays a large part. With feelings it's always hard to separate the real from the imaginary, and this is particularly true for young children.

● The feelings of young children are often sudden and intense. But how do you feel when your child throws a tantrum in the supermarket or violently resists a hair wash? It's important because your feelings partly determine what you do. (See *Bathtime* in Chapter 1, *Tantrums and tears* in Chapter 4.)

● Imaginative play helps your child to understand the world he's growing up in. How many times in the last week have you seen or heard your child: ask for a story? play with a 'person-toy'? pretend to be an object, such as a train? play at being someone else? (See *Stories* in Chapter 1, *Dolls and teddies* and *Playing mothers and fathers* in Chapter 2.)

● Be imaginative yourself. How many ways can you think of to use buttons or a piece of blanket or a saucepan and spoon as 'props' for imaginative play?

A review

Thinking

'Thinking' covers a very broad area. It's closely tied up with language: words are used to work out actions in advance. In this book we have looked at the development of different 'ideas' – of colours, number, size, weight, and at children's styles or ways of thinking. In the pre-school years, there's no substitute for experience. Children's ideas grow from what they see, and hear, and do. But they also need to be able to attend to what they are doing, and to handle materials that are at the right sort of level for them. And 'thinking' is catching – if you encourage your child to explore materials, solve problems, ask questions, he can see that 'thinking things out for himself' is a good and valued thing to do.

● how well do you think you estimate your child's level of understanding and abilities? (See *Learning styles* and *I can do it* in Chapter 4.)

● what ideas do you think a child may develop through playing with dough, water and bricks? How could you tell if your guesses are right? (See *Bathtime* in Chapter 1, *A dollop of dough* and *Woodwork* in Chapter 4.)

● how would you help your child choose the right size and price of a tin of beans for family tea?

Language development

Language development isn't just about the growth of vocabulary and grammatical skill. It's about the development of *uses* of languages: to describe, invent, question, answer, predict, recall, instruct, explain, and so on. Language is used to find out about and represent the world, and to fantasise. Pre-school children need practical experiences, but they also need the words to describe them.

● What do you think there is interesting to say or ask about growing some cress? What might your child be most interested in? It's not always the same thing.

● Questions take different forms and are asked for different reasons. Your answers are important, too. What aspects of the world do the following questions relate to, and what might be helpful answers to them? 'Will our cat have kittens?'; 'Me have sweetie?'; 'Can spiders get in my bed?' (See *All I get is questions*, Chapter 1.)

● How would you set about explaining to a four-year-old how to grate a lemon? (See *Instructions and explanations* in Chapter 4.)

Social development

Social development is about getting on with others and sharing activities. It includes being with others, talking to them, taking turns and dividing up the parts of a task or game, and the 'rules' of how to behave with others in many different situations.

● Your child throws sand at another child in play. Is this naughty? What would you do about it? (See *What's naughty and why?* in Chapter 3, *For their own good* in Chapter 6.)

● Two three-year-olds are playing side by side in a sandpit, doing the same things but separately. What type of social play is this? And what might happen if a third child came to join them? (See *Playing together* in Chapter 7.)

● What sort of birthday party, if any, would you give for a shy three-year-old? a bouncy four-year-old with a gang of friends at playgroup? (See *Children are different* in Chapter 1; *Playing together* and *Children's quarrels* in Chapter 7.)

Read more about it

The *Topic index* at the end of the book gives a complete list of all the topics in the course. It also shows the nine major themes on which the course is based. Five of these themes are the aspects of child development we have just been looking at: physical, emotional, intellectual, language, and social development. The other four are more general parental concerns: providing learning materials and situations, parent-child relationships, family life-styles, and community life.

The index uses blobs to show which theme(s) each topic is most concerned with. So, for example, you will find *Dressing* blobbed for 'physical development', and *Bathtime* blobbed for 'parent-child relationships' – even though these topics touch on other issues as well. *Mealtimes*, also in Chapter 1, contributes to two major themes: 'physical development' and 'thinking'.

If your interest is caught by a particular topic, you can use the index to find what other topics contribute to the same theme. Or, if you prefer, start by picking a theme and work through the topics listed under it. The topics are individual illustrations of the themes–they don't build up from chapter to chapter – so you can read them in any order you choose.

Because the development of language is so rapid, and so important in the pre-school years, the next topic is a special summary of it (*Words, words, words*).

Patterns of life

Routines of the day and week in Chapter 1, asks you to survey your child's activities and to review a typical day and week in your family's life. If you did so at the beginning of the course, go back now and repeat these exercises. If you haven't done them yet, why not do so now, and again in two, or six months time?

Changing together

Your child is changing from day to day. Often you don't realize it at the time. It's only after you've washed the last nappy, for example, that you realize that that stage is over. Making a record every so often helps you to stand back and see what things your child can do now that he couldn't do a week or six months ago.

You may also be changing the pattern of your child's life as a result of some of the ideas in the course. Perhaps you've tried out new play ideas; gone out somewhere different; helped your child to take more responsibility in taking care of himself; or found ways to involve him in day to day family work. Almost certainly some of these new ideas will fall flat:

your child is almost instantly bored by helping you tidy up, or looks with disgust at the lovely lump of dough you offer him. Don't give up. Perhaps it was the wrong time or the wrong activity for the stage your child is at or the mood he's in. Or perhaps you expected too much.

We looked at some of the ways adults get involved in children's play – the practical helper, the encourager, the talker and so on. You are all these and more to your child. By watching for his needs and interests, and caring as you do, you give him the support he needs to grow today, tomorrow, next year.

Your needs

You have your own needs too. At times the course looks very child-centred. But a child who rules your life is as badly off as the child who is dominated by his parents. Your child needs to learn to be sensitive to the needs and feelings of others. And he needs the self-confidence to be able to do things on his own. You help when you explain why you can't play now, rather than just shooing him away. You help by encouraging him to play on his own

while you work, and giving him his special time later. You help by giving him responsibility, for his personal care, for decisions and jobs around the house. You help by supporting him as your ways separate – he goes to a pre-school group, or a minder, for example, while you go to work, or do other things without him.

Most of all you help your child by being reasonably happy yourself. When you find living with pre-school children a strain, your child feels it too (see 'Unspoken words' in Chapter 5). There's no simple solution. In this book we invite you to 'take stock' of the pleasures of your life.

One of these may be work. Less time with your children is unlikely to be for the worse, unless you feel guilty, or are unhappy with the arrangements for care of your child. It simply means a different way of life. You may have less time to try out some of the ideas in the book. But they're not meant to be things you do all day, every day. They are suggestions, for you to pick and choose from, to build into your own family's pattern of living.

Anything goes!

Many of the topics in this book illustrate particular aspects of development by showing how specific materials are used in specific situations. But, with a little bit of imagination, anything goes. Try playing the activities fruit machine game.

The aim of the game is to come up with a different idea of something to do each time you play. The machine gives you two elements each time – you choose the third and work out an activity based on the combination of place, material and development.

● Get someone to call you out nine pairs of numbers from one to ten (for example three, six; two, seven). Write these in the table as follows:

Place and material: Enter the first three pairs of numbers in these columns. Your task is to choose from the list one type of development they could contribute to – and

work out an activity to do. For example (see table) the machine gave bedroom (one) and balls or bean bags (five). The *material* is usually considered an outdoor toy – but in a soft-furnished bedroom, bean bags especially are unlikely to do any harm. So for *development* we chose physical – large movements (two) – and for our *activity* either a target-hitting game for a wet day, or putting the bag in the child's waking-up basket, to buy some early morning peace.

Material and development: Enter the second three pairs of numbers in these columns. This time your task is to choose a place where you could carry out an activity, using the given material, that would contribute to the given development. For example, building blocks (two) and thinking-ideas (five). This was fairly easy – building blocks can be played with almost anywhere, and are a good practical material for developing

ideas about number, size, and so on. But to make a change from the usual, we chose for our *place* the stairs (four). And for our *activity* we chose the problem of 'have you enough bricks to make a long line all the way up the stairs?' – a task involving judgements about number and size.

Place and development: Enter the third three pairs of numbers in these columns. Now you have to choose a material to carry out an activity in the given place, with the given development in mind.

Played this way the activities fruit machine will give you hundreds of combinations, and it uses only a few examples of place, material and development. You can add your own. Not all of them are 'winners' – but you're only asked to try out nine games. We found it loosened up our thinking about what you can do, where and why. We hope it gives you some fresh ideas too.

Place		Material		Development			Place 1	Material 5	Development 2	Activity *target-hitting game*
1	Bedroom	1	Water	1	Physical – fine control of fingers					
2	Bathroom	2	Building blocks	2	Physical – large movements	1				
3	Kitchen	3	Books, catalogues	3	Emotional – imagination, fears	2				
4	Stairs	4	Large cardboard box	4	Emotional – independence, self-confidence	3				
5	Sitting room	5	Balls or bean bags	5	Thinking – ideas of numbers, size, cause and effect etc.	4				
6	Garden/yard	6	Food	6	Thinking – clearly and creatively	5				
7	Playground	7	Pebbles	7	Language – describing	6				
8	Playgroup	8	Old clothes	8	Language – asking questions	7				
9	Shops	9	Saucepans & spoons	9	Social – outgoingness	8				
10	Park	10	Cleaning things	10	Social – co-operation, sharing	9				

A review

Going on

The chart opposite maps out some of the topics in the book. There wasn't space to do the same for all the topics. Even if there had been, there would still have been some 'blanks' simply because the book cannot cover everything. But very often, the themes and activities developed in one setting can be applied, with a bit of change if needed, to settings the book does not consider. And in the settings that have been considered, it's often possible to bring in other themes than those we discussed. You can use the chart to work out new possibilities of things to watch for, and do. Here are some questions to get you started:

Using the chart

Quickly re-read the following topics, and then try to plot them on the chart:

Chapter 2 – *Children and television*
Chapter 2 – *New baby in the family*
Chapter 4 – *Cooking*

When you've got the 'feel' of the way the chart works, see how you can create more parts of it for yourself, by answering the questions below.

Same theme, different setting

How far can you apply to other settings what you have learned about the following developments?

1 *Numbers* These were considered in the settings of housework – table-laying and washing. How far can you help your child understand the numbers he meets when going out shopping – for example, the hour at which you leave, the number of the bus, the number of oranges you are going to buy, the number of pence you pay for a chocolate bar?

2 *Choosing* Choices and decisions were considered in the setting of shopping for food. Would your child be as interested, or as able to choose by himself, when shopping for his bedroom wallpaper, or gran's birthday present, or his shoes?

3 *Sharing activities with other children* We looked at this mainly in terms of sharing play in a pre-school group. How different an activity is two children sharing a household task?

Same setting, different theme

In most setting-based topics we considered only one or two types of development. But can you see how others could apply too?

4 *Tidying up* Here we looked at your child's ability to sort and group objects. But language is important too. What sorts of language do you and your child use in this sort of activity?

5 *Dressing* We looked at this mainly in terms of your child's growing skill with his fingers. But what other sorts of development are involved?

6 *Bathtime* We looked at this from the point of view of games to play, involving words and ideas, and some of the emotional fears that can arise. What other emotions can arise at bathtime?

Chart

This chart shows how the book was drawn up. Across the top are nine broad 'themes' of child development and parental concerns. Down the side are twelve common 'settings'—everyday situations and events. And plotted within this framework are some of the topics in the book. Like life, the chart's not neat and tidy. Some topics are specific to one setting, but span more than one theme. And some topics are specific to one theme but span almost every setting.

Settings	Child's development					
	Physical	Emotional	Thinking	Language	Social	Learning materials situations
Personal routines Getting up Eating Going to bed	Dressing Mealtimes	Day's end	Mealtimes			
Work and play Housework Making things Playing indoors	Woodwork	Dolls and teddies	Talking while you work Woodwork		Playing mother and fathers	Water in the sink Paint
Going out Going shopping Visiting/ Travelling Playing outdoors	Running, jumping and standing still	Wills of their own	Shopping Going places	All I get is questions		Learning about reading
Separating ways Meeting others Parents at work Children's groups		Working mothers Joining a group	Going to work— children's views		Hello stranger Playing together Children's quarrels	

Comment

We classified the three topics as follows:

Chap. 2 – *Children and television* – play indoors setting; the television is a learning 'material', and therefore of parental concern.

Chap. 2 – *New baby in the family* – emotional development (feelings about the new member of the family) across all settings.

Chap. 4 – *Cooking* – housework setting: development of thinking and language (always closely connected), and of physical skill with the fingers.

1 *Numbers* which stand for things such as hours, bus routes and prices are particularly difficult for young children to understand. Identifying the shape of the figures or the numerical value of the coins can be fun. But the most understandable experiences for a child are practical ones. Goods can be handled and counted in a way that is meaningful to your child; for example, counting oranges in terms of the people they are for – one for you, one for Sam, one for me and one for mummy.

2 *Choosing* It's probably more difficult for your child to make acceptable choices on his own for these goods. You need to 'set out' the choices for him in a more restrictive way.

A mistake in shoes for growing feet matters more than if he chooses a horrible pudding for one teatime. A present for gran is hard because he's likely to find it difficult to think what she would like rather than what he would like. And he's had less need to develop his 'taste' in wallpapers than his taste for different foods.

3 *Sharing housework* Many of the basic principles here are the same as for sharing play. Children need to be able to take turns and divide up the work between themselves – to cooperate – before the sharing will be successful. One important difference, though, is that you are much more likely to be on hand to supervise the activity, to guide and help them if needed. You'll probably try to help them cooperate, rather than leaving them to work it out for themselves as they do in play.

4 *Tidying up* This sort of activity involves language to *describe* and *name* objects, as an aid to sorting. There may be *questions* about what things are for. And certainly you will

Parental concerns		
Parent- child relationships	Family life-styles	Community life
	Waking	
Bathtime		
For their own good	Safety in the home	
What's naughty and why? Tantrums and tears	Routines of the day and week	
	Children in hospital	
		The generation gap
	Working mothers	
		Pre-school groups

need to give careful *instructions* that break the task down into child-sized jobs that can be carried out successfully. (See language topics in the Index at the end of the book.)

5 *Dressing* Again, language is involved, in giving instructions about what to wear, how to put it on, what to do next. Language is also involved in the learning of the 'ideas' of left, right, back, front and so on. And there is an emotional aspect – the 'unspoken words' by which you convey your feelings of the morning to your child.

6 *Bathtime* Bathtime is often a setting in which good or bad feelings can be aroused about nakedness; about sex; and about being 'clean and dry'. These issues are dealt with in separate topics (see the Topic Index). But they are part of every bathtime.

If you have found this exercise helpful in linking up parts of the book, or seeing how you can apply ideas in new ways – go on doing it. This book is only a beginning. Think about how each setting relates to each theme, and of ways you can apply those thoughts in practical terms. You may find you can make new opportunities for yourself and your child.

Words
Words
Words

A normal child will begin to say words at about one year old. By two, he will begin to form simple two- and three-word sentences. Just over two years later, at about four years old, he will have mastered almost the entire structure of his native language. This stunning intellectual achievement is routinely performed by every pre-school child.

Learning to talk is an amazing achievement. In just over two years a child learns to use a most complicated system of grammar, picks up thousands of words and uses language to organize his life. You don't have to sit down and teach your child what a question is: long before he can understand such explanations, he is already *asking* questions!

The exciting fact is (and nobody really knows the reason for it) that young children seem to be specially equipped to make sense of their environment and to communicate with the people in it. Fortunately, parents are equally well equipped – from the start they can often understand what their children are trying to say.

Communication for a purpose

Language is used to talk to other people, to share feelings, to give and obtain information, to cooperate and to *think*.

We adults carry on long conversations with ourselves in our heads, about what we are doing or have done, planning and making decisions or simply day-dreaming. Children think aloud, in conversations with another person, or by themselves as they play. They develop conversational skills in their talk with adults and these conversations help them to develop and use a wider range of language.

Some of the main uses of language which children normally meet in their everyday experience are listed below. The short conversations in the following exercise illustrate these uses in action.

Children use language:

1 **to obtain a desired object** – 'I want'
2 **to control other people's behaviour** – 'Do as I tell you'
3 **to describe relationships between people** – 'me and Mummy . . .'
4 **to describe themselves** – 'Here I come'
5 **to create imaginary situations** – 'Let's pretend'
6 **to exchange information** – 'I've got something to tell you'

Parents use language:

to help develop the child's ability to use language. They ask questions, give instructions, and respond to questions and suggestions. These are just some of the ways in which your responses can help your child. You may be:

A **asking a question** – 'What's she doing?'
B **making a comparison** – 'That's like a . . .'
C **giving an instruction** – 'I want you to . . .' or **an explanation** – 'You can't because . . .'
D **showing the child how** – 'You put it this way . . .'
E **giving positive encouragement** – 'That's good'
F **collaborating in an imaginary game or story** – 'I'll come into your little house'.

Identifying language uses

1 Read the first of the transcripts of taped conversations in the next column. A number or letter (according to the lists above) has been put beside each statement to describe the ways in which William and his mother are using language. As you can see there aren't always clear answers – and there are other questions to ask.
2 Now try marking the other three transcripts in the same way. Can you identify different uses of language in action?

Conversation

---

1 William (3 years) is watching TV with his mother.
William I'm doing what the lady's doing (puffing out his cheeks)

Mother What's she doing?

William Look I'm blowing too
Mother You look just like a fish. That's very clever.

---

2 Paul (2¼ years) has been told off for leaving a toy car under mother's feet.
Paul I nice boy
I only wanted to put it in that garage
Mother Yes, but it's in the way
Paul *You* bringed it in the room
Mother Well I don't want it left here. It's in the way
Paul It's not in the way (sobs).

---

3 Elizabeth (5 years) is pretending to take photographs.
Elizabeth What do I look through?
Do I look through that?
Father Yes
Elizabeth Do I have to push that one when I want to take a photograph?
Father No you have to press that one (Father shows her)
Elizabeth Please can I?
Father Yes, but there's no film in it
Elizabeth I did it.

---

4 James (3¾ years) and his father are playing trains.
James You go on there
Father There we are. I'll sit at the side. Off with the brake
James *I'll* start it up
Father Oh, sorry
James Dad, you don't steer it yet
(Pretending to start engine)
James There
Father Oh! That was a quick starting engine Very good
Have you shovelled enough coal on James?

We think . . .

In the next column we suggest what uses of language are in the transcripts. This is just one way of looking at the transcripts – which are, after all, only the 'bare bones' of speech. 'Live' conversations use gestures, pauses, tones of voice and facial expressions – all of which can make a great difference (See *Unspoken words*, Chapter 5.) But looking at language like this can help to point out the different ways children use language, how

Child's use of language (numbers 1–6)	Parent's response (letters A–F)
4 (describing himself) but also telling his mother so perhaps 4 and 6	
	A (asks for information)
4, 6	
	B (comparison) and E (positive encouragement). (Might it have been more helpful to ask William what *he* thought he looked like?)

Conversation game

Conversation begins at a very early age. Babies 'talk' to their mothers long before they can use words. Mothers talk to babies as they feed, wash, dress and play with them. The responsive, babbling baby of only a few months already recognizes talk as a most important form of communication.

Your job

Understanding what your child is saying can be difficult sometimes. You have to imagine what he is likely to be meaning in a particular situation. Remember that your child has to make an imaginative effort too. You may need to help him understand the situation as well as find the language for it. He needs to try it out for himself until he hits on what he wants to say the way *he* wants to say it. By using language, your child will discover what he is able to do with it. You can help by asking questions (which help him to say something in his own way or to discover an answer to something puzzling) rather than by giving him a piece of information or a correct answer.

Conversations are sharing

Ann ($2\frac{1}{2}$ years) is playing with her teddy.

Ann   Don't wake teddy up, will you Daddy?
Father No I won't. What's teddy doing?
Ann   My teddy's not very well
Father Isn't he? What's the matter?
Ann   Got a . . . teddy's got to have some Abidec (a vitamin preparation)
Father Has he?
Ann   And some aspirin
Father What are you going to give the aspirins to teddy for?
Ann   Cos . . . my teddy's not very comfy.

Notice how Ann's father enters into this conversation, treating Ann as his equal, asking questions which help her to explain what she is doing and extend her imaginative play.

Talking with our children is the way we find out about each other – we learn what they feel about things and they learn about us. As they hear about our experiences and expectations they begin to try out their own on us. Mealtimes, walks, bathtime and bedtime are occasions when you and the children are often particularly relaxed and can chat at length.

The best conversations take place when you treat the child as an equal, with ideas of his own. Discussing his ideas seriously helps him to feel confident about talking and listening. The ideas and feelings he is trying to express may be tentative and stumbling. Often, in the struggle to get an idea right, he will get words and grammar wrong. Give him time, and don't bother to correct the mistakes. Impatience makes a child more likely to stutter or stumble. Listen to the ideas and feelings he is trying to sort out and let him know how important you think they are. Children learn as they talk.

Following their lead

It is sometimes tempting to lead a conversation in the way you think it ought to go, trying to teach your child something new – especially if he asks about something that interests you. But you are far more likely to extend *his* interests and ability to use language effectively if you listen to him and follow his lead. When he asks you where the bath water goes, he may want to know the facts, or he may want to tell you what he feels about the gurgling, sucking noises made by the water going down the plug hole.

You can best find out what he wants – facts, permission, reassurance, or whatever – by trying out various ideas and seeing which one he responds to.

you help them, and how together you build up a pattern of conversation.

2 : *Paul* 4, 6 ; *Mother* C ; *Paul* 6, 3 ; *Mother* C ; *Paul* 6, 2.

3 : *Elizabeth* 1, 6 ; *Father* E ; *Elizabeth* 1, 6 ; *Father* D ; *Elizabeth* 1 ; *Father* D ; *Elizabeth* 4.

4 : *James* 2, 5 ; *Father* F ; *James* 4, 5 ; *Father* F , *James* 2, 5 ; *Father* F, E, A.

Looking forward to school

Your child is nearly five and about to start school. It's a big step for her – and for you too. How can you help her? Simply by continuing to provide her with the experience, support and encouragement that you have given her throughout her pre-school years.

Schools today

Compulsory school age is defined as the beginning of the term after a child's fifth birthday. In some areas children may be able to start sooner, on a full or part-time basis. But from five to sixteen your child is legally required to attend school. These are eleven important years in your child's development from helpless baby to independent adult. New influences, new ideas, new friends, new opportunities to learn new skills come into her life. To make the most of them, your child needs your continuing interest, support and encouragement.

'But it's all changed since my day—so how can I help?'

At various times in this book you have been asked to look back at your own childhood memories. However, in this case, looking back is not really the best way to start. 'How can I help with starting school?' is a question about the future. Today's children, their homes, their parents, their pre-school experiences, are not like yours were: their schools and the changing world outside are different too. So you need to look forward—school is something new for you to find out about, as well as your child.

How schools have changed

Much more is known now about the way young children learn than twenty-five or fifty years ago. The skills society wants from them when they leave school are different too, so you will probably find that teaching methods and subject-matter have greatly changed since your schooldays.

New knowledge has changed ideas about the best ways teachers can help young children to learn. Various changes have been made to meet the needs of new teaching methods. For example:

● new designs of school buildings,
● new kinds of teaching games and books,
● changes in the organisation of classes,
● changes in parent-teacher attitudes,
● more emphasis on self-discipline.

Changes in what is taught have been brought about also, to meet the work and leisure needs of modern society. There is greater emphasis now on:

● practical mathematics experience rather than just arithmetic,
● the development of spoken language,
● the development of creative skills,
● understanding the environment.

So, for example, you may find a class full of small groups doing different things, with the teacher going to each group in turn, instead of standing in front of rows of desks. Mathematics will be metric, and will include practical handling and sorting of objects before children go on to 'handling' numbers on paper. (See *Mealtimes* in Chapter 1.) You are more likely to find 'environmental and society studies' on a timetable than straight 'history' or 'geography'. A greater variety of ways of teaching reading are to be found— many schools now begin reading with the Initial Teaching Alphabet (i.t.a.). This is a special alphabet with extra letters so that, as nearly as possible, one letter stands for one sound. It is meant to be an easy 'bridge' between speaking and reading the traditional alphabet. Try reading the next paragraph, noting how the different sounds for 't' and 'a' single 'o' and 'oo' are written, for example:

tradiʃhonally wun ov ᚦe first tasks ov ᚦe infant scꭀl woz tꭀ teeᴄh ᴄhildren tꭀ reed. it iz still, kwiet rietly, a mæjor pre- occuepæʃhon, sins reeding iz a kee tꭀ muᴄh ov ᚦe lerning ᚦat will cum læter and tꭀ ᚦe possibility ov independent study.

What hasn't changed

For better or for worse some things are still the same in primary schools:

● there can still be up to 40 infants in one class, (30 is more usual);
● children are still expected to keep less exacting but necessary school rules;
● head teachers still have powers to keep parents out of schools and to punish children (though they use them less);
● a daily act of worship and religious education are still a legal requirement of all schools;
● infant schools are still primarily concerned with teaching the basic skills of reading, writing and mathematics.

By and large, primary schools still have less money and space per child than secondary schools. Teaching large groups of young children, often alone under difficult conditions, is not an easy job. Few schools are perfect in the eyes of teachers, parents or pupils but much can be achieved by parents at home and teachers at school finding out about each other and working together.

Home and school

All the research evidence shows that children do better at school when they have the understanding, support and encouragement of their parents.

In the pre-school years you will have been helping your child to learn – there's no reason to stop now. Your child still spends more time awake at home than at school, so don't feel you should leave everything to the school.

When children go to school, they have opportunities to learn from other children and from adults trained to guide them in specific ways. However, what they learn at home is still the major educational influence in their lives – home has the greatest effect on the educational progress of a child. So it makes sense for parents and teachers to work together.

School and home can begin to work together before a child starts school. They have a common first objective: they both want the child to get used to going to school regularly as quickly and easily as possible. Here are some of the things that can be done to ease children into school:

A school can

● encourage and support the setting up of a playgroup where pre-schooling provision is inadequate;
● seek contact with local nursery school or playgroup parents;
● welcome parents to look round the school;
● arrange meetings (formal or informal) for parents of incoming children;
● operate 'easing in' schemes, like inviting children to attend for some half days during the term before they start;
● arrange 'staggered starts' where only a few newcomers start on the same day;
● operate parent-helper schemes (parents helping in the classrooms);
● agree to half-day schooling in the first few weeks.

Parents can:

● keep an open mind about what others say about local schools (good or bad);
● take their child for walks past school at playtime. (Squat down and look at the playground from your child's point of view);
● give their child practice in getting used to separation from their mother at such places as nursery school, playgroup or friends' houses;
● arrange for their child to see parents chatting in a friendly way with their first teacher. (Get another parent to introduce you or collect neighbours' children and introduce yourself.)
● arrange visits to look round local schools, well in advance of their child's starting date;
● prepare their child (and themselves) as realistically as possible for the school their child will be going to . . .

It is impossible to describe the work of primary schools here in detail. But briefly and simply, here are some of the things you might see in a modern primary or lower school:

Teachers—teach to a flexible daily programme, not a rigid timetable;
—teach individuals and small groups sometimes, as well as the whole class together;
—encourage children to think for themselves.

Parents —are regarded as allies and encouraged to take an active interest and become involved in what goes on in the school.

Children—are not all doing the same thing at the same time;
—move about more freely;
—have more varied, purposeful activities to choose from;
—talk, read, write, draw, paint, and make models and music about what interests them.

'We went to see my school today'

School is less of a step into the unknown for the child who's been to some sort of pre-school group. Do you remember joining that group and the things you did then to ease life for your child? (See *Joining a group* in Chapter 7.) The same principles apply to school: your child gains her confidence through being able to see this 'unknown' and get to know it gradually, talking about it and looking forward to it while still at home. So a first visit will help her.

A first visit will help you to find out for yourself what the school is like, rather than depending on local hearsay. In the next columns some things you might do, ask, and look out for are suggested. The 'positive things to look for' list asks you simply to record your own first, general, impressions, rather than specific educational arrangements. Later on you'll be more interested in facts, but for both you and your child first feelings about a school may determine your relationship, good or bad, with it.

The list is split into two halves: *people* and *things*. Obviously, modern surroundings, and equipment are desirable, and often make life easier – but above all it is the atmosphere created by teachers and children that is important. A school can be cared for, lively, busy, happy, whatever its age.

● If you have been able to tick a lot of items you should have good reason to feel happy about your child settling.
● If there are less ticks than you would have liked, look at the balance between 'people' and 'things'. 'People' scoring more could indicate teachers working well in difficult conditions. 'Things' scoring more might indicate simply that you went on a bad day. Like homes, schools have them. Go again, perhaps after looking at other schools.
● A minority of parents may find that their impressions were so unfavourable that building up good relationships with that school would be difficult for them. If that is so in your case make every effort to look further afield if you can. In some overcrowded or underpopulated areas there is little choice. But in many areas, parents have more choice of first school than they realise. To find out what your rights and choices are, write to your local education officer – ask the library, or any local school or councillor for the name and address. Persistence may pay off.

If you do have to send your child to a school you are unhappy about – don't despair. If a school really is below standard you won't be the only worried parent: keep up relationships as best you can to support your child at the school, and get together with other like-minded parents to think about what might be done. And remember too – in one year a young child spends nearly twice as many waking hours at home as at school.

Making a first visit

Every school is different. The size and age of the buildings, the facilities provided, the staff, the children who go there and their families are the basic ingredients which make each school unique. So a first visit not only helps your child but also helps you to 'size up' the school from your point of view.

However, it's easy when you visit the school for the first time to be overwhelmed by the strangeness of the people and surroundings and the bustle of activity.

Schools are busy places so it helps to get relationships off to a good start if you are prepared. Here's what to do:

1 Call, write or phone the school to make an appointment with the head teacher. Ask if you (both parents if possible) and your child can look around during school hours.

2 Before you go think through the questions you want to ask. Write them down and take them with you if you prefer. Some of the things you may want to find out are:

practical/personal: dinner arrangements, clothes, times, the daily act of worship, discipline.

what is taught: what reading schemes and other new teaching methods are used, and what the results are, size of classes, standards attained on leaving, turnover of staff.

home and school: is there an 'easing in' scheme, how can you find out about your child's progress, are parents welcomed in Parent-Teacher's Associations or as helpers during school hours?

puzzling things: ask them about anything you see on your visit that you don't understand, or anything that worries you, and try to get as much explanation as you need.

3 Before you go, read through the list of 'positive things to look for'. When you get home, tick as many items as you honestly can.

4 During your visit, watch your child's reactions to the surroundings, the teachers and the other children. Tell the head teacher anything you feel is important about your child – though remember there'll be other visits and meetings where you can go into more detail as you and your child, and the school, get to know each other better.

Positive things to look for

People
Head teacher

Welcoming
Offered information
Listened to you
Answered your questions satisfactorily
Teachers seemed to like him/her
You liked him/her

Reception class teacher

Not embarrassed by visitors
Friendly
Explained what was happening in class
Attentive to needs of class
You liked him/her
Your child liked him/her

Other children

Busy – happily active
Not disturbed by visitors
Responsive to teachers
Willing to chat about what they are doing
Friendly towards your child
Your child knew/liked some of them

Things
Buildings

Cared for, even if old
Warm and cheerful inside
Lavatories clean and pleasant
Adequate washing facilities
No or few graffiti
Cloakrooms tidy

Classrooms

Children's work on display
Furniture arranged to allow small-group work
Toys and apparatus as well as books
Displays of plants, wallcharts etc.
Not overcrowded

Play areas

Not overcrowded
Things to do (e.g. climbing frames, hopscotch)
Living things (grass, tree, plants)
Hard surfaces in good condition
Supervised at playtime
In big schools – some area reserved for very young children

'I'll be going every day soon'

Successfully settling in at school depends, in part, on your child being able to cope with what she will be doing there. In the panel below are two lists, one of some of the things reception class teachers would like children to be able to do, the other of experiences that provide your child with these sorts of skills. To find out where your child needs more help, work through these two lists.

Checking these things is a way of finding out where your child may need extra help and support with schoolwork. If she has difficulty in handling things with her fingers it will be worth both telling her teacher that she has trouble holding a pencil or whatever, and giving her extra praise and encouragement at home for her drawing and writing efforts.

On your own?

Checking like this also makes you aware of how much your 'baby' has learnt to do for herself in such a short time. From day to day you may notice things she can suddenly do that she couldn't the week before. When you look back over five years, it's an amazing development. Over those five years, almost without noticing, you've been adapting to your baby's growing skill and independence; proud of her new achievements, you've encouraged her to do more.

Now when she starts school, you need to change again. You may feel a sense of loss – a child starting school often makes her parents realise that she does not need them as much as she did when she was tiny. In some ways this is true – your baby can now look after herself. She will always need your love and support but she is no longer a baby and will not want (except occasionally, when everything gets too much) to be treated as one. She needs the gap that her going to school will make in your life, to grow on her own. You need to find your own way to fill that gap, to be able to let her go willingly. It will help your child too to know that you are looking forward to the future on your own account as well as on hers.

Prepared for school?

Skills grow out of experience. The opportunities you give your child before school – to care for herself, to help you in family work, to play alone and with others – will help him when he gets to school. Tick off how often your child has had the following experiences, and how well he can do the following things.

Many of the things listed below are looked at in more detail in Chapters 1-7. With those things you have marked 'rarely' or 'not very well' your child may need more experience or simply more practice. The topics in earlier books may give you some new ideas of what to do, or how to help her. The important

thing is not to make her feel bad if she can't do certain things. Children differ in the age and rate at which they master new skills. Often all you need to do is give more time and encouragement to try, and praise for trying.

How often has your child:	Often	sometimes	rarely	How well can your child:	Very well	OK	Not very well
looked at picture books with you				put on her coat, socks, shoes			
looked at abc books with you				do up buttons			
looked at counting books with you				wipe her own bottom			
seen you reading and writing				wipe her own nose			
sorted and counted with you				wash her own hands			
had stories read to her				eat with a knife and fork			
been sung to				tidy up her own things			
been taken for walks				care for her own things			
helped you make things				share her own things			
got up and gone to bed at the same time regularly				speak clearly without shouting			
spent time away from you regularly				ask questions			
played with other children regularly				answer questions			
had responsibility for small jobs around the house				describe experiences			
talked with you				recite nursery rhymes and sing songs			
dressed and washed herself				name colours			
played with:				tell stories			
sand				listen attentively			
water				carry out instructions			
dough/clay/plasticine				climb confidently			
paint/crayons/pencils				kick a ball			
stick and paste				cut with scissors			
balls				copy simple shapes			
construction toys				spot details			
				do simple jigsaws			
				count objects			
				use a pencil			

'Children don't show any respect any more.'
'Teenagers today – they're all vandals and hooligans.'
'Old folk – they do nothing but grumble.'
'They're too fuddy-duddy even to enjoy themselves any more.'

The generation gap

A lack of contact across the generations leads to a lack of mutual understanding and respect. It becomes easy to make sweeping statements about whole age-groups. Yet there's much to be gained from contact across the generations. How do you and your child bridge the generation gap?

Who do you know... and where do you go?

Tick the columns as appropriate, to show what your friends, neighbours, workmates, acquaintances and the relatives you see often, are like – and what your child feels about them. Then check off the places you go to.

1 Are your:	Friends	Neighbours	Workmates	Acquaintances	Relatives
. . . older than you?					
. . . younger than you?					
. . . about the same age?					
. . . mixed?					
. . . the same status as you, that is:					
married					
single					
with children					
without children					
mixed					

2 How does your child feel about your:	Friends	Neighbours	Workmates	Acquaintances	Relatives
he's at ease with them					
he's shy of them					
he hardly ever sees them					

3 What places do you go to where you get to know people:

sports clubs ☐   churches ☐   pubs ☐
social clubs ☐   classes ☐   libraries ☐
other clubs ☐   pre-school groups ☐   community centres ☐

Generation gaps in your life?

Quite probably your friends are of a similar age and status to yourself. Different age-groups tend to have different values and interests, and it's often easiest to communicate with someone like yourself.

Your neighbours too may be like yourself. In recent years housing has often been built to appeal to 'newly weds', 'growing families' or 'retirement couples'.

Relatives are more likely to be mixed in age and status – but many people now do not see relatives often. Workmates are also more likely to be mixed; as are acquaintances who meet in places where there is a common activity to be shared, be it worship or football. Cross-generation friendships are more likely to grow here than in purely social settings for different groups – youth clubs, pensioners lunch clubs, singles clubs and so on.

'Typical' groups

So—you may have a lot of contact with other generations, or you may have little. What does it matter? It matters for everyone because when you know very little about the people who belong to a particular group, it's easy to draw a 'typical' picture – usually bad – of them. Grannies grumble. Children are noisy nuisances. Even when you know one or two, it's easy to make a special case for them which still allows you to keep your typical picture: 'Mrs G. – she's not like most divorcees, rushing after men . . .' 'He's a good lad . . . you'd hardly think he's still a teenager.' The better you get to know a number of people in a group, the less you will hold on to that group picture. You take each individual as they come, and accept what they are.

Getting older

As people grow up and working life ends, they sometimes feel they no longer have a part in life. More varied arrangements for retiring from work are an economic question. But it costs no money to change your view of the older people in your community. Pensioners don't always want, or enjoy, simple 'senior citizen' parties with balloons and jellies. Getting older may mean less physical activity, or less tolerance of noise and high-spirits. But it also means a wealth of experience, and often lots of time to be shared – if other age-groups will accept the offer.

Being young

Being young is not all fun, even though that's what adults often think childhood ought to be. Under-16s are kept out of many adult places of work and leisure, either by law or by their

parents' preference. They are often denied the chance to take responsibilities for themselves or for others, and are encouraged simply to play.

Yet children are naturally curious about what adults do, and are eager to be around to watch, talk, share in the activity, or simply to show friendship. As a baby your child would watch strangers with intense interest, from the security of your arms. Now, at 3 or 4, he has the mobility and words to go to other people. But he'll still want the security of your presence or approval when he approaches others.

Your child is also bound by the opportunities you provide for contact with other generations. Take James. He's never met his parents' workmates, they have few relatives or acquaintances, and their neighbours and friends are all of the same age. He's currently convinced that all old ladies are witches . . . The different generations can be confusing, as this conversation between Sally (4) and her new neighbour shows:

Sally: My daddy's 32 . . .
Tim: Oh, I'm only 22.
Sally: Is 32 bigger than 22?
Tim: Yes.
Sally: My daddy's older than you are?
Tim: Yes, but I'm not a daddy!
Sally: Are you a grandaddy then?
Tim: No, but I've got a mummy and daddy.
Sally: Mummy and daddy haven't got mummies and daddies . . .

Having people to observe, talk to, trust and admire is important to pre-schoolers. (See *Male and female* in Chapter 4). The more varied these people are, the more experience of life, and of relationships, they gain. And the gains to be had are not theirs alone as you can see in these case-studies.

Bridging the gap

Read through the six case studies below. As you do, consider what benefits the people concerned may gain from contact across the generations. There are no right or wrong answers. We suggest some gains below – but there may be more you wish to add.

Pre-schoolers may gain:

a a wider circle of known and trusted people
b experience of a wider range of life-styles and life-histories
c positive impressions of older people or 'models' to admire
d opportunities for more varied relationships than those of parent/child or child/child

Other people may gain:

a feelings of usefulness
b the affection of children
c freedom through the sharing of responsibility for children
d fresh perceptions of the world – from what they observe and what the children ask

Granny Austin

Granny Austin was lonely and beginning to get depressed by life when the playgroup leader invited her to visit. Now she goes five mornings a week. In the group milk is served continuously, as in a cafe, and Granny Austin's job is to pour the milk and ensure each child has some.

The playgroup is the highlight of her day, a reason for going out even in the wind and rain. She enjoys the children's chatter and cheerfulness – and the times in the local shops when they recognise her and speak or tug at their mother's coats to say 'Look, it's my playgroup grandma!'

Jane

Jane is fifteen. She's currently visiting a nursery class as part of her child development course at school. She's been getting some surprises, as this extract from her observation notes shows: 'I was looking around for something to appeal to two of the boys, and spotted a doll's house and a tub of furniture. Oh! I thought dismally, boys aren't interested in girlish games. But I was completely wrong. With children there is no real difference between boys' and girls' games.'

Shirley and Mrs Betts

Four years ago after Kate was born, Shirley found time on her hands. Through her local Council for Voluntary Social Service she began to visit Mrs Betts, recently widowed at 55 with no family of her own, who lived nearby. Today, Shirley and the children still pop in most afternoons. Kate and Mark ($2\frac{1}{2}$) treat her like an aunty or granny. Mrs Betts sometimes babysits for them.

Rick and Judy

Rick and Judy belong to a small sailing club which has members aged 6 months to 60. Mark, aged 4, sometimes goes in the boat with them. Often he prefers to stay and play in the club's riverside grounds. His parents let him do so, happy in the knowledge there'll always be someone on the bank who's got time for him, or will keep a friendly ear and eye open for him.

Ivor and Jacky

Greengrass Close is mostly occupied by young married couples. Most have children: Ivor and Jacky are unusual in not having a family. They do a lot of gardening and DIY and have become used to curious kids stopping to watch, talk and sometimes help. They like other people's children – and the children seem to like a change from 'families'.

Carol and Kathy

Carol and Kathy were both $2\frac{1}{2}$ when they met at the Mother and Toddler Club and became friends. Their mothers became friends too, often doing things together and taking care of each other's children. Kathy and Carol are both at ease in each other's households. Kathy likes the stories told by Carol's Nan while Carol – who has only a sister – is fascinated by Kathy's older brother.

Comment

Most of the gains, on both sides, do or could, apply to all the case studies. Mrs Betts, Shirley and her children provide an example of them all. If Jane stays long enough at the nursery, as well as gaining fresh perceptions of children she will feel more useful – and very likely to gain the affection of the children. As Mark gets older, his relationship with the other adults at the club is likely to become more than that of being 'minded' – particularly if the common interest in sailing appeals to him too.

Cross-generational contact is often a by product of people getting together, in a neutral meeting place outside the home, to share a common interest. This may be something directly for the benefit of children – for example, Mother and Toddler Clubs or playgroups. Or it may be something basically for the benefit of the adults, which children can nonetheless become involved in – for example the sailing club or a rambling club.

Sometimes contact is more deliberately set up – the playgroup leader inviting Granny Austin, Shirley offering to visit Mrs Betts, Jane choosing to do a nursery study. And sometimes, as with Ivor and Jacky, it just happens. Whichever way it comes about it can do no harm – and perhaps a lot of good.

Opportunities for

The need for play provision does not end once
a child starts school but continues and changes
as he grows older. Yet play opportunities for
older children are often inadequate and inappropriate.

What the children say . . .

Tom:

'Where I live there is hardly anywhere to play. We used to have a field to play in but now they are building an estate there and the other field's taken up with sheep, horses, cows, etc. If we do play there the farmer tells us off. When we play in the streets people say we are making too much noise.'

Jerry:

'I live on an estate. I am 11 years old. We have a road in front and a by-pass behind us. There is a field and now they are talking about fencing it off, we will have nowhere to play.'

Babs:

'I live in an area which contains a great number of children of all ages. I'm in the middle stage, just coming into my teens, but I still need a safe enjoyable place where I can run around and have laughs without grumpy grown-ups coming and telling you to 'clear off' or 'get up your own end'. We did have two nice grassy fields where grown-ups didn't come, or cars, but now the builders have settled there and are turfing up our play area both sides.'

Gordon:

'I used to play in a field at the bottom of my garden where everyone used to put their rubbish. We played for hours on end without being disturbed but now they are building houses on it and last year they said the foundations were not safe but now they say they are and they are spending a lot of money to make it safe to build on. I know people have to have houses to live in but the way in which they are having to build the houses it won't be very nice to live there. So all they are doing is filling houses with more children who will have nowhere to play.'

Jean:

'Where I live there is a small square of grass to play on, but the lady who lives in front of this makes us go away.'

Denise:

'We live in a maisonette on the second floor we have nowhere to play, the play centre is quite a long way from where we live and we are too young to go by ourselves.'

Adrian:

'My little brother and my big sister have nowhere to play. We used to go to the park across the road but now we can't as the men are digging it up to build houses and it is all muddy so we are not allowed and we can't go to the woods as Dad and Aunt May get too worried about us. We need a place where we can play as we get too fed up in the house all the time.'

What the papers say . . .

'Disaster start for holiday children...

Within days of the start of the school holidays, children's wards at hospitals are almost full. Hundreds of stay-at-home children looking for adventure in suburban gardens, derelict buildings and in busy roads are ending up in hospitals.'

'On wrong lines . . .

Children playing 'legs 11' or 'chicken' on railway lines are frightening the living daylights out of train drivers . . . In 'legs 11' a child hangs from a bridge over the line and swings his legs up at the last second as an express train goes underneath. In 'chicken' children vie with each other to see who is last across the line in front of an express.'

'In a spin...

Police are investigating reports that children are risking death by playing inside spin driers at launderettes . . . ten year olds were having competitions to see who could go round the most number of times.'

'Safety-lock plan to keep tower children off roof . . .

Housing chiefs are planning safety moves to stop children hanging over the edge of a 12-storey block of flats.'

'Caught! The vandal culprits aged 3 to 6...

Wreckers aged from three to six are blamed for vandalism on a council housing estate. The tear-away toddlers, some still at nursery school, have cost Chiltern District Council thousands of pounds in damage to car parks, garages and other property . . . There are more than 140 kids on the estate just running amok because they have nowhere to play.'

'Deadly game

Youngsters are playing a deadly new game – railway roulette. The aim is to jump on and off live railway lines without being electrocuted.'

'New play area plea after boys fall 15 ft . . .

Mothers demanded playground improvements for their children today after two playmates plunged 15ft to the bottom of an excavation.'

'Play time peril . . .

Police warned of play-time perils today after a spate of incidents in which children have been hurt in roof-top falls. Children are playing new danger games to relieve holiday boredom in the city's redevelopment areas.'

Facts and figures

Did you know . . ?

● That vandalism in England and Wales costs the community tens of millions of pounds a year . . . and the situation is getting worse.

● That deliberate fires, mostly caused by children, cost the nation an estimated £25,000,000 a year.

● That 1,000 children are killed on the roads each year and another 50,000 require hospital treatment following road accidents.

● That an area the size of the Isle of Wight disappears under concrete every year in this country.

older children

What sort of play?

Children need appropriately designed supervised playspaces where they can run and jump, climb, indulge in fantasy play, use their imaginations, test their courage and challenge both themselves and others, where they can socialise with other children. Where good play facilities do not exist, children may take risks or be exposed to dangers, when looking for such opportunities elsewhere.

The table below illustrates four different kinds of play facilities. For each one enter in the columns what opportunities you think are provided for children.

	What sort of opportunities are offered by the facility provided?			
	Danger/challenge experience within acceptable safeguards	Physical activity climbing, experimenting self-testing	Imitation and fantasy	Imagination curiosity and enquiry
Playing field				
Traditional unsupervised playground				
Architectural playground				
Adventure playground				

Now that you've tried the activity, perhaps you can see why streets, building sites, derelict houses, even railway lines provide fierce competition with so many of the common playgrounds for the explorative energies of your children. Streets have colour, movement, light, shade, people and danger; building sites have the basic materials for creative and imaginative play — bricks, timber, sand, gravel, soil mounds, scaffolding, empty and half-finished houses. Such opportunities for a wide variety of play experiences contrast sharply with playgrounds that contain only equipment with obvious and limited functions, or those which are architecturally contrived. Most of the time children are given what adults think they ought to have instead of what they need. Development has been seen too narrowly, in physical terms only, excluding intellectual, emotional and social considerations.

In planning playgrounds that are to be relevant to children's needs the basic activities of play must be catered for. If they are then the cost involved will always be justified. Imaginatively designed playspaces and supervised playgrounds can do much to remove the frustrations and insecurity of childhood. They will encourage satisfying experiences in a secure environment.

Opportunities for older children

Where to play?

Children play anywhere. Yet increasingly when they move away from the confines of home and garden, children are confronted by an X certificate world of restrictions where walking on the grass and ball games are censored. The 'do not' notices introduce a child to 'them' – people he does not know or see, but who restrain his freedom.

The children's letters at the start of this topic provide ample evidence that the 'go out and play' attitude of many adults reveals a lack of understanding that there's often just nowhere to go.

Why is play provision, though slowly improving, still far from meeting the real needs of children? Many reasons are given.

There is firstly a conflict between children and adults, a conflict which often takes the form of complaints about children making too much noise. This nuisance is closely related to the second most common difficulty – that of obtaining suitable sites. The proper location of play areas requires a balance between the privacy of adult residents and freedom from interference for the child. Rocketing land prices and decreasing availability of funds make it difficult to justify financially the use of land for play-

space. Vandalism to playgrounds makes them undesirable, though how much of this is due to the limited scope for play provided? Older children tend to congregate on playgrounds provided and designed for the lower age groups – does this point to the fact that facilities for the older age group are also inadequate or nonexistent?

Again, our local authority system is organised in such a way that it's very unclear who has overall responsibility for ensuring adequate play provision. A whole number of departments – planning, education, social services, recreation, housing – have powers and responsibilities for creating and maintaining playspace, for developing play facilities and opportunities. So any lack of co-ordination and communication results in little action being taken.

Added to all these reasons is the fact that many people still regard play as something children do when they have nothing better to do – a frivolous means of passing time. As long as people think this way those who make the plans and decide how to spend our money are unlikely to give play a higher priority than it has now or had in the past.

Building sites have all the basic materials for imaginative, creative and adventurous play.

How far does your neighbourhood meet children's play needs?

Apart from a secure and happy home children need good, sensible and varied play facilities within easy child-walking reach (not more than ¼ mile) from the home for the fives and upwards.

To find this you can either work alone or join with others living near you who are interested in children's play facilities.

The area

It is suggested you take an area of roughly ¼ mile (400 metres) from you own home or street. Treat the activity as a fact-finding exercise.

What you need

A map of your area. If you do not own one, your local library may have a large scale Ordnance Survey or other map covering your area. In this case you could trace your immediate neighbourhood from the map.

Make a sketch

Now try enlarging the map you have drawn onto a large piece of paper. Mount the sheet on a piece of hardboard with a clip.

● With your house (or street) in the centre of the paper rough out a ¼ mile circle taking up the whole area of the paper, so that it looks like the map on the page opposite.

● Now sketch in the streets, roads and footpaths copied from your original map. Try to measure lengths of streets to scale, so your map is in correct proportion.

● When you have done this, walk round the area and mark on your map using different colours and/or different letters for each feature, the following:
(a) open spaces
(b) parks
(c) community centres
(d) playgrounds with usual swings and play equipment
(e) pre-school playgroups, playschools, nursery school
(f) adventure playgrounds
(g) other playspace (if any)
(h) recreation centres
(i) youth clubs
(j) holiday play centres

● Now also mark in, in dotted lines, the route to walk from your home/street to each feature. Show clearly where these routes cross major or minor roads. Generally you can say a road is a major one if it is a bus or lorry route or carries a heavy volume of traffic.

Collecting information

If you have a group of three or four people so much the better. Each can work on a particular play or recreation feature.

● Arrange visits at different times of the day over a period of at least a week to each play facility you have marked on your map and make a note of the following:

(a) the place and date of visit
(b) the kind of equipment provided
(c) whether the condition of the equipment is (i) good (ii) poor (iii) dangerous (including the ground surface)
(d) whether the surface is soft (grass, sand, earth) or hard (gravel, tarmac, concrete, etc.)
(e) whether well-maintained or not
(f) whether any children are using it
(g) if so, rough ages of children
(h) the number of children
(i) the most popular piece of equipment
(j) distance from your home/street.

The greater the number of visits you are able to make to the same place, the more information you will have about its use by children. Bear in mind that your findings may depend on the time of year. Think about possible seasonal variations.

Other parents

● Try to find out the attitudes of some other parents in the neighbourhood to children playing in the street.

What are the attitudes of these parents regarding the adequacy of provision of existing play facilities near you?

The danger areas

On your map you can now draw in the following potential sources of danger for young children. These may be:
(a) canals, gravel pits
(b) railway lines (note if they are well-fenced or easily accessible)
(c) busy roads and bus/lorry routes

(d) car parks
(e) rubbish dumps
(f) derelict houses, buildings
(g) unprotected building sites
(h) others
● Now visit each of the dangers you have marked in and note:
(a) the number of children playing there
(b) their rough ages
(c) possible risks, for example children running on busy road from behind parked cars or lorries
(d) distance from home
● Observe and note areas where children tend to play such as:
(a) shopping areas
(b) car parks of public houses
(c) others (see *Safety outside the home* in Chapter 5).

Taking action

By doing this activity, you will be better informed about provision of play facilities for children in your neighbourhood. You will perhaps find how necessary it is for parents to become interested and involved in where their young children play.

Finally, you will perhaps have realised that for a variety of reasons many children lack the opportunity to play freely and safely. Perhaps you would like to take some action to improve children's play facilities in your area. This needs careful thought and planning and is probably more than one person alone can deal with. By joining with other parents in a Play Action Group or Play Association, you can work more effectively, and gain mutual support. In many areas such groups have developed successful play projects. Several organisations exist to help people do this.

Adventure playgrounds — imaginative play without undue risk

It's important to children to have protected places to play. Adults like their security and their own place of work, and place of leisure. The same is true for children.

An adventure playground is a playspace for children of all ages. Usually, it is enclosed by a wall, fence, or some other barrier, giving children a feeling of security. To many adults, the inside would seem a completely random mess of earth, rope, tyres, concrete tubes, wood and whatever else has been in use. Such play equipment may well be used for any number of imaginative games: making dens, for climbing through, swinging on, sitting on, making things with. And the children inside could be engaged on many other activities: painting, reading, talking, cooking, looking after animals.

Playgrounds of this type will often have a playleader – either a person specially employed for the job, or a local mum or dad, or a group of willing teenagers. Their role is not to direct play, but to support and encourage activities which are taking place. It's important, then, that the playleader is not seen as someone in authority to be obeyed at all costs, but instead as someone who can help if he's needed, and is there just in case.

While there is much in older types of playgrounds to admire – swings and roundabouts are still popular – it is the lack of possibilities for imagination which makes these playgrounds less suited to many of the play needs of children. A swing in a public park, or a see-saw, can serve only one purpose – swinging or see-sawing. A swing in an adventure playground may be a length of rope and an old tyre (the beauty of the equipment is not important). That swing may become the connecting link between a fortress and an Indian camp, or it may be the only bridge over a swirling set of rapids.

Authorities sometimes make mistakes in building playgrounds. They may decide to build an adventure playground which turns out to be no more adventurous than the older type. Here, all the equipment is safely embedded in concrete, so it cannot be moved away. While it may be necessary for large and heavy equipment (for instance, tree trunks and climbing frames) to be safely anchored, the scope for imagination will be lost if there is nothing children can move around and adapt to their own purposes.

Ideally, an adventure playground should be seen by children as their own area, where they may play without unnecessary interference from grown-ups, but are protected from the dangers of unofficial 'adventure playgrounds' such as building sites. Where children themselves have had a part to play in the constructing of the playground and in determining the layout and the activities taking place, the elements of imagination and play can become fused.

MAJOR ROAD

FACTORIES

CANAL

Key:
1 Sports club 4 Swimming pool 7 playgroup 9 Church yard and car park
2 Tennis courts 5 School 8 building sites 10 car park = back alleys
3 Scout hall 6 School and playground

Patterns of childrearing

The patterns in which people live together make up much of the child's world. Parents' jobs, housing, and interests are important, but relationships inside and between families may have an even greater effect on the way children grow up.

Several topics in Chapters 7 and 8 have considered the social development of children. *Playing together*, *Joining in*, *The generation gap* and *Hello stranger* have shown how the three-year-old, using his new fluency in speech and his confidence in independence from his mother may explore new relationships. How wide the circle is of people known to him, and how varied such people are, depends very much on the links that his family has with others.

In different societies, the number and kind of people who form the child's circle varies considerably. On the opposite page, four such societies are represented using the following symbols:

This is the immediate nuclear family, Mum, Dad and me . . . and brothers and sisters too. These are the people that a child feels at home with and knows well, in many moods. For better and for worse, they are part of each other.

These are the people outside the immediate family whom the child knows. They are the 'uncles and aunties', the neighbour who is 'one of the family', the milkman or shopkeeper who greets him, knowing his family and where he lives.

These are the unknown people, the strangers who crowd the pavement. The child sees them, is sometimes interested by them but does not recognise them, neither do they know him. They are unfamiliar, unpredictable and the world outside home is full of them. Some may be kind, but this is something the child is uncertain about and he treats them with reserve.

Think about your own neighbourhood. In the first column of the activity, fill in the spaces with YES ticks, NO crosses or ? for in-between answers such as 'sometimes' or 'perhaps'. Then, as you read the following brief descriptions of the four societies, fill in their columns. Sometimes you will have to use your imagination because the descriptions are so brief. There are few hard and fast, right or wrong answers, but doing the activity helps to pick out some of the differences between the societies, especially how differently crises are dealt with. Finally, compare the answers you gave for your neighbourhood with those for the four societies.

Families in society					
Characteristics of the neighbourhood	Stable society	Mobile society	Shared living	Friendly society	Your neighbourhood
Families know each other well					
Some relatives live near					
Adults know each other from childhood					
Children know what adults do at work					
Little children know: teenagers elderly people babies					
Children feel at home in several houses					
Little children hear old people tell of times past					
People can get away from their past					
Newcomers are treated with reserve					
Adults get to know each other by working together					
Mothers become socially isolated					
Do families have a big problem if . . .					
Family needs a babysitter					
Mother is unwell					
Parents need to leave children overnight					
A child needs guests for a birthday party					
Mother wants to go out for a day					
Both parents go out to work					
They want allies to help in pressing for a playground					

In a stable society

Children grow up among people of all
ages. Many people have grown up,
married and settled among people
they have known all their lives.
The children often join the adults
in work, play and ceremonies of joy and
mourning. From old people, children get an
idea of a time when the present was the
unknown future. The restrictions of a stable
society are felt more by adults than by young
children who have not yet explored the full
limits of their world. Such a society may
impose a rigid social system or fail
to offer work or opportunity.
Newcomers may be treated with
reserve, even suspicion.

In a mobile society

Young people and families move freely
in search of opportunities to work and
live in a way and place of their own choosing.
They are free to develop without restrictions which can
cramp those who remain in a stable society. People have not
known each other long. They are recognised first as
members of a family, or people who live in a certain house,
rather than as the individuals they are. Men are known
as husbands and fathers: their work lies elsewhere
and neighbours may know nothing about it. Earlier events
in people's lives are unknown, for instance
mother's work before having a child.

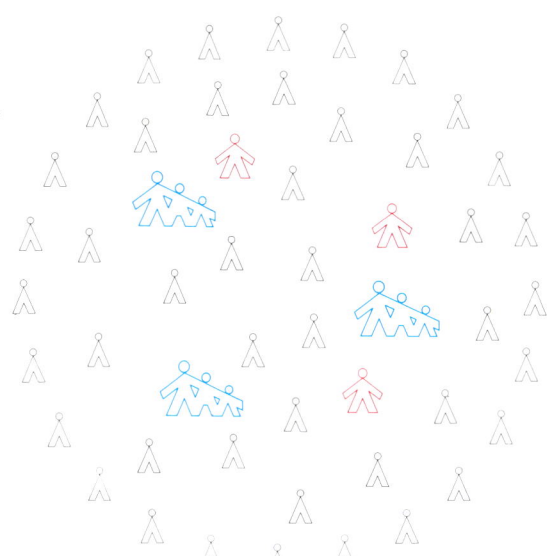

In shared living

Sometimes families choose or need to
live together. There are kinship homes in
which several related families live close together.
Old people and single relatives share the homes. There are
communes with single people and families which are
held together by an accepted bond. This bond may be
a wish to share work, cost of living, or childcare. The
success and stability of the groups depends upon whether
the bond is strong enough to overcome the problems raised
by shared living. The kibbutz in Israel is an extreme type of
commune in which children are cared for in houses for
different age groups, seeing their parents only after
work has finished, and usually returning to their
own houses to sleep.

In a friendly society

Here families, both newcomers and old residents,
are drawn together to use, or provide for their
children, facilities which they could not offer alone.
For pre-schoolers, the facility would be one of the groups that
have been described. If the group is really effective in drawing the
families together, it creates a pattern like that of a stable society so
that several families and other members of the community fall
within the circle of humanity known to children. Groups where
parents share work and responsibility are re-creating a society
in which families are known to each other: parents,
particularly mothers, find friends and help to
support each other in crises.

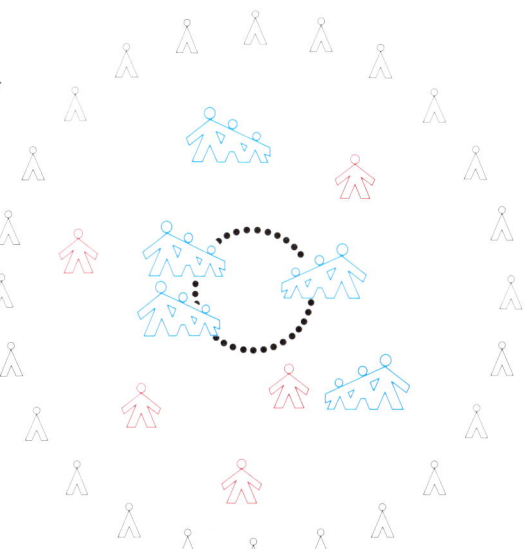

Patterns of childrearing

Problems and changes

In doing the activity, you probably found that families in a stable society knew most about each other, and their children knew many people, including old people from whom they would get a sense of continuity with the past. Children know about their parents' work and mothers are known outside the family.

You probably found that difficulties are coped with more easily and families have more friends in societies in which families are long-settled or drawn together by one bond or another. In a mobile society, incoming families starting a new life often do not have friends among their neighbours. Most have friends and relatives elsewhere who will be part of their children's continuing experience of people. These remote 'known people' have a special importance – a cousin is a cousin for a lifetime – but the fact that they are not seen from day to day lessens the contribution that they can make to children's lives.

Often, newcomers to a stable or a mobile society do not have the reassurance of a network of helpful friends. In this situation the small nuclear family can be unhelpful, even destructive, just because it is so small and so much is expected of it. It can become so isolated and shut in upon itself that it becomes fragile and is easily threatened by quarrels. If children in a family wanting and needing attention, concern, advice and companionship can turn only to their parents, there is inevitably rivalry between children. Matters may be worse if there is only one parent.

Knowing people

Children need to have adult friends, people outside their own family to whom they can go in need and get away from when they feel like it. Such people are available to children when families live together, in, for instance, the kinship home, the commune or the kibbutz. There, children can have relationships with adults which are not as intense as in the isolated families of the mobile society. But there are many problems in maintaining stability in these groupings. Although the kibbutz has been part of Israeli life for three generations, only 4 per cent of the population choose to live this way today. Stable communes are rarer still, and while they may contain children, they seldom have old people who have time and attention to give to children. While many of the problems of caring for children may be lessened in such a grouping, other problems may emerge, such as the difficulty of accepting regulation of day-to-day living that may be even more restrictive than that of the stable society.

Drawing families together

It is possible to make provision for children while doing nothing for the parents, or failing to achieve any drawing together of families in the pattern of the friendly society. A playgroup, nursery class or nursery school may give the child an enriching experience for 10 per cent of his waking hours and give the mother much-needed relief. For families with many friends, this may be all that is needed. But for newcomers, for shy, lonely, isolated mothers, a pre-school group which is an introduction to a wide circle of friends gives much more. They and their children can have many of the benefits of shared living without the enforced intimacy of a commune or the restrictions and inflexibility of a stable society.

Future developments

There are the beginnings of huge changes in society. One development is the creation of a new kind of extended 'family' to be the neighbourly replacement of that which most families lose in moving. This larger 'family' acts as a safety net in a crisis. It gives children a wider experience of adults, homes with different resources, values, interests and customs, and the assurance that there are friendly people outside the immediate family circle.

Other changes are those which allow fathers to share in childcare, especially in families where mothers continue to work. Sometimes shiftwork, flexitime or flexible jobs enable men to take on an equal share. Some are able to help with housework or babysitting. Other men take on all the work of childcare while their wives go out to work. The increase in leisure time in the future could make this sort of flexibility much more possible.

Such changes give children the chance to experience many different kinds of relationships with adults, and to see the different ways families allocate work and responsibilities. Children grow up confident in their ability to make friends outside the family. They gain an understanding of and tolerance for a variety of life-styles and relationships.

Taking stock

Life has its ups and downs for everyone. It is easy to feel overwhelmed when demands crowd in. Often it helps to pause and take stock. Most of this course has been about children – about how they learn, think and feel, how they come to terms with the world. What about the experience of becoming a parent?

Adapting to the first child

Before your first child was born, you had probably imagined what life was going to be like. Some people base their ideals on the 'cereal packet' family, smart, well-dressed, lively people, always smiling and happy. They may feel the need to live up to the well-run homes and lives depicted in advertisements. Most people can anticipate the housekeeping side of life clearly enough. What is more difficult is knowing how they would feel about living with a baby and young child.

Both parents have to adapt to greater responsibilities, more work, less money, disturbed nights (initially at least!), and the realisation that they have always to consider and care for another person. Both have to accept that for some years they will have less time for each other. It's important that each should think about how the other feels about life.

Mother's view

A mother, weighed down by chores and children, may sometimes think of her husband as having an easy, interesting time at work. She may resent:

- a loss of identity as an independent person;
- a feeling of inadequacy in her new role;
- loss of the companionship of others;
- not having any money of her own;
- being on call continually for a 24-hour day, seven days a week with no off-duty time;
- a sense of being tied for the indefinite future;

but she may also gain:

- freedom from the clock;
- freedom to choose which job to do first;
- freedom to vary the days;
- freedom to enjoy the children.

Father's view

A father, suffering from pressure or boredom at work, may imagine his wife enjoying leisure and interests at home. He may resent:

- alienation from his wife, who becomes preoccupied with the baby;
- a sense of being trapped by the new responsibilities;
- loss of his wife's company if he wants an evening out;
- difficulties in responding to his wife's tiredness or depression;
- a sense of panic and helplessness when he has to care for the baby;

but he may also:

- enjoy caring for and playing with the baby;
- share work with his wife and through that maintain and deepen their relationship;
- be able to help his wife if she's tired or depressed;
- find new friends and interests through meeting other parents;
- feel pride in being a father.

Taking stock

Encountering change

In any major change of way of life, adjustment can be seen as going through three stages. First, the initial shock of the change in which the snags and disadvantages, delights and pleasures of the new life are encountered for the first time.

Adjustment

After the encounter comes a period of adjustment. Life begins to settle down to a new routine in which people begin to realise the full extent of the change that has come over them.

Breakthrough

For most people, the stage of adjustment is followed by breakthrough in which they have come to terms with their new life, accepting that some past pleasures are not part of it but there are compensations.

Here are two accounts by women who have reached the breakthrough stage in learning to live with their children. As you read them, pick out the three stages of encounter, adjustment and breakthrough:

Diane: 'I loved the work I was doing. The last thing I wanted was to marry and stay at home, but, to my surprise, I got married and became pregnant. I was at the time looking forward to a new job and the impending baby scarcely affected my absorption with detailed plans for future work. I didn't go to antenatal classes or meet other pregnant women. When I did think of the baby it was as a small bundle which I would deposit at the crèche which was about to be set up at work. I would collect him in the evening and put him in his cot for the night. When he arrived, the first surprise was that he wasn't a bundle but a tiny person. When I looked at his intent face and his unfocusing eyes, I was unexpectedly aware of his individuality, of the man he would one day become.

The crèche did not materialise. I finally realised that no decision was involved. It was simply impossible for me to return to work.

This realisation did not leave me calm, happy, and magically transformed into a homey mum. I enjoyed caring for the baby, but I found housework tedious and irritating. I missed the interest of work, and the companionship. I'm afraid I found the company of other mothers a poor substitute. Three years later things have reached a comfortable equilibrium. I have finally begun to grasp how to organise the housework so that I am able to keep what I hope is a reasonably inviting and pleasant home. The strange thing is, things seem to have reversed themselves. While I was at work I was plagued by friends urging me to domesticity. These days, everyone I meet seems to ask when I am returning to work. And I must admit I am beginning to enjoy being at home, doing little odd jobs as they turn up and not having to live strictly according to the clock. But now it is I who feels guilty as I enjoy my unremunerative hours.'

Penny: 'I'd been working in a large town school for several years. Two months before Laura was born, I stopped working. It was a Friday, and on Saturday we moved from a flat in the town to a nice little cottage. Then, two weeks before she was born, we moved to an isolated cottage where we lived for a year. I did get very depressed. It wasn't the baby blues, it was just isolation. Laura was a good contented baby but I'd gone from living in a busy place and a busy job to living in an isolated place, not knowing a soul, never seeing anybody all day from eight in the morning to seven at night. I got very low. I reasoned out that it was the solitude rather than the baby alone. A baby's all right if you have other company as well, but the cottage was a long way from the village.

I had the idea that it would be nice to have a place where I could go with Laura and meet other mothers with young children, because there were several in the village. But it was very difficult to arrange because most of the others had cars and would go to the next town with their children. As I was the only one without a car, I was an outsider and found it impossible to do anything.

When I came to a bigger village, there were two or three other people interested in getting together with their young children and it was easier to arrange. The toddler group started two years ago when Laura was about eight months old and she's been going ever since. It took a lot of organising, though, getting the toys together and working it all out. We started a darts team and had netball and rounders matches.

Laura has learnt to mix well with children but I think the group has benefited the mothers more than the children! I think children are pretty adaptable, it's the mothers that aren't adaptable really.'

Different solutions

The two accounts are those of young, housebound mothers, for whom social isolation was the chief problem. It is one shared, though, by many single parents, whether mothers or fathers.

Others have different problems and different solutions. Many mothers manage, for instance, to work, or to maintain or develop other interests, while looking after the baby. Some fathers let their wives take on all housework and childcare, and may leave them at home in the evening to go out to the pub. Others find they enjoy caring for their child, and arrange to share work and play with their wives.

For some parents, however, adjustment may take a very long time, and stresses on the marriage and on the relationship with the baby may become intolerable, ending in breakdown rather than breakthrough. Some of the stresses, and where to get help, are described in *What sort of parent would harm their child?* in Chapter 6.

Contact with other parents can help towards a solution, not just by reducing social isolation, or by sharing problems and the care of each others' children. Perhaps one of the most important side effects of the contact is to see how other couples adjust, and to realise that there is no *one* solution to problems, even common ones – each couple has to reach their own.

Crying over spilt milk

Just carry out this check to see how much the reaction is caused by the parent's morale rather than by events themselves. There are many ways of reacting to each of the events listed, but three were chosen to illustrate the stages of adjustment. Think which might be the most likely reaction of Diane, Penny or yourself at each of the three stages. Put the letter corresponding to the probable reaction in the appropriate column. If you are a father, some of the events may seem more appropriate to mothers – try to use your imagination!

In these different stages, reactions to the same occurrence would vary considerably.

1 encounter;
2 adjustment;
3 breakthrough.

Stage	Diane 1 2 3	Penny 1 2 3	You 1 2 3
● The milk was spilt at teatime so there would be none for breakfast. Would she/you: (a) burst into tears or swear? (b) clear up the mess with a sigh or a groan? (c) laugh, recognising that nothing could be done about it.	☐ ☐ ☐	☐ ☐ ☐	☐ ☐ ☐
● She/you dropped and broke a wedding present teapot, a useful rather than beautiful one. Would she/you: (a) burst into tears or swear? (b) pick up the pieces but still feel shocked? (c) think 'Now when I have the money, I can buy one that I really like?'	☐ ☐ ☐	☐ ☐ ☐	☐ ☐ ☐
● The baby, alone with she/you in the car in difficult traffic, is suddenly drastically sick. Would she/you: (a) panic and stall the car? (b) attempt to clean up the baby with one hand and to drive (not very well!) with the other? (c) stay calm, find somewhere to park temporarily, and clean up the mess?	☐ ☐ ☐	☐ ☐ ☐	☐ ☐ ☐
● She/you cooked a new dish and it turned out really well. Husband/wife eats it without comment. Would she/you: (a) get cross? (b) eat without remarking on the silence? (c) ask what he/she thought of it?	☐ ☐ ☐	☐ ☐ ☐	☐ ☐ ☐
● She/you returns late, just before guests are expected. The table is only half-laid, children's toys are lying about, a child is crying and there's a smell of burning coming from the kitchen. Would she/you: (a) become angry or tearful? (b) rush about attempting (but failing) to get things under control? (c) deal with the crying child, burning food, litter of toys . . . and smile, even if the guests walk in while you're doing it?	☐ ☐ ☐	☐ ☐ ☐	☐ ☐ ☐

You probably found that there are mostly 'a's and 'b's for the two stages when the parents were adapting themselves to their new situations. You probably found more happy, confident, straightforward 'c's in stage 3 when they had completed the adjustment to the new kind of life. Those still in the first two stages may be helped by confidence in the fact that life will change.

It would also be good to realise what a difference it makes to new parents if someone realises the difficulties that they are passing through and is able to make some friendly gesture or give some practical help at the first and second stage. It is not enough just to be available, though that is better than nothing: a positive action would help much more.

Feeling good

It is interesting, sometimes, to think about the things that make life really worth living. You've probably found that what you enjoy changes as your life does. Take your adult life, for instance . . .

When you were on your own, probably working, free to make your own plans and to change them. When you shared life with another adult each with the other's needs to take into account, and adjust to.

With your first child, life becomes very different. It changes a little with later children but not so much as it did when the first was born.

What's been good?

Here is an activity for a time when the mind is leisured. Its purpose is to help you see how changes in your life have altered what things you enjoy, and how you enjoy them.

Think of those things you remember as particular pleasures in your life so far. They could be special events – a once-in-a-life-time experience; or regular happenings – a nice Saturday job or an evening class; or special treats of one kind or another, like going to a film or the theatre, or going away for the weekend. Put these in a list.

Then think out *three* things that you liked about these pleasures – for example, perhaps you enjoyed dancing because you went out, met people and enjoyed moving to music. Your experience may overlap with that of three parents who listed what they liked about remembered pleasures. These have been grouped under six different headings. Do you share some of these? Have you more to add?

Using the chart

On the chart, pick out any pleasures that you shared with the people who made the list, add your own and tick the 'When enjoyed' columns. Then under the six headings put your three ticks for what you liked about these pleasures, just what it was about them that made you feel good.

Having sorted out what's nice about the things you enjoy, add up the ticks in each column. The pattern of ticks will be different for everyone.

Perhaps you will find, if life is low, that by thinking back like this you may remember things you used to do that gave you a lift. Or you may realise which of today's pleasures will not be there in a few years time. Life will be changing again as your children get older. Some present pleasures will be as impossible then, as some of your old pleasures are not possible now. Perhaps these are the things that should be taking up a bit more time.

Still feeling low?

Should everyone expect to be happy all the time? Are, for instance, your children happy all the time? Hardly! Having to do things they don't want to do, not getting things they wanted, feeling tired, hungry and being bad-tempered . . . all these take the sunshine out of their living.

If the standards of childhood are applied to adult life it might be possible to learn something about how to adapt and how to accept the limitations of any stage of life. Living with children can teach parents a lot about themselves.

What's good about . . .

1 Being with adults: talking, laughing; working in a team; meeting new people; sharing an interest.

2 Being with children: seeing their pleasure and enjoyment; watching their faces; seeing them proud of doing something new; feeling them relax; feeling the grip of an anxious hand; getting the warm smell of their bodies.

3 Pleasures of the body: being active, relaxing, feeling the sun, wind, and rain, breathing fresh air, hearing and making music, feeling refreshed after sleep, seeing beautiful things, tasting good food, making love.

4 Pleasures of the mind: learning something new, stimulating the mind, finding out about myself, feeling useful, reading a difficult book, playing chess.

5 Enjoying the results: finishing something, earning money, getting satisfaction from being creative, making a change, achieving something difficult.

6 Getting away from it all: escaping in the mind, driving a fast car, going out, doing something new and challenging, getting drunk.

Pleasure	When enjoyed?			What's nice about it?					
	👤	👥	👨‍👩‍👧	Being with adults	Being with children	Pleasures of the body	Pleasures of the mind	Enjoying the results	Getting away from it all
Dancing	✓	✓		✓		✓			✓
Dressmaking									
Visiting art galleries and museums									
Belonging to a dramatic society									
Visiting the pub									
Visiting friends									
Making love									
Gardening									
Badminton									
Tidying a room									
Visiting community play facilities									
Walking in the country									
Going out for a meal									
Being alone sometimes									
Getting home									
Swimming regularly									
Playing at home with the children									
Going on an exploring bus ride									
Decorating									
Watching children									
Reading books									
Carpentry									
Eating a meal on your own									
Picnics									
Being at home in the summer									
Having nothing to do for a day									
Add others of your own...									
Number of ticks									

The changing parent

Two-year-old

The job of being a parent changes as children grow older. The concerns you had for your two-year-old are not the same as those you will have for your five-year-old or eight-year-old. Children change and parents change too but are these changes always in step? How do parents view themselves and what do children think of their parents?

The job of a parent

The job of a parent is to provide a sufficient range of opportunities for the child's developing abilities, while keeping the opportunities within limits that the child can cope with and that are acceptable to the parent. It's no good saying to a child he can do anything he likes, because he cannot cope with total freedom and because some of the things he comes up with may be unacceptable – for instance they may be dangerous or impolite. On the other hand the child may feel his parents are being unnecessarily restrictive and parents may feel that their child goes outside acceptable limits too often.

Of course, parents' standards change as the child changes. The question is – do they keep pace with the child's developing abilities, lag behind or run ahead? If parents lag behind the child will feel that even though they offer him more freedom they are always restricting him more than he feels is necessary. If parents' expectations run ahead of the child's abilities, if they expect him to do things he cannot or to handle freedoms he is not ready for, he will feel insecure and they are likely to be continuously disappointed.

Parents must keep pace with their child's changes, not holding him back and not expecting too much of him before he is ready.

Children's developing abilities

In their early years children are dependent on us. The food we give them and the love, care and opportunities we provide affect the way they grow. By the time they are five they are expected to be independent enough to face the challenging world of school.

During this time they develop a number of abilities. While this is usually a delight to parents, it may also raise concerns for them.

Parents may become concerned about the child's use of language – for example, using slang or swear-words. Children's increasing physical ability may cause concern about the dangers of bicycles, getting into forbidden places or opening cupboards. Emotional maturity may relieve parents of babyish crying but demands greater sensitivity from them. Wider social interests mean that children come into contact with ideas and influences other than those of the home. Not all of these may be to the parents' liking. Children's increasing ability to reason and choose can lead to challenges to parents' authority.

Some of these concerns may arise because a child begins doing something he hasn't been able to do before – for example, riding his bike outside. Others may arise because parents decide that behaviour that was acceptable for a two-year-old is not acceptable in the case of a five-year-old – for example, crying when told off.

Parents' concerns

As the child's abilities develop your concerns change. Some of these concerns may be positive – for instance, whether to let your child stay away overnight – or negative – for instance, stopping him from running into the road. By anticipating what might become concerns it may be possible to avoid over-hasty and negative reactions.

Which of the items on the list over page are likely to be the concerns of parents of a child of (1) age two, (2) age five, (3) age eight years? (You can tick more than one column if you wish).

These concerns have been placed roughly in order. The first concerns could apply mostly to two-year-olds, next five-year-olds and finally eight-year-olds. Every family will have a unique set of concerns that will change as the child gets older. The extent that any of the items in the checklist become serious concerns or are simply matters that parents deal with as they arise depends on a number of things. One of them has been mentioned already – that of keeping pace with the child's development. But different circumstances may make a particular item become a concern. For example, bedtimes and settling down times may not matter for a four-year-old but if a five-year-old stays up late regularly he may be tired at school. For other items, parents' standards will be important. We wouldn't expect a two-year-old to keep his room tidy, but we might encourage a five-year-old to, and if an eight-year-old refused to keep his room reasonably tidy we might get concerned.

Going to school can give rise to different concerns

Parents' Concerns	Age of child		
	2 yrs	5 yrs	8 yrs
Food fads	☐	☐	☐
Drawing on sitting room wall	☐	☐	☐
Running into road	☐	☐	☐
Waking early	☐	☐	☐
Temper tantrums	☐	☐	☐
Starting to play with other children	☐	☐	☐
Being 'dry' at night	☐	☐	☐
Politeness to visitors	☐	☐	☐
Helping round the house	☐	☐	☐
Bedtimes and settling down times	☐	☐	☐
Going off to play on their own	☐	☐	☐
Stay away overnight with grandparents on their own	☐	☐	☐
Watching certain TV programmes	☐	☐	☐
Riding bicycles outside	☐	☐	☐
Listening to child reading	☐	☐	☐
Playing one parent off against the other	☐	☐	☐
Child's need for privacy	☐	☐	☐
Handling money and making simple purchases	☐	☐	☐
Going on package holiday with parents	☐	☐	☐
Taking child to pantomime	☐	☐	☐
Child receiving punishment from others	☐	☐	☐
Undesirable friends		☐	☐
Criticising parents		☐	☐
Table manners		☐	☐
Obeying rules		☐	☐
Going away to camp		☐	☐
Dishonesty, lying		☐	☐
Receiving regular pocket money		☐	☐
Joining Cubs or Brownies		☐	☐
Keeping room tidy		☐	☐
Progress at school		☐	☐
Ignoring parents' advice		☐	☐
Unwilling to accept parents' authority		☐	☐
Child realising that parents don't know everything	☐	☐	☐
Stealing		☐	☐
Vandalism	☐	☐	☐
Masturbation	☐	☐	☐
Swearing	☐	☐	☐
Others (write in)	☐	☐	☐

Five-year-old

Parents' views of themselves

You learnt a lot about being a parent from your parents. Their influence affects how you behave as a parent, but does not necessarily make you simply do as they did. It could well go the other way so that you avoid doing what your parents did because you didn't like it and don't wish to impose it on your children. Or, now that times and circumstances have changed, you may be able to provide opportunities for your children that your parents could not for theirs.

Your views about being a parent are obviously important in determining the pace at which you are prepared to adapt to your child's changing abilities. You may believe that parents should act to restrain children so that there will be more occasions for them to learn what the limits to acceptable behaviour are. On the other hand, you may feel that children learn acceptable behaviour by being given a wide range of acceptable things that they can do.

Your knowledge and sensitivity are important too. If you know how your child is developing you can create opportunities for him before he demands them. You will be able to judge what your child can do and what opportunities he needs.

Your child will influence your view of yourself as a parent. If you find that many of the concerns become serious you will tend to see parenthood as a constant battle. If you are able to anticipate your child's needs and adapt to his changing abilities you may view parenthood as a rewarding and challenging experience.

A child's love and trust will help parents see themselves as lovable and trustworthy. Being loving and trusting involves respecting the child's developing abilities and need for independence. A parent who starts out wanting to be loved and trusted but who is not able to adapt to a child's changing needs may end up failing. A child who learns that telling the truth is likely to lead to punishment will probably tell lies. The parents will then have to face the fact that they have brought up a child to behave dishonestly. If a child is frightened of a parent, then this knowledge will affect the parents' view of himself.

Eight-year-old

Children's views of parents

As well as reviewing how you deal with the concerns you have, you can always discuss these with your child and ask him what he thinks. The questions you ask will depend on the age of the child. Many of his answers will show the the child's strength of feeling about what he thinks he should be allowed to do and what restraints you place on his activities. Usually he will accept them, but as he gets older he may feel differently.

During the pre-school years children tend to have an uncritical adoration for their parents – they think they know everything and can do no wrong. Only rarely do they think that parents make unreasonable demands or place unfair limits on them. But children need to feel that someone cares enough to keep what they do within limits. Children are not happy if they are allowed to behave unreasonably – and neither are parents. Imposing limits and controlling children may provoke resentment, but not doing so leads to children feeling guilty and scared.

The crucial question which must be asked continually is 'What does my child consider unreasonable and unfair?' The answer changes constantly as the child develops. A child who thinks that his parents are always imposing unfair limits will lose confidence in his parents and believe that they don't understand his needs or appreciate his abilities. But never having limits (or having very vague ones) will make the child feel insecure and that his parents do not care about what he does or about him.

As the child gets older he comes more into contact with standards outside the home. He hears about the limits placed on other children, and people other than his parents place limits on him. Parents hear that 'Johnny is allowed to watch a late TV show', or that 'Mrs Brown lets me slide down her banisters'. This provides him with a wider view to criticise his parents' standards and undermines his belief that they are always right. His growing knowledge of the world also supports his realisation that his parents are fallible. Parents must accept this but continue to provide reasonable limits within which their child can learn to act responsibly.

Looking to the future

Bringing up children is one of the most important things we do in life. How we go about it affects not only the future of the children concerned but also the future of our community as a whole.

Different starting points

The book as a whole is concerned with how parents can provide opportunities for their children to learn about the world. But all families have different starting points in terms of the experiences and opportunities they can offer to their children.

They also have different values. The way we see the situations of other families may be very different from the way they see themselves.

Five families

Here are five family situations. For each one try and answer the following questions:

1 What are the problems the family is facing, if any?

2 What effects, if any, is their situation having on the child(ren)?

3 What changes in circumstances are needed, if any, and why?

Joan and Martin live in a one-bedroomed flat, with no garden, over a sweet-shop. They have one child, Joanna, who is three. Martin works nights in a local bakery and Joan works full-time in a local boutique. They are saving hard to buy a home of their own in a different area, so don't go out much or know many people. Joanna is looked after by her grandmother for two days in the week, spends two days with her mother in the shop and the other days Martin is at home with her.

Do you think Joan and Martin are facing difficulties? Do you think Joanna is missing out on anything? *If* Joanna gets on well with her grandmother, *if* Martin enjoys having time to be with his daughter, and *if* she gets involved in the life of the shop and isn't told to go away and play, then she probably has a secure and stimulating life. Many families struggle to achieve a better standard of living. The children don't necessarily suffer because of it.

Shoonagh is the only child of a couple who own a business and are working hard to expand it. Her mother spends some time with her at the beginning and end of each day, but Shoonagh spends most of her time with a succession of mother's helps. Her own room in the flat, full of toys and books, is the only place she's allowed to play in and make a mess, and the extent of the mess depends on the attitude of the current mother's help. Occasionally she's taken to the park nearby where she meets other children.

Because Shoonagh is not invited to participate much in the lives of the people around her, she's likely to invent an imaginary world of her own, with fantasy companions and events. She may be shy and lacking in confidence when she does meet other children and adults. She has little chance to test herself out and learn about people's reactions to her, and her own capabilities with people. On the other hand, she's learnt how to rely on her own resources – but is too much independence expected of her? She may find school a frightening and over-demanding place, but it may be her first chance to make friends (and enemies!) and find out how to work and play with others.

Maureen and George live in a two-bedroomed flat on the twelfth floor of a large block. They have three children aged two, three and seven. George has been out of work for 18 months and is one of a large number of unemployed in his area. He spends most of his time sleeping or goes out. Maureen works three nights a week in a local pub just to get out of the house. The eldest child, Brian, often misses school, to be found in the park or roaming the streets. He's not interested in his younger sisters, who get on quite well together, though this may not always be evident. Maureen and George don't speak to each other much nor does the family do things together.

Maureen and George have a lot going against them – no work, no money, little self-respect which is all too easily communicated to the children. You might see them as a clear case where help from outside is needed for both parents and children. But do the problems seem beyond their own control? A job for George, a secure financial future, could change the parents' relationship and the family's pattern of life. But if things stay as they are, does anyone have the right to interfere? How do you think Maureen and George (and the children) would react to a social worker knocking at the door?

Kate is a single parent with a lively daughter of two called Polly. They live in a small bedsit which is part of a multi-occupied house. She shares a kitchen and bathroom with the rest of the household. Kate is looking for a job as she feels that more money would help to improve both her and Polly's life. She also wants the added interest of work so she can meet new people. At the moment she feels stifled by the 'mother and baby' talk which surrounds her.

Davy's father left home before he was born. His mum has a number of men friends who call, some of whom Davy gets on with OK, others of whom he doesn't like very much. At five years old he has a lot of freedom to play in the streets, do what he wants, play with other children in their homes and his. Some days he's well-fed and cared for; other days he's half-forgotten and has to fend for himself. Both he and his mum have fierce tempers which can create scenes from time to time.

When discussing such family situations we bring to bear our own experiences, prejudices, our own standards for how things should be done or could be better. How much did you find yourself focusing on the needs of the children as opposed to the needs of the family as a whole?

It could be easy for someone like Kate to feel that she's not being treated fairly by society – it's difficult to find suitable accommodation or decent childcare facilities. Are her and her daughter's lives hampered because Kate hasn't conformed to the accepted family structure of society? Is she responsible for the situation she finds herself in? Kate feels she could offer Polly a lot more if they could move and she could find work. What do you think?

Who knows what effect Davy's life is having on him. He seems happy enough now. But he's only a child. What sort of adult will he be? Davy's mother may think that neither she nor Davy have any problems or she may be depressed and unhappy about her lifestyle but doesn't know what or can't find the energy to do anything about it. What's Davy learning about life – that it's confusing, that you can never be sure about anything, that he's his own master, that if you want anything you have to get it for yourself? Quite harsh lessons for a five-year-old. What would you do about it? Do you think Davy's mum or even Davy would approve?

As long as he's happy!

Ask a number of parents what they want for their children and you will probably end up with a list like the one in the table.

In the first column tick the statements you agree with.

Then get three other parents to fill in the other columns – not just those with children of the same age as yours; grandparents too, *your* parents.

How do your ticks compare? What were/are their hopes for their children? Are there a number that you all share? Are there some that conflict with others? Because of the demands of everyday family life it's easy to forget that everywhere many other people share the same struggles and the same aspirations.

	You	Other parents		
		1	2	3
I want him to have the things we never had	☐	☐	☐	☐
I want him not to care too much for material things	☐	☐	☐	☐
I want him to appreciate the good things of life	☐	☐	☐	☐
I want him to be happy	☐	☐	☐	☐
I want him to be independent/able to make decisions	☐	☐	☐	☐
I want him to have a good career	☐	☐	☐	☐
I want him to enjoy life	☐	☐	☐	☐
I want him to care about other people	☐	☐	☐	☐
I want him to be self-reliant	☐	☐	☐	☐
I want him to take life seriously	☐	☐	☐	☐
I want him not to take life too seriously	☐	☐	☐	☐
I want him to have lots of friends	☐	☐	☐	☐
I want him to be healthy	☐	☐	☐	☐
I want him to be honest/tolerant/understanding	☐	☐	☐	☐
I want him to have everything he wants	☐	☐	☐	☐
I want him to be able to cope with life's problems	☐	☐	☐	☐
I want him to be free of worries	☐	☐	☐	☐

Tomorrow's adults

Today's children are tomorrow's teachers, tool-makers, hairdressers, town planners, lorry drivers, mechanics, doctors, poets, builders, parents. Our own children are our own special concern – but in the end they will marry other people's children, service other people's cars, be nursed and taught by others, work and play with others. Our children are as much a part of a larger community as we are ourselves. Our children need to experience being part of that larger community, and the community, as well as individual parents, has responsibility for the needs and future of its children.

Keeping an open mind

It's all very well knowing what kind of person we would like our child to be. But do we all share the same understanding of what it means to be 'happy', 'healthy', 'free from worries'? And how responsible should we feel for the way our children turn out?

Since the beginning of this century there has been enormous improvement in the physical health of the population. Much higher standards of public health, greater understanding of nutrition, near eradication of many diseases have given parents high expectations that their children will grow up physically healthy.

It's much harder to be sure that we are providing the right conditions for our children's mental and social well-being. Just by looking around at our friends and our families we can see that there's no one way of looking at things, no set pattern of childrearing to follow. There is constant debate on the rights and wrongs of parenting. You know your own situation better than anyone else ever can. It's important to have confidence in your judgement. It's also important to question, to keep an open mind, and to feel confident you can change when your familiar answers no longer fit.

Topic index

All the topics in the book are listed in chapter order here. There are nine basic themes running through the book, and each topic is related to one or sometimes two themes. Many of the topics in fact touch on a number of issues. But for simplicity we have marked only the most important themes.

If you are interested in following a particular theme through, just work your way through the topics marked under that heading. The topics are not in an order through the book, so you can start where you like. Each topic is like a 'spotlight' on a theme.

Child's development

● *Physical development:* the growth in skill of movement, body awareness and control over the body.

● *Emotional development:* feelings about self, about others, and about things, and the growth of confidence and independence.

● *Thinking:* the development of children's ideas about the world – such as number, colour, size, weight, length; and the development of styles of thinking and learning.

● *Language development:* the development of spoken language and its uses, and the comprehension of spoken, written and 'unspoken' body language.

● *Social development:* the development of relationships with other children and adults – getting to know them, and sharing of activities and experiences.

Parental concerns

● *Learning materials and situations:* providing the conditions and materials that will encourage your child to learn.

● *Parent-child relationships:* the way children and parents work out a pattern of living together including demands and conflicts of interest.

● *Family life-styles:* the way you organise and feel about your family's total life pattern and the support and encouragement your child needs to cope with and enjoy the changes that come about in it.

● *Community life:* beyond the family circle there are social groupings for parents and children that you may wish to get involved in.

Chap.	Physical	Emotional	Thinking	Language	Social	Learning materials	Parent-child	Family life-styles	Community	Topic
1								●		Routines of the day and week
1		●								Children are different
1								●		Waking
1	●									Dressing
1	●									Mealtimes
1			●							Food, glorious food
1							●			We all make demands
1							●			Bathtime
1							●			Clean and dry
1				●						Stories
1		●								Day's end
2				●						Talking to each other
2				●		●				Drawing
2								●		Children and television
2				●						Looking at books
2						●				Learning moments
2							●			Wills of their own
2		●						●		Babysitters
2		●								Breathing space
2		●								Dolls and teddies
2					●					Playing mothers and fathers
2								●		New baby in the family
2		●								Family relationships
3						●		●		Family work
3			●							Launder and learn
3	●					●				Water in the sink
3			●							Sewing
3								●		Safety in the home
3			●							What's naughty and why?
3			●				●			What's naughty – children's views
3				●						Talking while you work
3			●							Rhymes, songs and finger plays
3			●							Paint
3			●							All sorts of music
4			●							Stage by stage
4			●							All I get is questions
4			●	●						Male and female
4			●				●			Tidying up
4	●		●							Woodwork
4			●							Cooking
4			●				●			Making things
4			●							A dollop of dough
4			●							I can do it
4			●				●			Ways of learning
4				●						Instructions and explanations
4			●							Tantrums and tears
5						●				Shopping
5				●						Learning about reading
5				●						Your child's own books
5	●									Running, jumping and standing still
5								●		Pets
5		●								Safety outside the home
5			●	●						Unspoken words
5		●	●							What happens when you die?
5								●		Days in bed
5			●							Sorting things out
6						●		●		Going places
6					●			●		Hello stranger
6								●		Moving house
6							●			Parents have many faces
6		●								For their own good
6			●							Talking about sex
6										Ways of thinking
6						●				Puppets
6		●						●		Children in hospital
6		●					●			Could you harm your child?
7		●						●		Working mothers
7			●					●		Work: children's views
7								●		Feeling low
7					●					Playing together
7					●					Children's quarrels
7									●	Pre-school groups
7									●	Choosing a group
7		●						●		Joining a group
7								●		Coming together again
7									●	Other people's children
7								●		Children with a difference
8										A review
8				●						Words, words, words
8								●		Looking forward to school
8									●	The generation gap
8									●	Opportunities for older children
8									●	Patterns of child-rearing
8								●		Taking stock
8								●		The changing parent
8									●	Looking to the future

INDEX

baby-sitters 29, 52
bathtime 22–4, 230–1
books 44–5, 134–5, 139–41, 167

child-minding 195–7, 211, 218–19
choosing 14, 50, 59, 133, 230
comforters 55, 157
comics 139
cooking 70, 112–14, 230
counting and sorting 16–17, 72–3, 106–7, 158–9, 230

day nurseries 196, 209
death 149, 154–5
destructiveness 116
drawing 36–9
dressing 12–14, 230–1
dressing up 13, 88–9

family patterns 244–6
fears 24, 26, 30–1, 80–1, 102, 156, 177
food 18–19, 114, 216
    mealtime learning 15–17

going out 6, 163–7, 172–3
    to eat 19
    to the library 141
    to play 148, 150
    to shop 131–3, 163
    visiting 165, 169

handicapped children 220–3
harming a child 188–91

illness 156–7
    hospital 186–7
imagination 102–3, 167, 182–3, 227
imitation 80–1, 101, 105, 107

laundry work 72–3
learning
    right moments 46–8, 84–6, 229
    stages 99, 107, 142–3
    styles 122–3

making things 115–17
manipulative skills (handling things) 12, 15, 36, 70–1, 76–7, 108–9, 227
memory 10, 27, 86, 167
mess 15, 22, 74, 90, 107
Mother and Toddler clubs 11, 14, 196, 210
movement, development 142–8
moving house 171
music and rhymes 87–9, 94–5

naughtiness 49–50, 80–3
new babies 26, 37, 51, 58–60, 217, 230
nursery rhymes 17, 45, 140, 182
nursery schools/classes 208

obedience 20–1, 23, 61, 174–6

painting 39, 90–3
parents
    anxiety 14, 26, 49
    changing roles 251–2
    depression 195, 200–1, 247–50
    expectations 54, 61–3, 80–3, 104–5, 172–6, 191, 214, 247–52
    influence on personality 9, 105, 227
    pregnancy 58–9
    relaxation 11, 53
person-toys 54–5, 156
personality 9, 51, 122–3
pets 149
play 6, 67–8, 229
    in the bath 22–3
    in bed 10
    during illness 157
    learning through 46–8, 56–7, 158–9
    outdoor 142–8, 150, 240–3
    role play 54–7, 88–9, 156, 203
    types 202–6
playgroups 6, 60, 140, 149, 163–4, 190–1, 196, 210
privacy 26, 53, 207
puppets 184–5

questions 100–3, 113, 180–3, 228

reading 134–8, 234
regression ('babyish' behaviour) 26, 51, 81, 204, 217

repetition 13, 29, 179
routines
    daily 6–8, 199, 229
    sleep 10–11, 29
    television 40–1
    toilet 25
    weekly 8

safety 68, 71, 78–9
    outdoors 148, 150–1, 240–3
school, starting 234–7
security 51, 52, 152–3, 170, 171, 172–3, 215
senses, development 114, 115, 118–19
separation 51, 52, 59, 154–5, 187, 195–9, 214–15
sewing 76–7
sex
    education 59, 177–9
    roles, 54, 104–5, 227
shopping 131–3, 163
sleep 9, 10–11, 29–31
smacking 126, 176
social development (getting on with people) 50, 60, 62, 83, 102, 172–3, 202–6, 212, 217, 228, 230, 238–9
stories 27–8, 44–5, 134
    child's 37, 38
strangers 168–70

television 40–3, 140, 167, 230
temper 14, 19, 23, 49–51, 80–1, 116, 126–7, 227
    quarrels between children 207
tidying up 106–7, 230
toilet training 25–6, 80–1
toys 54–5, 111, 157, 167
    outdoor 147

water play 23, 74–5
woodwork 108–10
words and ideas 84–6, 100–3, 110, 124–5, 176, 180–3, 228, 232–3
work 6, 67–77, 120–1
working mothers 157, 195–7, 201, 229

Index by Ann Edwards